# The Peasant Economy
# and Social Change in
# North China

PHILIP C. C. HUANG

# The Peasant Economy and Social Change in North China

STANFORD UNIVERSITY PRESS
*Stanford, California*
1985

Stanford University Press
Stanford, California

© 1985 by the Board of Trustees of the
Leland Stanford Junior University

*Printed in the United States of America*

Published with the assistance of the
National Endowment for the Humanities

CIP data appear at the end of the book

# Preface

For empirical information, I am indebted above all to the researchers of the Japanese South Manchurian Railway Company (Mantetsu), who managed to compile possibly the best ethnographic data available on any peasant society of the early decades of the twentieth century, despite their ambiguous and suspect scholarly status as agents of a conquering power. The nature of those materials and the issues raised by the context in which they were gathered are discussed in detail in Chapter Two; readers with questions about those studies should begin there, although a real sense of their richness can probably only be gained by reading some of the material itself. In 1980, almost a decade after I first began working with the Mantetsu reports and when I was nearly finished with the book as it was originally conceived, I had the opportunity to do a year of research in China under the Senior Scholar Program of the Committee for Scholarly Communication with the People's Republic of China. That year gave me the chance to revisit two of the Mantetsu-studied sites for some oral history research to check and augment the Japanese materials, and to add a two-centuries' time depth to the book with the help of the Qing Board of Punishment archives and a nineteenth-century county government archive. I have of course been aided greatly throughout my research by the past studies of Chinese, Japanese, and Western scholars.

For theoretical concepts, I have drawn widely from the three major traditions of peasant studies and China scholarship: the mainly Marxist works of postrevolutionary China, the mainly "formalist" and "substantivist" (as I call them in this book) studies of the West, and the mainly Marxist and substantivist studies of Japan. Much space has been devoted to a dialogue with all three bodies of theory and research. (A Chinese version of this book will be published by Zhonghua shuju in Beijing.)

In working with both empirical information and theoretical constructs, I have chosen to proceed from historical reality to theory and back to reality, rather than the reverse, as is sometimes the practice in contemporary social science. I have tried to look to the most down-to-earth information for the largest ideas, and then to return once more to empirical material—to avoid the tendencies of starting with a given model and then seeking only facts that would support the model or of attempting to build abstract models independent of historical context.

This book could not have been finished without the luxury for uninterrupted research and writing provided by a year's fellowship from the National Endowment for the Humanities in 1978 and sabbatical leaves, in addition to the year of research in China. I benefited greatly from discussions with many Chinese historians and economists, especially Li Wenzhi and Liu Yongcheng. Outside China, I did much of the research for this book at the Hoover Institution, where curator Ramon Myers and the staff of the East Asian Collection were always most helpful. In the final stages of the work, friends and colleagues in several disciplines read different versions of the manuscript and gave me much appreciated encouragement and advice: Eugene Anderson, Norma Diamond, Arif Dirlik, Mark Elvin, Albert Feuerwerker, Linda Grove, Harold Kahn, Nikki Keddie, Diana Lary, James Lee, Eric Monkonnen, Gary Nash, James Palais, Charles Tilly, Frederic Wakeman, Alexander Woodside, and Ye Xian'en. Joseph Esherick, Michael Gasster, Victor Lippit, Elizabeth Perry, Andrew Walder, and Ernest Young, especially, gave enormous amounts of their time and helped shape the book in substantial ways. I also benefited from discussions with and comments from a number of my graduate students: Lynda Bell, Andrew Frankel, Kathy Walker, Phil S. Yang, and, especially, Honming Yip. Two undergraduate seminar papers on my manuscript, by Jewel Chung and Maurya Hogan, were helpful in my efforts to make this book more accessible to students. Noel Diaz, cartographer of UCLA's Geography Department, turned my rough sketches into real maps. Stanford University Press's Editor J. G. Bell placed me in the Press's debt by his considerate and efficient handling of the manuscript, as did Barbara Mnookin, whose rigorous editing greatly improved and tightened the book. Finally, Kate Peterson Huang, despite the rigors imposed by her return to graduate school, gave me the warmth of home and spirit that made this work possible.

*Los Angeles, California*                                    P. H.
*December 1983*

# Contents

APPENDIXES

# Tables

## APPENDIX TABLES

# Maps

# Note on
# Place-Names

The most common suffixes for villages in North China are *cun* and *zhuang* (both words mean village). Also common are *ying* (or "camp," suggesting that the community might have grown up around a military encampment) and *zhai* (or "fortress," suggesting that the community might have originated as an armed settlement). In referring to villages, the people of the North China plain seem always to include as part of the name the suffixes *zhuang*, *ying*, and *zhai*. They often drop the suffix *cun*, however, especially where a name denotes some entity in addition to the village, as for example Dabeiguan (or "big north gate" of the walled county seat) and Wangquansi (or "temple overlooking fountain"), and I have followed their lead, referring for example to Shajing village, not Shajingcun. The only exception to this practice is where the village's name would be reduced to just one syllable without the suffix (e.g., Macun), a problem similar to that presented by county names like Dingxian. All village and county names are rendered in full in the Character List.

This book is concerned primarily with the area of the North China plain encompassed by present-day Hebei province and the northwest portion of Shandong. Except for parts of Daming prefecture, Henan, that area substantially overlaps the Qing Zhili and Republican Zhili and Hebei portions of the North China plain (compare Maps 2.1 and 6.1). Thus, even where precision would require Zhili, I have preferred to use Hebei through all periods, reverting to the proper historical name only on rare occasion for clarity.

# I

# BACKGROUND

# CHAPTER I

# The Issues

## THE CHINESE PEASANT

The peasant in prerevolutionary China had three different faces. He was first of all someone who to some degree produced directly for household consumption; his production decisions were accordingly shaped in part by considerations of household needs. In this respect, he was very different from contemporary urban residents, for whom the activities of production and consumption, of workplace and home, are generally distinct and separate. Second, he was also something of an entrepreneur, for most peasants produced in part for a market, and had to base production decisions on considerations of prices, supply and demand, and costs and returns. In this respect, the peasant farm possessed some characteristics we usually associate with a capitalist enterprise. Finally, we can think of the peasant as a member of a stratified society under a state system, whose surplus supported the consumption needs of the nonagricultural sectors.

### Three Traditions of Peasant Studies

Each of these different dimensions of the peasant has been illuminated by a major tradition of scholarship. The peasant as entrepreneur has been well studied by economists of the Western world, most importantly in Nobel Laureate Theodore Schultz's now-classic study *Transforming Traditional Agriculture* (1964). Schultz argued powerfully in this book that the peasant, far from being lazy, inept, or irrational in his economic behavior, as popular conception might make him out to be, was in fact an enterprising and optimizing user of resources, within the constraints of "traditional agriculture" (before the coming of modern inputs like mechanical power and chemical fertilizer). Traditional agriculture might have been poor, but it was highly efficient. It in fact tended toward an "equilibrium" level in which "there are comparatively few significant inefficiencies in the allocation of factors of production" (p. 37). Schultz's peasant is "Economic Man" no less than any capitalist entrepreneur (see esp. his Chaps. 2 and 3). Consequently, in Schultz's view, the way to transform traditional agriculture is to leave the small family farm structure of productive organization intact, rather than tampering with it as was done in the Soviet Union, and to provide modern "factors of production" at prices within the economic reach of the small peasant. Once proper economic incentives for innovation are present, the entrepreneurial family farmer will innovate to modernize agriculture, in much the same manner as had happened in American agriculture (ibid., Chaps. 7 and 8).*

More recently, Samuel Popkin has elaborated on the implications of Schultz's type of analysis for our comprehension of peasant political behavior. For Popkin, the peasant farm is best described with the analogy of a capitalist firm, and the peasant as political actor, by extension, with the analogy of an investor in the political marketplace. In his view, peasants act to maximize gains by rationalizing production and balancing short- and long-term interest, in the same ways that a capitalist firm or investor does, hence the title of his book: The Rational Peasant (1979).†

Critics of this peasant-as-capitalist-entrepreneur analysis have stressed the subsistence producer–consumer dimension of the peasant. The classic theoretical analysis is presented by A. V. Chayanov in his studies of the Russian peasants in the 1920's (1966a, b). Chayanov argued convincingly that peasant economies cannot be understood in the conventional terms of a discipline developed for the study of capitalist economies. Capitalist profit accounting cannot be applied to a peasant family farm on which there is little or no wage

---

*The American family farm has in fact been the economists' favorite illustration of a near-pure capitalist enterprise (see, for example, such textbooks as Mansfield 1980). The multitude of small producers makes for an ideal model of competition in an open market (as opposed to the oligopolistic situation in automobiles, for example). A wheat farmer's decisions illustrate well the relationship between prices and supply and demand. And the wheat farmer's choice of how best to combine different quantities of inputs of land, labor, and capital illustrate well the principles of optimizing the use of scarce resources for the purpose of minimizing costs and maximizing returns.

†Popkin does attempt to improve on Schultz's analysis by taking into account the element of risk in peasant agriculture. Here he borrows heavily from Milton Friedman's class analysis (1948) of consumer choice under conditions of risk (in which "utility maximizing" carries with it calculated "gambles" and "insurance"). He also borrows from Michael Lipton's analysis (1968) of the nature of "rational" behavior when sheer survival, not profit, is the paramount consideration. In criticizing James Scott's substantivist analysis (1976), Popkin draws also on Marxist ideas. But his argument is at bottom a formalist one.

labor, where the family's own labor input cannot be readily disaggregated into unit labor costs, and where the farm's annual yield is a single "labor product" that cannot be readily disaggregated into units of income. Most of all, the peasant family farm produced for the satisfaction of the family's consumption wants, not for profit maximization.

Some 30 years later, the argument against the use of conventional economics to study peasant economies was joined, from a different angle, by Karl Polanyi. To Polanyi and his associates at Columbia University, the analytical concepts and methods of conventional economics are predicated above all on the existence of "price-making markets." The application of such concepts to premarket economies is in fact nothing more than the universalizing of "utilitarian rationalism," of the view of man as "utilitarian atom" out to "economize." In place of this kind of "formal" economics, which presupposes choice and the ready marketability of land, labor, and capital (all quantifiable in terms of money), Polanyi suggested the use of a "substantive" economics that would stress the social relationships in which economic behavior in premarket societies was "embedded." Relationships of "reciprocity" (as of mutual aid and obligation among kinship groupings) shaped economic behavior in the ancient world, not market relations and profit maximization. A separate and different approach to economics as "instituted process" was required for studying precapitalist economies (Polanyi et al. 1957: esp. Chaps. 12 and 13).

Polanyi's views found support among many economic anthropologists studying premarket subsistence communities and partly commercialized peasant communities. These "substantivists" (as they are sometimes called) have challenged the "formalists" (like Raymond Firth and Melville Herskovits), who led in advocating the application of the categories and analytical tools of conventional economics to the study of non-Western and preindustrial communities. The debates on just how and the extent to which conventional economics may or may not be applicable continue. (See Dalton 1969 and the accompanying commentaries for the range of issues involved.)

James Scott has elaborated on the implications of Chayanov's and Polanyi's analyses for our understanding of peasant mentality and political behavior. In *The Moral Economy of the Peasant: Rebellion and Subsistence in Southeast Asia* (1976), Scott argues that peasant economic behavior is guided by the principles of "risk avoidance" and "safety first," and by a "subsistence ethic" involving "reciprocity" between "patron and client" of the same moral community.

Peasant collective action, by extension, is basically defensive and restorative against threats to subsistence and intrusions by the capitalist state and the impersonal market forces of capitalism.

In contrast to both the formalist and the substantivist view, the Marxist emphasis is above all on the third main dimension of the peasant. In conventional Marxism,* peasant economy is "feudal," characterized above all by a particular set of class (or production) relations: in this case mainly between landowning lord and producing peasant. Surplus in a feudal economy is extracted from the peasant producer principally in the form of land rent, whether as labor-rent, rent-in-kind, or cash-rent. The peasant under feudalism is neither the entrepreneur of the formalists nor the subsistence member of a moral community of the substantivists, but an exploited cultivator whose surplus goes to support a ruling class and a state structure. (Marxists of course recognize the existence of the small owner-peasant under feudalism, but maintain that the primary class relationship is the one between lord and tenant. See esp. Mao 1939; Stalin 1940; Lenin 1956: 190–218; Marx 1967, 3:782–802.)

## An Integrated Analysis of a Differentiated Peasant Economy

The approach taken in this book is an integrated one. The three separate traditions of analysis outlined above have each contributed much to our comprehension of the dimension it has singled out for emphasis. Yet, this one-sidedness has also given rise to much unresolvable debate—between Marxists and non-Marxists, and between the formalists and substantivists in economic anthropology, a debate recently replayed in political science between Popkin and Scott. It seems to me pointless to continue to insist on one or another of these characteristics to the exclusion of the others. This book maintains, first of all, that the key to comprehending the Chinese peasant household is to see it as an entity that fused the characteristics of entrepreneur, subsistence producer–consumer, and exploited cultivator into a single, inseparable unit. Each of the three faces tells about one aspect of a multidimensional being.

But we need also to differentiate among different kinds of peasants, for the mix of these characteristics varied with peasants of different social strata. An upwardly mobile rich peasant-farmer using hired labor and producing a substantial surplus conforms to a much

---

*By "conventional" here I mean to include mainly those who would adhere to the formula, made official in the dominant Marxist tradition through Lenin, Stalin, and Mao, that historical development follows five successive modes of production: the primitive, slave, feudal, capitalist, and socialist.

greater extent with the formalist model of analysis than the downwardly mobile tenant-laborer struggling on the margins of hunger while paying high rents and receiving low wages for the labor he did for others. The latter fits much better the Marxist model of analysis. An owner-cultivator producing mainly for family consumption, on the other hand, closely resembles the substantivist image of the peasant.

What we need is an integrated analysis that distinguishes among different kinds of peasants. North China peasants who took up cotton cultivation after the sixteenth century may all seem to have been merely making an entrepreneurial response to market demand and the relatively higher returns offered by cotton farming. But closer examination will show a complex of motivations that varied with different strata of the peasantry and with the different production relations in which they were involved. The larger and more well-to-do farms were unmistakably motivated to a great extent by considerations of profit when they chose to include cotton in their total cropping "portfolio." Yet even the largest and most commercialized farms still devoted a substantial proportion of their cultivated area to subsistence crops for household consumption. They also paid a part of their surplus in tax to support a state structure. In the case of poorer peasants, survival considerations often figured more prominently than profit motives in a switch to cotton. By the eighteenth century, social stratification and population pressure reduced many poor peasant farms in North China to a size too small to produce enough foodgrains to sustain their households. Many of those households were impelled to place abnormally large proportions of their farms under cotton, at greater risk and sometimes also reduced average returns, because cotton offered fuller employment for their surplus labor, and the possibility in any given year for returns high enough to meet their subsistence needs. For those poorer peasants who were tenants, there was often no choice at all: once rental terms on land that could grow cotton came to be set according to the market potential of that crop, no tenant could really afford to grow cereals. Yet when market conditions changed, poorer households could and did adjust their cropping portfolios accordingly, in ways not unlike the more well-to-do farms. Thus, all three sets of considerations figured in peasant responses to cotton, with entrepreneurial calculations looming much larger for the richer farms, and subsistence considerations (albeit through cash-cropping rather than cereals grown directly for household consumption) and production relations much more important for the poorer farms.

In a related phenomenon, large farms using hired labor and small farms worked by family labor responded to population pressure in different ways. Reliance on wage labor gave the large farms the flexibility to adjust their labor supply to the optimal needs of their farms: they could hire labor as needed, and fire excess labor. But family farms had no such flexibility. A family farm could not simply fire its excess family members; where alternative employment was not available, it had to tolerate the existence of surplus labor and the underemployment of its labor. Under those conditions, subsistence pressures could drive such farms to intensify labor input on their farms to a very much higher degree than the farms using wage labor would tolerate. Labor input could be pushed to levels well beyond the point at which diminishing marginal returns set in. Chayanov pointed out the existence of this phenomenon in the agriculture of prerevolutionary Russia (1966b: 113–16). Clifford Geertz has given the same phenomenon, in rice farming in Java, the catchy term "agricultural involution" (1963).* Population pressure on the Hebei–northwest Shandong plain, as will be shown, often forced the marginal product of labor on the poorer family farms below the market wages for a laborer and the subsistence needs of the cultivator's household.

The contrasting behavior of wage-labor-based large farms (or "managerial farms," which will be defined fully in Chapter Four) and family-labor-based small farms can be comprehended through the combined use of formalist and substantivist analyses. The large farms were impelled by the profit motive toward optimal combinations of land with labor, and hence would not tolerate the existence of surplus labor. The small farms, on the other hand, were driven to involute severely by the combination of subsistence pressures and the distinctive characteristics of family labor. Their behavior would make no sense in terms of a profit-oriented enterprise. Why should any enterprise continue to apply labor when its marginal costs exceed marginal returns? That would mean choosing to operate at a loss.

Still, we should not hasten to conclude that the economic behavior of those family farms was somehow "irrational" and not comprehensible in the terms of "formal economics." Involution can in fact be readily rationalized in the terms of conventional microeco-

---

*If we think in terms of a graph in which the vertical axis represents output and the horizontal axis labor input, "involution" occurs when the line showing the relationship between output and labor input begins to level off—i.e. when the marginal output of labor diminishes.

nomics theory, provided one approaches the question not as a simple matter of profit maximization, but as a matter of both enterprise behavior and consumer choice. The small peasant with surplus labor intensified labor input to such levels because of the very low "opportunity cost of labor" to the farm enterprise (because of the lack of alternative employment under severe population pressure), on the one hand, and the very high "marginal utility" of the marginal increments of produce to the peasant consumer (struggling on the margins of subsistence) on the other hand. The advantage of using the concept of "utility" (from microeconomic theory about rational consumer choice) rather than the concept of profit maximization (from theories about enterprise behavior) is that "utility" allows for subjective preferences related to particular environments and circumstances. Most of all, the family farm needs to be understood as an entity that was at once producer and consumer.

Peasant behavior in the above two examples—the one having to do with commercialization and the other with population pressure —can only be comprehended through an analysis that differentiates among peasants through the integrated use of the formalist, Marxist, and substantivist traditions of scholarship. This view is basic to my approach to the central historical question posed in this book: what were the patterns of agrarian change in China in the several centuries before the Revolution?

### PATTERNS OF AGRARIAN CHANGE

For the "classic" pattern of agrarian change in the modern age, we of course look to England's transition to capitalism. Peasants came to be differentiated into capitalist farmers and wage workers, and agriculture modernized along with capitalist industrialization. In the process, the society and the economy became so completely transformed that it no longer made sense to speak of an English peasant.

Comparisons of different national or regional experiences in the Western world, to be sure, bring out striking contrasts. The peasant family farm, for example, was more tenacious in France than in England both before and during the process of industrialization (Brenner 1982). And the American experience, more than any other, calls attention not only to a differentiation process, but also to the emergence of the modernizing and capitalizing family farm as a major social form in the transformation of traditional agriculture. In comparison with China, however, all this is just a matter of degree, for what is most striking is that in China the differentiation did not end in the complete transformation of agrarian society, as happened in the West, but remained within the framework of the existing small peasant society. It led not to a capitalist industrial economy, but to a differentiated peasant economy.

## Past Scholarship

The question of patterns of agrarian change in China raises the issue of the nature and direction of change both before China's contact with the modern world and as a result of that contact. To characterize change in modern China one needs first to define a clear premodern baseline for comprehending that change.

Formalists have spotlighted especially the fact of great population pressure in "late traditional" and modern China. The major book is Dwight Perkins's monumental quantitative study of Chinese agriculture in the six centuries from 1368 to 1968. In his use of empirical data, Perkins built on the earlier work of Ho Ping-ti (1959), who paved the way for the systematic and critical use of imperial cadastral and demographic data. For his conceptual framework, Perkins adopted a model of analysis spelled out by Ester Boserup (1965): population growth, Boserup argued, was the major dynamic behind development (or intensification) in traditional agriculture, from the one crop in 20 to 25 years "forest-fallow system" (slash-and-burn agriculture), to the one crop in six to ten years of the "bush-fallow system," to the two crops in three years "short-fallow system," to annual cropping, and finally, to the multiple cropping regimes of densely populated peasant economies.

According to Perkins, Chinese population expanded seven- to ninefold in the centuries from the beginning of the Ming down to 1949, and agricultural output grew at roughly the same rate. In this period, farm technology and "institutional" patterns (of land tenure and production relations) remained essentially unchanged; hence, population growth itself was the crucial dynamic behind the increased agricultural output. An expanded population led to migration and a roughly fourfold increase in the total cultivated area. This accounted for one-half of the increase in output. The other half was the result of a doubling in the average output per unit area, which was again a development powered by the population growth. Increases in capital inputs in this period were mainly in the form of labor-intensive water-control projects and organic fertilizers, both made possible by an expanded population and labor force. There was an intensification of labor inputs per unit area, with an increased frequency of cropping and the adoption of higher-yield, more labor-intensive crops, also the result of an expanded labor force. In these ways, agricultural output grew with an expanding population, until a crisis point was reached in the twentieth century, when new frontiers for migration were exhausted and intensification in land use along existing lines had reached something of a plateau (Perkins 1969: esp. 184–89). Perkins' analysis brings out most clearly the view of "late traditional" Chinese society as undergoing only quantitative changes in response to population growth, not qualitative changes of the type that characterized the Western experience.

To this model of intensification powered by population increase, Mark Elvin has added the refinement of the notion of the diminishing marginal product of labor (when other inputs—like land, capital, and technology—are held constant). As Chinese agriculture intensified to a higher and higher degree with the population growth of the late imperial period, the marginal productivity of labor steadily declined, and with it, the surplus above subsistence produced by the small peasant farm (Elvin 1973: esp. Chap. 17). The peasant economy, in other words, involuted along the lines suggested by Geertz's analytical model.

Whereas Western scholars have focused on population, scholars in China have studied mainly production relations. The dominant theoretical model has been that of "incipient capitalism." First set forth by Mao (1939), this model maintains that capitalism had "sprouted" in China long before the coming of imperialism, as evidenced by the increased commercialization of the economy and the development of capitalist wage-labor relations. But this path of development had been skewed by imperialist intrusion, which reduced China to a "semi-feudal, semi-colonial" country and prevented the capitalist sprouts from developing into full-fledged capitalism. It is an analysis with obvious ideological uses: the first part of the argument has the advantage of placing China within the Stalinist five-modes-of-production formula (that all societies follow the unilinear path of development through the primitive, slave, feudal, capitalist, and socialist stages), and the second the advantage of an unambiguous condemnation of imperialism.

Economic historians in China have worked mainly under the first half of this conceptual scheme.* On agriculture, important new re-

*Though "incipient capitalism" remains the dominant analytical framework in Chinese studies of the social and economic history of the Ming–Qing period (Nanjing daxue 1980: 2 lists 218 titles of this school by 1979), the last few years have seen the publication of studies using other approaches. In two major works in particular (Hu Rulei 1979; Fu Zhufu 1980), we find sustained analyses of the differences between the socioeconomic structure of imperial China and that of the precapitalist West, though

search came first from Jing Su and Luo Lun, who used oral-history research to demonstrate the existence of substantial numbers of "managerial landlords" operating wage-labor-based farms in 1890's Shandong (Jing & Luo 1959; Wilkinson 1978). Li Wenzhi subsequently showed that the seventeenth and eighteenth centuries saw the rise of "commoner landlords" (*shumin dizhu*; as opposed to "gentry landlords," *jinshen dizhu* or *shenfen dizhu*) through profitable commercialized farming (1963a, b; 1981). More recently, the evidential base for these "capitalist sprouts" in farming has been enlarged by scholars working with the Board of Punishment archives in the Ming–Qing Archives in Beijing. The most important new contributions have come from Liu Yongcheng (1963; 1979b).*

For reasons both of ideology and of availability of source materials, most "incipient capitalism" scholars have concentrated mainly

---

still within the conceptual boundaries of a "feudal" China and of the five-modes-of-production formula. For Hu Rulei, the key lies in the differences between Chinese "feudal landlordism" (*fengjian dizhuzhi*) and European "feudal manorialism" (*fengjian lingzhuzhi*). In the European feudal manor, landownership or economic power was merged with military, administrative, and judicial powers; each manorial lord exercised the entire range of those powers. The state system of manorialism was thus one in which sovereignty was parceled out. In Chinese landlordism, by contrast, political authority came to be separated from economic power through private landownership and the frequent buying and selling of land. This made possible the centralized imperial state system. Landlordism and the centralized imperial state thus made up an interdependent politicoeconomic system that must be distinguished from European manorialism. Hu's is an analytical model that can help explain the differences in the nature of the premodern Chinese and European politicoeconomic systems and hence also their different paths of sociopolitical change in the modern era.

Fu Zhufu has pointed to another difference between manorialism and landlordism. In the serf-based manorial system, the lord had to look to the subsistence and reproduction of his workers, lest the very basis of the manorial economy be undermined. But the Chinese landlord was under no such constraints. He could seek the highest possible returns that the land-rental market would support (Fu 1980: 9–10, 201–2). Though Fu skirts the issue here, it is obvious that such principles became harshest when the pressures of social stratification were joined by the pressures of population; under those conditions, a tenant who failed to survive could always be replaced by another. Landlordism could become an institutional system in which the poor tenants were pressed below the margins of subsistence.

*As this book went to press, I received in the mail a new book by Li Wenzhi, Wei Jinyu, and Jing Junjian, *Ming-Qing shidai de nongye zibenzhuyi wenti* (The problem of the sprouts of capitalism in agriculture during the Ming–Qing period), Beijing: Zhongguo shehui kexue chubanshe, 1983. This book provides additional support and elaboration, on a nation-wide basis, for several of the themes of my Chapters Five and Six. The first part (242 pages), by Li Wenzhi, supplies for the incipient capitalism analysis the richest documentary support and most sophisticated analytical elaboration to appear since 1949, though Li still steers completely clear of any consideration of the effects of population increase. Readers interested in pursuing the subject further should go to that book; it arrived too late for its research to be incorporated here.

on production relations, to the neglect of "productive forces," the other of the pair of factors that are crucial in the Marxist conception of a "mode of production." The general tendency has been to equate "capitalist sprouts" mainly with the supposedly capitalist relations of wage labor. Where changes in productivity are discussed, the tendency has been to simply assume, rather than demonstrate systematically, that advances in productivity accompanied capitalist relations (Jing & Luo 1959; Liu Yongcheng 1962, 1979b; see also ZRD 1957 and Nanjing daxue 1980). (The question raised by the second half of the "incipient capitalism" formula, of the effects of imperialism on China's agrarian economy in the modern century, has turned out to be too close to the present and too politically sensitive to permit sustained academic research.)*

Among substantivists, Chayanov has furnished the most distinctive and fully elaborated model for comprehending change in the precapitalist peasant economy. According to Chayanov, the fortunes of peasant farm families rise and fall mainly with the changing consumer-to-laborer ratio of the family (which varies with the age of the family and the numbers and ages of its children). The families' economic fortunes are at their height when the adult parents are without children, giving a one-to-one ratio of consumer and laborer, and lowest when the number of nonworking members reaches the maximum in the family cycle (1966b: Chap. 1). Change in prerevolutionary rural Russia thus consisted of cyclical "demographic differentiation" rather than the linear social differentiation argued by Lenin in his study of the development of capitalism in Russia (Shanin 1972: Chap. 3). (More recent substantivist scholarship, such as that of James Scott, has focused on the question of the influence of world capitalism on the precapitalist economy rather than on patterns of premodern change. We will discuss that aspect of substantivist analysis under the section on the role of imperialism.)

Chayanov's scheme has yet to be applied to the study of Chinese history. It is an understandable gap: detailed data on Chinese family farms are limited by and large to the cross-sectional field survey data of the 1930's. We do not have household information of sufficient time-depth to permit the testing of Chayanov's model. Unless such

*Scholars in China have not been able to go beyond the initial compilation of source materials by Li Wenzhi (1957) and Zhang Youyi (1957) of the Institute of Economics in the 1950's. Those three volumes remain indispensable reference tools for anyone working on the subject, but they have not been followed by substantial analyses or further research. (Yue 1980 is a text intended for college students and does not go beyond the Li-Zhang collection.)

data become available, we can only speculate on the possible limitations and relevance of Chayanov's scheme: it clearly does not take sufficient account of unequal distribution in land and other property. The neglect is possibly more defensible in the context of the Russian *mir*, which redistributed land periodically (though to an unknown extent—Shanin 1972: 79–80), than in China where there was little practice of that kind. On the other hand, Chayanov's notion of family cycles, especially if it can be made to take account of the downward pressures of partible inheritance in China, could probably help explain the different economic fortunes over time of families that begin with the same landholdings. In contemporary China, where landed property is no longer a significant determinant of income, Chayanov's scheme is of obvious relevance: the most well-to-do households of a given village are generally those with the most favorable consumer-to-laborer ratio.

## Population and Production Relations

This book is concerned mainly with long-term patterns of agrarian change. (If and when the necessary data become available, we might be able to take fuller account of short-term cyclical change linked to the biological rhythms of families, as suggested by Chayanov.) To define secular agrarian trends before China's contact with the modern capitalist world, this book maintains that we need to pay simultaneous attention to population and to production relations, to synthesize the formalist and Marxist approaches.

Formalist scholarship has certainly shed much light on the critical role of population. Nineteenth- and twentieth-century family farms in China were, on the average, only about one-sixtieth the size of the contemporary American farm, and about one-tenth the size of the French farm. This basic difference set certain constraints on China's agriculture, indeed on the Chinese economy as a whole. One major difference between China's agrarian economy and American, English, or European agriculture is its singular reliance on crops to the virtual exclusion of livestock. Animal husbandry still forms only a small part of Chinese agriculture (about 16 percent of the total value of output, compared with 60 percent for the United States, and 57 percent for France), and that small share involves, not grazing herds, but mainly scavenging animals such as hogs and hens (Chen Ping 1981; also 1979). The crucial difference, of course, lies in the size of China's population relative to its arable land. High population density effectively rules out grazing livestock and dictates a reliance on crops, for it takes several pounds of feed to produce one pound of meat (or milk or cheese).*

This crops-only agrarian economy is distinctive for its very high land productivity and very low labor productivity. Kawachi Jūzō, working with John Lossing Buck's data, has shown that Chinese agriculture in the 1930's in fact attained a much higher crop yield per unit of cultivated area than the much more modernized American agriculture of the day. Yields per unit of cropped area in Buck's "winter wheat–kaoliang area" (which encompasses the Hebei–northwest Shandong plain studied in this book) were comparable to those of the midwestern United States. But China's "winter wheat–kaoliang area" cropped with a higher frequency: a three-crops-in-two-years system of sorghum, wheat, and soybeans, compared with a two-crops-in-three-years system of wheat, fallow for grazing, and wheat in the Midwest. If one takes into account these differences in cropping frequency, the Chinese yields work out to roughly 216 to 247 catties annually per mu of cultivated area, or 647 to 740 kilograms per acre, as opposed to about 133 catties per mu, or 400 kilograms per acre, in the United States.† This was of course almost entirely the result of much more intensive cultivation: a ratio of about 23 : 1 in labor use for wheat, and 13 : 1 for sorghum (Kawachi 1963; see also Grove & Esherick 1980: 423). This combination of high land productivity and low labor productivity documents the fact of agricultural involution in recent centuries.

The "incipient capitalism" analysis, on the other hand, directs our attention to agricultural commercialization and to the social differentiation accompanying that commercialization. Agrarian China should not be seen as undergoing only quantitative changes under the pressure of population. Increased proportions of peasants came to be involved in cash-cropping and to be differentiated into a wide spectrum of groups positioned differently in two sets of production relations. The conceptual category of "feudalism" emphasizes the axis of rent relations, and distinguishes between those who paid one-half of the produce of their farms in rent and those who lived off such rent without farming themselves (as well as owner-cultivators who worked their own farms). The incipient capitalism model em-

---

*Buck (1937a: 12) points out that an acre of land produces six to seven times as much in crops used directly for human consumption as one used for the production of milk.

†These figures do not take account of the fallow year when the field was used for grazing.

phasizes the second major axis of production relations in the pre-revolutionary peasant economy—wage labor—and distinguishes between those who hired labor (generally for about one-third of its produce) and those who hired out for a meager wage. Attention to both of these axes permits a systematic classification of rural society into the categories of landlords, rich peasants, middle peasants, poor peasants, and agricultural workers, as was done in the Land Reform Law of 1950 (discussed in Chap. 4 below). It also brings out the central patterns of agrarian social change in the three or four centuries before the Revolution.

To take account at once of production relations and of population, this book draws on the mass of Japanese field surveys and on the Qing Board of Punishment archives for a comparative history of managerial and family farming in Hebei–northwest Shandong. The two kinds of farming differed in production relations, one relying principally on wage labor and the other on family labor. Shifts from family farming to managerial farming tell about the spread of wage labor and the rise of larger farms. The two kinds of farms also differed in the ways in which they responded to population pressure, one adjusting its labor supply according to the changing needs of the farm while the other often could not. A comparison of differential labor use in the two kinds of farming thus reveals the workings of population pressure on the family farm economy.

A comparative analysis of farm productivity in these two kinds of farms tells about development as well as stagnation in agriculture. The managerial farms were the largest as well as the most successful farms in the North China countryside. Their rise along with the spread of agricultural commercialization attests to agricultural development in the area. Their inability to effect qualitative breakthroughs in farm productivity, on the other hand, illustrates the roots of agricultural stagnation.

The twin stories of managerial and family farming attend at once to the twin factors of production relations and productive forces, and will bring out clearly the fact of social change in a context of economic involution. Such a pattern of change differs from the separate projections both of formalist and of Marxist analysis. The North China countryside underwent neither simply involution nor simply the beginnings of a transition to capitalism. What happened was differentiation within the context of a tenacious and involuting small peasant economy.

The absence of dynamic economic growth along Western lines

meant a pattern of social change different from the pattern that accompanied the rise of capitalism. Western Europe in the early modern and modern periods saw a long-term process of differentiation characterized by the rise of a capitalizing rural bourgeoisie and a proletarianizing peasantry. The latter part of this process—termed proletarianization in the current literature—saw more and more people coming to rely on wage labor for a living, from the landless agricultural laborer to the wage worker in rural industry, small-scale manufacturing, urban services, and, finally, industrial factories (Tilly 1978, 1979). Peasant society thus gave way to industrial capitalist society. In North China, by contrast, the process of change did not lead to the end of the small peasant economy, with capitalizing managerial farms developing into modern capitalist farms and the severing of an increasing proportion of peasants from their family farms as under proletarianization. Rather, it led only to the rise of labor-employing but noncapitalizing managerial farms and to the partial proletarianization of an increasing proportion of peasants, who came to rely at once on family farming and on wage labor for a living. Some of those peasants came to be employed in nonagricultural activities, but the majority remained tied to agriculture, most of them working as agricultural day-laborers, and others as year-laborers. I shall refer to this process variously as the increase in numbers and proportions of partly proletarianized peasants, or as the formation of a "poor peasant" economy and society or, simply, as semiproletarianization. In using the term semiproletarianization, I do not mean to suggest that it was transitional to capitalism and complete proletarianization, as if those represented some inevitable stage of historical development (Mao 1926), but rather to characterize a process of social change distinctive of a peasant society and economy under the combined pressures of social differentiation and intense population pressure, without the outlet and relief provided by dynamic capitalist development. I wish also to spotlight the partly proletarianized peasants' involvement in agricultural wage labor, as was the case in Hebei—northwest Shandong, rather than in nonagricultural labor, as the term "semiproletariat" is often meant to suggest in current usage.

This book suggests that under semiproletarianization, the majority of peasants took on new characteristics. It was not that they changed simply to nonpeasants or lost one of the three faces outlined earlier to another. Rather, the change consisted in a marked alteration in the relative proportions in which the three characteristics were mixed together, and in the addition of the new dimension of the peasant as part wage worker.

## The Issue of Underdevelopment

The question of how agrarian change in China differed from that of the West unavoidably raises the issue of why the Chinese economy did not undergo capitalist development.* Elvin went on from his analysis to argue that population pressure caused underdevelopment in two ways: it eroded the surplus above subsistence of the peasant farms, thereby precluding significant capital formation by them. It also powered the development of traditional agriculture to a very high level, and this became a disincentive to innovative investment. Chinese agriculture was thus caught in a "high level equilibrium trap" (Elvin 1973: esp. Chap. 17).

Elvin's views are consistent with Theodore Schultz's. Chinese peasants, no less than European or American farmers, were optimizing users of scarce resources who drove traditional agriculture to an efficient equilibrium level. Moreover, the example of England shows that despite the constraints of "feudal" land rents, the capitalist tenant-farmer could be the cutting edge of the modernization of agriculture. It thus makes no sense to seek agricultural modernization by restructuring the small family farm mode of productive organization or altering social relations through revolution.†

Elvin goes on to draw further political and prescriptive conclusions from his analysis. On the emotionally charged issue of the role of imperialism, he writes: "It was the historic mission of the modern West to ease and then break the high-level equilibrium trap in China" (1973: 315). Imperialism had stimulated economic development in China by opening the country to the world market and by making available modern technology. If the forces of international trade and technology transfer were only allowed to work their natural results, substantial industrialization would ensue and the enter-

---

*I use the word underdevelopment here to refer to nondevelopment of capitalist industrialization, or retarded development relative to what occurred in Western Europe. But as the following discussion should make clear, I do not wish to suggest a simple causal connection between imperialism and underdevelopment, as the dependency school does.

†Here both Elvin and Schultz echo Buck, who prefaced his work with an explicit rejection of social revolution and collectivization in favor of a program of population control and improved marketing and technology (Buck 1937a: 21–22; see also 1930: 159–66). American rural sociologists of his day had similarly argued for American-style family farming in preference to Soviet-style collectivization. (Sorokin & Zimmerman 1929 is the classic in the field; see esp. pp. 625–28.)

prise and inventiveness of China's peasants would reappear to modernize Chinese agriculture (pp. 315–16, 319).*

Since Marxists regard the peasant under "feudalism" as an exploited toiler whose surplus above subsistence was extracted by the landlords, they see little sense in asking, as Elvin does, why the small peasants did not accumulate capital to generate development. Those who controlled the surplus available for investment were the landlords, and it is to them that this question should be addressed. As long as feudal landlords expended the agricultural surplus for consumption rather than productive investment, the economy would stagnate. The capitalist transformation of the economy would take place only with the process of capital accumulation by a new class, leading to both new production relations of wage labor and new productive forces of capitalist development. The transition to a new mode of production comes through the interplay of production relations and productive forces: a given set of production relations will obtain until they become fetters on the development of the productive forces. A genuine transition to a new mode of production would come with changes in both production relations and productive forces. The rise of the bourgeoisie accompanies the capitalist development of the economy.†

Paul Baran, elaborating on the process of capital formation, drew a useful distinction between "actual surplus" after consumption and "potential surplus." The latter includes that portion of the surplus produced by peasants that is extracted from them and expended by the ruling classes for consumption. If existing class relations are altered, it is a surplus that can be mobilized for productive investment, hence the term potential surplus.‡ Victor Lippit has applied the concept of potential surplus to prerevolutionary China, attempting to quantify the amounts taken from peasants in the forms of rent, "surplus" above wages paid, interest on loans, and tax. The

*This is of course not the only prescriptive conclusion that can be drawn from analyses such as those outlined above. Perkins 1967, for example, in comparing 19th-century China and Japan, ascribes Japan's faster pace of development to the role played by the state: the late Qing government did not so much obstruct economic development as fail to lead it, in the manner of the Meiji government.

†This overarching analytical framework was of course best capsulized by Marx himself in his "Preface to *A Contribution to the Critique of Political Economy*" (Marx 1968: 182–83).

‡Lippit 1983 points out that Baran included in his notion of potential surplus not just the difference between necessary consumption and actual consumption, but also the difference between actual output and potential output in the economy. The latter is a much more nebulous concept and is not easily quantifiable. I restrict myself to the former idea here in referring to Baran's notion of potential surplus.

computation of the potential surplus extracted as rent is the most obvious: if about one-third (to round off Lippit's figures) of the farmland was rented, and the rent rate was usually about one-half of the agricultural output, then about one-sixth of the output was collected as rent. Repeating this procedure for the net produce of labor not paid in wages, for the interest that peasants paid to usurers, and for the taxes that smallholders paid to the state, Lippit arrives at a total surplus of just under 30 percent of the agricultural output, or about 19 percent of the total output of the economy (Baran 1957: esp. Chap. 2; Lippit 1974).

In Lippit's view, then, China's failure to develop stemmed not from a lack of surplus, as Elvin suggests,* but from the fact that the surplus was controlled by a ruling class committed to expending it for luxury consumption rather than for productive investment. In those circumstances, development could come only with social revolution. The economic meaning of China's land reform was that the state, through social revolution, wrested this potential surplus from the old ruling classes and redirected it toward productive investment and the improvement of the lot of the poorer members of society (Lippit 1974, 1978; see also Riskin 1975).

Lippit's demonstration of the existence of a substantial potential surplus is an important corrective to that part of Elvin's trap thesis. When production relations are brought into consideration, there can be no doubt that some members of the society controlled a surplus, and that an analysis of the roots of China's underdevelopment needs to be made socially specific and not be predicated on some abstract average family farm. For agriculture on the North China plain, my materials spotlight especially the managerial farmers who, unlike the landlords, were directly involved in production and who, unlike the small peasants operating family farms, possessed the capacity for capital accumulation and innovative investment. An analysis of their failure to do so lends concrete substance to the question of the hows and whys of surplus use in the pre-1949 agrarian economy.

The second part of Elvin's trap thesis, about how population density might have affected surplus use, still requires attention. It is an analysis that can usefully be integrated with the Marxist attention to production relations. The question then becomes one of how population and production relations interrelated to shape the use of surplus in the economy. The story of managerial agriculture supplies in

---

* Although Elvin acknowledges the existence of a surplus in his discussion (1973: 285–316), his graph of the "high-level equilibrium trap" (p. 313) argues that population pressure had whittled away the surplus above subsistence.

this case a concrete illustration of how a differentiated peasant economy under severe population pressure constrained capital formation in agriculture. It also documents the influence of China's distinctive sociopolitical system on capital formation.

The agricultural sector of the economy alone, of course, cannot tell the full story of the economy as a whole. Development in agriculture might help the industrial sector by supplying, for example, the needed surplus for investment; and underdevelopment in agriculture might obstruct development in industry by limiting, for example, the domestic market. Conversely, a dynamic industrial sector might pull up an agricultural sector, and a weak industrial sector might do the reverse. Whereas Lippit attempts to provide an explanatory framework for the entire economy, Elvin is primarily concerned with agriculture. To move toward an analysis of the larger question of how population pressure and social structure interrelated in China's underdevelopment, we will need to consider much more than just the agricultural sector. On that question, this book attempts to take only one step in the direction of a full analysis, by pointing to some ways in which the involuted but differentiated peasant economy shaped the formation and use of capital in China's infant industrial sector.

## The Issue of Imperialism

Another question is how rural North China was affected in the twentieth century by contact with the expanding capitalist economies of the West and Japan. Since formalists see the development of a market economy as crucial to economic growth, they tend to see the influence of world capitalism as beneficial. Elvin, as has been seen, maintains that imperialism provided China with its only opportunity to break out of a trap of stagnation. To explain why China nonetheless failed to develop, he points to constraints on the influence of a free market economy and to the obstructive role played by high population density. Along these same lines, the influential formalist theory of "economic dualism" maintains that the impact of world capitalism created two separate and distinct economies in China, a "modern sector" concentrated in the treaty port cities, and the "traditional economy" of the hinterland. The two supposedly largely went their separate and independent ways with minimal interpenetration. Labor-intensive and low-priced goods produced in the traditional sector retained their grip on the rural consumers of the traditional market. The often-cited example here is handwoven cloth, which not only survived, but grew in the face of competition from machine-woven cloth. Goods produced by the modern industries tended to be more capital-intensive and higher priced, hence beyond the means of the consumer of the traditional sector. Those goods were therefore largely restricted to the cities, as was the influence of the modern sector of the economy. Rural China thus remained substantially unaffected by imperialism and the modern urban economy (Hou 1963, 1965: esp. Chap. 7; Murphey 1977).

Few Marxists agree with an argument that sees imperialism as benign. According to one major current of Marxist analysis in the West, imperialism imposes a system by which the advanced capitalist economies extract surplus and raw materials from third-world countries. Within those countries, the cities in turn extract surplus from the countryside, thereby forming a two-tiered system of surplus extraction, or a "metropolis-satellite" and "core-periphery" relationship. Thus, far from being benign or inconsequential in its effects, imperialism actually prevents development in the victimized countries, imposes dependency, and causes and perpetuates underdevelopment (Frank 1967, 1978).

Immanuel Wallerstein (1974, 1979) has added to "dependency theory" the concept of a capitalist "world-system" in which the national economies of the world are integrated by a world market into a single economic system. It is a concept that has the advantage of helping to remove the emotional issues of exploitative intent from the discussion of imperialism, by emphasizing the impersonal, systemic, and transnational character of the phenomenon. It also has the virtue of highlighting the interconnectedness of similar phenomena worldwide, all linked to the expansion of the "capitalist world economy."

Substantivists have also emphasized the deleterious effects of imperialism, though from a different angle. In James Scott's view, the intrusion of impersonal capitalist market forces and relations undermines the personalized patron-client relations of the precapitalist moral community. And the increased extractiveness of the capitalist colonial state undermines the autonomy of the insulated precapitalist village.

Although all three of these theories hold much relevance for modern China, they share a common weakness in their neglect of the internal dynamics of change in peasant China before contact with the capitalist West. This book suggests that once that pattern of change is clearly defined and the effects of imperialism are seen against the span of several centuries, it will be clear that the economic dualism analysis, though substantially correct about the continued vitality of rural handicraft weaving, seriously underestimates the effects of accelerated agricultural commercialization on rural life; the dependency analysis, though correct about the disruptive effects of machine-spun yarn on handicraft cotton spinning, and about the implications of Japanese economic expansion into Shandong, overlooks the fundamental continuity of the small peasant economy and of "modern" patterns of change with the earlier, internally generated patterns of change; the moral economy analysis, finally, though correct in emphasis if not in specifics about the effects of world capitalism on rural socioeconomic relations, overestimates the role that moral constraints played in those relations before the modern period.

With regard to the question of the relationship between imperialism and modern China's underdevelopment, we need to look at the interactions between imperialism and the indigenous economy and social structure. The effort to isolate the single "factor" of imperialism, as if it were something that could be introduced or removed at will in a controlled experiment, seems to me fundamentally misguided. Once introduced, imperialism came to be merged and interconnected with other parts of the socioeconomic and sociopolitical system to form a single structure of underdevelopment. This book will suggest one possible new way of approaching the question: by focusing on the process of capital formation, in which imperialism was only one of several determinants.

THE CHINESE VILLAGE

The villages of the North China plain, like their peasants, merged into a single unit the several characteristics projected separately by formalist, substantivist, and Marxist analyses. Most village families to some extent produced for the market as individual units. From this perspective, the village was more a neighborhood of separate peasant families pursuing their individual interests than a solidary collectivity. Yet most villages were also, to one extent or another, self-contained economic units in which the community's residents consumed part of what they produced. The village marked off not only the boundaries of residence, but also to some extent the boundaries of production and consumption. Those ties of residence and workplace, moreover, were often reinforced by ties of kinship. From such a perspective, the village was an insular, and perhaps also solidary, community. At the same time, rent and wage-labor relations obtained in most villages. Focus on those relations results in a picture of the village as a stratified society in which some villagers extracted a surplus from others.

As with the differentiated peasant economy, an understanding of North China's village communities and of the ways in which they changed in recent centuries will require an analysis that integrates the formalist, Marxist, and substantivist analyses, and distinguishes among different types of villages. Most villages possessed all three faces, but the relative proportions in which the three sets of characteristics were mixed together varied with village economic and social structure, and with the nature of external power acting on the village.

*Past Scholarship*

American historians' image of Chinese villages has been shaped mainly by scholarship from the formalist perspective, most powerfully by the work of G. William Skinner. Skinner set out to correct mainstream anthropology's substantivist tendency to concern itself exclusively with the small community, to the neglect of the larger world beyond the village. As he put it:

> Anthropological fieldwork on Chinese society, by focusing attention almost exclusively on the village, has with few exceptions distorted the reality of rural social structure. Insofar as the Chinese peasant can be said to live in a self-contained world, that world is not the village but the standard marketing community. The effective social field of the peasant, I will argue, is delimited not by the narrow horizons of his village but rather by the boundaries of his standard marketing area. (1964–65: 32)

The standard market town, according to Skinner, is the lowest tier in a three-tiered hierarchy of local marketing systems. This is where "all the normal trade needs of the peasant household" are met—where the upward flow of agricultural products and craft items begins and the downward flow of goods destined for peasant consumption ends. The typical standard marketing town in China is the central place for a community encompassing about 1,500 households in 18 or so villages deployed in a hexagonal pattern over an area of about 50 square kilometers (pp. 3, 6).

A peasant in Kao-tien-tzu (Gaodianzi), the market town where Skinner did three months of fieldwork in 1949,

> had, by the age of fifty, attended his standard market three thousand times. He had, at least one thousand times on the average, been jammed into a small area along one street with the same male representatives of

every other household in that community. He made purchases from peasant vendors whose homes lay in all directions from the town, and more to the point, he socialized in the teahouses with fellow peasants from village communities far removed from his own. . . . Few persons who went to market failed to spend at least an hour in one or two. Codes of hospitality and sociability operated to bring any community member who entered the door quickly to a table as somebody's guest. Inevitably an hour in the teahouse enlarged a man's circle of acquaintances and deepened his social knowledge of other parts of the community. (1964–65: 35)

In this picture of the peasant's social world, every peasant had a "nodding acquaintance with every adult in all parts of the marketing system." The standard marketing community defined the operating parameters of matchmakers, secret society lodges, annual fairs, religious societies, dialects, and so on. It was, in a word, the "effective social field of the peasant" and the basic unit of Chinese society (pp. 40–41).

Skinner has since extended his marketing model to incorporate an eight-tiered hierarchy of "central places," ranging from the standard market upward through county seats to regional cities and central metropolises. And the local marketing systems have been extended upward to become functionally integrated "regional systems" within eight "macroregions" in China, each centering around regional or central metropolises. Skinner has also added a powerful diachronic dimension, extending the marketing structures and regional systems backwards in time to encompass "cyclical rhythms" spanning centuries (Skinner 1977a, b).

It is a testimony to the power and influence of Skinner's work that what he had intended as a corrective to an overemphasis on the village has ended by virtually exterminating its opposition. A generation of American historians has come to take for granted that villages in China were so highly integrated into larger trading systems that there is no need to give serious attention to the village as a unit. This assumption, implicit in much of our past scholarship, is perhaps best expressed in the words of Theda Skocpol, a comparativist who was totally dependent on the secondary literature for her picture of the structure of Chinese society:

We must note that the basic unit of community in traditional China was not the individual village . . . but the marketing community composed of a cluster of villages. . . . Though they resided and worked in individual villages, the marketing community was the significant local world of the peasants. There they regularly bought and sold at the peri-

odic market, obtained craftman's services, secured loans, participated
in religious rites, and found marriage partners. (1979: 149)

This downplaying of the village community, predicated on the basically formalist perception of the village as little more than an atomized neighborhood of a larger economic and sociopolitical market
system, has received unwitting reinforcement from several other
sources. Scholars in the United States have concentrated on the state
and the gentry in their study of the political structure of late imperial China. Commoner peasants, except for times of violent rebel-
lions, have been seen largely as passive subjects of imperial rule and
gentry leadership. K. C. Hsiao's classic *Rural China: Imperial Control in the Nineteenth Century* (1960) perhaps best exemplifies the
use of a dualistic state-gentry model of analysis. His baseline for
nineteenth-century changes comes from the ideal projected by the
imperial bureaucracy itself, in which all rural households were systematically grouped into artificial decimal groupings of households
for tax purposes (the *lijia* system) and for purposes of police control
(*baojia*). By this means, state power and bureaucratization supposedly penetrated inside natural villages to reach individual households. Hsiao also equates virtually all organized activity in society
with the gentry: "It is not an exaggeration to say that the gentry constituted the keystone of rural organization. The village could and did
exist without the gentry; but villages without gentry could hardly
show any high degree of organized activity" (p. 317). In this picture
of a passive peasantry, changes in the sociopolitical structure of imperial China consisted mainly in alternating shifts of power between
the two poles of state and gentry. In the nineteenth century the formal state apparatus declined, and political power gravitated toward
the pole of informal gentry power. The village did not figure as a separate entity in this process.

Ch'ü T'ung-tsu (1962) and Chang Chung-li (1955) employ substantially the same model in their influential studies. Like Hsiao,
Ch'ü equates all leadership in local society with the gentry. Beyond
the apparatuses of county governments, he examines only the relationship between government and gentry. No consideration is given
to the possibility of endogenous political structures in village communities, and of the relationship between them and the state. And
Chang, also like Hsiao, stresses the all-pervasive nonofficial functions that the gentry performed in local society, without consideration of the possible leadership roles played by commoner villagers.

Philip Kuhn (1970) has built on these analyses to point out the long-term trend of "militarization" that began with the formation of local *tuanlian* under gentry leadership in the late eighteenth century in response to the White Lotus Rebellion. This trend, with the accompanying shift of power from state to gentry, was the background to the local "self-government" movements of the twentieth century, when the gentry arrogated to themselves ever-greater political power. Kuhn sees the rise of local bullies and tyrants in the 1920's and 1930's as part of a long-term process of the devolution of state power to the gentry. That has prompted him to suggest that these men originated from the lower gentry of old (Kuhn 1975). In a more recent article (1979), Kuhn has studied the Guomindang's attempts to re-bureaucratize local government with this same framework of alternating shifts of power between the state and the local elite.

All these studies assume that villages were completely integrated into larger systems either through an intrusive state apparatus or through the pervasive influence of the gentry. This view easily complements Skinner's model of villages as units that were socially and economically integrated into larger trading systems. Thus, even if villages were in fact often made up wholly of commoners, with neither gentry nor officials in residence, we can still maintain that we need only study the state and the gentry to understand village organization and political life.

As it happens, this picture of villages has also been reinforced by the post-1949 studies in China on peasant wars. In that massive body of scholarship, peasants have generally been depicted as a single "peasant class" that transcended villages and acted as one. There have of course been lively debates over the specific ideological and behavioral characteristics of "the peasants" (see *Zhongguo lishi nianjian* 1979; K. C. Liu 1981), but there has been little consideration of whether peasants might have acted on occasion simply as members of their village communities.

Most Chinese studies of the Revolution have similarly stressed class action to the exclusion of community bonds. Whether we read Mao's writings, or the Land Reform Law of 1950, or the immense body of scholarship on the history of the Revolution itself, we will not find much consideration given to the village as a unit worthy of analytical attention. The village community, we are led to believe, was of no consequence in the social dynamic of the Revolution— and yet, in the subsequent restructuring of rural society, the village was left intact as a basic unit of Chinese society.

Where this dominant "class model" approach is qualified, it is done from the point of view of kinship organization, not of village community (see, most recently, Fu Yiling 1979). Kinship, it is acknowledged, often cut across class lines and greatly complicated peasant class action. But the village as such is merely subsumed under the broader categories of class and kinship. In this respect, the perspective accords with recent anthropological studies by Western scholars, who have tended to focus mainly on elite lineage groups to the neglect of communities of commoners. (See Watson 1982 for a thoughtful summary of this body of work.)

The substantivist emphasis on the village as a collectivity has received sustained attention only in Japanese scholarship on China. One of its first spokesmen was Hirano Yoshitarō, who argued that Chinese and Japanese villages alike embodied a *kyōdōtai*, or collectivity, with an endogenous political structure and shared religious institutions and beliefs. But this was an unfortunate beginning for the Japanese substantivist school, for Hirano's intentions were not merely academic, but also political. He went on to maintain that this East Asian kyōdōtai was distinct from the individualistic societies of the West and could form the basis for a Great East Asian Co-prosperity Sphere. Hirano's critic, from a combined formalist and Marxist perspective, was Kainō Michitaka, who maintained that the Chinese village was atomized and stratified: it had neither a fixed boundary nor community property, its families farmed or worked only for themselves, and its leadership was based on class and power, not community consensus. Kainō's intent was to advocate the path of development that he had idealized for the West—in which private property and peasant individualism led to the development of capitalism, democracy, and a genuine kyōdōtai based on the equal political participation of all the members of a community (Hatada 1973: 35–49). Kainō's criticisms of Hirano are reminiscent of Popkin's (1979) more recent critique of Scott.

Despite its unfortunate beginnings, the substantivist emphasis on the village as community has shaped subsequent Japanese scholarship. Japanese wartime field investigations in China drew on a strong ethnographic tradition and accumulated much concrete information about the community structures of Chinese villages. Later academic analyses, even from formalist and Marxist perspectives, have kept the issue of kyōdōtai at the center of discourse and research. Shimizu Morimitsu (1951), for example, has gone on to posit a connection between isolated village communities and "Oriental despotism," in the tradition both of substantivist analysis and of Marx's notion of an "Asiatic mode of production." Niida Noboru (1963: 365–83) has addressed kyōdōtai mainly in terms of kinship and class, whereas Imahori Seiji (1963: 42–61) has argued that various forms of kyōdōtai are nothing but ways of cloaking and maintaining class rule and exploitation. Hatada Takashi (1973) has presented some of the most balanced and concrete analyses of Chinese villages, while sharply distinguishing his views from the overstated case of Hirano and Shimizu.

## North China Villages

One major reason for the differences between Western formalist and Japanese substantivist scholarship is that each has drawn on different empirical bases. Western scholars have studied mainly the most highly commercialized areas of China (e.g., the Sichuan basin in Skinner's studies, the lower Yangzi in much of historical research, and Fujian-Guangdong and Hong Kong–Taiwan in most of the recent Western anthropological research), where market development is most advanced, social stratification most pronounced, and lineage organization most highly developed. They have therefore understandably stressed the side of the village that is integrated into supravillage market systems and elite kinship networks.

Japanese scholarship, especially on China's modern period, has by contrast been influenced to a considerable extent by wartime field studies carried out on the North China plain. Here dry farming and lack of water transport made for a much less highly commercialized agrarian economy than the lower Yangzi or the Sichuan basin. Peasants produced for the market to a much lesser extent and spent much less time in marketing outside their villages. The low degree of agricultural commercialization, with relatively little agricultural surplus, made for a society composed mainly of owner-cultivators whose production activities seldom took them outside their home villages. This preponderance of owner-cultivators made for a greater presence of the state, which since the eighteenth century had levied taxes only on landowners and not by head. And the greater presence of the state tended to contribute to a fuller articulation of a village political organization to cope with state demands. The low level of social stratification and rarity of elite members in rural lineages, finally, meant also the absence of elaborate and powerful kinship groupings such as those in the lower Yangzi or the Pearl River delta. Here lineages typically comprised only peasants, possessed only a modicum of corporate property (a few mu of burial ground), and seldom crossed over the boundaries of villages or village and town. Such lineage structures reinforced the insular-solidary character of most village communities.

In the present context of Western formalist and Chinese Marxist scholarship, we need first to redress the imbalance between the formalist-Marxist views and the substantivist view, and to bring the relatively uncommercialized and "inward-oriented" village (Migdal 1974) back to our attention. The recent work of Elizabeth Perry (1980: 152–207) shows how the Red Spears of the North China plain in the 1920's were a movement of dispersed village communities, typically comprising mainly owner-cultivators, that took to arms to protect themselves from banditry, excessive state taxation, and, during the Sino-Japanese war, foreign invasion. The character of these armed communities was well summarized by Liu Shaoqi in 1938 in a report on the Communist efforts in North China. According to Liu, the Red Spears, the Heavenly Gate Society (Tianmen hui) and the Lianzhuang hui (lit., "association linking villages") alike were "purely self-defense organizations" that would only fight when their homes were threatened, but would not "come out to engage actively in resistance, to attack bandits, or fight as guerrillas" (1938: 51). Skinner, as if to encompass phenomena such as the Red Spears, and as if to correct his own earlier overemphasis on the standard marketing community, himself supplied a model of analysis that attempts to take into account both the village highly integrated into larger systems and the village that is primarily an isolated unit. In that model, villages undergo cycles of "opening" and "closure" along with periods of stability and instability in dynasties (1971).

To test for possible correlations between community organization and village economic and social structures, this book draws on 1930's Japanese field studies of 33 villages of the Hebei–northwest Shandong plain to develop a typology of seven different kinds of villages in the area. The typology distinguishes the relatively uncommercialized villages from the moderately and the highly commercialized ones (these classifications are defined in the next chapter), the villages with little handicraft industry from those with highly developed industries, the truly rural villages from the suburban ones, the villages that saw little migration from those that were home communities of migrants who worked on the Manchurian frontier, and the villages that were relatively untouched by twentieth-century man-made disasters of civil war and invasion from those that were severely affected by them. Information about community structures in the villages that remained relatively unaffected by twentieth-century developments help to fill out a baseline picture of village communities in the Qing period.

For pre-twentieth-century village-state relations, this book draws on a county government archive of the nineteenth century to reconstruct the details of tax collection and document more precisely the nature of state power over the village. Oral history materials about different ways in which villages responded to twentieth-century state efforts to impose artificial administrative structures on them also help to fill out a bascline picture. I shall suggest that most pre-twentieth-century North China villages were socially and politically far more insular than we have assumed.

## Twentieth-Century Changes

A clearer grasp of village-state relations in the nineteenth century helps to bring twentieth-century changes into sharper relief. The important works of Frederic Wakeman Jr. (1966), Philip Kuhn (1970), and Joseph Esherick (1976) have shown well how the gentry increased their political power at the expense of the state, first through "militarization" to deal with rebellion, and then through elite leadership in modernizing reforms and local "self-government." At the same time, K. C. Liu (1978) and Stephen MacKinnon (1980) have shown well how this was paralleled by state efforts to re-bureaucratize in order to reverse the trend of gentry-led militarization and self-government. Ernest Young (1977), finally, has shown how the coincidence of those two trends gave rise to complex patterns in which decentralization was meshed with the centralizing efforts of the state, and militarization and local assemblies with the bureaucratizing efforts of the central government.

Preoccupation with these late Qing trends, and the unavoidable divisions in scholarly opinion, have kept scholars from turning to changes in the nature of village-state relations in the twentieth century. In the Western world, the expansion of state power vis-à-vis local communities was part of the rise of the centralized modern nation-state from the parcelized sovereignties of the feudal age. The combined process, termed "modern state-making," has been grasped with crystal clarity (Tilly 1975a, b). In China, however, scholarly attention has been drawn mainly to the more dramatic developments: the state's partial loss of sovereignty to imperialism, the decline and collapse of the imperial state, and the rise of decentralized warlordism. Contrasts between the imperial state and the Republican state, moreover, have been blurred both by our tendency to attribute modern characteristics to the imperial state (after all, it was remark-

ably modern in some respects, especially in its examination system),
and by the fact that the Republican state was not nearly as modernized as its contemporary Western counterparts.

This book draws on village-level documentation to reconstruct a
picture of changes in village-state relations in the twentieth century.
The emphasis, once again, is on taxation, that critical locus of state-
village relations. Twentieth-century county governments, I shall
suggest, took on expanded political functions and became substantially more intrusive and extractive vis-à-vis villages than their predecessors in the Qing.

Village-state relations in the twentieth century were shaped not
only by the nature of governmental power, but also by the internal
structures of villages. Semiproletarianization, I shall show, brought
with it a progressive dissolution of the insular, solidary village community. As owner-cultivators gave way to poor peasants who worked
part of the year outside and whose partial or total alienation from
landed property weakened their identification with the interests of
the community, tightly knit villages began to give way to less insular, solidary villages. When these tendencies were reinforced by the
heightened instabilities of the twentieth century—from man-made
and natural disasters, and from frontier and urban migration—
villages became increasingly atomized.

Where the trends of bureaucratization and semiproletarianization
intersected, severe new stresses resulted. These were especially apparent in village governments, those critical points at which heteronomous state power met indigenous village political organizations.
In the more extreme cases, as will be seen, this intersection gave rise
to the abuse of villages by "local bullies and evil gentry" (*tuhao
lieshen*) and "evil tyrants" (*eba*, the more common term in the
north), which drew such widespread commentary from contemporary observers, including revolutionaries like Mao Zedong (1927),
academics like Fei Xiaotong (1948), and novelists like Ding Ling
(1949). The rise of that phenomenon, as much as anything else, indicates how the larger processes of agricultural involution and social
differentiation studied in this book affected village communities and
their relations with the state.

# CHAPTER 2

# The Sources
# and the Villages

The study of peasants and villages in Chinese history has been severely limited by the lack of adequate source materials. For the elites, historians have been able to draw on large quantities of official sources, elite writings, and elite genealogies, and for more recent centuries, on the large numbers of elite biographies in local gazetteers for quantitative analysis. These sources often have a richness of texture and depth of time that are the envy of historians of other countries. For the "little people" of Chinese history, however, we have yet to gain access to the kinds of materials that have informed the best of the recent studies of social history in other countries. Local government archives, such as those used by Georges Lefebvre (1934) in his monumental study of the peasants of Nord, or long runs of cadastral records, such as the *compoix* of Languedoc used by Emmanuel Le Roy Ladurie (1974), are still beyond the reach of China historians. Materials like village parish registers (the *shūmon aratamechō* in the case of Japan), which have made possible the recent breakthroughs in demographic research by the "reconstitution" of the demographic histories of individual villages across several centuries (e.g., Levine 1977; T. Smith 1977), may not exist at all.

Still, the fact that China's peasant society remained intact into the mid-twentieth century means that China scholars have access to masses of modern ethnographic data far richer than the materials available to the historians of peasant Europe. Those data have yet to be fully exploited. This chapter discusses the large body of materials on 33 villages in the Hebei–northwest Shandong plain compiled by Japanese social scientists in the 1930's; they form the backbone of this study. My choice of a geographical area was largely determined by those materials. The Board of Punishment archives of homicide cases in the Qing period and records in the fragmentary Baodi county government archive on tax collection at the lowest levels of sub-county government in the nineteenth century have been valuable for placing the twentieth-century data in historical perspective.

### THE MANTETSU SURVEYS

The Japanese field survey data consist of three main groups of materials, most of them compiled under the auspices of the Japanese South Manchurian Railway Company (Minami Manshū Tetsudō Kabushiki Kaisha—or Mantetsu, for short) during the years 1935–42. The first group of data grew out of a systematic investigation of northeastern Hebei between the years 1935 and 1939. On May 31, 1933, Japan took its first step south of the wall, imposing, through the so-called Tanggu Truce, a "demilitarized zone" down to a diagonal line joining Yanqing, Baodi, and Lutai, just north of Beijing and Tianjin. Two years later, in preparation for the full-scale invasion and occupation to come, Japanese military intelligence created an investigative corps to study village conditions in the northeastern Hebei area (Kitō chiku nōson jittai chōsahan). The 30-men corps included seven intelligence agents assigned by the army, researchers of the Mantetsu research staff (mainly from its Tianjin office and Economic Research Section), and nine Japanese students studying in China under Mantetsu auspices at the time. These researchers met for weeks to set up a research design and questionnaire, and then, between April 22 and May 15, 1936, went into the field in 14 squads to gather basic information on 25 villages in 16 counties (MT, Kitō 1936a).

In the following year, four villages in four counties—Dabeiguan in Pinggu, Xifanzhuang in Baodi, Michang in Fengrun, and Qianlianggezhuang in Changli—were selected for in-depth study by five-men investigating teams. This time the studies were done without the participation of military intelligence, and the teams were made up in the main of researchers from the Mantetsu's Tianjin Office, which now assumed full responsibility for the investigations. The teams spent four weeks in the field, from February 16 to March 17, 1937, gathering detailed statistical information on each household in 16 categories, including landownership, wage labor, cropping, marketing, taxes, capital equipment, and income and expenses. The results on three of the villages were considered satisfactory for publication (MT, Kitō 1937a–c). The fourth village, in Baodi, was deemed to require further investigation. That survey was never published.

A third study was undertaken in 1937–39, this time centering only on cotton-producing Michang village, in Fengrun county. A resident Chinese researcher was assigned to the village to help 14 selected households keep detailed records of every item of income and expense. The result was three volumes of statistical data—undoubtedly the most detailed ever compiled on any single group of village households in Chinese history (MT, Hokushi jimukyoku chōsabu 1938–41).*

The second group of field survey data is the product of the combined efforts of Mantetsu investigators and academic researchers from the law faculty of Tokyo University and the economics faculty of Kyoto University. Between November 1940 and December 1942, 16 researchers (including two Chinese investigators) made seven field trips of from three to five weeks each to study six villages: Shajing in Shunyi, Sibeichai in Luancheng, Lengshuigou in Licheng, Houxiazhai in Enxian, Houjiaying in Changli, and Wudian in Liangxiang. The researchers usually went into the villages in groups of four, but sometimes either singly or in groups of as many as ten at a time. One or two researchers were assigned to collect data on a specific topic: the village (including especially village government and community organizations), landownership, land sale and purchase, tenancy, water control, land deeds, tax, credit and trade, and kinship. (Uchiyama 1980: 52–54 gives a useful tabulation of the division of responsibility and the different field trips; see also KC, 6:8–9.)

The approach was to interview villagers, sometimes several at a time and sometimes individually, usually about one topic at a time, and to record the questions and answers verbatim. These interviews produced 114 reports (listed KC, 1:57–61), later published in six massive volumes totaling, in large 2,400-character pages, about 3,200 pages. Maps of the counties (from gazetteers) and detailed maps of the villages are appended. The best of the surveys have detailed household-by-household data. The published volumes, edited by Niida Noboru, also contain a detailed and very precise index. The most thoroughly studied villages were Shajing (KC, vols. 1 and 2) and Sibeichai (vol. 3). Shajing was visited six times by the investigators, Sibeichai four.† This group of surveys is particularly rich in the kind of information that can be covered well in interviews but not in

---

*I have drawn extensively on both Michang studies in this book. It is important to keep in mind that the household numbers assigned in the later study do not correspond to those used in the 1937 study.

†Many of the investigators later published scholarly articles on their areas of special responsibility. I have drawn on several of these to supplement the raw data. (For a list, see KC, 1:63–65.) See also Myers 1970 for a glimpse of the extraordinarily rich data available in these materials, and for a large and useful bibliography of the Mantetsu and related Japanese surveys.

statistical surveys (e.g., village government, community organizations, and qualitative information on production relations). The northeastern Hebei survey was much stronger in data on the agricultural economy.

The third group of field survey data I have drawn on consists of anthropological monographs on individual villages written by Mantetsu researchers and others. As descriptive-analytical studies, these are a valuable adjunct to the raw data of the other groups of material. Four are especially useful for their rich information on farm technology, labor schedules, cropping patterns, the use of animal power, and other aspects of agriculture: those on Lujiazhai in Zunhua, Xiaojie in Tongxian, Macun in Huailu, and Qizhai in Gaotang. Three others have detailed household data: those on Nanquanfuzhuang in the Jinan suburb, Dongjiao in the Shijiazhuang suburb, and Tiaoshanying near Mancheng.* Of the three groups of materials, this is the least explored, by either Japanese or Western scholars.

Compared with other rural survey data of the time, the Mantetsu materials stand out for their richness of detail on individual villages and households. All three groups of investigations took individual villages as their unit of analysis. The 13 best studies (see Map 2.1 for the villages) give detailed data on every household in the village. In many, like the studies on Shajing and Sibeichai, one can read extended conversations that the investigators had with dozens of individual villagers. Indeed, Michang village was so thoroughly studied that one could write entire chapters on a single household from the mass of data gathered over the four years 1936–39. In all cases, individual households and villages can be examined up close through these data.

By contrast, virtually all other rural survey materials from the 1920's and 1930's show us the outlines of the forest, but seldom the trees and the foliage. Consider, for example, John Lossing Buck's national surveys (1930; 1937a, b). The approach used was drawn from urban sociology: to sample a number of households across the map of China, much as one might pick names out of a telephone book to survey the population of a city. The first study surveyed 2,866 farms, the second 16,685. There was no systematic formula for selecting households from villages. The first study surveyed as few as two households and as many as 102 in nine villages in Hebei. The second

_____

*Three other studies deserve special mention for the quality of their detailed information: those on Laowazhuang in the suburb of Taian and Gaojialou in the suburb of Weixian (MT, Hokushi keizai chōsajo 1940b, c); and the one on Xihangezhuang in the suburb of Qingdao (MT, Hokushi jimukyoku chōsabu 1939).

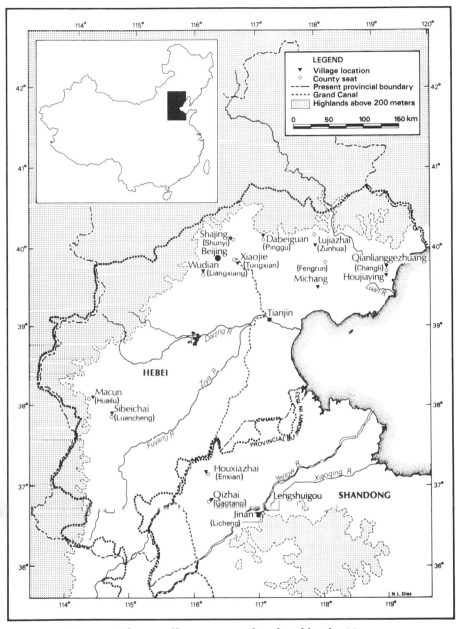

MAP 2.1. The 13 villages surveyed in detail by the Mantetsu

surveyed only one household in 21 of 101 villages studied in Hebei, but 100 households in two of the villages (Buck 1930: 6, 102, 235; 1937b: 465–66). These surveys, as we will see, are far from representative. But in any case, however useful the aggregate figures are for an overview, Buck's data do not give us a picture of individual villages and households.

The Land Commission of the Guomindang used an improved version of the same method for its surveys. The overall strategy, in ten provinces (of 22 studied) selected for special emphasis, was to survey one-fifth of all households in one-fifth of the counties. In the end, a total of some 1,800,000 households were surveyed, by some 3,000 investigators mobilized for the project (Tudiweiyuanhui 1937: 1–6). This produced a reasonably representative sample, with the result that the average per capita cultivated area of the farming population was a realistic 4.2 mu in Hebei and 3.7 mu in Shandong (3.2 mu and 2.7 mu, respectively, if the nonfarming population is included), as compared with Buck's abnormally high national average of 7.4 mu per capita in 1930 and his still unrealistic 7-mu average in the "winter wheat–kaoliang area" in 1937 (Tudiweiyuanhui 1937: 23, 24; Buck 1930: vii, 1937b: 291). Buck's was really a sampling of the rural well-to-do; but though the Land Commission's sampling was much more representative, it too affords no more than an overview.

Several studies by Chinese social scientists that focused on individual counties or groups of counties bring us somewhat closer to the ground. The Li Jinghan group's investigation of Dingxian is the best known (Li 1933). Research on this county went beyond rural surveys to include studies of land taxation (Feng Huade 1936) and rural industry (Zhang Shiwen 1944: 13–14). Similar though less detailed studies were made of Qingyuan county in central Hebei and a group of 24 northeastern Hebei counties (Zhang Peigang 1935; 1936–37); all these studies give us a more detailed picture of the localities than the national surveys of Buck and the Land Commission. But like them, they paid little attention to the village as a unit of study and typically presented their data in aggregated averages of household samples that cut across numerous villages. One searches in vain in these studies for profiles of individual villages and households.

Other available Chinese and Western qualitative data—as opposed to Buck's and the Land Commission's largely quantitative data—have been assembled in three volumes by the Institute of Economics in Beijing (Li Wenzhi 1957; Zhang Youyi 1957). These materials—large portions of which are anecdotal observations by urban intellectuals, officials, journalists, and travelers—help to round out the overview we get from Buck and the Land Commission.* But, once again, they do not permit us to see the villages and households up close.

There are some notable exceptions to these general observations about the nature of the available Chinese and Western materials. For my geographical area, David and Isabel Crook (1959) have given us an anthropological-journalistic account of revolution in the village of "Ten Mile Inn" in Wu'an county at the foot of the Taihang mountains in southern Hebei. Though their book lacks the quantitative data of the Mantetsu-surveyed villages, it provides good information on the process of revolution during the Sino-Japanese war years in the liberated zone—something that the Mantetsu materials of course lack. And Sidney Gamble's *North China Villages* (1963), based on the Li Jinghan group's study of Dingxian, supplies useful information on village government that complements the Mantetsu materials. If we move outside of the immediate geographical focus of this book, then there is also William Hinton's *Fanshen* (1966), documenting the tribulations of "Longbow village" near Changzhi in southeastern Shanxi during the civil war years 1945–48, when the village underwent the paroxysms of violent land reform. Like the Crooks' account, it is a useful complement to the Mantetsu materials.

A CRITICAL ASSESSMENT OF THE MANTETSU MATERIALS

To take full advantage of the rich Mantetsu materials, one must squarely face their limitations. As one of the original members of the Mantetsu staff has asked, given that the research was sponsored by conquerors for their use in colonial administration, how objective could the findings be, regardless of the intentions of the individual investigators (Noma 1964)? Further, the investigators gained access to the villages through the military authorities and the collaborationist county governments; on occasion, they had to be protected by armed guards to carry out their research. And once inside the villages, they often relied heavily on the village elite for their information. Sometimes, as one cynic has pointed out, the Japanese investigators were even entertained at village expense, at heavy cost to the villagers (Furushima 1955; see also Uchiyama 1980).

*The Rural Reconstruction Commission of the Executive Yuan (Xingzhengyuan nongcun fuxing weiyuanhui 1934a, b) conducted a series of surveys with a different, on-the-ground method that focused on individual villages. Those studies are useful supplements to the Land Commission's overview. But they did not cover Hebei and Shandong.

Defenders of these studies have countered that some of them were in fact academic efforts that were little influenced by the occupation authorities. The joint Tokyo University–Mantetsu study of six villages, especially, was guided largely by an academic research model designed by Professor Suehiro Itsutarō of Tokyo University's law faculty. Suehiro was particularly interested in capturing the customs of Chinese society, not as abstractions but as they were actually being lived by the people of the society. His aim was to discern the special characteristics of Chinese society through its living and changing customs. It was a research model born of the discipline of legal sociology that rose above the immediate concerns of occupation, and lent academic substance and objectivity to the work. (See especially Niida Noboru's preface to the six volumes: KC, 1 : 1).

All this is true enough. Nevertheless, I think there can be no denying the intelligence-gathering aspects of the six-villages study. The Mantetsu was a semiofficial company with intimate ties to the government. It sponsored myriad research projects that were directly concerned with occupation intelligence. The six-villages study was undeniably part and parcel of these activities. (J. Young 1966 provides a good overview and bibliography of this research.)

Likewise, the fact that the research was sponsored by a conquest government undoubtedly limited the field investigators' access. In the case of Lengshuigou (about 25 kilometers east of Jinan in Shandong), the least satisfactory of the six studies, only the initial investigation, in November–December 1940, could be conducted inside the village itself. So hostile were the villagers toward the alien investigators that the researchers had to conduct their second and third investigations, in 1941, from the county seat, by summoning villagers there for interviews. A reading of these interviews shows that the villagers sometimes engaged in a kind of passive resistance to the study: they answered questions with a perfunctory "yes" or "no," or provided contradictory testimony (e.g., KC, 4 : 147, 157, 158). In 1942 the research group had to abandon this study altogether and shifted instead to a neighboring village, where security was less of a problem. (KC, 4: p. 9 of Intro., 9, 11, 55; KC, 6 : 8–9.)

But contradictory and sketchy as much of the Lengshuigou material is, the interviews are still exceptionally rich in concrete information, especially about community organizations and the rain ceremonies, and I will be drawing on that information in this study. It is simply that with the data on this village, even more than others, the user would do well to heed the advice of one of the most down-to-earth of the original investigators, Andō Shizumasa: one must read the materials in toto for a full view of the village, keeping in mind the contradictory testimony and taking care not to accept a one-sided view of things; to merely look up a few details, via the index, in order to illustrate one's favorite themes (as many younger Japanese scholars have done; see Uchiyama 1980 on this point; also Hatada 1981), is to risk falsifying the real situation in the village.*

The Lengshuigou study was not typical, in any case. To quote from Hatada Takashi, one of the principal investigators (who went on to become a leading historian of both China and Korea):

> We had a very close relationship with the villagers [of Shajing]. There were occasions when we gathered with the children, the youth, and the old people for an athletic meet on the grounds of the grammar school, and passed a happy day together. There were times when the children would see us off at the station, and wept at the parting. . . . We were asked to mediate disputes, to help in resisting an attempt by a monk in the county town to take over the village's temple land. . . . The relationship between us was more than merely one of investigator and subject; it was much more affectionate and trusting. . . . We cannot forget that at the end of the war, when things were difficult for us, villagers who were living in Beijing came with sacks of American flour for us. This affectionate relationship we had with the villagers was one important reason we were able to carry out a scientific investigation despite the undeniable fact that it took place within the context of Japanese military occupation. (KC, 1:68)

I was able to confirm Hatada's fond memories when I restudied Shajing in April and November, 1980. Eighty-year-old Zhang Rui— the wealthiest member of the village at the time of the Japanese investigation, deputy village head (*fu cunzhang*) from 1936 and village head (*baozhang*) in 1942 (KC, 1:99–100, 177), recounted for me once more how the Japanese investigators helped them. Shajing village owned 20 mu of temple land, and neighboring Shimen village 23 mu. The villages had used the rent from this land to support a resident temple monk until around 1885, when they ceased to maintain a resident monk. In the twentieth century, the rent came to be used for special tax levies, the expenses of the new village school, and other needs of village government. Then, in 1942, a certain village tough of Shimen, Fan Baoshan, who had just returned from three years' imprisonment, conspired with the head monk of the Chenghuang temple in town to take over the temple land, claiming that it really belonged to the village temple, not the village, and

---

*Andō's no-nonsense investigative style is well illustrated in KC, 5:572–91.

that the local temple was under the jurisdiction of the Chenghuang temple in town. Since the two men were powerfully connected, and Fan especially was feared by everyone in the two villages, the people were at a loss what to do. The Shajing leaders decided to appeal to the Mantetsu investigators for help, and it was Hatada who took on the task. He systematically collected the evidence by interviewing everyone concerned, and gathered together the relevant documents and tax receipts (the village leaders had receipts for tax payments on the land dating back to 1915), then called a meeting with the head monk and county officials. Presented with Hatada's incontrovertible evidence, the officials berated the monk for his groundless claims; Hatada then arranged on the spot for the man to sign an affidavit renouncing all claims to the land. Zhang Rui and other elderly Shajing villagers whom I interviewed in 1980 still remember with gratitude the help that the Mantetsu scholars had given them in this matter (interview with Zhang Rui, April 1980; the full details and documents are in KC, 1:194–203).

This anecdote, in illustrating the kind of relationship that the researchers sometimes managed to establish with the villagers, gives credence to Hatada's claim that many of the researchers, despite the handicap of working under the auspices of occupation authorities, were serious scholars who managed to gather information of substantial academic value (Hatada 1981; see also Uchiyama 1980). In my re-investigation of Shajing village, in fact, I was able to verify the Mantetsu data. The elderly villagers often marveled at the degree of precision and detail of the information on their families. The land reform data I was given also corroborate the household surveys done by the Mantetsu researchers.

Still, even the best of the Mantetsu studies have their limitations. Most paid little attention to villagers' attitudes, values, and thoughts. The strength of the materials is in concrete social and economic data. It was an intentional emphasis of the original research design. Under the circumstances, this was probably a wise decision: matters of consciousness are at best elusive even under the most ideal of research conditions; any effort to study villagers' attitudes under wartime conditions would no doubt have run into insurmountable difficulties. In any case, the investigators generally stayed in the field for only short periods, instead of the preferred anthropological method of "participant observation" for a year or more, and few could communicate with the villagers without interpreters.

This weakness is particularly glaring with respect to the thoughts and aspirations of the lower strata of the villagers, since the Mantetsu investigators tended to rely on the established village elite as their informants. As critics like Noma Kiyoshi (1964) and Uchiyama Masao (1980) have pointed out (and as Niida in KC, 1:1–5; and Hatada 1973: 267–74; 1981, among others, have repeatedly acknowledged), these investigations did not, could not, focus on the stirrings of revolution in the countryside. These materials aimed to define the "old" China as it was, not to search out the "new" China in the making. For that kind of data, we must await materials from the liberated areas outside of Japanese control.

The reliance on the village elites of course means that we cannot take at face value one-sided testimony from the established and powerful. One rather extreme example will serve to illustrate this point. Highly commercialized Sibeichai village was dominated by an exceptionally rich and powerful landlord, Wang Zanzhou. Wang had managed to take advantage of natural disasters and instability to triple his landholdings by lending money to impoverished peasants at usurious rates against the titles to their land. Wang and his father had also managed to impose a fixed rent-in-kind system that worked very much to their advantage. In a period of rising cotton prices and natural calamities, they were thereby ensured a stable income regardless of poor harvests or inflation. (Wang's activities are discussed in detail on pp. 174–77.) In Wang's testimony to the Japanese investigators, however, his rental system becomes one for the mutual convenience of the tenant and himself, his land-pawning system a way of providing credit to the needy, and his lot a difficult one in the face of rising prices. To accept such testimony at face value is to place oneself completely at the mercy of the worst built-in bias in these materials.* Here, as elsewhere, a careful reading of the entire corpus of material is a must.

For all these limitations, the Mantetsu surveys stand as the most precise and detailed body of information available to us on pre-Revolution Hebei-Shandong villages. If, when the materials from the many oral-history projects undertaken in China in the 1950's and early 1960's become available, they prove to be more substantial than the few pieces that have been published or have otherwise found their way into collections outside of China, perhaps the Mantetsu surveys can be superseded. If not, with all their imperfections, they will remain our primary source for a close-up examination of the Hebei-Shandong villages in the 1930's.

*Myers 1970 does just this (see, for example, pp. 70–74, 77–78), a weakness that seriously detracts from a book otherwise rich in detail.

## THE VILLAGES

A critical question that remains is: how representative were the villages selected for study? Were they chosen only because they lay along strategic routes and near major cities of special interest to the occupation authorities? To what extent can they be considered representative of the broader Hebei–northwest Shandong plain area?

Map 2.2 locates the 33 surveyed villages I have used in this study against the major rivers, railroads, and urban centers (100,000+ population in the 1930's) of the Hebei–northwest Shandong plain. The basic social-economic profiles of the villages are given in Appendix A, numbered in the same order as on the map.

There is no question, as we can quickly see, that the choice of the villages does reflect to some extent Japan's strategic concerns. For a start, the villages are concentrated in the northeastern Hebei plain area. Fully 22 of them lie inside the Tanggu demilitarized zone between the Tianjin–Beijing railroad and the great wall. This emphasis was a direct result of the dictates of Japanese militarism, which launched the first group of studies in 1935 in preparation for full-scale invasion. Moreover, a substantial number of the villages are clustered along the railways, eight of them along the strategic Tianjin–Tangshan–Shanhaiguan line. And two of the villages are suburbs of Shijiazhuang and Jinan. In short, it will not do to consider these villages a representative, random sample of the vast Hebei–northwest Shandong countryside.

To guard against an overemphasis on any one type of village in my own study, I defined each of the 33 villages by a set of 12 social and economic criteria to see more precisely just what kinds of villages are represented in the Mantetsu selection. As shown in Appendix A, the villages in fact fall readily into seven types, the first four of which might be considered more widely representative, and the last three rather more selectively so.

Types I–III, which account for 20 of the 33 villages, can be considered the basic types; they are all predominantly farming communities, differentiated mainly by their degree of commercialization, of involvement in a market economy. Type I, the relatively uncommercialized villages (3), are those in which less than 10 percent of the cropped area was under cash crops, such as cotton, peanuts, tobacco, and fruits. Type III villages (7) are the highly commercialized ones, with more than 30 percent of their cropped area under cash crops. Type II villages (10) fall between these ranges and are grouped as moderately commercialized villages.

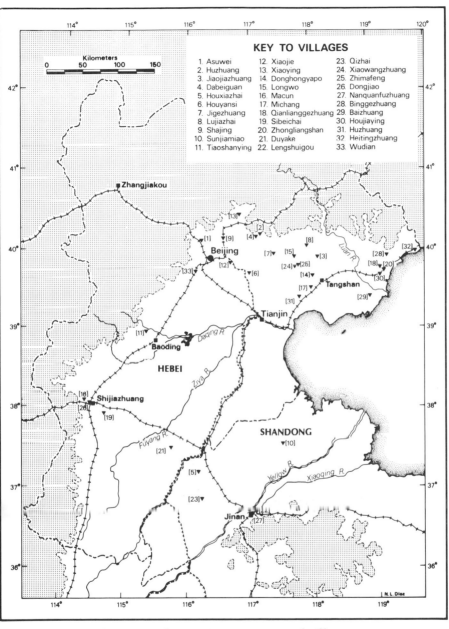

**KEY TO VILLAGES**

| | | |
|---|---|---|
| 1. Asuwei | 12. Xiaojie | 23. Qizhai |
| 2. Huzhuang | 13. Xiaoying | 24. Xiaowangzhuang |
| 3. Jiaojiazhuang | 14. Donghongyapo | 25. Zhimafeng |
| 4. Dabeiguan | 15. Longwo | 26. Dongjiao |
| 5. Houxiazhai | 16. Macun | 27. Nanquanfuzhuang |
| 6. Houyansi | 17. Michang | 28. Binggezhuang |
| 7. Jigezhuang | 18. Qianlianggezhuang | 29. Baizhuang |
| 8. Lujiazhai | 19. Sibeichai | 30. Houjiaying |
| 9. Shajing | 20. Zhongliangshan | 31. Huzhuang |
| 10. Sunjiamiao | 21. Duyake | 32. Heitingzhuang |
| 11. Tiaoshanying | 22. Lengshuigou | 33. Wudian |

MAP 2.2. The 33 Mantetsu-surveyed villages

Type IV (5) is the major variant to this primary grouping of villages. Here handicraft industries were so highly developed that the villages depended on them for a substantial portion of their income.

Types V–VII are less widely representative. Type V villages (2) are adjacent to major urban centers, really suburban communities with semiurbanized economics. Type VI villages (4) are the home communities of migrant workers; large proportions of their adult males took employment on the Manchurian frontier. And Type VII villages (2) are shell-shocked villages, whose position along strategic pathways had repeatedly subjected them to the ravages of civil war and foreign invasion.

These different types of villages, though by no means exhaustive of all types of villages on the Hebei–northwest Shandong plain, clearly do include a considerable range. I shall draw on the Mantetsu-surveyed villages to illustrate specific processes—of the results of commercialization, of the development of handicraft industries, of urban or frontier employment, and of shell-shock; I shall not attempt to use the surveyed villages as if they were a randomly selective sample of *all* villages of the North China plain.

Still, with this typology in hand, it is clear that the Mantetsu investigators tried to choose a broad range of villages for their in-depth follow-up studies. The nine most thoroughly studied villages—three in the northeastern Hebei study and six in the Tokyo University–Mantetsu collaborative study—are both geographically and typologically more widely representative than the total 33-village sample. As shown in Map 2.2, two of these villages are in northwestern Shandong (Houxiazhai, 5; Lengshuigou, 22), two in southern and central Hebei (Sibeichai, 19; Wudian, 33), and five in northeastern Hebei (Dabeiguan, 4; Shajing, 9; Michang, 17; Qianlianggezhuang, 18; Houjiaying, 30). Five of my seven types of villages are represented in these villages, excluding only Type I, the uncommercialized village, and Type V, the suburban community. I shall be drawing extensively on my reconstructions of these nine villages to illustrate generalizations about the larger area.

ARCHIVAL MATERIALS

For questions of long-term change, the Mantetsu data are useful but not sufficient in themselves. Close study of the best-surveyed villages, which contain data going back three generations, yielded information suggestive of secular trends. A comparison across different kinds of villages also suggested certain patterns—of the kinds of changes that accompanied commercialization or the development of handicrafts, for example. But preindustrial agrarian change was generally a slow and gradual process that seldom emerged with full clarity over a mere three-generation time span.* Moreover, the conflicting forces at work on rural society in the twentieth century often resulted in patterns of change that resembled whirlpools more than straight currents. Peasants who improved their status through farm profits, for example, were frequently pressed back downward by the counter pressures of population acting through partible inheritance. And commercialization itself was, in different areas and at different times, countered by the de-commercializing effects of civil war, banditry, and invasion. We need therefore to look at a longer time frame in order to gain a clear grasp of the more enduring trends.

Yet conventional historical data on village society and economy in the Qing period are sketchy at best, and do not easily permit us to test hypotheses suggested by the very much more detailed Mantetsu data. Past scholarship has given us only very hazy glimpses of the rent and wage labor relations in Hebei (or Zhili as it was called until 1928) and northwest Shandong in the seventeenth to nineteenth centuries, or of the rich-peasant agriculture, or of village-state relations. To discern long-term patterns of change in these basic socioeconomic and sociopolitical relations, we need richer historical data than those we have worked with in the past. If data can be found to lend a deeper time perspective to the Mantetsu materials, then a case will have been made for bridging the disciplines of anthropology with history, for using twentieth-century field survey data in conjunction with historical materials. The richer twentieth-century materials would permit us to fill out our sketchy pictures of earlier centuries. The time depth of the historical data would bring into sharper relief trends of change suggested by the twentieth-century materials.

It was with this in mind that I spent a year in Beijing in 1980 in search of Qing records to complement the twentieth-century story. That search turned up two sources of some value.

The first is the Board of Punishment reports (*xingke tiben*) in the Ming-Qing Archives (Ming-Qing dangan guan; also known as the Diyi dangan guan, or First Archives, as opposed to the Second Archives, which house the government records of the Republican period). Under the Qing, any case involving killing (*ming an*) had to be

---

* A short time frame seems to me a major weakness of Ramon Myers's book on the peasant economy of this area.

reported all the way up the judicial apparatus, from the county magistrate, to the provincial judge (anchashi), to the provincial governor, and finally to the Board of Punishment and the emperor. The heart of this material is the magistrate's report, which until the nineteenth century contained fairly detailed testimony by the immediate family of the deceased, by the accused murderer, and by witnesses, neighbors, or employers, together with an autopsy report and the magistrate's summary analysis and recommended action. As the report went up the judicial ladder, it was jacketed by the opinion of the provincial judge, then the governor, and finally the Board, which made an abstract (tihuang) for the emperor's quick perusal. There are hundreds of thousands of such cases in the Ming-Qing Archives. In the category land- and debt-related cases, the number ranges from a few hundred a year (308 cases in 1739, for example) to nearly 1,500 (1,495 in 1836).

In the nineteenth century, the Board's records became more and more abbreviated, probably in order to cut down on the immense volume of paperwork involved. Only a barebones summary of the nature of the crime and of the punishment was kept; personal details and the testimony of the parties involved were no longer recorded. But the rich eighteenth-century records give important clues to life in the countryside.

Take, for example, this relatively well-documented case from that period. On the sixth day of the fifth month, 1735, in the independent district (zhili zhou) Yizhou, in the highly developed western part of central Hebei, four agricultural year-laborers got together to drink and pass the day because heavy rains kept them from the fields. One of the four, Liu Jincai, provided the liquor, which he sold to the others. All were drinking at his place. When one of the workers demanded more liquor but was unable to pay for it, a fight broke out. In the ensuing brawl, the worker Wang Cheng was killed by the worker Wang Mingjiu, who ran away with Liu Jincai.

The record of the case contains brief statements (ca. 100 words each) about the workers by their employers, and the testimony of the brother of the deceased, and of the three other workers involved. The longest testimony, about 500 words, was the statement of the accused murderer, Wang Mingjiu. The department magistrate (zhizhou) summed up the case and recommended death by strangulation. The provincial judge concurred. The governor of Zhili supported the recommendation. And, finally, the Board reviewed the case and presented it to the emperor, with a brief one-page abstract.

In this case, the document was actually marked by vermillion brush "approved as recommended." (1736, bao 82, 6.17.)

Eighteenth-century records like this are truly valuable sources for social history. Many of the cases involve disputes between creditors and debtors, between employers and workers, or between landlords and tenants, and these provide some indication of the texture of social relations—the kind of texture that is not normally available in the standard sources of the period. Scholars in China have led in the use of these materials for Qing social and economic history. My debts to their research are indicated in relevant parts of this book.* I myself spent a total of four months examining all cases related to Hebei and Shandong for the four years of 1736, 1737, 1796, and much less productively, 1896—a total of about 3,000 cases. Chinese scholars often compare work in these archives to "trying to scoop up a needle from the bottom of the sea" (haidi laozhen); I myself would compare it instead to fishing: exciting moments interspersed with long periods without so much as a nibble. It is painstaking work, often for low returns. But until better materials can be found in local archives, these Board of Punishment materials take us about as near to a close-up view of the basic levels of rural society as we can get for the Qing period. For my purposes, these materials have helped to fill out, for example, hazy outlines derived from more conventional sources about the development of agricultural wage labor in the eighteenth century. The story of the development of agricultural wage labor, in turn, has helped me to link up the larger process of commercialization, documented in gazetteers, with social and economic change at the village level.

The second of the sources that turned out to be of value is the hitherto totally unexplored Punishment Office archives of Baodi county, east of Beijing, in the northeastern Hebei area—which happens also to be the main area of emphasis of the Mantetsu investigations. I was fortunate to find these materials in the course of my work at the Ming-Qing Archives. It is not a complete county government archive (about which I will have more to say shortly), but only a collection of documents spanning the years 1800–1911 and consisting mainly of records of court cases. The cases involve all sorts of

---

*I am particularly indebted to Professor Liu Yongcheng of the Institute of History of the Chinese Academy of Social Sciences of Beijing, who first introduced me to these materials in 1979 and later helped me find my way through them. Liu has worked with these records since the 1960's, concentrating especially on the Qianlong (1736–95) period. At the time of my research, the fruits of some of his studies had just been published (Liu 1979a, b; 1980), and other works were in press.

matters, from marital and inheritance disputes to the suppression of popular movements.

These county records differ from the central government's Board of Punishment archives in a number of important respects. They include the original complaint filed by the party bringing suit, and sometimes also the hand-recorded original depositions of the parties involved. To this extent, they are much richer than the final magistrate's summary report filed with the Board of Punishment.

The main body of the Baodi fragments consists of 300-odd cases pertaining to the selection, appointment, and dismissal of quasi-officials at the sub-county level, especially an officeholder called the *xiangbao*. This xiangbao, it turns out, was the lowest level quasi-official for tax collection. In Baodi each xiangbao oversaw an average of 20 villages. He was usually someone nominated by the supra-village and village elites, and then confirmed and formally appointed by the county yamen. He was the conduit through which delinquent taxes were collected and special levies allocated. Any tensions between state and village over taxation resulted in pressures on the xiangbao, who had to answer to both the county government and the local notables who nominated him.

In the triangle of the state, gentry, and village, our past studies have concentrated largely on the relations between the state and the gentry. (Chang 1955, 1962; Ch'ü 1962; Eberhard 1965; Kuhn 1975, 1979). The emphasis is understandable, given the nature of the materials available. But such studies have not been able to take us down to the level of the villages, stopping at the market towns or county seats, where the gentry usually resided. To link up with the villages, we need sources that tell us about the interrelationships in the other legs of this triangle: between the gentry and the villagers, and between the state and the village. The materials in Baodi are distinctive in affording us a view of state-village relations in the crucial matter of taxation and at the critical juncture of the xiangbao. They provide a baseline against which to compare changing state-village relations in the twentieth century.

## LOCAL ARCHIVES AND SOCIAL HISTORY

I must emphasize that my work with local archives has been limited to the fragments for a single county and is at best a beginning and preliminary effort. The one fairly complete county government archive that has surfaced in China gives us a good indication of the exciting possibilities that such bodies of material hold for social and economic history research. This is the Baxian (Sichuan province) archive, with more than 100,000 items spanning the years 1757–1941.* About 80 percent of the documents come from the county Punishment Office, and include massive records of lawsuits involving family disputes, creditor-debtor disputes, and the actions of sub-county quasi-officials.

It is not clear whether the Baxian archives contain cadastres of the Office of Revenue and Population (Hu fang). But some indication of what such materials might be like is provided by another set of materials that has surfaced: about 300-odd cadastres (called *bianshence*) of Huailu (Huolu) county near Shijiazhuang in Hebei. These span the reigns of Kangxi, Yongzheng, and Qianlong (1662–1795); most are concentrated in the second quarter of the eighteenth century, a critical time when the head tax was formally merged into the land tax (*tanding rudi*). Each of these volumes has entries on landholdings and tax assessments, recorded every five years, which show the landholding five years before, the amount of land sold or purchased, and the tax equivalent of the land held.† These cadastres seem to be intermediate registers, one step before the final "red registers" (*hongbu*) recording the actual tax assessments and receipts that were used in the studies of Dingxian and Jinghai counties (Feng Huade 1935, 1936).

A summary of the preliminary findings based on the Huailu cadastres (Dai 1980: 347–48) shows the possible uses to which a long run of such materials can be put. With a complete run of such materials for the Qing and Republican periods, we should be able to identify long-term trends in land-distribution patterns and perhaps also to correlate demographic trends with landholding patterns. Such work would fill a major gap in our understanding of the social and economic history of late imperial China.

---

*These files surfaced only because, during the Sino-Japanese war, the county authorities removed them to a local Guandi temple as a precaution against bombing raids. Unfortunately, after the war the documents were left unguarded, and many were used as waste paper before they were discovered by Feng Hanji, of the Southwest Regional Museum, in 1953. The files were then turned over to the history department of Sichuan University for sorting and cataloguing. Substantial progress was made until 1964, when the Party Central Committee placed all pre-Revolution archival materials under the unified management of the State Archival Bureau. The files were then removed to the Sichuan Provincial Archival Bureau in Ya'an, where they sit to this day, out of the reach of historians (Wu Shiqian 1979).

†I am grateful to Pan Jie of the Qing History Institute of the People's University of China for sharing with me the details of his work with these materials.

As I write this, an unknown number of Chinese local government archives still lie buried in the offices of county, municipal, and provincial authorities. If historians of peasant China can gain access to those archives, we would be able to combine the advantages of Europeanists and Third-World historians—of detailed official records over a long span of time with modern ethnographic research.

# CHAPTER 3

# The Ecological Setting

A historian of court politics, or of gentry ideology, or of urban development, does not necessarily have to take into account climate, topography, water, and the like. But the historian studying the people of an agrarian society can ill afford to overlook these features, for the natural environment is what shapes the life and orders the day of the peasant. A rural social history needs to begin with a consideration of the interrelationships between the natural environment and the sociopolitical economy.

Such interrelationships, which I shall call *ecological* relationships, can be projected backward in time to tell us about historical changes in the countryside. Just as historical demographers often rely on modern census data for a baseline for historical analysis, and just as I use 1930's anthropological data in this study to help fill out an earlier story, so modern geographical research can be used for ecological observations about earlier centuries. The historian, in fact, is on firmer ground with ecological observations than demographic or anthropological ones.

Map 3.1 shows my area of study: the lowland areas of Hebei and northwest Shandong. The area may be divided into four major zones: northeastern Hebei north and east of the Beijing–Tianjin railroad; central Hebei north of the Jinan–Shijiazhuang railroad; southern Hebei; and northwest Shandong, including the Xiaoqing river valley and the area north of the Yellow River. These are mainly locational references for convenience, rather than ecological divisions. A more substantial and ecological division, as will be seen, is between the shaded western portions of Hebei and the area of Shandong north of the central Shandong hills, on the one hand, and the lighter eastern sections, on the other. Map 3.1 also shows the major navigable rivers—a crucial indicator in preindustrial economies of the potential for water transportation and the development of a market economy.

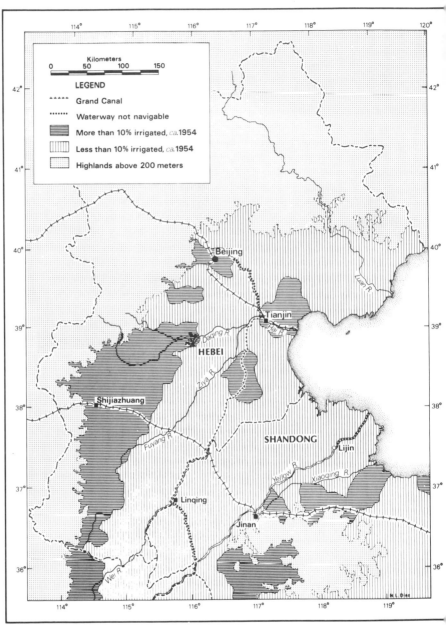

MAP 3.1. Irrigation, drainage, and water transportation
on the North China plain

The major navigable rivers in Hebei are the Wei River–Grand Canal, the Ziya–Fuyang River, and the Daqing River. The Luan River in northeastern Hebei is navigable only by small junks in its lower reaches (Sun Jingzhi 1957: 37–38, 74–75). The Yellow River is navigable down to Lijin, before the delta area. The Xiaoqing connects Jinan with the sea. The importance of the section of the Grand Canal between the Yellow River and Linqing declined after the mid-nineteenth century owing to a shift in the Yellow River's course in 1855,* the opening of Tianjin with a consequent increase in sea transport after 1860, and the completion of the Tianjin–Nanjing railroad in 1911 (*ibid.*, pp. 120–21, 146; *Cihai* 1979: 2141). The section of the Grand Canal north of Tianjin fell into disuse after the completion of the Beijing–Shanhaiguan railway in 1901 (Sun Jingzhi 1957: 74).

WATER CONTROL AND POLITICAL ECONOMY

Water control in this area, as in most of the North China plain, consisted of either colossal dikes for flood control or diminutive wells for irrigation. No visitor to the dikes along the Yellow River could fail to be impressed by their immense scale. Flowing eastward from its sources in the mountains and plateaus in the west, the river's rate of flow slows as it enters the plains, as does its capacity for carrying the silt picked up along the way. The result is a continual build-up, so that now, 100-odd years after the river last changed course, the riverbed rises from three to more than ten meters above its former level for a stretch of some 1,800 kilometers across Henan (east of the Beijing–Hankou railroad) and northwest Shandong. The massive dam that regulates the river along its lower stretches towers over the surrounding countryside. Whatever one might think of the extravagant claims made by Karl A. Wittfogel (1957) for the determinative impact of hydraulics, one cannot help being powerfully reminded of the state apparatus required to build and maintain such a project; for a society without modern technologies, it was an enterprise that demanded the work of hundreds of thousands of people.

Irrigation, by contrast, was very much a matter of individual en-

---

*This is only one of nine major changes in the river's course. But it has usually flowed north of the central Shandong hills into the Hebei–northwest Shandong plain. The three periods when it did not were 1194–1493, when one channel was north of the hills and one south; 1494–1855, when the river ran fully south; and 1938–47, when the dikes at Huayuankou were blown up in a futile attempt by Chiang Kai-shek (Jiang Jieshi) to slow the Japanese advance (Hsieh 1973: 115; Ren et al. 1979: 167; *Cihai* 1979: 4712).

terprise, involving thousands of small wells. Most rivers on the
North China plain have the same basic characteristics as the Yellow
River: originating in the mountains and plateaus to the west, picking up a great deal of silt as they flow downward toward the plain,
slowing their flow as the gradient levels out, and building up great
silt deposits. These rivers tend to become very shallow in the spring
growing season, after the dry fall and winter, for 70 percent of the
rainfall in the plain occurs in the summer months, especially July
and August. Water flow on the Yellow River decreases in the spring
to less than 100 cubic meters per second, and many of the smaller
rivers simply dry up. The total river water flow relative to unit area
has been estimated to be merely one-sixth to one-eighth of that of
the Yangzi valley (Sun Jingzhi 1957: 4). These environmental features set severe limits on the use of river water for canal irrigation as
well as on water transportation. By best estimates, before the Revolution, only some 7 percent of the total cultivated area in Hebei and
less than 3 percent in Shandong was irrigated; and almost all of this
was by wells (80 percent in Hebei, 90 percent in Shandong; *ibid.*, pp.
53, 125).*

A typical well in the Shijiazhuang area of central-southern Hebei,
where this form of irrigation was the most highly developed before
the Revolution, was seven to ten meters deep, the water level being
five meters or so below ground. It took five or six men about a week
to construct a brick-lined well, which could irrigate from five to as
much as 20 mu of cropland. An unlined earth-well (*tujing*), really
just a hole in the ground, could be dug by five men in a day, and had
about one-fifth the irrigation capacity of the brick wells (KC, 2:293–
94; KC, 3:365). Both kinds of wells were usually dug on the initiative of the individual landowner, and were usually privately owned
(though drinking wells were often community property). Table 3.1
shows the number of private and public wells in seven Hebei and
Shandong villages, located in both the poorly irrigated areas and the
highly irrigated ones. This was household- or neighborhood-level irrigation—of an entirely different scale from the mammoth flood-
control projects on the North China plain.

The contrast in the scale of these two types of water-control projects is suggestive of the contrast in the structure of the political
economy: between a giant centralized imperial state apparatus and a
small peasant economy. In this respect, the North China plain differed sharply from the lower Yangzi delta or the Pearl River delta,

*By 1973 an estimated 45% of the cultivated area of the Hebei–northwest Shan-
dong plain was irrigated (Zhongguo kexue yuan 1980: 351).

TABLE 3.1

Wells in Seven Villages in Poorly and Highly Irrigated Areas of Hebei
and Shandong, 1930's

| Village | Wells | | | Number used for irrigation |
|---|---|---|---|---|
| | Total | Private | Public | |
| Northeastern and eastern Hebei | | | | |
| Shajing | 10 | 7 | 3 | 7(?) |
| Wudian | 8 | 4 | 4 | 4 |
| Houjiaying | 8 | 4 | 4 | 3(?) |
| Dabeiguan | 1 | | 1 | 0 |
| Northwest Shandong | | | | |
| Houxiazhai | 0 | | | 0 |
| Southern Hebei | | | | |
| Sibeichai | 80 | 60 | 20 | 60 |
| Piedmont plain, northwest Shandong | | | | |
| Lengshuigou | 50 | 50 | | 50 |

SOURCES: *Shajing,* KC, 2: 293–94; *Wudian, Houjiaying,* KC, 5: 297–316, 410; *Dabeiguan,* MT, Kitō nōson 1937a: 1; *Houxiazhai, Lengshuigou,* KC, 4: 169, 284–85, 459; *Sibeichai,* KC, 3: 365–66 (compare p. 27, which shows 42 irrigation wells and 12 drinking wells).

where networks of canals channeled river and lake water for irrigation or provided drainage, and shore dikes were used for flood control and land reclamation. Such projects typically involved as few as
a dozen or so people up to perhaps thousands—a scale manageable
by a well-organized lineage.

There, as we know, lineage organizations were in fact highly developed and powerful, more so than in the North China plain; the
scale of the organizing capacities of lineages was thus relatively well
matched to the scale of irrigation works. We might accordingly
think of those dimensions as interlocked parts of an *ecosystem*—in
which the natural environment and the social structure of the area
constituted a single interdependent system. Matsuda Yoshirō (1981),
who has documented the expansion of cultivation in the Pearl River
delta through reclaimed marshland (the *shatian*) in the mid-Ming to
early Qing period, has shown that control over the shatian was the
economic basis for the local gentry's expanding control over local
and village political and fiscal structures during this period.

DISASTER-PRONE DRY FARMING AND POPULATION DENSITY

Some comparativists have made the error of equating Chinese agriculture with intensive wet-rice cultivation, seeking thereby to explain elements of China's political economy by the distinctive characteristics of rice growing.* But in fact the two areas that were historically the most critical in shaping China's political economy and society, the Guanzhong plain of the northwest and the Yellow River plains of the north, were primarily dry-farming areas. In the Hebei and northwest Shandong portions of the North China plain, rainfall averages only about 500 mm (19.5 inches) a year, which coupled with the lack of irrigation, virtually ruled out the cultivation of wet-rice. Peasants there typically raised spring crops of sorghum or millet (or maize in more recent times) and a winter crop of wheat, usually followed by a summer-sown crop such as soybeans.[†]

Further, the growing season is quite unlike that in the wet-rice areas. The frost-free period ranges from only six months a year in northeastern Hebei to seven and a half months in northwest Shandong. This puts great pressures on the double-cropper, who must harvest his spring crop and plant his winter wheat within the space of about six weeks, before the frost sets in. The abbreviated growing season, together with other problems—lack of irrigation, lack of fertilizer, and alkaline soil—has severely limited the possibilities of land use over the winter months. In 1949 the sown-area-to-cultivated-area figure (in other words, an index of double-cropping) was 116.3 in northeastern Hebei, 139.3 in central Hebei, and 143.7 in southern Hebei (Zhongyang renmin zhengfu nongyebu 1950: 53–55). A 1934 survey showed substantially the same pattern: 122.6 for Hebei province as a whole, and 143.7 for Shandong, compared with 167.1 for Jiangsu and 204.7 for the southeastern province of Fujian (Tudiweiyuanhui 1937: 19). Longer growing seasons permitted more frequent cropping in the rice regions than in the Hebei–northwest Shandong plain.

Rice growing, moreover, gives a higher yield per crop. As early as Song times, the lower Yangzi valley had attained a yield of 300–400 catties of unhusked rice per mu (Perkins 1969: 21–22, 315).[‡] In the

---

*See, for example, Wallerstein 1974: Chap. 1. This is not to detract from Wallerstein's stimulating "world system" analysis, which I draw on in Chapter Seven.

[†] However, where there were the requisite canal irrigation systems and labor, small pockets of rice cultivation did spring up in increasing numbers during the Ming–Qing period, as Brook 1982 has demonstrated. In English the identification of a crop by season can variously refer to the time of sowing, harvesting, or even growing. Chinese terminology is more precise, with terms such as "crops sown in the spring" (*chungeng zuowu*), "crops that cross the winter" (*yuedong zuowu*), and "crops harvested in the summer" (*xiashou zuowu*). I use the term "summer-sown crop" here to distinguish soybeans from crops planted in the spring (Shenyang nongxue yuan 1980).

[‡] The ratio of unhusked to husked rice is generally about 10:7.

1930's the area's average rice yields ranged from 260 catties to more than 700 catties per mu. This compares with yields of from 70 to 150 catties for wheat, maize, millet, and sorghum in Hebei and Shandong. Converted to cash values, the difference was about three to one: nine to 13 yuan per mu for the rice, as opposed to three or four yuan per mu for the northern crops (Tudiweiyuanhui 1937: 20–21). Even if one compared North China's cotton to South China's rice, the difference in cash value per mu is still about 50 percent (the per-mu yield of cotton in Hebei and Shandong was 55 to 65 catties of unginned cotton, with a cash value of six to eight yuan). Rice farms in the south, in other words, did much better per unit of land, both in terms of absolute yields and in terms of the cash value of the yields.

There was (and is) thus a great difference in agricultural productivity between the North China plain and the lower Yangzi. As one sixteenth-century observer put it: "Land in the south . . . is irrigated and can yield two or three crops of several *shi* each year.* The land in the north, whether of medium or lower grade, is very different in value and in produce. Even the best land cannot be compared with the land in the south" (Ge Shouli, quoted in Kataoka Shibako 1962: 157). The government's "National Program for Agricultural Development, 1956–1967," promulgated in 1957, spoke therefore of target productivity figures of 400 catties per mu north of the Yellow River, 500 south of the Yellow River and north of the Huai, 800 south of the Huai and north of the Yangzi, and more than 800 south of the Yangzi. The differences were summed up in the exhortations to peasants in North China to "cross the Yellow River" (*kua Huanghe*), or exceed 400 catties per mu, and to "cross the Yangzi" (*guo Changjiang*), or exceed 800 catties per mu (Lau et al. 1977: 0487, 0667, 1797).

Beyond this, agriculture on the North China plain must contend with constant threats of natural disasters. According to historical records, the Yellow River has burst its dikes at least 1,593 times (Ren et al. 1979: 168).† On the poorly drained eastern half of the Hebei plain and all of the northwest Shandong plain, waterlogging during the torrential downpours of July and August is a frequent and serious

---

*A shi was actually a volume measure of varying weight; here it can be read as equivalent to roughly 160 catties in weight.

†Another count, based on just the *Tushu jicheng* for the Han to the Ming, and the *Qing shi gao* for the Qing period, tallied 1,521 recorded floods for the provinces of Hebei and Shandong (Yao 1942).

problem. Records kept for the period 1949–72 show that in the North China plain as a whole, an average of 30,000,000 to 50,000,000 mu of farmland (or about 10 percent of the total cultivated area) were affected by waterlogging each year (Zhongguo kexue yuan 1980: 352). The worst areas become marshes, which in turn become breeding grounds for locusts—a third major natural calamity of the area.

The obverse of floods and waterlogging is of course drought. The rainfall in this area fluctuates greatly: a wet year can have seven or eight times as much rain as a dry year. The threat of drought is especially serious in the spring growing season, a relatively dry season at best, with only 10–15 percent of the total annual precipitation. From the Han to the end of the Qing, the provinces of Hebei and Shandong were drought-stricken on at least 1,078 occasions (Yao 1942: 308). More recent figures tell the same story: between 1949 and 1972 the North China plain saw seven years of drought severe enough to affect an average of 40,000,000 to 60,000,000 mu of cultivated land each year (Zhongguo kexue yuan 1980: 350, 352).

These conditions make for a very harsh agrarian regime, and this though the soil of this region, a mixture of windblown loess and a loess-like alluvium, is constantly renewed and easy to cultivate.* Under other historical circumstances, such environmental conditions might have kept the population level down. But the fact that this area was for so long the heart of Chinese civilization and the political center of the empire no doubt worked in the other direction; so, probably, did the fact that the imperial state identified its interests with a small peasant economy and periodically encouraged the expansion of the owner-cultivator segment of that economy. Whatever the causes, this area has been densely populated throughout most of the history of imperial China.

The core lowland areas of the Guanzhong plain and the North China plain were in fact densely populated as early as the Han. Hsü Cho-yun (1980: 21 and Chap. 5) estimates that the average per-capita farm area in the Han was four to five mu (present-day shi mu),† or less than an acre per person. Hsü suggests also that the twentieth-century cropping pattern of spring crops (usually millet) followed by winter wheat was probably already established by then on the Guanzhong plain (Chap. 4). Ning Ke (1980), similarly, suggests an average of 15 mu of cultivated land per farm laborer in Han times. This puts

---

*Ho 1969 shows that these properties go far to explain how loessland became the "cradle" of Chinese civilization.

† 1 shi mu equals 1.45 Han da (big) mu, or 3.47 Han xiao (small) mu.

the population density at even that early date very much higher than in the rural areas of twentieth-century America (where the average family farm had 873 mu in 1925) or France (135 mu in 1908). And the figure was not too far removed from the average for China in the 1930's: 4.21 mu per capita of farm population in Hebei, 3.70 mu in Shandong, and 5.02 mu in Shaanxi (Tudiweiyuanhui 1937: 24, 28).*

High population density rules out the type of mixed farming-livestock agricultural system employed in France and the United States, for it takes several pounds of feed to produce one pound of meat, or milk, or cheese. A moment's reflection will show the relevance of this difference in explaining the contrast between the respective dietary habits of these countries. Chinese peasants have long been in effect vegetarians, not by choice, but by the dictates of the Chinese agrarian system. And the distinctive Chinese dietary pattern, consisting of a main foodgrain, supplemented by dishes in which relatively little meat is used, in contrast to the three-part division of the Western diet of meat, potato, and vegetable, is of course a direct reflection of China's more intensive agrarian system.

The intensity of land use on the North China plain is shown also in its cropping system. Two basic methods were used to achieve more than one crop a year. One was the three-crops-in-two-years rotating method. Sorghum or millet was planted in May/June and harvested in September/October. Winter wheat followed, planted as soon after the harvest as possible, before frost set in. This was then harvested the next summer, in July, too late for planting sorghum or millet; the wheat was therefore followed by soybeans, to be harvested in October/November. The land was then allowed to lie fallow, replenished by both the nitrogen-rich soybeans and the fallow period. Cultivators had to take careful account of both the supply of available labor and the amount of available land. Every effort was made to maximize their use, alternating the fallow period from one plot to another.

The other method used to maximize cropping was interplanting. Here, winter wheat was planted in every second or third row; and then, in the spring, millet or maize was planted in the open rows. The wheat was harvested *after* the planting of the spring crop. Given enough hands or machinery to cope with the fall rush and sufficient fertilizer, peasants could by this means increase their land use to the equivalent of double-cropping. Before 1949, however, interplanting

---

*The 1930's figures, of course, are not just for the lowlands but include the by now well-settled highlands.

in the North China plain appears to have been little more than a variation on the three-crops-in-two-years theme.

In any event, by one or the other method, cultivators of the North China plain maximized the intensity with which their land and labor could be used within the constraints of the existing agricultural technology. What was distinctive about this ecosystem was that it was born of the conjunction of a harsh natural environment that dictated an agrarian regime of low-yield, disaster-prone dry farming, with an imperial state system that chose to locate its capital in this area and thereby contributed to its high population density. The combination of the two resulted in severe scarcity, and a standard of living much below that of such areas as the lower Yangzi valley.

In this connection, we must not be misled by a simple comparison of the two regions' population-to-cultivated-land ratios, which would show a somewhat higher density in the lower Yangzi provinces: 3.80 mu per capita in Jiangsu, 3.76 in Zhejiang, and 2.56 in Anhui, against Hebei's 4.21 and Shandong's 3.70. The correct comparison is between the population-to-cropped-area ratios, which takes into account the longer growing season in the lower Yangzi. Here the difference largely disappears: 4.85 per capita in Jiangsu, 3.44 in Zhejiang, and 2.99 in Anhui, compared with 3.95 in Hebei and 3.88 in Shandong (Tudiweiyuanhui 1937: 24, 25). What we are left with is the considerable gap in productivity between wet-rice farming and dry farming—the basis, in turn, for the substantially higher standard of living in the lower Yangzi area. Severe scarcity was a second major ecological characteristic that underlay the development of the social and political economy of the North China plain.

WATERLOGGING AND THE SOCIOECONOMIC STRUCTURE

The problem of water control not only sets this area apart from others like the lower Yangzi, but also provides the most telling contrasts within the region itself. The dark areas in Map 3.1 are those in which more than 10 percent of the cultivated land was irrigated by 1954 (when the Institute of Geography undertook a systematic survey). In general, these include the piedmont plain areas and the western portion of the Hebei plain. Here the gradient of the land is generally more than 1/3,000 (one foot per 3,000 feet), compared with 1/5,000 to 1/10,000 in the unshaded eastern sections of the Hebei plain and virtually all of the northwest Shandong plain. It is a critical difference: the eastern zone, with a less sharp gradient and poor drainage, is much more prone to flooding and waterlogging (Sun Jingzhi 1957: 35, 37, 119; see also Ren et al. 1979: 181–83).*

This difference in drainage accounts for other sharp differences between the two areas. Because waterlogging leads to the salinization of the soil (by raising the level of the underground water and by deposits left from evaporation; Ren et al. 1979: 192), about one-sixth of the land in the poorly drained eastern zone of Hebei is highly alkaline and therefore relatively unproductive. Moreover, in many areas of the saline soil zone, fresh water lies as much as 50 to 100 meters below ground, putting irrigation wells out of the technological reach of most peasants. Before the Revolution the total irrigation picture in this zone was consequently dismal.† According to the 1954 survey, only 1.9 percent of the cultivated area in northwest Shandong was irrigated, compared with about 25 percent in the western zones of Hebei shown on the map. Most of these Hebei areas were irrigated by wells that tapped ample fresh water lying only five to ten meters below ground (Sun Jingzhi 1957: 63, 131).

These differences are reflected in the data presented in Table 3.1. Sibeichai, in well-drained southern Hebei, had a developed well-irrigation system in the 1930's. So did Lengshuigou, in the similarly well-drained piedmont plain area just north of the central Shandong hills. The other villages in the table, all in the poorly drained northeastern Hebei and northwest Shandong areas, had little or no irrigation at that time.

As one would expect, the difference in irrigation and drainage dictated different cropping patterns. On low-lying, easily waterlogged land, peasants typically chose to grow flood-resistant but low-yielding sorghum. Sorghum is a low-investment subsistence crop requiring little or no fertilizer when grown on waterlogged land. Accordingly, we find a high proportion of the cultivated land in easily waterlogged northeastern Hebei and northwestern Shandong devoted to that crop—15 percent and 10 percent, respectively, in 1949,

---

*There is further variation within the western and eastern zones, where the floods have resulted in an uneven surface. In general the areas beyond the main course of floods are high-lying land, the areas of overflow gently sloping land, and the bays formed in the wake of the floods low-lying land. These differences correspond roughly with gradations in the stability and productivity of the farmland (Zhongguo kexue yuan 1980: 350).

†The two shaded pockets in eastern Hebei shown in Map 3.1 are exceptions to this statement. Here improvements made on pre-Revolution channels (the Machang jianhe and Jiedi jianhe), the construction of new ones (the Chaobai xinhe and Duliu jianhe), and the building of irrigation canal systems brought a high degree of irrigation by 1954. Major parts of the area between Tianjin and the Bohai Gulf are even planted under wet-rice (Sun Jingzhi 1957: 38, 53, 65).

compared with only 9 percent in southern Hebei. Cotton, the major cash crop, is by contrast a high-investment crop that cannot stand soaking. Understandably enough, few peasants living in areas prone to waterlogging were willing to take a risk on it. In northeastern Hebei only 5.5 percent of the cultivated area was under cotton in 1949—generally on the high-lying and relatively secure land along major transport routes. This compares with fully 19.2 percent in southern Hebei, especially the western section, where cotton growing was encouraged not only by the relative security of the land from waterlogging, but also by the greater availability of irrigation and water transportation (Zhongyang renmin zhengfu nongyebu 1950: 53–55; Sun Jingzhi 1957: 2, 63–65, 119, 125, 131).*

The relative preponderance of these two crops in the cropping patterns of a given area tells us a great deal about the degree of that area's commercialization—and something about the process of social differentiation as well, for as Part Two of this book will show, up to a certain point commercialization was associated with increased social differentiation. Cash-cropping increased the opportunities for some owner-peasants to become rich peasants or even large farmers and landlords. But it also increased the element of risk by requiring a substantial investment in fertilizer and labor, and therefore also reduced many owner-peasants to tenants or wage laborers. At very high levels of commercialization, resident landlordism and rich peasant farming tended to give way to absentee landlordism. Again, to the extent that commercialization was linked to certain patterns of class relations, we might speak of a single ecosystem in which elements of the natural environment (the gradient of the land, the availability of underground fresh water for irrigation and river transport) and elements of the social and economic structure (cropping patterns, degree of commercialization, class relations) were interconnected.

### ECOLOGY, RESIDENTIAL PATTERNS, AND COMMUNITY STRUCTURES

Like much else in the ecology of the North China plain, the threat of floods and waterlogging dictated the residential patterns of villages. A visitor to North China and to the Chengdu plain of the Sichuan

---

*Irrigation was not always used for cotton growing in this area, but its availability added to the security of the crop, which requires water in the spring. The Sibeichai villagers usually irrigated their cotton crop twice a year: once early in April before planting and again in early June before the summer rains (KC, 3:129–32, 365).

basin cannot help being struck by the great contrast between the nucleated residential pattern of the one and the dispersed pattern of the other. In North China, villagers built their homes in a cluster on high ground to guard against flooding and, perhaps, also to cope collectively with it. In the Chengdu plain, where there was no comparable threat, the Min River having been conquered as early as the third century B.C. by the Dujiang weir, villagers simply built their homes conveniently near their fields. A single village thus embraces many widely separated small clusters of houses, usually defined by a bamboo grove, which are called *ba, yuanba,* or *yuanzi.*

The community structures in these two regions were as disparate as the residential patterns. The nucleated and relatively uncommercialized villages of North China tended to be more tightly knit and inward-looking, whereas the dispersed and more commercialized villages of the Chengdu plain tended to be less cohesive as single communities and more a part of what G. William Skinner calls a standard marketing community. In the North, we have greater intravillage solidarity, but intervillage dispersion; in the Chengdu plain, intravillage dispersion, but greater intervillage integration.

The fact that lineage organizations figured less prominently in rural society on the North China plain may also have contributed to the comparatively strong village structure there. The Hebei–northwest Shandong villages were generally multiple-surname communities, in contrast to the many single-surname villages common in provinces like Guangdong, Fujian, and Jiangxi (Hsiao 1960: 326–27). Where multiple-surname villages predominated, the lines of kinship and the lines of community were different, and rural residents could identify with the one group as much as the other. If, in studying social relations in the south, we need to consider above all the twin axes of class and kinship, in North China we need to look closely at village community as well.

I have not tried here to develop a complete characterization of the ecosystem of the North China plain, only to set the context for the history of the social and political economy of this area. To recapitulate: this Hebei–northwest Shandong core area of the North China plain was characterized by (1) colossal and diminutive water-control projects that well matched a political economy consisting of a towering imperial state system based on small peasant farming; (2) a conjunction of low-yield, disaster-prone dry farming with high population density that laid the basis for severe scarcity in this area throughout much of imperial history; (3) a basic divide between poorly drained and relatively well-drained regions; and (4) a pattern of nucleated settlements that, coupled with a low level of commercialization and weak lineage organization, set the ecological basis for a high degree of community insularity. These four characteristics must be kept in mind if one is to understand the changes in the social and political economy of this area.

# 2

# ECONOMIC
# INVOLUTION
# AND SOCIAL
# CHANGE

# CHAPTER 4

# Managerial Farming and
# Family Farming
# in the 1930's

## SOCIOECONOMIC CATEGORIES AND DEFINITIONS

Rural society in prerevolutionary China can be usefully differentiated along two different axes of production relations: rent and wage labor, the one focusing on land relations and differentiation between landlord and tenant, and the other on labor relations and differentiation between employer and laborer. Along the lines of land relations, we speak of landlords, owner-cultivators, and tenants and part-tenants. Along the lines of labor relations, we speak of rich peasants who employed hired labor and agricultural laborers who hired out.

The two sets of production relations were in fact intertwined in twentieth-century China. Some landowners both leased out land and used hired labor; some small peasants both rented land and hired out as laborers, and others, more well-to-do, rented land and employed wage labor instead of hiring out. To take account of the complex realities of village social structure, the Land Reform Law of 1950 used a classificatory scheme that attempted to take account of both sets of production relations. Thus landlords were those who depended mainly on rent for a living, rich peasants those who hired one or more year-laborers,* middle peasants those who did most of the farmwork themselves, poor peasants those who hired out, usu-

---

*To distinguish rich peasants from middle peasants, the Land Reform Law called for complex calculations of how much of the household's total income was "income from exploitation." In the civil war period, the divide was drawn at 15%; in the period after 1950, at 25%. Two general and inconsistent rules of thumb were used in the civil war period. By one relatively lenient measure, a rich peasant was someone who hired more labor than he and his household put in. But at the same time revolutionary practice called for doubling the computed income from exploitation if the household owned more than twice as much land as the average per-capita amount held by middle peasants, which meant in effect that many who hired just one year-laborer fell into the rich peasant class. In 1950 the State Council amended the law to raise the line of divide above one year-laborer. (Beijing zhengfa xueyuan 1957: 42, 44; Hinton 1966: 405, 409.)

ally as day-laborers, in addition to cultivating their own or a rented small farm, and agricultural laborers, those who hired out for a living. (On the genesis of these categories, see Huang 1975a.)

These are all useful categories, and I will need to employ them in this book. For the present, however, I begin with the broader distinction between the sea of small family farms, whether self-owned or rented, whether farmed by well-to-do peasants or poor, that were worked mainly by the family's own labor, and the islands of larger farms worked mainly by hired labor. It is a distinction that takes account of population as well as production relations, for the contrast between these two fundamentally different kinds of labor organization becomes clearest under conditions of severe population pressure. A small family farm cannot "fire" its excess labor; under the combined pressures of social relations and population, and given limited outside employment opportunities, a poor peasant farm could be forced to tolerate substantial underemployment of its available labor. And this, as we will see, is the fix that the majority of small farms in the Hebei–northwest Shandong plain were in in the 1930's.

The larger farms based on hired labor, by contrast, could hire only as much labor as they needed and could fire any excess labor. Where this flexibility in labor organization was combined with a managerial outlook to maximize profits, underemployment of labor was not tolerated. In the Hebei–northwest Shandong plain of the 1930's, most managerial farms were able to use labor much more efficiently than the small family farms, achieving substantially the same yields at a cost of fewer days of labor per mu.

These managerial farms, for complex reasons that will be discussed and documented in Chapter Ten, were generally of 100 mu or more. It is enough for now to note that in this area one adult male, using the best methods then available, could farm 15 to 30 mu in the 1930's; and since many well-to-do peasant households were joint families (of married sons living in one household), it was not uncommon for a household to farm upwards of 50 mu mainly with its own labor. Only when a farm was large enough to require the work of four or more adult males was there a good likelihood of its being farmed mainly by hired labor. As for the "rich" peasants who worked alongside a hired worker to cultivate a farm of 30-odd mu, most were still tied to the outlook and expectations of a family farm; not managerial farmers, yet not small family farmers, they should be seen as transitional between the two groups.

In terms of the categories of the Revolution, my use of the term managerial farmers (and managerial farms) approximates the term *jingying dizhu* (lit., "managerial landlords"). The 1942 "Resolution of the Central Committee of the Chinese Communist Party on Land Policy in the Anti-Japanese Resistance Base Areas" explicitly recognized the special nature of these farmers and distinguished them from leasing landlords: "[We] recognize that the capitalist mode of production is a relatively more progressive mode of production in China at the present time. . . . The mode of production of the rich peasants carries characteristics of capitalism. . . . Among the landlords those who manage their land in a capitalistic mode (the so-called *jingying dizhu*) will be treated the same as rich peasants" (Beijing zhengfa xueyuan 1957: 381).

Later, in 1950, the Party Central decided to treat these "managerial landlords" simply as landlords, drawing the basic divide between those who labor and those who live off the labor of others: "Since labor is the main standard for differentiating between landlords and rich peasants, those who only hire laborers to cultivate their land and do not engage in exploitation through rent, usury, and the like, and those who oversee production themselves, but do not engage in principal labor, will be treated as landlords" (*ibid.*, p. 39).* Such a division, however, although it made good sense from the standpoint of revolutionary justice, can obfuscate a subject of fundamental importance for socioeconomic history: the managerial farmers, as we will see, were the most successful farmers in the pre-Revolution countryside and were very different indeed from leasing landlords.

### THE VILLAGE "RICH" AND MANAGERIAL FARMING

When asked by Japanese investigators to define a *caizhu*, or someone "rich," the peasants of this area responded: "Someone owning more than 100 mu" (KC, 1:124). I was given this same answer about the prerevolutionary usage of this term by elderly Shajing villagers in 1980.†

---

*Less than four months of labor a year or lighter agricultural work such as weeding was defined as "supplementary" rather than "principal" agricultural work.

† The meaning of "rich" households here should not be confused with the Land Reform category "rich peasants." It was clear to the investigators that the peasants made a distinction between the rich and those respected for their learning and character, who were called simply "teacher" (*xiansheng*). The term gentry (*shenshi*), however, caused some confusion. For one village teacher, it retained the anachronistic meaning of a degree-holder (KC, 5:43). To others, it either meant someone of learning and moral character, without regard to property (KC, 1:96), or meant the same thing as the term caizhu (KC, 4:401).

The question I want to ask here is: how prevalent were managerial farmers among the resident village economic elite, among those whom villagers considered rich? Table 4.1 shows all the "rich" village households in the 33 Mantetsu-surveyed villages, divided into those who leased out their land and those who cultivated their land with hired workers. As we quickly see, most of the resident village "rich" were managerial farmers, accounting for 40 of the 55 rich households in these villages. If we exclude the rather unrepresentative villages of Types V–VII and restrict ourselves to the more widely representative villages of Types I–IV, the picture is essentially the same: managerial farmers account for 34 of the 46 rich households.

As will be seen, managerial farming brought better returns than leasing landlordism. This was in part because most managerial farmer households did some farm labor themselves, whereas those who leased out their land did not. But it was also in part because the managerial farmers were able to use labor much more effectively compared with the small tenant family farms on which leasing landlordism was based. The income differences might seem minuscule to us, but to the "rich" people who owned 100 or 200 mu in the Hebei–northwest Shandong plain, they were important enough to make managerial farming more attractive than landlordism.

### PROFILE OF THE MANAGERIAL FARMER

Let us take a closer look at two of the managerial farmers in Table 4.1. Dong Tianwang of highly commercialized Michang village in Fengrun county in northeastern Hebei owned 128.3 mu of land (a year later, in 1937, and including his house area). He farmed this land partly with his household's own labor (a total of 193 man-days for two adult males), but mainly with hired labor (a total of 1,198 days). He grew cotton on 50 percent of his land, mainly for the market—destined ultimately for Tianjin, via cotton merchants in nearby Hetou and Xuanzhuang. The rest was given over to subsistence crops, some for the market, but mostly for consumption by his own household of eight and his four hired year-laborers: 32 percent for sorghum, 7 percent for maize, 3.4 percent for soybeans, 2.9 percent for barley, and 4.1 percent for vegetables, mainly cabbage.

Dong's household economy was pretty simple and straightforward. Almost all of his cash income (650 yuan of 843 yuan) was derived from his cotton crop, the rest from small portions of his sorghum, maize, and vegetable crops. He had no significant income from nonfarm sources; the main item was a small loan of 30 yuan he made to a friend in 1936, at a monthly interest of 2 percent. (MT, Kitō 1937b: Tables 11–13, 15; MT, Hokushi jimukyoku chōsabu 1938–41, 1: Tables 2, 9, 40.) Dong had inherited only 85.8 mu from his father, but by this means he had managed to expand his landholdings over the past several years, recalling (incompletely) purchases of 5.8 mu of land in 1931, 2.2 in 1933, 10.5 in 1935, and 10.0 in 1936. The key to his success was very simply profits from cotton farming in the boom market of the 1930's (MT, Kitō 1937b: Table 2).

Our second example, from a moderately commercialized village, is Zhang Chonglou of Dabeiguan in Pinggu county, also in relatively underdeveloped northeastern Hebei. Zhang owned 218 mu in 1936. Of this, he rented out 30 mu, and farmed-managed the rest, with the aid of three of the four adult males in his household of 14 members, and four hired hands. He gave most of his land to meeting the needs of his household: 28 percent to millet, 16 percent to sorghum, 17 percent to maize, 9 percent to beans. His main cash crops were cotton and sesame, 19 percent and 5.3 percent, respectively, of his total cropped area. In addition to these cash crops, he raised 22 pigs in 1936.

Zhang's cash income of 535 yuan came mainly from cotton (314 yuan); most of the rest came either from the pigs he raised (141 yuan) or from the land he rented out (71 yuan). On this mode of operation, he had been able to steadily expand his original landholding of 150 mu in the past 20-odd years. He could recall acquisitions totaling 65 mu since 1913. (MT, Kitō 1937a: Tables 2, 5, 11, 13, 15, 16.)

That this type of upwardly mobile managerial farmer was by no means exceptional can be seen from the Mantetsu materials. For nine of the surveyed villages, the Mantetsu data permit a reconstruction of the rich households in the village over a three-generation time span (1890's, 1910's, 1930's). The information on three of the villages shown in Table 4.2—Michang, Dabeiguan, and Qianlianggezhuang—were systematically collected and tabulated by the Mantetsu researchers. For the remaining six, I have compiled the information from the transcripts of the Japanese investigators' interviews with the villagers (the information on the earlier generations may be fragmentary and incomplete). The villages once again are grouped according to the typology shown in Table 4.1—these nine villages include five of the seven types; only the relatively uncommercialized and suburban communities are not represented.

We have already seen in Table 4.1 that the majority of the village rich were managerial farmers rather than leasing landlords. For these nine villages in the 1930's, the proportion was 14 of 20.

## TABLE 4.1

### Managerial Farming and Resident Landlordism in 33 Hebei and Shandong Villages, 1936–1942

(Land in mu)

| Village | Total cultivated area | Managerial farming | | | Resident landlordism | | | |
|---|---|---|---|---|---|---|---|---|
| | | Number of farmers | Area managed | Percent of total cultivated area | Number of landlords | Area leased | Percent of total cultivated area | Percent of total cultivated area rented |
| Type I. Relatively Uncommercialized Villages | | | | | | | | |
| Asuwei | 1,527 | 0 | | | 0 | | | — |
| Huzhuang | 2,400 | 0 | | | 0 | | | <10.0% |
| Jiaojiazhuang | 2,502 | 0 | | | 0 | | | 9.2 |
| Type II. Moderately Commercialized Villages | | | | | | | | |
| Dabeiguan | 2,438 | 3 | 124, 212, 189 | 21.5% | 0 | | | 8.2 |
| Houxiazhai | 2,530 | 0 | | | 0 | | | 3.6 |
| Houyansi | 5,012 | 3 | 320a | 6.4 | 0 | | | — |
| Jigezhuang | 1,575 | 2 | 116, 104 | 14.0 | 0 | | | 0 |
| Lujiazhai | 2,497 | 3 | 100, 105, 200 | 16.2 | 0 | | | <10.0 |
| Shajing | 1,182 | 1 | 110 | 9.3 | 0 | | | 17.2 |
| Sunjiamiao | 1,037 | 0 | | | 1 | 176 | 17.0% | 24.4 |
| Tiaoshanying | 1,230 | 0 | | | 0 | | | 5.5 |
| Xiaojie | 2,692 | 2 | 266, 127 | 14.6 | 1 | 190 | 7.1 | 41.2 |
| Xiaoying | 3,025 | 2 | 120, 220 | 11.2 | 3 | 150, 270, 143 | 18.6 | 34.5 |
| Type III. Highly Commercialized Villages | | | | | | | | |
| Donghongyapo | 1,143 | 1b | 80 | 7.0 | 1 | 240 | 21.0c | 19.2% |
| Longwo | 524 | 1 | 110 | 21.0 | 0 | | | 10.5 |
| Macun | 4,209 | 4 | 695a | 16.5 | 0 | | | 24.2 |
| Michang | 2,237 | 3 | 183, 120, 109 | 18.4 | 0 | | | 34.6 |
| Qianlianggezhuang | 1,564 | 0 | | | 5 | 660a | 42.2c | 36.0 |
| Sibeichai | 2,053 | 0 | | | 0 | | | 66.8 |
| Zhongliangshan | 2,000 | 2 | 159, 100 | 13.0 | 1 | 100 | 5.0 | 18.5 |

## Type IV. Villages with Developed Rural Industries

| | | | | | | | |
|---|---|---|---|---|---|---|---|
| Duyake | 1,558 | 2 | 280$^a$ | 0 | 18.0 | | | <10.0 |
| Lengshuigou | 4,200 | 3 | 125, 125, 175 | 0 | 10.1 | | | < 5.0 |
| Qizhai | 2,245 | 2 | 165, 102 | 0 | 11.9 | | | 3.4 |
| Xiaowangzhuang | 1,036 | 0 | | 0 | | | | 20.0 |
| Zhimafeng | 676 | 0 | | 0 | | | | 5.3 |
| SUBTOTAL | 53,092 | 34 | 4,839 | 12 | 9.1% | 1,895 | 3.6% | 17.9%$^d$ |
| **Type V. Suburban Villages** | | | | | | | | |
| Dongjiao | 1,459 | 2 | 255$^a$ | 0 | 17.5 | | | 30.0 |
| Nanquanfuzhuang | 279 | 0 | | 0 | | | | 15.0 |
| **Type VI. Home Villages of Emigrants** | | | | | | | | |
| Binggezhuang | 1,200 | 0 | | 2 | | 130, 100 | 19.2 | >45.0 |
| Baizhuang | 1,860 | 0 | | 0 | | | | 30.0 |
| Houjiaying | 2,979 | 4 | 170, 170, 150, 114 | 1 | 20.3 | 160 | 5.4 | 12.1 |
| Huzhuang | 1,943 | 0 | | 0 | | | | 47.5 |
| **Type VII. Shell-Shocked Villages** | | | | | | | | |
| Heitingzhuang | 1,799 | 0 | | 0 | | | | 72.7 |
| Wudian | 1,100 | 0 | | 0 | | | | 54.5 |
| TOTAL | 65,711 | 40 | 5,698 | 15 | 8.7% | 2,285 | 3.4% | 22.1%$^d$ |

SOURCE: See Appendix A.

NOTE: Relatively uncommercialized is defined as less than 10% of cropped area in cash crops, moderately commercialized as 10%—30% in cash crops, and highly commercialized as more than 30% in cash crops.

$^a$ Total for all farmers or landlords.

$^b$ This man owned 320 mu, of which 240 were rented out.

$^c$ The figure is larger than the percentage for the total cultivated area rented because it includes some land owned outside the village.

$^d$ In computing this average, I have treated <10% as 5%, and <5% as 2.5%. The two villages for which the percentage of rented land is unknown are not included in this figure.

TABLE 4.2

"Rich" Households (100 Mu) Across Three Generations in Nine Hebei and Shandong Villages, 1890's–1930's

(Land in mu)

| Village | 1890's Name of owner | 1890's Land owned | 1910's Name of owner | 1910's Land owned | 1930's Name of owner | 1930's Land owned | Reason for movement into or out of "rich" category |
|---|---|---|---|---|---|---|---|
| | | | | Type II. Moderately Commercialized Villages | | | |
| Houxiazhai | Wang | 500 | Wang | 100 | x | | Household division: 3 brothers |
| | | | Wang | 100 | x | | ? |
| | | | Wang | 100 | x | | ? |
| | ? | | Wang | 100 | x | | ? |
| | | | Liu | 140 | x | | Household division: self and 2 sons |
| | Wang | 150 | x | | x | | Household division: 5 brothers |
| Dabeiguan | Guo | 160 | x | | x | | Household division: 3 brothers |
| | Guo | 230 | x | | x | | Household division: 3 brothers |
| | Zhang | 172 | x | | Zhang | 145 | Household division: 2 brothers |
| | Zhang | 180 | *Zhang* | 86 | x | | Profit from farming |
| | Zhang | 300 | x | | Zhang | 243 | Household division: 2 brothers |
| | | | Zhang | 150 | Zhang | 218 | 1910's–1930's, profit from farming |
| | Zhang | 300 | Zhang | 150 | x | | 1910's–1930's, profit from farming |
| | | | x | | | | Household division: 3 brothers |
| Shajing | Li | 200 | Li | 100 | x | | Household division: 5 brothers |
| | Chong | 500 | Li | 100 | x | | ? |
| | Du | 700 | ? | | x | | ? |
| | Yang | 270 | ? | | x | | ? |
| | ? | | x | | x | | Household division: 3 brothers |
| | x | | Zhao | 140 | x | | Household division: 3 brothers |
| | | | x | | Zhang | 110 | Urban employment |
| | | | Type III. Highly Commercialized Villages | | | | |
| Sibeichai | Xu | 200 | Xu | 100 | x | | Household division: 5 brothers |
| | | | Xu | 100 | x | | ? |
| Michang | Dong | 150 | x | | x | | Household division: 2 brothers |
| | Dong | 165 | x | | x | | Household division: 3 brothers |
| | ? | | Dong | 140 | x | | 1890's–1910's, profit from farming; 1910's, 1930's, household |

The following table classifies villages by type and traces landholdings (in mu) across three generations of lineages.

| Village | Generation 1 | Generation 2 | Generation 3 | Remarks |
|---|---|---|---|---|
| Qianlianggezhuang | *Dong* 46 | Dong 86 | Dong 130 | Profit from farming |
| | *Dong* 20 | Dong 150 | Dong 157 | Profit from farming |
| | *Dong* 93 | Dong 120 | Dong 109 | Profit from farming |
| | ? | Bai 546 | Bai 185 | |
| | | | Bai 192 | |
| | | | Bai 172 | |
| | Fu 210 | Zhang 130 | x | Household division: 2 brothers |
| | | *Fu* 90 | Fu 118 | 1890's–1910's, ?; 1910's–1930's, profit from farming |
| | *Wang* 40 | *Wang* 40 | Wang 104 | Employment in Manchuria |
| **Type IV. Villages with Developed Rural Industries** | | | | |
| Lengshuigou | ? | Li 100 | x 125 | Household division: 3 brothers |
| | ? | Wang 250 | Wang 125 | |
| | ? | ? | Yang 175 | ? |
| **Type VI. Home Villages of Emigrants** | | | | |
| Houjiaying | Liu 400 | Liu 160 | Liu 170 | ? |
| | | Liu 160 | Liu 170 | |
| | | Liu 160 | x | |
| | | x | Hou 150 | Commerce in Manchuria |
| | | x | Hou 114 | Commerce in Manchuria |
| | | x | Hou 160 | Service to official |
| **Type VII. Shell-Shocked Villages** | | | | |
| Wudian | Yu 100 | x | x | Household division: 3 brothers |
| | Zhao 200 | x | x | Household division: 4 brothers |
| | ? | Yu 100 | x | Household division and warlord requisitions |
| | | Guo 300 | Guo | Moved to county seat |

SOURCES: *Houxiazhai*, KC, 4: 444–4 , 506, 556–63; *Dabeiguan*, MT, Kitō 1937a: 6–11; *Shajing*, KC, 1: appended chart; *Sibeichai*, KC, 3: 529, *Michang*, MT, Kitō 1937b: 6–12; *Qianlianggezhuang*, MT, Kitō 1937c: 6–11, 16ff; *Lengshuigou*, KC, 4: 206; *Houjiaying*, KC, : 5–6, 151, 179 193; *Wudian*, KC, 5: 430–31, 588.

NOTE: Men with less than 100 mu (non-rich) are in italic; question marks show no information is available; x's show no one in that generation owned 100 mu.

Among these nine villages, Qianlianggezhuang was something of an anomaly. As far back as anyone could remember the villagers had grown fruit, especially pears, for the Manchurian market. Profit-oriented managerial farming had been quite highly developed here until the Japanese closed the Manchurian frontier to trade with China proper in 1931. After that, the village economy had declined steadily, and managerial farming had given way to leasing land-lordism. By 1936 all of the village rich had become landlords of sharecroppers in a de-commercialized economy (MT, Kitō 1937c: 12–16). If we exclude that anomalous case from Table 4.2, the pre-ponderance of managerial farmers over leasing landlords among the resident village rich is greater still: 14 of 15. The only leasing land-lord, in Houjiaying village, was a man who had made his wealth through service to an official.

Of the ten rich households of the 1930's who could be traced back clearly for three generations, one-half had become so only in their own or their father's generation. More important, of the 13 instances in which the cause of upward movement could be positively identi-fied, eight had risen through profits from farming. And three of the others were a result of frontier commerce or employment in Man-churia, a situation peculiar to the counties in adjacent northeastern Hebei.

At the same time, the data suggest that few rich households main-tained their status for more than a generation or two. Of the 19 households identified as rich in the 1890's, only three still had rich descendants (a total of five) in the third generation in the 1930's. The main reason for downward movement was the division of family property among sons—fenjia—an established custom in Chinese society since the Han (Fu 1980, 1:222–23). The property of these households, rich only compared with their poor neighbors, was rela-tively meager; a single partition drove a rich household down to middle or poor peasant status. Few could survive such downward pressures through income from farming alone. (This, as we will see, added to the pressure on the more successful ones to leave farming for more lucrative pursuits.)

The typical rich village household, then, was that of a managerial farmer who owned 100 to 200 mu of land and cultivated his farm with hired labor. Such farmers outnumbered leasing landlords by a ratio of about 3:1 among the rich households. Most of these farmers had been peasants who had managed to acquire more land through profits from commercialized farming. They outnumbered those who became rich by other avenues, such as urban and frontier employment, by about 2 : 1. Most of these households were managerial farmers for only the first or second generation, for very few (three of 19) managed to survive as rich households into the third generation against the downward pressures of partible inheritance. These rich households, finally, tended to be found in relatively commercialized villages; the uncommercialized villages generally had neither rich managerial farmers nor landlords.

A QUANTITATIVE ESTIMATE

The evidence presented above shows only that managerial farmers were the majority among villagers considered rich by fellow villagers. That is far from claiming that managerial agriculture was the dominant mode of farm organization in Chinese agriculture of the time and farther still from saying that rural North China was mainly capitalist, or that it was ready for or well launched on the road to capitalist development. To place managerial farming into the larger perspective of agriculture in North China as a whole we need first of all some sense of the relative quantitative scale of managerial farming.

The Guomindang's Land Commission counted a total of 4,122 *farms* (as distinguished from landholdings) that were larger than 100 mu in a total of 391,170 farms surveyed in Hebei and Shandong. This amounted to 1.05 percent of the farms surveyed, and 9.95 percent of the total cultivated area of the surveyed farms.* These data suggest that about 10 percent of the total cultivated area in these two provinces was under managerial farming (Tudiweiyuanhui 1937: 26).

Another way to try to estimate the extent of managerial farming is to look at the data on wage labor. We have a number of such surveys, none of them fully satisfactory. The most substantial is a nationwide survey conducted by Chen Zhengmo in 1933, when questionnaires were mailed to county "agricultural investigators" in 726 counties. No explanation is given on how the information was gathered by

*The 9.95% figure is arrived at by assigning an average farm size of 125 mu to farms in the 100–150 range, 175 to those in the 150–200 range, 250 to the 200–300 range, and so on, and simply 500 mu to those of "more than 500." In spite of this rather high proportion of cultivated area under large farms, this survey counted only 1.57% of all rural households as those of agricultural laborers. The discrepancy probably stems from an excessively rigid definition of "agricultural laborer" that excluded anyone who owned or rented any land at all. As I will show in Chapter Ten, most year-laborers were in fact first-generation hired laborers who still maintained minuscule family farms, usually worked by other members of their household.

each investigator—presumably much depended on the person on the scene, so that the investigations could vary from conscientious data-gathering with field studies to rather arbitrary assignments of figures by clerks sitting in county offices. This study found that 10 percent of the rural population in Hebei and 12 percent in Shandong worked as long-term agricultural laborers (10 percent nationwide). No effort was made to study the scale of day-labor. (Chen Zhengmo 1935: 1–4, 58.)

John Lossing Buck's surveys yielded several figures for the proportion of farmwork done by hired labor. His two national samples, of 2,866 and 16,685 farms, show totals of 19.5 percent and 15 percent, respectively (Buck 1930, vii, 234; 1937a: 293). In the second, more complete survey, 70.7 percent of the work was done by year-laborers. For Hebei, where Buck surveyed households in nine counties, he got an average of 23.4 percent for the work done by hired hands, and in northwest Shandong, where he surveyed only two counties, an average of 16.5 percent (1937b: 305). All these figures are probably biased upward, however, because of the exceptionally large farms Buck selected for his surveys (which averaged an unrealistic seven mu per capita in our area, for example).

Finally, a survey carried out by 61 Qinghua (Tsinghua) University students in 1922, under the direction of C. B. Malone and J. B. Taylor, found an average of 16.5 percent of farmwork done by hired labor in three counties in Hebei—Zunhua, Tangxian, and Handan in northeastern, central, and southern Hebei, respectively. For Shandong, where the survey covered villages in only one county, Zhanhua, along the highly alkaline lowermost reaches of the Yellow River, the figure was a low 3.3 percent (Malone & Taylor 1924: 25).

Though none of these studies is completely satisfactory, there is enough general agreement among them to make "ball-park" guesses about the scale of hired labor. Applying Buck's ratio of year-labor to day-labor to Chen Zhengmo's data yields a figure of 14–17 percent for the proportion of farmwork done by hired labor in Hebei and Shandong. If we adjust Buck's own figures downward somewhat to correct for the bias in his sample, they come very close to this same figure.

The figure is also corroborated by the Mantetsu data. We have complete and reliable information on year-labor in 22 of the 25 villages of the basic Types I–IV, and on day-labor as well for 12 of them. For this group of 25 villages, 12.5 percent of all village farming households had a member who hired out as a year-laborer, and 36.2 percent had one or more members working as day-laborers (computed from data shown in Appendix A). However, the 12.5-percent figure needs to be adjusted downward somewhat in order to reflect the actual proportion of farmwork done by year-laborers, for many wage workers still had a small plot farmed by other family members (see pp. 199–201). In terms of the proportion of total farmwork done, the figure would be close to 10 percent.

Day-laborers generally hired out for an average of about 40 to 50 days a year, and year-laborers for about 200 days (see p. 199). In terms of total farmwork done, therefore, the ratio of year-labor to day-labor suggested by the Mantetsu surveys was about 5 : 3 (compared with Buck's 7 : 3 for the nation as a whole). This suggests that another 6 percent or so of total farmwork was done by day-labor. The combined total of year- and day-labor is thus very close to the figures of Buck and Malone and Taylor.

In addition to corroborating the survey figures, the Mantetsu data permit us to differentiate between the large managerial farms of over 100 mu and the smaller farms using hired labor. As I have shown in Table 4.1, in the 25 villages of the basic Types I–IV, 9.1 percent of the cultivated area was under managerial farming. This corroborates very closely the Guomindang Land Commission's 10-percent figure for large farms over 100 mu. Since the managerial farmers' own households often did a part of the labor on their farms (16.1 percent and 11.6 percent of the total labor, in the cases of two of the managerial farmers of Michang village, for example; see Table 10.1), we might estimate that, of the 16 percent or so of total farmwork in the rural economy that was accounted for by hired labor, perhaps one-half was employed by managerial farms, and the rest by smaller rich- and middle-peasant farms.

All these estimates are of course rough and tentative. However, until better data come to light, these are probably the best guesses we can make about the extent of managerial farming in the Hebei–northwest Shandong plain area in the 1930's: the Mantetsu data, the Guomindang Land Commission surveys, and the Chen Zhengmo, Buck, and Malone and Taylor surveys all point to a figure of about 9–10 percent of total cultivated area under managerial farming.

### MANAGERIAL FARMERS AND LEASING LANDLORDS

If the picture presented above is substantially accurate, we need to correct the common misconception that the village rich were usually leasing landlords. Several things have contributed to this mistaken notion. It stems, first of all, from the failure to distinguish between absentee landlords and resident landlords. Most of the rented land in Hebei-Shandong was leased by either absentee landlords or absentee small landowners resident in town or in neighboring villages.* That is why many of the villages in Table 4.1 show the apparent anomaly of no resident landlords owning more than 100 mu and yet a high incidence of rented land. Consider highly commercialized Michang, for example: 34.6 percent of its land was rented, but there was not a single rich landlord in the village. This was because most of the rented land (663 mu of 774) was owned by outsiders: 411 mu by big absentee landlords owning over 100 mu, and 252 mu by smaller owners living outside the village (MT, Kitō 1937b: 4, 27, 39–50). Similarly, in Sibeichai, also highly commercialized and a cotton-producing village, almost all of the 1,372 mu of rented land was owned by absentee landlords resident in town, especially one Wang Zanzhou (KC, 3:5–6, 177–86, 525–33 and appended map of landholdings). In moderately commercialized Shajing, by contrast, most of the rented land was owned by small landowners outside the village. Of the total of 426 mu owned by outsiders, 307.4 mu were owned and farmed (except for 45 mu) by small peasants resident in the nearby villages of Shimen and Wangquansi; the rest was owned mainly by petty merchants resident in town (KC, 1:464–67).

A second source of the misconception is the loose revolutionary usage of the term landlord. We have already seen how "managerial landlords," identified with rich peasants and a supposedly "capitalist mode of production" in 1942, were simply lumped together with landlords by the Land Reform Law of 1950. In fact, during the social revolution, "landlord" came to include virtually all undesirable elements in the villages. Thus the "evil tyrant" (eba) and "landlord" Qian Wengui of Nuanshuitun village (in Zhuolu county, Hebei), immortalized in Ding Ling's *The Sun Shines on the Sanggan River*, turns out to have been a middle peasant who farmed 60+ mu with his two adult sons. Qian had earned the wrath of the villagers not because he was a landlord, but because of his unprincipled wheelings and dealings. Similarly, the "landlord Sheng Ching-ho" of William Hinton's "Longbow village" (near Changzhi, Shanxi) turns out

---

*According to the Guomindang Land Commission, 15% of the farm households in Hebei and Shandong were tenants or part-tenants, who rented 13% of the total cultivated area (Tudiweiyuanhui 1937: 34, 36). These figures seem low. As Joseph Esherick (1981) has argued, the National Agricultural Bureau's figures of 28% for tenant or part-tenant households in Hebei and 26% in Shandong are probably more reliable. If one works back from those figures to estimate the proportion of total cultivated land that was rented, one comes closer to the 17.9% figure I show in Table 4.1 for the 25 Type I–IV villages.

to be a managerial farmer who worked his 138 mu of land with the help of two hired laborers; the entire village in fact had only one tenant household. Nor was there a resident landlord in David and Isabel Crook's "Ten Mile Inn," where the wealthiest landowner was an absentee landlord.* (Ding 1949: 8, 451–53; Hinton 1966: 29–32, 592; Crook & Crook 1959: 5, 18–19, 129.)

These distinctions between managerial farmers and leasing landlords, and between resident and absentee landlords, far from being just so much hairsplitting, are critically important to our understanding of the dynamics of change in the farm economy. The fact that most of the village rich were managerial farmers indicates the degree to which upward social mobility accompanied the commercialization of agriculture. And a closer examination of the nature of managerial farming, as we will see, tells us much about some crucial characteristics of the family farm economy. Moreover, whether a member of a village's elite was a managerial farmer or a landlord is important to our understanding of the nature of village political structure. A "rich" landlord who did not work in the fields was more socially distant from the villagers than a "rich" managerial farmer who worked alongside his hired laborers—and the absentee landlord the more so. Finally, most absentee landlords, as will be seen, took little interest in the affairs of a village of which they were not inhabitants; the resident landlords, on the other hand, generally did involve themselves actively in village affairs.

### MANAGERIAL AND FAMILY FARMING

The data presented in this chapter suggest that no social or economic historian can afford to ignore wage-labor-based farming. If it is true that about 16 percent of the total cultivated area on the Hebei–northwest Shandong plain was farmed by hired labor, that 12.5 percent of rural households had long-term agricultural workers, and another 36.2 percent short-term agricultural workers, then no picture of the rural society and economy of this area can be complete without a close look at agricultural wage labor. More households, in fact, were involved in wage labor than land renting, which here involved just over one-quarter of the rural households. If it is true, furthermore, that the managerial farms were the most successful farms and employed about one-half of the total hired agricultural

---

*The wealthiest landowner was Fu Hsin [Xin], an absentee landlord who lived in the market town of Yangyi (Crook & Crook 1959: 5, 18–19, 129).

wage labor, then no analysis of agricultural development and under-development in this area can afford to overlook these farms.

Yet it will not do to exaggerate the extent of managerial farming or of wage-labor-based farming in this area before the Revolution. Most of the cultivated area, 84 percent by the figures of this chapter, remained under small family farms. This figure would be larger still if one included those farms in which family members did at least half of the work. That would include all middle peasant farms that used some hired day-labor in busy seasons, and many of the farms that the Revolution classed as "rich peasant." The total cultivated area under family farming by such a reckoning would come quite close to all of the area not under managerial farming, or 90 percent of the total cultivated area.

The history of the farm economy of this area, I suggest, needs to be seen through the twin phenomena of change and stagnation. In the development of managerial farming we find clear evidence of dynamic change in the area's small-peasant economy. But the continued preponderance of small family farms in the 1930's just as clearly attests to the inability of this new pattern of agriculture to supplant and replace the old one. A comparative analysis of the two kinds of farming will reveal their basic characteristics and help us find the roots of both change and stagnation in the agriculture of this area.

# CHAPTER 5

# The Small-Peasant
# and Estate Economies
# of the Early Qing

Massive depopulation of the North China plain during the Ming–Qing dynastic transition left large areas open to resettlement by smallholders, under the active encouragement of the state. At the same time, Zhili, as the capital province, saw the creation of numerous large serf-based estates. The result was the coexistence of an estate economy with a smallholder economy, which affords us a rare view of the competitive development of the two systems.

In the smallholder economy, I shall show that the first century and a half of the Qing saw a long-term process of social stratification that accompanied agricultural commercialization. In that process, former smallholders came to be differentiated between labor-employing rich peasants and managerial farmers and labor-selling poor peasants and agricultural workers, and between land-leasing commoner landlords and land-renting free tenants. In the estate economy, on the other hand, the institution of serfdom gave way before the pressures of population increase and commercialization. Managerial and leasing estates came to be based first on serf-like intermediate categories of people, until they finally gave way to labor and rent relations that had been born of the small peasant economy. By the late eighteenth century, the lines between the estate and small peasant economies had blurred, and agrarian Zhili–northwest Shandong had taken on the basic landholding patterns and production relations that were to remain down to the twentieth century.

## SMALL HOLDINGS VERSUS LARGE ESTATES
### IN THE EARLY QING

Wars of the Ming–Qing dynastic transition depopulated possibly one-quarter to one-third of the arable land in Hebei-Shandong (see pp. 114–16). In these areas, the Qing undertook to encourage the development of a smallholder economy. Three times in the Shunzhi reign (in 1649, 1651, and again in 1652), the government ordered that drifters (*liumin*) living on uncultivated land be given permanent title to it, regardless of their place of origin. At the same time, the Qing made a practice of granting the land that had belonged to the estates of the Ming aristocracy to their original cultivators, thus again encouraging the expansion of the smallholder economy.

Parallel to these moves, the state took steps to check the expansion of large estates. It forbade the *touxian* practice of the late Ming (whereby smallholders sought shelter from heavy taxation under the tax-exempt big estates), which had given the big estate owners opportunities to expand their holdings. It restricted the tax-exempt privileges of the bureaucracy and the gentry, first by limiting the exemption from corvée to the individual bureaucrat or gentry landowner. Later, in the second quarter of the eighteenth century, it merged the corvée into the land tax (*tanding rudi*), so that assessments came to be based on the amount of land owned, regardless of the owner's legal status. Against gentry who were delinquent in tax payments, it pursued a vigorous policy of collection. In 1661, for example, no fewer than 2,171 upper gentry and 11,346 holders of the lower degree of shengyuan were reduced in status or lost their status altogether in the four lower Yangzi prefectures of Suzhou, Songjiang, Changshu, and Zhenjiang alone (Li Wenzhi 1963a: 78–85; 1981: 144–45).

The Qing state's encouragement of a smallholder economy at the expense of big estates is not particularly surprising. Smallholders, after all, were a more accessible source of tax revenue than the powerful big estate owners. From the point of view of the central government, they were also far less politically threatening. The success of the Qin state, for example, had very much to do with a small peasant economy (Hsü 1980: 13; Elvin 1973: Part 1). The Tang, similarly, installed the "equal field" system of small cultivators for a time. And the Ming likewise had moved in this direction, decreeing in 1372, for example, that resettlers of the vast areas devastated by the wars of dynastic transition could not claim more land than they could farm themselves (Li Wenzhi 1981: 144). Through much of imperial history, therefore, the beginnings of new dynasties were associated with renewed assertions of the small peasant economy. It is in the periods of dynastic decline that one witnesses the rise of big powerful estates to challenge the central government's authority. That the Qing was a conquest dynasty only made this calculation that much more pertinent.

Yet even as the Qing was strengthening the small farming economy, it was also creating large numbers of big estates. Like other dynasties before it, the early Qing rewarded its own kin and meritorious followers with grants of land. The largest of these grants, the imperial estates (*huangzhuang*), totaled perhaps 4,000,000 mu. After them came the estates of the kings and princes (*wangzhuang*), and of the meritorious officials. If we include the parcels granted to the bannermen (usually 30 mu), some 20,000,000 of China's 740,000,000 mu of arable land was doled out by the court (Li Wenzhi 1963b, 1:73; Yang Xuechen 1963: 176–81; Perkins 1969: 240). Bannerland loomed especially large in the capital province of Zhili, accounting for 17,600,000 mu in 1657, compared with 42,700,000 mu of privately owned land, or roughly 29 percent of the total arable (Ju Zhendong 1977: 39615–22).*

The court's beneficiaries typically got an estate (*zhuang*) of 720 mu, ten serfs (*zhuangding*) under a headman (*zhuangtou*) and six to eight oxen. In the Shunzhi period (1644–61), at least, as Yang Xuechen has shown conclusively on the basis of archival material (1963: 177, 184), the court's intention was to create a serf-based system. Some 400,000 *ding* of serfs were granted to the court-created estates during the period.

As Li Wenzhi has shown (1963a: 78), the Li Zicheng revolt in the late Ming had sounded the call of "equalize the land between the rich and poor" and in general had seen the rich plundered and killed. The revolt had dealt a devastating blow to big estates in Hebei, Shandong, and Henan. The Qing measures reversed the trend toward the disappearance of large estates in this area and in so doing, created the potential for the rise of large-scale managerial agriculture.

MANAGERIAL ESTATES

The estate system created by the Qing court was not a viable one. Since most estates were essentially fixed in size, they could not long maintain a serf population that was growing along with the rest of the population. By 1700, as even the court recognized, much of the estate land was in fact being leased out to free tenants. The court divested itself of the serfs on the imperial estates in 1744 by permitting them to become commoners (*liangmin*), and the ruling was extended to the estates of the nobility of the eight banners soon after. By the middle of the eighteenth century, serfdom no longer figured

*Zhili's unusual situation should not be generalized to all of China. Mark Elvin's speculation (1973: Chaps. 6, 15) that a "manorial economy" predominated until the 18th century seems an exaggeration even for Zhili.

prominently in the agricultural system, even in this area where the capital was located (Yang Xuechen 1963; see also Muramatsu 1962: Part 1).

On estates that were operated as large farming units, or managerial estates, as opposed to estates leased out in small parcels, serfs gave way to hired worker-serfs, the *gugongren*, a category of people already prevalent in the Ming. The worker-serf was defined in the Ming code as an individual who was generally "hired by a written contract, for a fixed period of years," and who was below the commoner in status. He was more harshly punished for an offense against his employer-master than someone who committed the same offense against an equal; by the same token, his employer-master could deal with him with more impunity than with someone of his own status. Thus, for example, an employer-master who beat his worker-serf without causing permanent injury would not have been legally liable at all, whereas the reverse offense was punishable by three years at hard labor plus 100 strokes with a heavy stick; if two commoners were involved, the offender received only 20 strokes, and then with only a light stick. In the "New Precedents" appended to the Ming code in 1588, laborers "hired for only short terms of months or days, and paid only small amounts" were specifically excluded from this worker-serf category. But long-term agricultural laborers continued to be so categorized on the assumption that they were all employed by upper-status, nonpeasant estate owners (Jing Junjian 1961a, b). The Ming code remained in effect in the early Qing, until new social realities brought a redefinition of the law in 1788.

The worker-serf system was more viable under population pressure than the serf system, for unlike the serf (*zhuangding*), the worker-serf was not permanently attached to land and could be contracted for only as needed. But the worker-serf was not yet a rural wage worker (*gugong, changgong, niangong*) either, for his employer-master held extra-economic powers over him, as the serf-owner did over the serf, which were reinforced by the law's recognition of his superior social status. The worker-serf system died out only when the more equal wage-labor relations born of the small-peasant economy came to predominate in rural society as a whole.

Thanks to the research of Liu Yongcheng (1982: 115–16), we have a documented example of a managerial estate in eighteenth-century Zhili.* In a homicide case recorded in the Board of Punishment ar-

---

*Kataoka Shibako's earlier painstaking research with the gazetteers (1959: 81–90; 1962) had failed to turn up a single example of a North China estate of this type.

chives, we hear of the estate of a Mongolian aristocrat in Xincheng county that was operated as a large farm, mostly with a long-term labor force, under a Han zhuangtou named Qian Jin. The deceased in this case, Yu Tunzi, was one of the temporary hands the farm hired to supplement its regular workers in the busy seasons. He had been sent out to harvest wheat, along with some 50 to 60 other temporary workers, each of whom was given a plaque that was to be turned in at the end of the day for pay. (Yu, apparently, had asked that he be paid a lump sum on the completion of the harvest. But Qian accused him of trying to get double pay. In the end, Yu was beaten to death by the servants of the estate.)

We also have a fictionalized account of a late Ming managerial estate in one of Feng Menglong's collected tales. Its protagonist is Lu Nan, a brilliant and rich dilettante (holder of the lower examination degree of *jiansheng*), who owned a large estate in Junxian in southernmost Bei Zhili (present-day northern Henan). Lu had built an exquisite garden of 200 to 300 mu on this estate and farmed the rest with some 100 worker-serfs. He customarily paid these workers in silver in the twelfth month, in advance of their work for the coming year. As the story tells it, Lu made a habit of calling out the workers' names himself and of personally handing them their pay, lest his servants cheat them. He would then fill the workers with wine and food, and they would "prostrate themselves in gratitude as they withdrew."*

It is impossible to get any precise sense of the proportion of estates that were operated as managerial estates. The evidence cited above tells us that such estates existed in Zhili, but cannot give us any indication of the proportion they occupied in the province as a whole. Still, the fact that the late Ming and early Qing code equated all long-term agricultural workers with worker-serfs of managerial estates suggests that these estates might have been quite common in that period.

---

*Feng Menglong 1958, 2 juan 29: 597–627; quote at p. 612. One of these worker-serfs, Niu Cheng, had been an impoverished peasant, and being "somewhat lacking in character," had been unable to rent any land to farm. He had therefore taken employment with Lu Nan. His brother had been sold as a slave to a minor bureaucrat. In the story, Lu, the benevolent master, was framed by the jealous county magistrate on a trumped-up charge involving this worker-serf Niu and Niu's wife. He languished in prison for more than a decade, until a principled new magistrate arrived on the scene and uncovered the truth. One of Lu's servants had coveted Niu's wife and had loaned Niu money in an attempt to get at her. When she rejected him, the servant got angry and had Niu beaten. Niu died from the beating. The evil county magistrate had seized this opportunity to frame Lu. The new magistrate, in his review of the case, pointed out that in any event, since Niu had been Lu's worker-serf and was therefore of a legally inferior status to him, the supposed offense did not call for such harsh punishment.

### THE SPREAD OF RICH-PEASANT AND MANAGERIAL
### FARMING IN THE EARLY QING

While the institution of serfdom was giving way to that of the hired worker-serf in the estate economy, a new set of employer–wage laborer relations was spreading within the small-peasant economy. As commercialization proceeded and the population grew, small peasants became increasingly differentiated (for reasons that will be analyzed in the next chapter) into labor-employing rich peasants and managerial farmers on the one hand, and labor-selling poor peasants and wage workers on the other. By the eighteenth century, in fact, most agricultural laborers were employed on the farms of former small peasants, rather than on estate farms.

Of the 2,337 "land- and debt-related" homicide cases for 1736, 1737, and 1796 in the Board of Punishment Archives, 234 pertain to Hebei and Shandong. From these cases (57, 70, and 107 for the respective years), I have culled profiles of 52 wage workers (both long-term and short-term), as shown in Tables 5.1–5.3.*

What these cases reveal, first of all, is that upper-class employers were the exception rather than the rule.† Only one of the employers involved in these 52 cases was a degree-holder, and he was a lowly shengyuan. There was a bannerman who employed two workers, and a zhuangtou in charge of a bannerman's 300 mu, who rented out most of the land and employed one laborer with additional day-labor help to cultivate the rest. Finally, there was one employer who did not hold a degree but clearly maintained a big, wealthy household: this man, Chen Butian, employer of Li Ming, had a gate guard and two bondservants, male and female (1796, bao 80, 5.20). (Chen's household entered the Board of Punishment's archives because Li Ming was carrying on with the female servant, whom the master had already betrothed to the male servant. When this was discovered, Li became desperate and murdered his employer. The case was judged to be a dispute between a worker-serf and his master, and Li was given the severest sentence—death by slicing.)

---

*In the archives, cases are labeled by the lunar month and day and grouped by *bao*, or bundles, according to the year. In the text I identify these cases first by year, then bao number, then month and day.

†It can of course be argued that the elites tended to be underrepresented in the Board of Punishment records, not only because people of this status were less likely to have direct altercations with a worker than the commoner employer, but also because, in many instances, they would have been able to pull strings to keep from being held accountable. To the extent that these qualifications are valid, the Board of Punishment materials should not be considered conclusive evidence. My case here is based on the totality of several kinds of evidence, as will be seen below.

TABLE 5.1

Agricultural Laborers Cited in Homicide Cases in Hebei and Shandong, 1736

| Laborer's name | Laborer's recorded origin | Location of case | Employer Status | No. of workers | Source[a] Bao no. | Date |
|---|---|---|---|---|---|---|
| Yuan Liang | Deserter | Central Hebei (Yizhou) | | | 95 | 2.28 |
| Shi Yulong | Next village | N.W. Shandong (Qihe) | Managerial farmer | 3+ | 99 | 6.6 |
| Wang Yong | In-migrant | N.W. Hebei (Xuanhua) | Peasant | 1 } | 99 | 6.11 |
| Liu Meiyu | Local(?)[b] | | Shengyuan | 1 } | | |
| Wang Cheng | In-migrant | S. Hebei (Yizhou) | Peasant | 1 } | 82 | 6.17 |
| Liu Jincai | In-migrant | | Peasant | 1 } | | |
| Wang Jinli | In-migrant | | Peasant | 1 } | | |
| Wang Mingjiu | In-migrant | | Peasant | 1 } | | |
| Cui Lin | In-migrant | Kaizhou, Daming fu[c] | Peasant | 1 | 83 | 6.18 |
| Zhao Zigang | In-migrant | North of wall | Peasant | 1 | 83 | 6.20 |
| Li Shiqing | In-migrant | N. Shandong (Shouguang) | Peasant | 2 } | 98 | 6.21 |
| Li Shiming | In-migrant | | Peasant | — } | | |
| Xin Yong | In-migrant | | Peasant | 1 } | | |
| Han Yuxian | In-migrant | Near Beijing (Shunyi) | Peasant | | 103 | 11.12 |
| Liu Wenju | In-migrant | North of wall (Shizigou) | Peasant | | 107 | 12.1 |

[a] Ming-Qing Board of Punishment Archives, Beijing. The dates are by lunar month and day.
[b] Many of these cases do not indicate how the worker came to be on the scene. In this and the following tables I have guessed that he was a local(?) man.
[c] Present-day Puyang, Henan.

TABLE 5.2

Agricultural Laborers Cited in Homicide Cases in Hebei and Shandong, 1737

| Laborer's name | Laborer's recorded origin | Location of case | Employer Status | Employer No. of workers | Source[a] Bao no. | Source[a] Date |
|---|---|---|---|---|---|---|
| Cui Liu | In-migrant | North of wall | Peasant | 1+ | 51 | 2.2 |
| Huang Han | In-migrant | Near Beijing (Wanping) | Peasant (kin) | 1+ | 52 | 2.2 |
| Zhang Gui | Next county | | | | | |
| Li Bingrui | Local | Central Hebei (Boye) | Peasant | 1 | 63 | 6.20 |
| Zhang Da | In-migrant | North of wall | | | 65 | 7.7 |
| Zhang Liuer | Local(?) | N.E. Hebei (Tongzhou) | Bannerman (zhuangtou)[b] | 1+ | 67 | 7.7 |
| Xin Da | Local(?) | | | | | |
| Zhang Guangzeng | Local(?) | Central Hebei (Cangzhou) | Bannerman | 2 | 77 | 11.14 |
| Yin Ertuzi | Local(?) | | | | | |
| Zhao Er | Local(?) | | Managerial farmer | 3+ | | |
| Li Gao | Local(?) | | | | | |
| Liang Yazi | Local(?) | | | | | |
| Li Xiaogou | Local | N. Shandong (Changyi) | Peasant (kin) | 1 | 76 | 11.22 |
| Liu Er | In-migrant | North of wall (Babanggou) | Peasant | 1 | 76 | 11.29 |
| Zhang Ba | In-migrant | North of wall | Peasant | 1 | 77 | 11.30 |
| Jia Da | Local(?) | S.W. Shandong (Ziyang) | Peasant (tenant)[c] | 1 | 60 | 12.3 |

[a]Same as Table 5.1.   [b]Zhuangtou was overseer of 300 mu.   [c]Tenant farmed 30 mu.

TABLE 5.3

Agricultural Laborers Cited in Homicide Cases in Hebei and Shandong, 1796

| Laborer's name | Laborer's recorded origin[b] | Location of case | Employer | | Source[a] | |
|---|---|---|---|---|---|---|
| | | | Status | No. of workers | Bao no. | Date |
| Zhang Xiaowu | In-migrant[b] | N.W. Shandong (Ningjin) | | | 109 | 2.23 |
| Li Huaicheng | Local(?) | | | | | |
| Zhang Yuekuan | Local(?) | | | | | |
| Zhang Zihe | Local[b] | | | | | |
| Liu Haoxue | In-migrant | N.W. Hebei (Huailai) | | | 90 | 3.27 |
| Wang Lian Yi | Ir-migrant | North of wall (Chengde) | | | 111 | 4.20 |
| Li Ming | Ir-migrant | W. Shandong (Jining) | Upper class | 1 | 80 | 5.20 |
| Liu Anbang | Local | N.W. Shandong (Qihe) | Peasant | 1 | 120 | 5.26 |
| Zhu Laicheng | In-migrant | Central Hebei (Shenzhou) | | | 107 | 8.17 |
| Liu Niuer | Local | Central Hebei (Qingyuan) | | | 112 | 8.17 |
| Wang Lu | In-migrant | N.E. Hebei (Luanzhou) | | | 83 | 8.30 |
| Ma Gubao | Local | N.W. Shandong (Huimin) | Peasant | 2 | 115 | 12.2 |
| Zhao Xuan | Local | | | | | |
| Chen Ming | In-migrant | North of wall (Pingquan) | Peasant | 1 | 103 | 12.13 |
| Yin Tianxi | In-migrant | N.W. Hebei (Zhangjiakou) | Peasant | 1 | 69 | n.d. |
| Li Zhen | In-migrant | N.W. Hebei (Zhangjiakou) | Peasant | 1 | 84 | n.d. |
| Dong Er | In-migrant | | ? | | | |
| Zhang Shibao | In-migrant | | ? | | | |
| Zhang Shengde | In-migrant | North of wall (Huaikou-beidao) | | | 107 | n.d. |
| Zhang Shengxiang | In-migrant | | | | | |
| Zhang Shen | In-migrant | | | | | |

[a] Same as Table 5.1.   [b] Muslim.

To judge by these materials, the typical employer was a commoner, generally a peasant himself. This relatively well-to-do commoner peasant would hire one man, sometimes even two, to help him in his farmwork. Most of these laborers were either migrants from another county or province (frequently men who left when famine struck their own localities) or peasants from the same village or a neighboring one. The terms of employment were typically reached orally; no written contract was drawn up. The year-laborers often stayed for more than one year. The day-laborers, on the other hand, were generally hired and paid by the day. (In the case of the worker Li Xiaogou, a daily cash wage of 50 *wen* was noted; 1737, bao 76, 11.22.)

Two of the employers are clearly identifiable as managerial farmers of the type I have been discussing. One was Qu Er of Cangzhou, central Hebei, who employed three long-term workers, Zhao Er, Li Gao, and Liang Yazi, to work in his fields of millet and cotton. (Qu's nephew Zhang Wenju had killed a little village girl for picking his crops, and Wenju's father had tried to hush the whole thing up, bribing the girl's father to keep quiet. But the truth came to light when Qu's workers told what happened; 1737, bao 77, 11.14.) The other managerial farmer, Yang Kun of Qihe county near Jinan, had had one of his workers hire Shi Yulong to help two other workers hoe the ground. The two had agreed on a daily wage of 90 wen, but after Shi came to work, Yang tried to cut this down to 62. When Shi protested, Yang killed him. (Yang in the end was let off on a technicality; the crime had been committed before the Yongzheng Emperor's general pardon, granted on the third day of the ninth month, 1735; 1736, bao 99, 6.6.)

Most of the cases collected in Tables 5.1–5.3 occurred in one of two kinds of areas: either the relatively commercialized core zones surrounding cities like Beijing and Jinan and the relatively well-developed parts of central and southern Hebei, or the frontier "periphery" zone, the part of Hebei north of the wall. This area "beyond the passes" (*kouwai*), as it was commonly known, saw heavy immigration in the eighteenth century, especially the eastern portion, named the Chengde prefecture (*fu*) in 1777 (Rehe province in the Republican period). Within this prefecture, Pingquan county (Pingquan *zhou*, known before 1777 as the Eight Gullies area—Bagou ting; Zhao 1955: 8) seems to have been particularly unruly—a frequent scene of brawls resulting in deaths.

The employer in this frontier zone was typically a settler who had been in the area for some time, a proprietor-peasant on his way up the economic ladder. The wage worker was typically a more recent arrival, one of many who came in response to the employment opportunities of this growth area, "to hire out for a living" (*yonggong duri*). In 1736, for example, two such individuals made their way into the Board of Punishment archives. The employer, Yang Lianting, and his worker, Zhao Zigang, were killed by a friend of Yang's, Li Wanliang, who was passing through the area. Li had stayed at Yang's house, and Yang had borrowed 3,000 wen from him. When Li sought payment, Yang refused, on the grounds that he had repaid Li in the form of room and board. But Li had in fact paid for his own food. A fight ensued, in which the worker Zhao, who had been drinking with his employer that night, took Yang's side. Li killed the worker, along with his employer (1736, bao 83, 6.20).

### RECENT CHINESE SCHOLARSHIP

Figures presented in Li Wenzhi 1957: 111, though inconclusive, tend to support the view that wage labor spread in the small-peasant economy during the eighteenth century. The number of homicide cases involving wage laborers jumped dramatically between 1723 and 1820, from an average of 0.9 a year in 1723–35 (12 cases in the Board of Punishment archives), to 4.3 a year in 1736–95 (259 cases) to 17.5 a year in 1796–1820 (437 cases).*

Other information culled from the homicide cases also tends to support this view. In 68 of 140 cases involving year-laborers, the relationship between employer and worker was explicitly said to be one in which "they address each other as equals," "normally eat and sit together," and "are not differentiated like serfs from masters." In the remaining cases, 67 carried no explicit identification of the nature of the relationship, and four specified that there had been a written contract. In only one case was the relationship clearly stated to be that between "master and serf" (Li Wenzhi 1963a: 107–8). Like the other legal cases discussed, this material suggests that most year-laborers were employed by commoner peasants by the end of the eighteenth century.

---

*It is important to note here that, if my own four-year sample is any indication, only a small fraction of these cases would have involved disputes between employers and their laborers; they mostly involved only other workers or other segments of rural society. Liu Yongcheng (1962: 113) has added 180 cases from various other sources to the Li Wenzhi sample that expand the time frame to 1644–1840. But he does not seem to have combed the Board of Punishment archives for the 1644–1722 and 1821–40 periods, and his 888-case sample therefore seems to me less useful than Li's, which is based on a single source.

Two very different explanations of how this came to be have emerged in Chinese historical circles. Liu Yongcheng (1979b) stresses the role of commercial capital. According to him, the development of handicraft industry led to the demand for agricultural raw materials and the consequent commercialization of agriculture; the entrance of commercial capital into agriculture led to the differentiation of the peasantry and the consequent increase of wage labor. Liu's picture of the labor-employing farmer is of someone who was merchant in origin, employed at least five or six laborers (but usually more), and combined commercial farming with food processing, handicraft manufacturing, and so on. Liu's stress is on the "sprouting of capitalism," not in the sense merely of the existence of some enterprises with capitalistic characteristics, but in the sense of the dawning of the inevitable stage of capitalism, following the dusk of "feudalism."

Li Wenzhi (1963a: 99–109), on the other hand, emphasizes the rise of the "commoner landlords" (shumin dizhu), as distinguished from the degree-holding "gentry landlords" (jinshen dizhu). These commoner landlords generally became "wealthy" through farming (linong zhifu). Among them, the "managerial landlords," who oversaw production themselves, must be distinguished from the bigger gentry landlords, who could not be bothered with matters of agricultural production and were normally absentee rent-collecting landlords.

Li's is the better explanation for Hebei-Shandong, where the commoner employer was a more important and pervasive phenomenon than the merchant-farmer. My data for the years 1736, 1737, and 1796, as noted, suggest that the typical employer of agricultural wage labor was the relatively small-scale rich peasant or managerial farmer. The 1930's data presented in Chapter Four, of course, suggest the same.

This is not to say that the larger-scale merchant-farmer did not exist in the area. We know of an eighteenth-century Shanxi merchant named Niu Xiwu, for example, who rented a sizable amount of land in the suburb of Beijing for commercialized farming, and operated a money-changing shop as well (Liu Yongcheng 1982: 102). And from Jing and Luo (1959: 68–72) we learn of another case, that of the peasant Bi Fenglian, residing in the well-drained and well-irrigated piedmont plain area of Zichuan county (Lijiazhuang village), Shandong, who began with less than 30 mu of land and was able to move up the social and economic ladder through silk-weaving. At the time of his death in 1840, Bi Fenglian (according to his descendants' oral testimony) had succeeded in expanding his weaving activities into a substantial enterprise, with more than 20 looms, all operated by hired workers. By then, his landholdings exceeded 300 mu. Under the management of his grandson Bi Yuanrong (1814–96), the family's fortunes grew. Their landholdings tripled, to some 900 mu, the bulk of which, 600-odd mu in the village of Lijiazhuang, was operated as a managerial farm, with a regular work force of more than 30 long-term laborers, assisted by some 50 day-laborers in the busy seasons. The family now owned a hat-making shop as well as the silk-weaving shop, and employed about 100 workers in each.

Such operations, however, were relatively rare. Indeed, it is clear even in Jing and Luo's own sample of 331 "managerial landlords" in Shandong in the 1890's, that the more land and wealth these men accumulated, the more they tended to give up direct farm management for other activities. Whereas the group owning less than 200 mu (in their more detailed sample of 131 managerial landlords) kept fully 87.5 pecent of their land under their management, the entire group of 331 placed only 20.7 percent of all their holdings under managerial farming and leased the rest out in small parcels (Jing & Luo 1959: App. 1, 2; see also Wilkinson 1978: 17–21, 35).

### THE LEGAL RECOGNITION OF NEW SOCIAL REALITIES

On the typical commoner-owned managerial farm of 100 to 200 mu, as on the even more modest rich peasant farms, the employer generally worked together with his hired hand, and the social distance between them was not nearly so great as on the larger, elite-owned managerial estates or large-scale merchant-farmer type of operation. It was the rise and spread of these small managerial farms that led to a fundamental redefinition of the legal status of agricultural workers in Qing law.

The eighteenth century appears to have been a crucial period of transition during which the law found itself caught between old principles and new social realities. In 1735 an employer in Xincheng county, Zhili, Liu Qidazi, killed his wage worker, Shi Maoer. It is clear from the records of the case that Shi did not fit the 1588 definition of a worker-serf; he had not been "hired by a written contract, for a fixed period of years." The records also show that Shi and Liu were fellow villagers, and that their relationship was sufficiently equal for them to have gone drinking together at the marketplace. However, the governor-general of Zhili ruled that the case should be treated as a dispute between an employer-master and a worker-serf;

and though the Board of Punishment disagreed, the governor stuck to his guns and prevailed in the end (Jing 1961b: 55). In 1757, however, another case in Zhili involving a commoner-employer and his wage worker (in this case the worker, Zhang Gouer, raped his employer's wife) was judged to be one between two commoners. By 1760 the Board of Punishment was ready to recognize the reality that "the commoners in managing their farms, in planting and harvesting, often need help, [and that] relatives and members of the same status employ each other." In such situations, the Board held, the wage workers should not be treated as worker-serfs and as men of a different status from their employers (*ibid.*, p. 60).

In one case in Zhili in 1784, and in two in Shandong in the following year, all of which involved workers hired at an agreed-on annual wage, the Board overruled the governors' recommendations and held that the hired workers should be treated as commoners rather than worker-serfs (Jing 1961b: 62). Three years later, in 1788, the law formally recognized the new social realities, noting that hired agricultural laborers were generally men who were "hired by the peasant and tenant households to perform agricultural labor, . . . who normally sit and eat with their employers, and address them as equals, and are not differentiated from them as serfs are from masters." Such workers, the law now stipulated, should be excluded from the category of worker-serfs and should be treated as commoners equal in status to their commoner employers (*ibid.*, p. 63).

From the point of view of the social elites—the nobility of the eight banners, the officials, and the degree-holding gentry landowners—it made little sense to put labor-employing peasants among the upper-status groups, distinct from their workers; they were all commoners who got their hands dirty in the lowly and menial task of farming. It was the recognition that most agricultural workers were being employed by commoners rather than by members of the elite that prompted the Qing to redefine the legal relationship between rural employer and wage worker.

In the end, the new production relations born of the small-peasant economy came to prevail on the court-granted estates as well. More and more of this land fell into private ownership, despite the Qing court's repeated attempts (four times in the Qianlong reign) to arrest the trend. High living placed many of the Manchu and Mongol nobles in debt to Han Chinese merchants, leaving them with no recourse but to pawn or sell their bannerland. A mid-eighteenth-century observer noted that this had happened to some 50 percent to 60 percent of the court-granted estate land (Li Wenzhi 1963a: 89–93;

Woodside 1978: 23–28). As these lands passed into private hands,* the social relations on them gave way increasingly to those that had taken hold in the small peasant economy. The worker-serf became a rarer and rarer phenomenon—to the point where, by the 1890's, the large elite-owned managerial farms in Shandong typically employed wage workers on the same terms as those prevailing on the smaller peasant farms (Jing & Luo 1959: 118–24, 147–53).

CHANGING RENT RELATIONS

Parallel developments occurred in rent relations even earlier. In the Song and Yuan, tenants were still generally bound to the land and were of a lower legal status than commoner landowners. In the Ming, however, this kind of "serfdom" gave way to freer relation-ships: some intermediate between serfs and free tenants, such as the tenant-serfs (or tenant-bondservants; *dianpu*) and bondservants (*shipu, nupu*) who farmed parcels on leasing estates. Others were freely contractual, and free tenants came to be recognized by law as of commoner status (Li Wenzhi 1981: 148–50; Niida 1963: 138–44).

The Qing had tried to revert to earlier rent relations on the estates it created. But leasing estates based on tenants tied to the land, like managerial estates based on laborers tied to the land, could not ac-commodate to the problem of maintaining an expanding population on a fixed amount of land. They were soon replaced by a system that allowed the estate owner to retain some economic control over ten-ants but gave him latitude in adjusting the number of tenants to the size of his estate. Sometimes, especially on land sold into private hands, rent relations became more purely economic and contractual, as in the small-peasant economy.

The operation of a free-tenancy system side by side with a system that still had earmarks of serfdom led to disputes over differing ex-pectations in rent relations. Materials in the Board of Punishment archives permit us to catch a clearer glimpse of the process than has hitherto been possible.†

*By the end of the Qing, except for the estates of the imperial clansmen, almost all bannerland had been sold to private owners, and what remained had become virtually indistinguishable from private land (Li Wenzhi 1963b: 93). In Wudian village, of Liangxiang county south of Beijing, in the 1920's, for example, the only difference between so-called bannerland (*qidi*) and the usual private land (*mindi*) was that the bannerland was taxed at a slightly higher rate, and thus fetched slightly less on the market. The two kinds of land were otherwise identical, in this village where 70% of the land had been bannerland (KC, 5:513, 521).

†Kataoka Shibako (1959) has found five references to rent relations in the gazet-teers of this area during the Ming–Qing transition: one in the Wanli period (1573–

TABLE 5.4

Landlords and Tenants Cited in Homicide Cases in Hebei and Shandong, 1736–1796

| Tenant's name | Rented land | | Landlord | | | | Source[a] |
|---|---|---|---|---|---|---|---|
| | No. of mu | Type | Location of case | Name | Description | Form of rent | |
| Chen Yu | | | N. Shandong (Anqiu) | Liu Gan | Absentee | Share of crop | 1736, 83, 6.8 |
| Liu Si | 10.0 | Bannerland | N.E. Hebei (Changping) | Zhang Guoyi | Zhuangtou | Share of crop | 1736, 105, 12.13 |
| Pang Zhengxi | 25.0 | | N.W. Hebei (Huaian) | Liu Zhu | Son of gongsheng | Share of crop | 1736, 78, n.d. |
| Chen Simin | | Bannerland | N.E. Hebei (Wuqing) | | Absentee | Cash | 1737, 52, 2.2 |
| Cui Jie | 70.0 | | E. Hebei (Nanpi) | Zhang Rujiao | Jiansheng | Share of crop | 1737, 57, 4.7 |
| Shi Youcai[b] Xie Da[b] | | Temple land | North of wall North of wall (Xigou) | | Temple monk | Share of crop | 1737, 56, 4.27 1737, 65, 7.7 |
| Xin San | 10.0 | Bannerland | N.E. Hebei (Tongzhou) | Li Dingguo | Zhuangtou | In kind | 1737, 67, 7.7 |
| Li Nengshi | 65.0 | | S. Hebei (Feixiang) | Li Xiude | Jiansheng | In kind | 1737, 69, 12.6 |
| Nie Wancang[b] | "A few" | Waterlogged | Chengde fu (Jianchang) | | Mongol | 50% share of crop; 50% fixed in kind | 1796, 75, 6.8 |
| Huang Fengqi | | | N. Shandong (Shouguang) | Meng Laining | Rich peasant | Share of crop | 1796, 92, 7.6 |
| Zhang Shijie | | | E. Shandong (Laiyang) | Tang Jipu | Big; absentee | Share of crop | 1796, 82, 10.9 |
| Wang Zhongfu[b] Liu Lianjun | | | North of wall E. Shandong (Laiyang) | Yan Haoming Zhang Yuling | Rich peasant[b] Shengyuan | Share of crop | 1796, 117, 10.24 1796, 70, n.d. |
| Liu Xi | | | E. Hebei (Cangzhou) | Zhang Tingying | | Share of crop | 1755, Liu 1980: 61 (3.15) |
| Li Maozhe | 29.5 | Bannerland | N.E. Hebei (Luanzhou) | Tong Dun | Small | | 1776, Liu 1979a: 60; 1980: 74 (n.d.) |
| Qiao Youzhi | 3.0 | | S. Hebei (Jize) | Tian Genzi | | Share of crop | 1788, Liu 1980: 63 (5.n.d.) |
| Zhang Jie | | | E. Shandong (Gaomi) | Dan Fu | Absentee | | 1790, Liu 1979a: 65 (n.d.) |

Table 5.4 presents 18 homicide cases involving such disputes in Hebei and Shandong: 14 from my own samples of 1736, 1737, and 1796, and four for other years, culled from the works of Liu Yongcheng. Together, these two sets of cases allow us to look backward and forward across the critical transitional years of the Qianlong period.

The first thing we see is that a large portion of the landlords involved in these tenant disputes were smallholding members of the lower gentry. These relatively weak landlords, it appears, were trying to exercise the prerogatives that the owners of the more powerful large estates took for granted, at a time when their tenants were demanding the prerogatives now commonly accorded tenants in the commercializing small-peasant economy. Thus, in 1736 in Huaian county in northwestern Hebei, the small landlord Liu Zhu (son of a lower-degree—*gongsheng*—holder) tried to rescind the lease on a 25-mu parcel of riverbank land farmed by Pang Zhengxi. Liu charged that Pang was illegally and secretly leasing the land out to someone else, but this was apparently merely a pretext for Liu's wish to lease the land to another tenant for a higher rent. Pang, however, refused to give up the land, contending that his family had cultivated it for three generations, and that their work in bringing what had been uncultivated "raw" land to its present "ripe" state entitled him to permanent tenure. The dispute came to a head when Liu simply went ahead and planted the land himself. (In the ensuing fight, Liu was killed by Pang's maternal uncle, who lived and farmed with Pang.) In another case of a similar nature, in eastern Shandong in Gaomi county in 1790, Dan Fu, an absentee landlord, ordered his tenant, Zhang Jie, to haul some coal to his house in town; Zhang refused to perform the service, and a dispute ensued. In yet another case, this one from Tongzhou in northeastern Hebei in 1737, a zhuangtou of a Mongol estate of 300 mu had engaged a tenant's son to do some day-labor for him. The young man, Yin Da, understood that he would be paid by the day. But the zhuangtou, Li Dingguo, refused to pay for the work. Xin raised a fuss, and was beaten to death by Li's son and nephew. Such cases illustrate the tensions born of conflicting expectations in rent relations as the new arrangements took hold in the small-peasant economy. It was no accident that the tension was greatest on the relatively small holdings of the lower gentry.

---

1620), one in the Kangxi period (1662–1722), and three in the Qianlong period (1736–95). These references all suggest that sharecropping was the usual form of rental arrangement, either through a simple division of the crop or, when the landlord supplied the draft animals and seed, at a somewhat higher rate. But none indicate how the rental forms or relations might have changed over these years.

Other cases illustrate tensions born of the rapid agricultural change and development under the impact of commercialization. In 1788, in Jize county in highly commercialized southern Hebei, a landlord who sharecropped his land tried to make his tenant convert to tobacco from foodgrains, in order to reap the great returns of the new cash crop. When the tenant refused to comply, the landlord, Tian Genzi, wanted to break the rental agreement, and a fight ensued. In the socially fluid society of the eighteenth century, sometimes the fortunes of landlord and tenant could be reversed. In one case, in Luanzhou, northeastern Hebei, in 1776, a small landlord borrowed over a period of time some 66,000 wen from the tenant who rented his 29.5 mu of bannerland. When the landlord was unable to pay off the debt, the tenant, Li Maozhe, offered to let the sum stand as security for permanent rights of tenure. The landlord was to agree to not raise the rent or try to lease the land to another.

Although Liu Yongcheng (1979a: 55) has found a strikingly high proportion of cash-rent arrangements in Zhili in the Qianlong period—27 of 47 cases, or 57.4 percent, compared with an average for all provinces of 28.5 percent—I suspect that this finding simply reflects the disproportionate number of court-created aristocratic estates in the capital province.* Most of those estate owners, as has been seen, were high-living nobles who opted for the leasing mode of operation over the managerial, and it seems likely that they required this cash payment to maintain themselves in style in the towns or cities where they resided. As we know from the 1729 account books of one of these estates, some 89 percent of the total rent receipts were collected in silver (Muramatsu 1962, 1:59). We should therefore not be misled by Liu's data into exaggerating the degree of agricultural commercialization in this province. Liu's figure for Shandong (six of 19 cases in cash rent, or 31.6 percent) is probably more representative of the actual scale of the change.

Further, in the frontier areas in particular, land renting frequently took place between earlier migrants and later arrivals, on a much more equal basis than between upper-status owners and commoners in the older and more tradition-bound areas. In one such case, in the frontier area north of the wall, a recent in-migrant (Wang Zhongfu, from Shanxi), was shown to have sharecropped the land of a rich peasant with more land than he could farm himself (see Table 5.4).

In the face of these trends, some estate owners tried to hold

---

*Liu's figures are based on 888 explicit identifications of rental forms, culled from the homicide reports of the Qianlong period. Liu himself does not offer any explanation for the high incidence of cash rent in Zhili.

on to their traditional prerogatives and treat their tenants as sub-commoner bondservants. State officials, on the other hand, sought to enforce the legal prescription that tenants were to be treated as commoners unless they were actually bondservants serving in their lord's household. The ensuing tug of war was finally settled in 1809 by decree of the Jiaqing Emperor and reaffirmed by the Board of Punishment in 1825: "Even if [tenants] rent the land of the big owner, are buried in the burial sites of the big owner, and live in the house of the big owner, so long as there is no formally defined relationship of master and bondservant between them, they should not be pressed down to the status of bondservants" (cited in Liu Yongcheng 1980: 60). By the end of the eighteenth century, the rent relations on the large leasing estates had become much more like the rent relations in the commoners' economy than those that had obtained on the large estates before the Ming–Qing transition.

### LANDHOLDING PATTERNS IN THE EIGHTEENTH CENTURY

From the Huailu county government Office of Revenue's (Hu fang) tax records (300-odd volumes of *bianshence*) for the Kangxi, Yongzheng, and Qianlong reigns (1622–1795), the Chinese historians Pan Jie and Tang Shiru have reconstructed the county's landholding patterns in the second quarter of the eighteenth century.* Their figures, presented in Table 5.5, reveal a picture of land distribution very much like that of the twentieth century. The households of this relatively developed and densely populated piedmont plain area of Hebei owned an average of just under 15 mu of land (compared with 11.6 mu in 1930). Similarly, as we can see, landownership was highly fragmented at this point, which again fits the twentieth-century pattern. In the eighteenth century, then, Huailu was clearly already under a densely populated, small family farm economy.

The patterns of stratification that characterized the twentieth century had also taken shape by this time. About one-quarter of the households were landless, presumably tenants and wage laborers. Another third owned ten mu or less, part-tenants and part-laborers. There were relatively few big landowners, the largest grouping being in the 100–200 mu range, as Table 5.6 shows.

*Pan points out that the unit they used was the cadastral ding, or adult male, not the cadastral hu, or household, which encompassed anywhere from a few up to 180 people. The 91 *jia* covered by their data took in 21,000 + households and 315,000 + mu of cultivated land, which probably covered a large part of the county. (Interview with Pan Jie, Sept. 1980.) By the Guomindang Statistical Bureau's count there were 42,200 households and 491,000 mu of arable in the county in 1930 (compiled in Kahoku sōgō 1944b, 1:78).

TABLE 5.5
Land Distribution in Huailu County, Hebei, ca. 1725–1750

(Land in mu)

| Land owned | Number of households[a] | Percent of households | Total land owned | Percent of total land owned |
|---|---|---|---|---|
| 0 | 5,331 | 25.3% | 0 | 0.0% |
| <1 | 888 | 4.2 | 439 | 0.2 |
| 1–5 | 3,507 | 16.7 | 10,207 | 3.2 |
| 6–10 | 3,172 | 15.1 | 22,948 | 7.3 |
| 11–15 | 2,137 | 10.1 | 26,157 | 8.3 |
| 16–30 | 3,332 | 15.8 | 70,006 | 22.2 |
| 31–40 | 967 | 4.6 | 33,205 | 10.5 |
| 41–50 | 498 | 2.4 | 22,313 | 7.1 |
| 51–60 | 334 | 1.6 | 18,195 | 5.8 |
| 61–100 | 540 | 2.6 | 40,534 | 12.8 |
| >100 | 340 | 1.6 | 71,225 | 22.6 |
| TOTAL | 21,046 | 100.0% | 315,229 | 100.0% |

SOURCE: Dai Yi 1980: 347.
[a]In 91 jia.

TABLE 5.6
Large Holdings in Huailu County, ca. 1725–1750

(Land in mu)

| Land owned | Number of households | Land owned | Number of households |
|---|---|---|---|
| 100–200 | 310 | 401–500 | 20 |
| 201–300 | 86 | 501–1,000 | 33 |
| 301–400 | 25 | >1,000 | 4 |

SOURCE: Based on Pan Jie's figures for 139 of the county's 181 jia. I am grateful to Professor Pan for sharing these unpublished data with me.

This configuration of landholding patterns permits us to understand some of the land-purchasing records that researchers have unearthed for this period. Records of the Li lineage of Zhangqiu county, owners of an atypically large managerial farm, show that they acquired their holdings piecemeal, purchasing scattered small parcels over an extended period of time. The Lis bought an average of 5.46 mu a year, in 36 separate transactions, over the years 1793–1868. The leasing-landlord Meng lineage of the same county had a similar record of land acquisitions: 154.7 mu acquired between 1718 and 1850 in 18 transactions.* Fish-scale registers and land-purchase records of

---

*Both lineages continued to expand their holdings by the same process. Between 1870 and 1905, the Li family bought an average of 5.01 mu a year, through 40 trans-

Jiangnan from the late Ming down to the nineteenth century show the same pattern of purchases (Chao 1981). Such land-acquisition patterns are further testimony to the predominance of a small-family-farm economy in the area. In landholding patterns as well as in production relations, late-eighteenth-century Hebei–northwest Shandong had taken on the basic outlines that were to remain down to the twentieth century.

---

actions. In 1905 they owned a total of 515 mu, acquired over a period of 144 years in 105 transactions. Over the years 1854–1911, the Mengs added 610.7 mu to their holdings, purchased in 60 transactions (Jing & Luo 1959: 50–53, 81–85).

# CHAPTER 6

# Commercialization and Social Stratification in the Qing

The spread of rent and wage labor relations in the countryside took place in the context of long-term agricultural commercialization, population increase, and the development of a market-oriented household handicraft industry. This chapter will show how the spread of cotton cultivation led to the social stratifications of the small peasantry. Cotton brought far greater returns than foodgrains, thereby providing the opportunity for some peasants to profit from farming and to move up the socioeconomic ladder. But it also increased the risks of farming, because it required considerably more capital and labor input than foodgrains. And since a failed cotton crop was much more devastating than a failed sorghum crop, many peasants who turned to cotton slid down the ladder, too.

Population pressure and commercialized handicraft production had ambiguous effects on this fundamental process. Although population increase added to the pressure for agricultural commercialization and aggravated the downward pressures on peasants, it also obstructed through partible inheritance the development of large farms. Similarly, although rural handicraft industry added to the incentives for agricultural commercialization, it also helped to sustain an undifferentiated owner-cultivator economy. The emphasis of this chapter is on the forces leading to the social differentiation of the small peasantry. The ways in which population pressure and handicrafts contributed to the persistence of the small peasant economy are considered more fully in Chapter Eleven.

## THE TWENTIETH-CENTURY CHANGES

The story of agricultural commercialization in Hebei–northwest Shandong has above all to do with cotton, which took hold and spread in this area from the sixteenth century on. Before turning to the historical evidence, however, I would like first to illustrate the basic pattern of change with the help of the twentieth-century field-survey data.

Let us begin with Michang village in northeastern Hebei. Michang had grown mainly grain until the 1910's, when cotton was introduced. By the 1930's, all the better land of the village, land that was not easily waterlogged by the summer rains—about 30 percent of the cultivated area—was given over to the crop. The reason for the change was of course cotton's superior returns per mu. Table 6.1 compares cotton cultivation with sorghum cultivation on the four middle peasant farms surveyed in 1937 that owned most of their own land and farmed it mainly with their own household labor (rich peasant and managerial farms that used mainly hired labor or poor peasant farms that rented land would introduce other considerations, to be taken up in Chapter Nine). As we see, their gross income from cotton per unit cropped area was nearly three times that for sorghum. Cotton, of course, did require more investment in fertilizer, whereas sorghum, grown mainly on low-lying, easily waterlogged land, required little or no fertilizer (because the waterlogging itself constantly re-enriched the land). It also needed nearly two times as much labor per mu. But in this area, where land rather than labor was the scarce and more expensive resource, cotton brought a superior net income as well, more than twice that for sorghum. Under these circumstances, cotton cultivation was irresistible to most peasant households in the village.

But there were ecological constraints that operated against their turning all the way to cotton. As in so much of northeastern Hebei, Michang village suffered from severe problems of waterlogging on the low-lying land with poor drainage, and cotton is easily damaged

TABLE 6.1

Average Income from Cotton as Compared with Sorghum on Four Middle Peasant Farms, Michang, Hebei, 1937

(Yuan)

| Item | Cotton | | Sorghum | |
| --- | --- | --- | --- | --- |
| Gross income per mu | | $17.7 | | $6.1 |
| Expenses per mu | | | | |
| Fertilizer[a] | $4.6 | | $0.0 | |
| Wages | 1.7 | 6.3 | 1.2 | 1.2 |
| Net income per mu | | $11.4 | | $4.9 |

SOURCE: MT, Hokushi jimukyoku chōsabu 1938–41, 1: Tables 3, 28, 29, 32, 33.
[a]Includes both fertilizer purchased and the cash equivalent for family and animal wastes used as fertilizer.

by water. Sorghum, which is highly water-resistant, therefore continued to be grown on the low-lying land even after cotton had become entrenched in the village. At the same time, there were economic constraints on the proportion of farm area that a household could wisely put under cotton. An unbalanced "cropping portfolio" with nearly all of the cultivated area under cotton posed the double problem of concentrating the peak labor needs within a single period and "putting all of one's eggs in one basket." Drought in the spring could bring total disaster to a household completely dependent on cotton. Under these conditions, most peasant households that had a choice tended to opt for a diversified cropping portfolio, regardless of their motivations for adopting cotton.

In Chapter Nine we will see the very different considerations that motivated cotton cropping by managerial and rich peasant farms as opposed to poor peasant farms. For now the important point is the differentiating effects of cotton cultivation. A doubling or tripling of the value of the yield from the land meant that the luckier households—those with a more favorable land-to-population ratio, a more favorable adult-male-laborer-to-consumer ratio in the household, those fortunate enough to be spared sickness and extraordinary expenses—might even be able to save a little to buy more land, to move slowly from subsistence farming to some small measure of profit- and accumulation-oriented farming. This had indeed been the pattern, as we saw in Chapter Four, with Dong Tianwang and the other managerial farmers in the village.

But cash-cropping could cut both ways. The smallholder found that, though his returns became higher, so too did his expenses. The risks from natural or man-made disaster were thus correspondingly greater. A ruined cotton crop was much more devastating to the smallholder than a ruined sorghum crop, often starting him on a downward spiral in which he was forced to offer his land as security for a loan, only to lose it and become first a tenant, then a part-laborer, and finally a landless wage worker. Thus was the supply of labor demanded by the new managerial and rich peasant farms created.

This process of social stratification in Michang village is verified by the data on land purchases and sales the Mantetsu investigators gathered in their interviews with the villagers.* They found that

* Such interview data, though almost certainly imperfect and incomplete, seem to me nonetheless highly credible. Land sales and purchases, after all, were matters of utmost importance to the villagers. Most of them were able to give the Mantetsu investigators the precise amount of land bought or sold to the decimal point and the

fully 424 mu of the 538.39 that had been sold between the 1890's and 1936 had been purchased in the last 20 years, after the coming of cotton cultivation. Much of this land (207.85 mu) had been bought by managerial farmers who had profited from this commercialized agriculture. Well-to-do middle and rich peasant households (farming between 20 and 100 mu) accounted for another 265.84 mu (MT, Kitō 1937b: 5–10; Yoshida 1975: 16). The sellers, of course, were mainly downward-moving peasants who were becoming part-tenants, tenants, day-laborers, and year-laborers.

Where the switch was from a three-crops-in-two-years agrarian regime (for convenience, I will use three-crops system in this section) to a single annual crop of cotton (which was planted in April and could not be harvested until October/November, thereby ruling out the possibility of a winter crop to follow), the change was less dramatic, although the principles involved were much the same. It was less dramatic, first of all, in terms of the degree of commercialization because wheat had long been a highly commercialized crop. We know from a great variety of twentieth-century sources that wheat was the staple of the urban and upper classes, and sorghum, maize, and sweet potatoes the staples of the lower classes. In 1940, in Shajing village, near Beijing, a shi of wheat cost 34 yuan, and a shi of sorghum only 18 yuan (KC, 2: 55, 69, 238, 252). In 1942, in Houxiazhai village in northwestern Shandong, a shi of wheat cost 40 yuan, a shi of sorghum 25 yuan (KC, 4: 402, 460). In Martin Yang's childhood, the poor peasants of Taitou village (near Qingdao) ate sweet potatoes "at every meal every day throughout the year," whereas the more well-to-do enjoyed millet, wheat, and even meat and rice (1945: 32–33). The village of Lengshuigou, near Jinan city in Shandong, had a "society of wheat buns" (*bobo she*): each member paid 20 cents a month toward the bulk purchase of wheat flour at reasonable prices to ensure his having wheat flour buns as a special treat at New Year's (KC, 4: 408, 19). Even today, Shajing brigade takes special pride in being able to guarantee its members one meal of "fine grain" (*xiliang*; i.e., wheat flour buns or noodles) a day, at midday; most North China peasants continue to rely principally on "coarse grains" (*culiang*) like maize and sorghum (interviews with Shajing brigade leaders Zhang Linbing et al., April 1980).

approximate year of the transaction. In general, I think the informant's data are probably very dependable for his own generation, somewhat less so for his father's generation, and even less so for his grandfather's. For my purposes here, the crucial data are those on the 20 years immediately before the investigations. (See Yoshida 1975: 16 for a systematic tabulation of the land-purchase data under seven socioeconomic household groupings.)

This social differentiation in foodgrains, between the "fine" grains like wheat (and rice in the south) and "coarse" grains, dates back at least to Qing times. The Juye county (southwestern Shandong) gazetteer for the Kangxi period (1662–1722) noted, for example: "The wealthy households eat mainly wheat; the poor have sorghum for their staple." Similarly, the Haiyang county (easternmost Shandong) gazetteer for the Qianlong period (1736–95) reported: "The cereal of the rich is made from rice, their cakes from wheat flour; the poor eat millet gruel and the residue from soybean milk" (cited in Kataoka Shibako 1959: 96). The poor, therefore, commonly sold their wheat crop and used the cash to buy coarse grains, thus making their limited resources go farther. Where cotton displaced a winter wheat crop, consequently, it was not so much a matter of turning from an uncommercialized subsistence crop to a cash crop as a process of pushing commercialization one step further.

The switch from a three-crops system to cotton was also less dramatic in terms of the degree of agricultural intensification (and of returns from the land) than the switch from an annual crop of sorghum to cotton. The two most authoritative surveys of cropping and yield patterns in this area show that yields from the spring sorghum crop were generally somewhat higher (in volume and in weight) than the winter wheat or summer soybean crop (a ratio of about 10:8, according to Tudiweiyuanhui 1937: 20–21). Nonetheless, total yields from the three-crops system were higher than those from annual cropping (a ratio of about 5:4 over a two-year period, according to Tudiweiyuanhui, or about 6:5, according to Zhongyang renmin zhengfu 1950: 68). Gross receipts from the three-crops system for the two years 1934–35 worked out to an annual average of about nine yuan per mu in Hebei and Shandong, compared with about six yuan per mu when sorghum alone was cropped annually. In terms of labor use, the three-crops system of sorghum, winter wheat, and soybeans required a total of about 20 days per mu in a two-year period (7.2, 7.8, and 5.7 days, respectively; MT, Hokushi jimukyoku chōsabu 1938–41, 1: Table 46), compared with about 14 days per mu for two annual crops of sorghum. The three-crops system was thus a more intensive and higher return system than the single-crop system, so again the switch to cotton was not so dramatic a step toward commercialization as the switch from a single annual crop of sorghum.

But it was an important step nonetheless. The switch from the one-sorghum-crop-a-year system to the three-crops system raised foodgrain yields about 20–25 percent over a two-year period, and their cash equivalent value some 50 percent. The further switch to cotton brought the cash value of the crop to more than double the value of the single sorghum crop.

For the sake of clarity, I have discussed cotton cropping and sorghum-winter wheat-soybean cropping as if they were distinct and separate systems. In practice, of course, peasant farms often mixed these systems. One very common pattern (Buck 1937b: 259–60) was to alternate cotton cropping with the three-crops system in rotation across plots, so that a farm had all three stages of the mixed system going in any given year:

|  | Plot 1 | Plot 2 | Plot 3 |
|---|---|---|---|
| *Year 1* | | | |
| Spring | Cotton | Sorghum | (Wheat) |
| Summer | (Cotton) | (Sorghum) | Soybeans |
| Winter | Fallow | Wheat | Fallow |
| *Year 2* | | | |
| Spring | Sorghum | (Wheat) | Cotton |
| Summer | (Sorghum) | Soybeans | (Cotton) |
| Winter | Wheat | Fallow | Fallow |
| *Year 3* | | | |
| Spring | (Wheat) | Cotton | Sorghum |
| Summer | Soybeans | (Cotton) | (Sorghum) |
| Winter | Fallow | Fallow | Wheat |

Most peasant farms, furthermore, cultivated many other crops, the most common in this area were millet, maize, barley, sweet potatoes, and cabbage. The typical process of agricultural commercialization, therefore, did not involve blanket shifts from a subsistence crop to a cash crop, but rather the gradual incorporation of an increasing proportion of cash crops into a highly complex and diversified system.

The basic principles at work in this area, however, were no different from the more dramatic Michang example from northeastern Hebei. The spread of cotton cultivation, with its higher returns and higher risks, unavoidably encouraged social differentiation. A few among the petty proprietors could take advantage of the increased returns to move upward into rich peasant and managerial farming; others slid down the socioeconomic ladder to become tenants, day-laborers, and landless year-laborers.

COTTON CULTIVATION IN THE MING AND QING

The turn to cotton in this area in the sixteenth century began when market demand for the raw material in the lower Yangzi and Fujian-

Guangdong made cotton cultivation more lucrative than the cultivation of foodgrains.* By the Jiajing period (1522–66) cotton was being grown all over Shandong. The northwestern prefecture of Dongchang led the province. As the provincial gazetteer put it: "[Cotton was planted] in all six of the prefectures. It is especially widespread in Dongchang. The merchants sell it in the four directions. The profits are quite substantial."† Gaotangzhou and Enxian in particular became quite highly commercialized, according to the prefectural gazetteer: "The soil here is suited for cotton cultivation. The merchants from Jiangsu and Anhui trade in the cotton, and the residents are enriched as a result" (Cong 1981: 62).

Cotton cultivation was also highly developed in southwestern Shandong's Yuncheng county, where the soil was likewise said to be well suited for the crop: "The merchants sell it to the lower Yangzi valley and store it for trading on the market. Profits from cultivating the five grains do not come to half as much" (*Gunzhoufu zhi*, juan 4, cited in Chen Shiqi 1959: 30; see also Kataoka Shibako 1959: 97). In Hebei, too, cotton was widely grown by the late Ming. Even Jizhou and Luanzhou in the relatively underdeveloped northeastern section were growing cotton by the Jiajing or Wanli period (1573–1620). The areas of highest concentration were in central and southern Hebei —in the prefectures of Baoding, Hejian, Zhending, Daming, and Guangping—and particularly in the sections near the Henan and Shandong borders (Cong 1981: 62, 75).

The expansion of cotton cultivation produced a relatively abundant and cheap supply of raw material for the more highly developed areas to the south. As the agronomist Xu Guangqi noted in the early 1600's: "Nowadays in the north the cotton is cheap while cloth is expensive; in the south the opposite is true. Cotton is therefore shipped to the south, while cloth is shipped to and sold in the north" (Xu 1956: 708; see also Cong 1981: 67).

Cotton continued to spread in the Qing period. A 1754 source noted that "in the past in the area south of Baoding in Zhili, those with good land generally planted wheat, but now they cultivate cotton" (Huang Keren, cited in Jian 1957: 351). And in 1765 the governor general of Zhili reported that "eight or nine of ten peasants" cultivated cotton in Jizhou, Shenzhou, Dingzhou, and Zhaozhou,

---

*The lower Yangzi itself was a cotton surplus area. The North China cotton often went on from there to markets in Fujian-Guangdong (Xu 1981: 26–29).

†Cong Hanxiang 1981: 61. Cong, a historian at the Institute of Modern History of the Academy of Social Sciences in Beijing, has painstakingly combed through all the Ming gazetteers for evidence on cotton cultivation. Her work has superseded the earlier research of Nishijima Sadao (1966) on this subject.

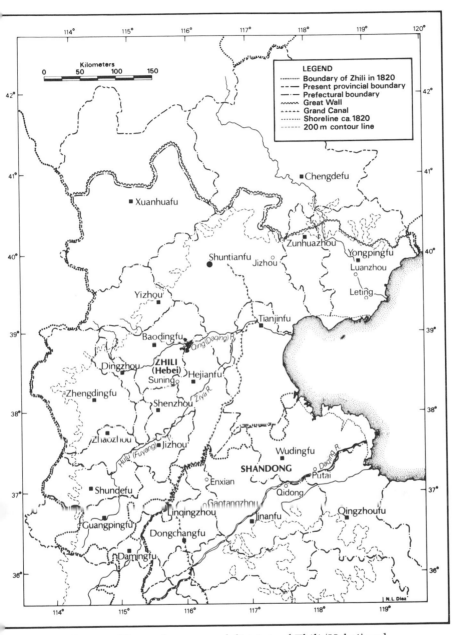

MAP 6.1. The prefectures and districts of Zhili (Hebei) and
Northwest Shandong, ca. 1820

that "in the area near the capital" cotton was grown on "about a fifth to a third of the land," and that "when the new cotton comes to market, merchants from distant places gather, rubbing shoulders and tangling up each other's feet. The speculators line up at the market to accumulate it. The traders bring their carts for the market" (cited in Shang 1957: 184, 197).

The social and economic changes that accompanied the spread of cotton cultivation are best summed up in this remarkable observation by the magistrate of Jining, Shandong, in the second quarter of the nineteenth century: "[In] Gaotang there is more land sown under cotton than under foodgrains. The rich do not store grain, and the poor rely entirely on hiring out and the board that comes with wage labor. Once confronted with natural disaster and bad harvests, they are at a complete loss. . . . Nowadays there is sometimes drought in the spring. Confusion follows: the poor have no place to turn for loans; the rich are afraid of robbers, of litigation for the fair distribution of grain. The entire area is disturbed" (cited in Jing & Luo 1959: 33). This was an advanced state of social stratification in a highly commercialized cotton-growing area.

### AGRICULTURAL COMMERCIALIZATION AND POPULATION GROWTH

In the early Ming, Hebei-Shandong was something of a frontier area, for the Mongol campaigns against the Jin in the second decade of the twelfth century had left large parts of the land devastated. The Ming *Veritable Records (Shi lu)* abound with references to this devastation, and to the efforts to encourage immigration, especially from Shanxi. A 1388 entry noted, for example, the repopulation of Linqing by people from Zezhou and Lu'an prefectures in southeastern Shanxi. Another entry, in the following year, called for the resettlement of underpopulated Dongchang prefecture. Gaocheng county, in the heart of southern Hebei, it was noted, was resettled in 1416 by people from Shanxi (cited in Kataoka Shibako 1959: 85–86; 1962: 139–41). Three of the Mantetsu-surveyed villages—Shajing, Sibeichai, and Houxiazhai—were founded at the beginning of the Ming by migrants from Hongdong county in Shanxi, according to village oral tradition (KC, 1:59, 67; KC, 3:27, 150–51; KC, 4:397). The two provinces had a combined population of only around 7,000,000 in 1393. (See Appendix B for a discussion of the available data on the demographic history of the area.)

Parts of the two provinces remained sparsely settled even in the late Ming. In the Wanli period (1573–1620), for example, the "strong peasants" in Jingzhou (in the poorly drained eastern part of central Hebei) were said to cultivate "as much as 200 or 300 mu. Farms of less than 100 mu are considered small" (*Jingzhou zhi*, juan 1; see also Kataoka Shibako 1959: 80). As I show in the next chapter, in the 1930's one adult male under the best conditions could cultivate 20 to 30 mu of land that was partly under cotton. In a sparsely populated area where family farms could average 100 mu or more, the smallholder would have enjoyed the option of farming a larger area less intensively. For the same amount of labor devoted to one mu of cotton, he could farm two mu of sorghum. And his returns would be comparable or perhaps even better, since he did not have to put up cash for fertilizer. Where land was abundant and labor scarce, therefore, a twofold cash return per unit of land from cotton cultivation would not necessarily have been sufficient incentive to power a switchover from sorghum to cotton. Agricultural commercialization, as one form of the intensification of farming, required a certain minimum population density to take hold.

Hebei-Shandong did not remain a frontier-like area for long, however, for as we have seen, cotton had begun to take hold in the more developed parts of the two provinces by the sixteenth century. The Ming centuries, in fact, saw the beginning of a secular trend of population growth that brought the combined total figure to perhaps 50,000,000 by 1800, a sevenfold increase since 1400. This long-term increase was briefly interrupted by the devastations of the wars of the Ming–Qing dynastic transition. A memorial of 1644 noted that in Shandong "the land lies waste. In some households, only one or two are left" (Shang 1957: 169). This depopulation was confirmed by the governor of Henan: "In the prefectures and counties north of the river, 9,450,000 mu lie waste." He urged that the land be settled with soldiers, and that taxes be waived for three years (Nankai daxue lishi xi 1959: 59). As late as 1683, the magistrate of Lingshou county, in central Hebei just north of Shijiazhuang, reported that resettlement in his area had not proceeded very far, that the harsh conditions made many reluctant to cultivate the depopulated land (Chen Zhenhan 1955: 288). If we take the cadastral figures of 1724 as approximating full settlement (70,000,000 mu in Zhili and 99,000,000 mu in Shandong), and those of 1661 as roughly representing the amount of cultivated acreage at the start of the dynasty (46,000,000 mu in Hebei (Zhili) and 74,000,000 mu in Shandong; Table C.1), then as much as one-quarter to one-third of the cultivated land in the two provinces may have been depopulated in the dynastic transition. But this was only a temporary dip in a long-term trend of population growth.

By the eighteenth century cultivated acreage per capita had declined from 15 + mu in the early Ming to less than 4 mu (Tables B.1, C.1). As land became scarcer, the prospect of doubling the returns from each parcel was difficult to resist. For the relatively well-to-do farms that had the means to hire labor and make the necessary capital investments, cotton offered the opportunity for upward mobility, to rich peasant and managerial farmer status. For the "average"-sized family farm of 20 to 30 mu, cotton offered the opportunity for fuller employment of the family's labor than planting just foodgrains. For the poorer and smaller farms under even more intense pressures of land scarcity, the increased returns per unit of land from cotton cultivation meant improved chances for meeting the family's subsistence needs. Rich and poor peasants alike thus joined to power agricultural commercialization.

The combined pressures from population and social stratification were even more apparent in the case of the adoption of the sweet potato, a New World crop that made its way into China in the late Ming via the Philippines and Burma (Chen Shuping 1980: 198–99). In our area, it was first planted in Jiaozhou in Shandong in 1749, in response to famine conditions. Its appearance is also recorded in 1746, in Dezhou, on the northwest border with Zhili along the Grand Canal. From there it spread in a few years as a staple throughout western Shandong. In Zhili, at about this time, "many people came to rely on it for subsistence" in Tianjin prefecture, according to the governor. The Qianlong Emperor in fact ordered that information about it be disseminated through the land in order to "aid in the feeding of the people" (ibid.). By the twentieth century more than 7,000,000 mu (or roughly 3.5 percent of the cultivated area) in Hebei and Shandong were under the crop (Perkins 1969: 236, 254).*

The dynamic behind the spread of sweet potato cultivation was mainly population pressure on land. As a crop that required two to three times the labor investment required for foodgrains such as sorghum or millet (though no greater investment in fertilizer), but repaid the farmer with a considerably higher per-mu yield in grain

---

*Maize, a crop whose yields can be increased much more than sorghum with added inputs of fertilizer, was known in Shandong and Zhili in the late Ming (Chen Shuping 1980: 192). But sorghum is a more water-resistant crop. In easily waterlogged areas peasants were not willing to risk growing a crop more susceptible to water damage than sorghum. Only with the systematic improvements in drainage in the decades after the Revolution has maize come to replace sorghum as the dominant crop in this area.

equivalent,* the sweet potato could both absorb surplus labor and expand the carrying capacity of the land. This point did not escape the official Lu Yao, who pointed out in his agricultural treatise "On Sweet Potatoes" (1776): "One mu of sweet potatoes can yield one thousand catties, and surpasses the five grains in yield severalfold" (Chen Shuping 1980: 201).

The sweet potato, however, then as now ranks below even the "coarse" grains as a food of the poor. It was planted as a substitute grain and adopted as a staple only when poverty and population pressure forced the choice. Its spread in the North China plain, and the prominent role that it came to occupy in the diet of the most hardpressed of the peasants, tell the story of high population density as well as of a social stratification reflected in the increased commercialization of the "fine" grain wheat.

As I said at the outset of this chapter, population growth both encouraged agricultural commercialization and impeded it. The most important obstruction to the development of managerial farming was partible inheritance. A family might in one generation move from family farming upward to managerial farming, but a single partition among two or more sons was apt to force each household back into family-farm status. That is why, as we saw in Table 4.2, few village "rich" were able to remain rich across several generations. Of the 19 households in the nine villages who could be clearly identified as rich in the 1890's, only three still had rich descendant households (a total of five) in the 1930's. This constant check on upward mobility explains the anomaly of a village like Houxiazhai, which was moderately commercialized (with perhaps 20 percent of the cropped area under peanuts and another 5–10 percent under cotton; see Table A.2) but did not have a single rich landlord or managerial farmer in the 1930's. By then partible inheritance had eliminated all the rich households that had existed in the two preceding generations.

Inheritance, of course, acted in the same way on the family farms: rich or middle peasants could be pressed downward into poor peasants, and poor peasants into agricultural laborers. Poor peasants and agricultural laborers, in turn, furnished the labor supply for managerial agriculture. This subject is discussed in detail in Chapter

---

*Sweet potatoes are roughly three parts water and one part solid. Accordingly, the State Statistical Bureau in China has followed the practice of equating four catties of potatoes with one cattie of grain. Computed in this way, the available data for the period 1931–37 shows a national average of 263 catties per mu for sweet potatoes, compared with 114 for wheat, 193 for maize, 170 for sorghum, and 160 for millet (Perkins 1969: 276–79).

Eleven. Here it suffices to note the ambiguous ways in which population pressure affected managerial agriculture.

## MANAGERIAL FARMING AND COMMERCIALIZED HANDICRAFT PRODUCTION

The development of a market-oriented household handicraft industry likewise had ambiguous effects on the growth of managerial farming. The added income from handicraft products increased the returns from a raw material such as cotton, and therefore furthered the commercialization of agriculture. That same added income, however, helped to sustain a family farm economy that might otherwise have collapsed under the weight of population pressure and social stratification.

Let us look first at the historical record on the development of handicraft production in the Ming and Qing. As has been seen, by the late Ming, North China had become economically tied to the lower Yangzi in a kind of "periphery" to "core" relationship.* Raw cotton grown in North China was shipped south to the lower Yangzi and beyond, and cotton cloth produced in the lower Yangzi was shipped to the north in exchange. There was a limited amount of cotton cloth production in the most developed pockets of the North China plain, as for example in Suning county (Hejian prefecture in central Hebei). As the well-known agronomist Xu Guangqi noted in the early seventeenth century: "The cloth produced by Suning . . . totals one-tenth of that produced by Songjiang. . . . Its fineness and density are comparable now to the middle grade of Songjiang's products. Its price is about seven- or eight-tenths. That's . . . because the cotton is cheaper" (cited in Cong 1981: 67). But this was one of a very few pockets of cloth production in the whole of the North China plain (Wenshang and Dingtao counties in southwestern Shandong were others; *ibid.*, p. 67).

Population growth and the spread of cotton cultivation, however, soon furnished the conditions for the development of commercialized handicraft production in North China itself. By the eighteenth century the southern and central parts of Zhili had become major cotton cloth production centers themselves, as Governor Fang Guancheng observed: "In Jizhou, Zhaozhou, Shenzhou, and Ding-

---

*I use the vocabulary "core" and "periphery" here to refer simply to a more developed area and a less developed area that had economic ties, leaving out of this discussion the additional baggage that comes with Skinner's "regional systems" (1977a, b; for here we are witnessing interregional relationships as well as intraregional ones), or with the "dependency" or "world-system" theories about the flow of surplus from the periphery to the core (Frank 1967, 1978; Wallerstein 1974, 1979).

zhou, eight or nine of ten peasants cultivate cotton. The output is greater than in the lower Yangzi, and the quality of the weaving also matches that of Songjiang. . . . The surplus is transported to the areas north and south of the Yellow River. Even in the foothills and the coastal areas, and as far as Korea, people buy their cloth from the merchants" (cited in Shang 1957: 184). From Putai county in Shandong, similarly, we have this report for the Qianlong period: "The households diligently engage in spinning and weaving. . . . Having satisfied their own needs, they sell to merchants who sell it as far south as Yishui [on the southern side of the Shandong hills] and as far north as Manchuria" (*Putai xian zhi*: juan 2; see also Kataoka Shibako 1959: 98). The same observation was made of nearby Qidong county by the Jiaqing period (1796–1820): "The people carry their cloth to the periodic markets, five or six times a month, and return home after trading. It's called a cloth market, and reaches into Manchuria. The quantity traded in a year is calculated in the hundreds of thousands" (cited in Kataoka Shibako 1959: 93).

All these early centers of handicraft production were in lowland areas with convenient access to water transportation and relatively favorable ecological conditions for agriculture. In Hebei, Jizhou, Zhaozhou, and Shenzhou all lay along the navigable Ziya and Fuyang (Hulu) rivers, and Dingzhou had access to the Daqing (Qing); in northwest Shandong, both Putai and Qidong lay along the navigable Yellow (Daqing) and Xiaoqing rivers. (See Map 6.1.)

As the lowland areas became fully populated, people began to settle the frontier areas. As early as 1709, the Kangxi Emperor noted that "many people from Henan, Shandong, and Zhili have gone to open up frontier land," and again in 1712: "More than 100,000 people from Shandong have gone back and forth to open up land beyond the wall" (Jian 1957: 346). Initially, these frontiers bore a periphery-to-core relationship to the settled lowland areas much like the earlier relationship between the North China plain and the lower Yangzi, as noted, for example, in the Leting county gazetteer for the Qianlong period: "The merchants of this county generally go beyond the passes to trade. . . . The millet comes from beyond the passes, for the consumption of the people of the county, while the cloth is assembled by Leting." Of the total cloth produced in Leting, only "10 or 20 percent is used inside the county; 80 or 90 percent is transported to other places." "Trading cloth for millet," the gazetteer added, "was actually one way the poor people manage to keep themselves fed" in this more fully populated and differentiated area. The same pattern of trade was noted by the Luanzhou county gazetteer for the Jiaqing (1796–1820) period (both cited in Kataoka Shibako 1959: 93).

By the nineteenth century parts of the far northern prefecture of Chengde had begun to engage in household handicraft production. The prefectural gazetteer of 1831 observed: "Formerly cotton was unheard of beyond the wall. Now Chengde prefecture has it all over. But people had only made cotton-wool with it, and had not woven cloth." The official who compiled the gazetteer, a man named Hai-zhong, went on to boast of the measures he had taken to teach people to spin and weave, so that the sound of the spinning and weaving machines was now heard "all over the area beyond the wall" (*Chengde fu zhi* 1831: juan 74, "Products," 2).

From the perspective of the development of managerial farming, the greatest effect of commercialized handicraft production was the stimulation of the spread of cotton cultivation. Just as the handicraft spinning and weaving industry in the lower Yangzi and Fujian-Guangdong stimulated cotton cultivation on the North China plain by its demand for the raw material, so the development of commercialized handicraft production in the core areas of the Hebei–northwest Shandong plain helped to stimulate cotton cultivation in the peripheral zones of the area. But household handicraft production also often helped to sustain small family farms that might otherwise have collapsed under the pressures of population. A family with less land than its labor could farm, less land than was adequate for meeting its consumption needs from farming alone, could supplement its income by spinning yarn and weaving cloth to sell on the market, and so stave off tenancy or landlessness.

To sum up briefly, there is no question that the small peasant economy of North China underwent dynamic change long before China's contact with the modern world economy. Commercialization and cottage industry, and population increase and migration, set into motion a process that saw greater and greater social differentiation between upward- and downward-moving smallholders. Those who moved up the economic ladder hired labor to varying degrees to supplement their family labor and, if they could, to expand their farms; those who moved down hired out to varying degrees to supplement the inadequate incomes from their shrinking family parcels. Managerial agriculture encompassed the terminal rungs of this ladder: the most successful farmers and the year-laborers. It was this development that prompted the Qing to redefine the nature of wage labor relations in the rural economy in 1788.

# CHAPTER 7

# Accelerated Commercialization
# in the Twentieth Century

How was the peasant economy of Hebei–northwest Shandong affected by imperialism? This chapter will show that world market demand, foreign economic intrusion, and domestic development together powered the accelerated commercialization of the peasant economy. Three centuries of the spread of cotton cultivation was at least doubled in the short span of three decades in the twentieth century. Through agricultural commercialization, imperialism made its impact felt in many small villages of the North China plain. In this respect, analyses based on the model of "economic dualism" require serious qualification. On the other hand, "dependency theory" and "world-system" analysis tend to overstate the role of imperialism. The historical record will show that imperialism did not fundamentally reshape the small-peasant economy, but only caused acceleration along the preexisting patterns of involution and commercialization.

## CHINESE AGRICULTURE AND THE WORLD ECONOMY

Chinese agriculture came to be integrally linked to a world commodities market in the nineteenth and twentieth centuries. International demand greatly stimulated the cultivation of a number of major cash crops, including tea, silk, cotton, sugar, peanuts, and soybeans. In the North China plain cotton and peanuts were particularly important. At the same time, international competition sometimes cut into the expanded cultivation undertaken in response to the world demand, as was true of tea, silk, and sugar, for example. Cyclical movements in the international market, furthermore, affected agriculture inside China in unprecedented ways. The great depression of 1929 affected the prices of nearly all of the cash crops involved in export. Where once commercialized Chinese agriculture had been influenced only by the domestic market, it now responded to market forces worldwide.

Consider, first of all, the example of tea. International demand greatly stimulated tea cultivation in China in the nineteenth century. Exports reached 2,000,000 piculs in 1880,* about one-half the total tea production in China. Thereafter, however, international competition increasingly cut into China's share of the world market. Indian and Ceylonese tea took over the English market, Japanese green tea the North American market, and Indian, Ceylonese, Japanese, and Javanese tea the Russian market. As a result, China's exports declined steeply, to an average of only about 651,000 piculs a year between 1918 and 1927, or just 16 percent of total domestic production. (Zhang Youyi 1957, 2:137–38, 148; 3:408–9, 419–20, 628–29; Perkins 1969: 285; Yue 1980: 65–67.) Later, during the great depression, the price of export-oriented Qimen (Anhui) red tea dropped 57 percent between 1931 and 1933, with severe consequences for the growers (Zhang Youyi 1957, 3:629). The effects of such changes on the local society and economy of the major tea-growing areas—of such provinces as Fujian, Jiangxi, Guangdong, Hunan, Hubei, and Anhui—await detailed investigation.

Silk was second only to tea in its importance as an export commodity (accounting for 32.6 percent of China's exports in 1867, compared with 58 percent for tea). Exports of raw silk rose from a mere 10,000 piculs in 1840 to 102,000 in 1890, 139,000 in 1910, and 168,000 in 1925 (Zhang Youyi 1957, 2:149). By the late nineteenth century, 30 percent to 40 percent of all the silk produced went to the foreign market.† Some Chinese localities became heavily dependent on this export commodity. One rather extreme example is Shunde county in Guangdong, where some 70 percent of the cultivated land was under mulberry trees in 1923 (*ibid.*, p. 224). Wuxi county in the lower Yangzi delta was another major silk-producing area.

These production centers were hard hit by the competition of the government-subsidized and technologically superior Japanese silk industry. By 1925 Japanese silk held some 60 percent of the world market, which China had dominated in the nineteenth century (Yue 1980: 89). Export demand for Chinese silk sank further during the great depression, when Chinese producers were faced with massive dumping by Japanese silk manufacturers. The results were devastat-

---

*Or *dan*: 100 catties, or 110 pounds.

†Perkins, 1969: 286. Perkins gives the figures in cocoons; they can be converted to silk at a ratio of 13:1.

ing. Between 1931 and 1932 silk prices fell by more than 30 percent, and export values with them (from 147,000,000 yuan to 56,000,000). In Wuxi the acreage under mulberry trees dropped from 251,000 mu in 1930 to a mere 84,000 in 1932. In Shunde mulberry leaves went unpicked when their market price fell below labor costs (the wage for picking one picul of leaves ran about 60 cents, which was all the grower could obtain for them; Zhang Youyi 1957, 3:623, 626–27).*

Sugar tells a similar story. Exports reached an all-time high of 1,570,000 piculs in 1884, then fell to the competition of the sugarcane plantations of Java and the Philippines and the sugar-beet fields of Europe, which eventually captured much of the domestic market as well. Exports dropped to 780,000 piculs in 1894; by 1906 China was importing 6,540,000 piculs and exporting a paltry 170,000 (Zhang Youyi 1957, 2:139). In the Shantou area alone, sugar exports dropped from a high of 200,000 piculs a year in the early 1880's to a mere two-year total of 20,000 piculs in 1890–91 (Li Wenzhi 1957: 453). In time, Shantou lost some of the domestic market as well. Its shipments to the Yangzi area fell from a high of at least 8,000,000 piculs a year in 1899 to some 2,000,000 in 1911 and 1912. During the First World War, when Javanese sugar exports were interrupted, Shantou regained some ground, sending 8,800,000 piculs of sugar to the Yangzi area in 1918. But Java's reentry into the market after the war brought decline once more to Shantou's sugar growers. By the 1930's Guangdong province had changed from an exporter of sugar to a net importer (Zhang Youyi 1957, 2:140, 146; 3:661).†

With the story of soybeans we come closer to our region. By 1920 China accounted for 80 percent of the world production, and the bulk of this (60–70 percent) was produced in Manchuria, most of it (75 percent) for export (Perkins 1969: 133). But soon thereafter Manchuria began to lose its market share, for though soybean production continued to grow dramatically (by 50 percent in the years 1924–30), this growth paled in comparison to the more dynamic expansion in American production, which doubled during these years. U.S. soybeans cut not only into the American market for Chinese soybeans, but also into faraway markets like Australia as well. At the same time, with advances in chemical fertilizer production, the use of

---

*The relationship between world capitalism and the export-agriculture economies of Shunde and Wuxi are studied in two dissertations at the University of California, Los Angeles: So 1982 and Lynda Bell, in progress.

†Marks 1978 links the up-and-down movements in the world sugar market to the peasant movement in the Hailufeng area.

beancake for fertilizer fell off badly. When the great depression struck, soybean prices sank, with disastrous consequences for the heavily export-dependent peasants of Manchuria (Zhang Youyi 1957, 3 : 639).*

The expansion of tobacco growing is a two-sided story, stimulated not only by export demand, but also by increased domestic consumption (actively promoted by the British American Tobacco Company). Exports grew from a mere 4,000 piculs in 1870 to 19,000 in 1880, 93,000 in 1890, 134,000 in 1900, 218,000 in 1910, and 277,000 in 1920. The spread of tobacco cultivation was especially dramatic in Shandong, where total production grew from a mere 2,400,000 pounds in 1916 to fully 120,000,000 by 1937 (Zhang Youyi 1957, 2 : 149, 201). Some 920,000 mu (about 0.8 percent of the province's total cultivated area) was under tobacco by the 1930's (Perkins 1969: 262). This acreage was heavily concentrated along the Jiaozhou–Jinan railroad, especially in Yidu and Weixian, which became greatly dependent on this cash crop. The full story of the effects of the violent market swings in this crop on the local society and economy of the tobacco-growing areas has yet to be told.[†]

The story of peanuts returns us still more centrally to the area under study. Peanuts could be grown in sandy and otherwise unproductive land. Once export demand set in and the prices rose, the crop spread rapidly. It was in production in Yutian, Fengrun, and Luanzhou counties, all in northeastern Hebei, by the 1880's and 1890's, and also in the hilly and arid areas north of the Great Wall, which alone produced 500,000 to 600,000 *haiguan* taels' worth of peanuts a year by the 1890's. Factories for pressing peanut oil sprang up first in Tianjin, then spread into the growing areas. Southern Hebei was exporting peanuts to Guangdong by the 1900's (Li Wenzhi 1957: 436–37). The value of peanut exports from China grew from 500,000 taels in 1908 to 10,800,000 in 1928. Hebei had more than 2,000,000 mu under peanuts by 1914–18, and in excess of 4,000,000 by the 1930's. Shandong's acreage grew just as fast, exceeding 3,000,000 mu in 1920 and 5,000,000 in the 1930's. By then peanuts accounted for about 4 percent of the cultivated acreage in the two provinces and was second only to cotton as a cash crop (Zhang Youyi 1957, 2 : 227; Perkins 1969: 259, 361).

---

*In Shandong soybean prices fell from 8.0 yuan per picul in 1929 to 4.5 in 1933.

†The tobacco acreage in China as a whole changed sharply even from year to year. Taking 1926 as 100, the figures look like this: 364 in 1921, 140 in 1922, 252 in 1924, 138 in 1925, 94 in 1927, 242 in 1928 (Zhang Youyi 1957, 2 : 202). Yip Honming's dissertation (in progress at the University of California, Los Angeles) compares Weixian and Linqing counties from the Ming to the 1930's.

Once again, cultivation was heavily concentrated in certain localities. In 1924 peanuts accounted for 20 percent of the cultivated area in Hejian county in central Hebei, for example; and in Zhangqiu and Jiyang counties in northwest Shandong, for a whopping 50 percent and 40 percent, respectively. Almost all the output in these two northwestern counties was for export—an estimated 90 percent of the crop in 1924—much of it sent via Qingdao to be forwarded to places as distant as Marseilles (Zhang Youyi 1957, 2:227, 232).

To tell the full story of the social and economic consequences of peanut cultivation in modern China, we will need studies with a narrow enough focus to differentiate export-dependent pockets like Zhangqiu and Jiyang from areas such as northeastern Hebei, where peanuts were a minor cash crop, but with a broad enough focus to take into account world market trends and their impact on the Chinese growers. A peanut-producing peasant in Zhangqiu, Shandong, in the 1930's, for example, found himself at the mercy of forces beyond his control when Indian peanuts began to penetrate the English, Dutch, and Australian markets. This increased competition, coupled with the world depression, caused the price of (shelled) peanuts in Qingdao to fall from 12.9 yuan per picul in 1929 to 8.5 in 1934 (Zhang Youyi 1957, 3:638). The ways in which developments and cycles in the world commodities market affected Chinese peasants engaged in export agriculture still await systematic studies.

### THE GROWTH OF COTTON PRODUCTION

Since cotton was the major cash crop of the Hebei–northwest Shandong plain, its incorporation into the world market seriously affected the political economy of the area. But before we take up that subject in detail, let us look at the scale of cotton production in China in general and our region in particular in the twentieth century.

Two economists have done painstaking work with the available (and often sketchy) statistics to give us convincing pictures of the broad trends in the decades between the 1870's and the 1930's. Richard A. Kraus uses county-by-county data compiled by the Chinese Cotton Millowners' Association (Huashang shachang lianhehui) spanning the period 1918–36. On the basis of fairly reliable series for 12 to 13 counties in each of nine provinces, he constructs first provincial estimates, and then, with the help of the National Agricultural Research Bureau's figures (from 1929), national output figures. He then draws on the relatively credible figures for 1918–36 to make some educated guesses about the preceding 50 years. It is a shaky procedure, but probably the best that can be done given the limited data available. This was a period of bust and boom, Kraus concludes.

> [In] 1870–1900 both the Chinese peasant and the economy were hit hard as handspun yarn production was cut by half and cotton production by a fifth. A painful reallocation of resources is a certainty. A lower standard of living a probability. . . . Then from the turn of the century to the early twenties growth of the factory yarn industry benefited both the peasant and the economy by prompting an enormous (perhaps 50%) increase in cotton production. (1968: 167)

Cotton output grew again in the period 1933–37, after a setback from flood and famine in 1931 (Kraus 1968: 30, 145, 167). These conclusions have since been substantially supported by Chao Kang (1977: 224).

This upward trend in output, by all evidence, did not stem from any important change in yields, but reflected instead increases in cotton acreage; the short-term fluctuations were due largely to the vagaries of weather (Kraus 1968: 37–42). Within this picture for China as a whole, Kraus supplies some highly credible figures for Hebei (the best data of any province) and Shandong, which I tabulate

TABLE 7.1

Cotton Acreage in Hebei and Shandong, 1927–1936

(Millions of shi mu)

| Year | Hebei | | Shandong | |
|------|-------------------|-------|-------------------|-------|
|      | Shanghai study | Kraus | Shanghai study | Kraus |
| 1927 | 2.3 | 2.5 | 2.9 | 3.2 |
| 1928 | 1.9 | 2.1 | 3.1 | 3.3 |
| 1929 | 2.4 | 2.6 | 3.9 | 4.2 |
| 1930 | 2.7 | 3.0 | 6.1 | 6.5 |
| 1931 | 2.7 | 3.0 | 7.4 | 8.0 |
| 1932 | 4.8 | 5.1 | 6.3 | 6.8 |
| 1933 | 5.7 | 6.1 | 5.0 | 5.5 |
| 1934 | 7.2 | 7.8 | 5.1 | 1.3 |
| 1935 | 5.8 | 6.3 | 1.7 | 5.8 |
| 1936 | 9.7 | 10.4 | 5.7 | 6.1 |
| 1937 | 13.9 | — | 5.6 | — |

SOURCES: *Zhongguo mianfang tongji shiliao* 1950: 114–15; Kraus 1968: Appendix B.

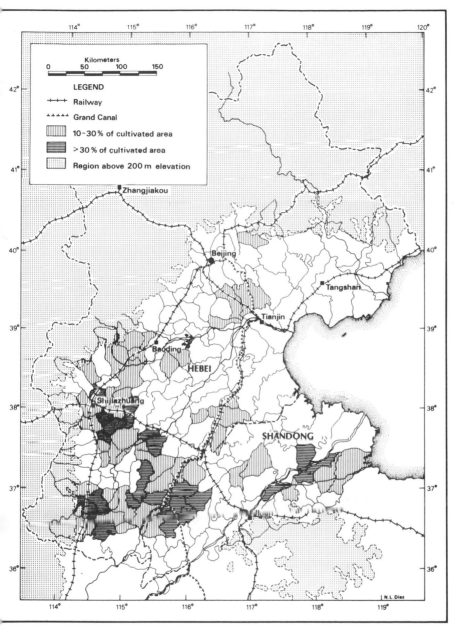

MAP 7.1. Cotton cultivation in Hebei and Northwest Shandong, 1936.
Based on Amano 1936: 305–11; Hebei sheng mianchan gaijin hui 1937;
and Kraus 1968: Appendix B.

in Table 7.1, next to a set of figures compiled by Shanghai municipal authorities in 1950 (using the same sources Kraus used, but with more complete data than he had in hand).

Though the amount of acreage fell off in the 1920's, according to the Shanghai study, the long-term trend was unmistakably upward. If we apply to Hebei and Shandong Kraus's guess that cotton acreage in 1900 was perhaps half what it was in 1925 (2,700,000 mu for Hebei and 2,900,000 for Shandong, by the Shanghai study), then neither province would have had more than 1,500,000 mu under cotton at the turn of the century. That would mean a threefold to fivefold increase by 1936. In terms of total cultivated acreage in the two provinces, cotton's share rose from about 2–3 percent to as much as 10 percent in Hebei and 6 percent in Shandong in this period (see Perkins 1969: 236, 261).

A figure of 6 percent to 10 percent of course cautions us against excessive emphasis on the influence of the world economy along the lines suggested by world-system theory. Yet, at the same time, we must not underestimate the importance of an increase of this scale. As Map 7.1 shows, a significant number of counties in Hebei–northwest Shandong had more than 30 percent of their cultivated area under cotton in 1936, and many others had from 10 percent to 30 percent. Such a commitment of land, as we will see in later chapters, was sufficient to alter the sociopolitical as well as the economic structure of the cotton-growing villages.

## COTTON AND THE WORLD ECONOMY

The story of Chinese cotton cannot be viewed in isolation from the world economy. This point was made dramatically to merchants and producers in the Shanghai area in 1863—when cotton prices rose in a single two-week period from 9.8 taels per bale to 25 taels per bale in face of an international scarcity caused by the Civil War in distant America (Li Wenzhi 1957: 396). In 1923 the Chinese Cotton Mill-owners' Association petitioned the government in Beijing to restrict cotton exports when overseas shipments of nearly a million piculs so depleted the domestic stock that the Chinese textile manufacturers had to buy Indian cotton and Japanese yarn (Zhang Youyi 1957, 2:167–68). The price drops during the great depression are further forcible evidence of how closely Chinese cotton production was tied to the movements of the world market. In Zhaoxian in southern Hebei, for example, the price of cotton dropped by about a quarter in the 1930's; and in some places in Shandong the price drop was even sharper, falling from 21 yuan per picul to 10 yuan (*ibid.*, 3 : 634).

Although Hebei's cotton economy was very much linked to the world market, much of its cotton went to the Chinese textile mills. But Shandong's situation was quite different. By the 1930's, in fact, most of the province's cotton went to the eight Japanese textile mills in the treaty port of Qingdao. Wu Zhi, of that remarkable Nankai Institute of Economics, has shown very clearly what this foreign domination meant for the province's cotton production. In 1935 the eight Japanese mills, with 500,000 spindles, processed about 1,200,000 piculs of cotton each year, compared with 300,000 for the Chinese-owned mills (of which there was only one in Qingdao, and three in Jinan). Almost all of the cotton for the Japanese mills was supplied by growers in Shandong (Wu Zhi 1936: 67–68).

Jinan and Zhangdian (about 100 kilometers east of Jinan on the railroad) were the two main cotton-purchasing centers for the Japanese mills in Qingdao. Most of the cotton grown in the western part of the Shandong plain found its way over land by animal cart to Jinan, and thence by railroad to Qingdao (744,962 piculs in 1934). The cotton grown in the Xiaoqing river valley and the piedmont plain area was transported either by boat down the Xiaoqing River to Jinan or by animal cart to Zhangdian, and thence by rail to Qingdao. Zhangdian accounted for about 200,000 piculs of the cotton spun in Qingdao in 1935 (Wu Zhi 1936: 36–37, 55, 61–62).

The Japanese mills in Qingdao purchased their cotton exclusively through Japanese brokerage firms. Zhangdian had four such firms, which (in 1935) handled fully three-fourths of all the city's cotton destined for Qingdao. The more than ten large Japanese brokerage houses in Jinan likewise accounted for most of the cotton purchases there (Wu Zhi 1936: 37, 46).

Such a production and sales structure meant complete domination by the Japanese firms. The Japanese mills in Qingdao determined the level of demand for raw cotton; the Japanese brokerage houses in Jinan and Zhangdian set the standards and the prices. The role of Chinese merchants was largely limited to the lower levels of the trading hierarchy—purchasing from peasant producers in the small periodic local markets, and ginning, baling, and transporting the cotton to Jinan and Zhangdian, where the Japanese firms made their bulk purchases for the Qingdao mills.

The Japanese-imposed economic system profoundly altered the

structure of commercialized agriculture in Shandong. The Xiaoqing river valley was a new area of cotton production, one that arose in response to the demand generated by the Japanese mills in Qingdao. In the older cotton-growing areas, such as Linqing, Chinese cotton seed gave way to American "trice 36" seed, which produced the finer and longer fibers demanded by the Japanese mills in Qingdao. Perhaps half of all the cotton grown in that county in 1934 was of the American variety. The proportion was even higher in neighboring counties such as Xiajin, Gaotang, Qingping, and Enxian. More important, perhaps, was a basic realignment of the flow of trade. Most of the cotton grown in this western section of the northwest Shandong plain had been transported up the Grand Canal to Tianjin; but by 1934 Tianjin was receiving only 30 percent and Jinan all the rest (Wu Zhi 1936: 15, 28).

This same pattern of "dependency" between peasants and modern industry existed in the tobacco industry, where the producers of Weixian and Yidu were subject to the whims of the British American Tobacco Company. As Sherman Cochran shows (1980: 142–44, 202–7), BAT can indeed be said to have extracted the "surplus" from the peasant economy of Shandong in the sense that the company reinvested only about 7 percent of its profits in the years 1913–41. In the language of "dependency theory," the surplus flowed out of the "satellite" to the "metropolis." To induce peasants to grow the needed "bright tobacco," BAT provided seed and guarantees of purchase in the early years, only to withdraw those subsidies in the 1920's and 1930's. From the company's point of view, the system worked well: the local tobacco was very nearly comparable to American tobacco in quality, but cost only eight to ten cents a pound, compared with about 43 cents for tobacco shipped from the United States. The company's profit rate in China (about 17 percent of sales) was in fact much higher than could be obtained in the United States. For the peasants who cultivated tobacco, the returns were attractive so long as the added labor required could be furnished by surplus labor with little possibility for other employment (in other words, by labor of little "opportunity cost" to the peasant farm). Once involved, peasant growers tended to be locked into this relationship of dependence.

Cash-cropping peasants in Hebei were not nearly so dependent on foreign-owned industry as their counterparts in Shandong. Of the 1,000,000 to 2,000,000 piculs of cotton grown annually in Hebei in the early 1920's, only about 10 percent to 20 percent was exported out of Tianjin, mostly to Japan.* Chinese textile mills consumed the bulk of the remainder—200,000 to 300,000 piculs by the mills in Tianjin alone (Qu 1931: 15, 103). Here indigenous industrialization held greater influence over the peasant economy than foreign industry.

The new mills of Tianjin (with some 200,000 spindles) drew on a combination of old and new cotton-producing centers, linked with the city through a combination of old and new transportation networks. The essential continuity with the traditional transportation networks is reflected, for example, in the persistence of the old nomenclature for the cotton trade among Tianjin merchants down to the 1930's. Hebei cotton was differentiated by its river system: "west rivers cotton" (*xihemian*), which was grown and transported along the "upper west river" (*shang xihe*; i.e., the Daqing River) and the "lower west river" (*xia xihe*; the Ziya River and, in its upper reaches, the Futuo and Fuyang rivers); "royal river cotton" (*yuhemian*), which was grown and transported along the Grand Canal south of Tianjin (Nan Canal); and "east and north river cotton" (*dongbeihemian*), which was grown and transported along the "east river" (Luan River) and the "north river" (Bei Canal, or the Grand Canal north of Tianjin; Qu 1931: 307). That these terms remained in general usage in the cotton market in Tianjin for a decade or more after the completion of the railroad networks in Hebei shows the continued importance of the premodern structure of cotton cultivation and marketing. At the same time, the new railroad networks also played their role. Cotton-growing areas around Baoding and Shijianzhuang, for example, came to rely on a combination of river and rail transport to supply Tianjin. Map 7.1 reflects how cotton followed both the old and the new routes.

When Japan carried economic expansion to the extreme of colonization, it sought to turn North China into a gigantic cotton-producing area for Japanese industry. Textiles in the early 1930's had accounted for one-quarter of all Japanese exports, and raw cotton (mainly from India and the United States, and only secondarily from China) for one-third of all Japanese imports (Ye Duzhuang 1948: 167–68; Zhang Youyi 1957, 3:585). The militarist 12-year plan of development for the North China provinces of Hebei, Shandong, Henan, and Shanxi called for expanding cotton acreage from

---

*Japanese industries found special use for the short, coarse cotton produced in Hebei: for stuffing material, for bandages, for explosives, and, mixed with wool, for blankets and rugs (Qu 1931: 4).

5,000,000–6,000,000 mu in 1939 to 30,000,000 mu by 1950 (Ye Duzhuang 1948: 222–23). The vital interest that cotton held for Japanese militarism was of course one reason why occupation authorities promoted so many systematic surveys of cotton-growing villages in North China.

Contact with the world economy affected cotton spinning and weaving differently. Spinning went into drastic decline. The share of handspun yarn in China's total yarn supply fell from 98 percent in the 1870's to 40 percent in the 1900's and to only 25 percent by the late 1920's (Feuerwerker 1970: Chao Kang 1977: 232–33). Imports of machine-spun yarn, especially of Indian yarn, made the first inroads into the handicraft market. Thereafter, yarn produced in textile mills in China took over.

A peasant spinner simply could not overcome the overwhelming advantage of a technology by which, according to one estimate, he could be outproduced by as much as 8,000 percent by a worker using a power spindle (Yan 1963: 59–69, 251–55). The result was a product so cheap that it sometimes sold close to the cost of raw cotton. In these circumstances, spinning hardly paid as a sideline activity. In Dingxian, for example, the net annual income of spinners had fallen to a mere 3.26 yuan a year by the 1920's, compared with 22.15 yuan for handweavers (Chao Kang 1977: 179–83, 185).

Handicraft weaving, in contrast to spinning, survived quite well against mechanized competition. As late as 1932 hand-woven cloth still accounted for 66.3 percent of the total cloth output in China (86.8 percent in 1928–31). More important, even though its share of the total cloth market in China declined, output still expanded in absolute terms, from 1,876,000,000 square yards in 1905–9 to 2,845,000,000 square yards in 1924–27—this in the period of the Chinese machine textile industry's most dynamic growth (Chao Kang 1977: 232–33). The reason, as both Yan Zhongping and Chao Kang have pointed out, was the relatively lesser technological imbalance between the power loom and the hand loom, especially the "iron-gear loom" (tielunji), which became widespread in China in the 1920's. With an iron-gear loom a worker could produce about one-fourth as much as a worker running a power loom, thus putting the peasant household within competitive range of the textile mills.

The expansion of handicraft weaving, stimulated by the increased quantity and improved quality of yarn supply, brought into being a number of new weaving centers in Hebei and Shandong. Most notable among these were Gaoyang in central Hebei, which at the height of the boom in 1926–30 had 50,000 weavers and produced 3,800,000 bolts of cloth (including 6,000,000 bolts of rayon-cotton) a year;* Baodi, in eastern Hebei, which reached its height earlier, in 1923, producing 4,600,000 bolts with 10,469 weaving households; and Weixian, in north-central Shandong, which during its peak years of 1926–33 had 150,000 weavers and produced 10,000,000 bolts a year (Yan 1963: 243; Chao Kang 1977: 191–96).

### CHANGE AND CONTINUITY

The cotton story, then, tells a tale of both change and continuity in rural Hebei–northwest Shandong. The combined influences of the world commodities market, of Japanese intrusion, and of indigenous industrialization led to a cotton economy far different in structure from that of the earlier centuries. The earlier system was one that was integrated, first of all, within the boundaries of China, within its local, regional, and interregional trading systems. As we have seen, the spread of cotton cultivation on the North China plain was first stimulated by the demand for raw cotton by the developed handicraft production centers of the lower Yangzi and Fujian-Guangdong. In time, southern and central Hebei and northwest Shandong became handicraft production centers themselves and supplied new frontier regions north of the wall and beyond. It was also a system that was integrated at the level of the household: the same household that grew the cotton generally also produced cloth for the market.

This earlier system was a relatively stable one. In the absence of natural and man-made calamities, supply and demand were fairly predictable. There was a certain built-in equilibrating mechanism even in abnormal times: when the crop was poor and the supply scarce, prices rose to compensate the cultivators for their poor harvest; when the harvest was abundant, prices dropped. The socially differentiating tendency of agricultural commercialization did operate, to be sure, but it was a differentiating force without the violent upswings and downswings characteristic of a capitalist world market.

The twentieth-century system, by contrast, involved forces far beyond China's borders. The cotton and textile economy was no longer

---

*Linda Grove's forthcoming study of the rise and fall of the handicraft weaving industry in the Gaoyang area promises to throw much light on this complex subject.

affected only by local, regional, or interregional developments. And farm households no longer performed the complete cycle of cotton farming, yarn spinning, and cloth weaving. By the 1930's much of the cotton left the countryside to be machine-spun in the cities and abroad (especially in Japan), and much of the machine-spun yarn, in turn, was sent back to the countryside to be woven there. In all phases of the production system, farm households had to face stiff international competition. Thus, the cotton grower of Sibeichai village found that the prices he could obtain for his cotton depended very much on what cotton merchants in Tianjin and Qingdao were willing to pay, which in turn depended very much on the cotton supply from faraway places like the United States and India. The erstwhile spinner of yarn, meanwhile, found this source of the household's supplementary income supplanted by the cheap machine-spun yarn produced in China and abroad. For the household weavers, twentieth-century commercialization was a mixed blessing. Their fortunes were improved with machine spinning, which supplied more and often better quality yarn. They also benefited from improved transportation, which allowed them to work in places like Gaoyang, Baodi, and Weixian, where cotton was neither grown nor spun. On the other hand, they found that their fortunes were now tied to entirely unpredictable developments abroad. The world depression, which brought a whiplash effect to many cotton-growing localities after the boom of the 1920's, is one example. The rise of Japanese militarism, which led to the Japanese conquest of Manchuria and the policy to sever Manchuria from the North China economy, is another; its effects were devastating for North China village weavers who had come to depend on the booming Manchurian market.

With the rise of the new weaving centers, moreover, came also new forms of productive organization. Merchant capital entered into the production process in unprecedented ways. The old system in which weavers took their products to market to sell gave way to a putting-out system in which merchants supplied yarn to the household weaver and specified the kind of cloth to be produced. By 1923 some 72 percent of all looms in Baodi operated under this system, run by 67 merchant stores. Similarly, in Gaoyang in 1932 some 65 percent of the looms were controlled by 80 stores (Chao Kang 1977: 204).

This new putting-out system—based on the combination of merchant capital with household industry—initiated socioeconomic and politicoeconomic changes that have yet to be systematically studied. It certainly meant that many farm families came to engage in a kind of hiring-out for a piece-rate wage to town merchants, as I shall show. Whether this kind of system represented a step toward industrial capitalism is a question that needs to be considered in conjunction with the small family farm economy. I will return to this question in Chapter Eleven. Beyond that, such a production system raises an entire range of questions about the changing composition of the merchant class, and consequently also of the local elite and of their role in the evolving local political structures of twentieth-century China. The whole story of the cotton economy and of its related sociopolitical changes deserves a separate study.* In this chapter I have merely tried to point to the broad outlines of some of the structural changes that the Chinese cotton and textile economy underwent in the present century.

The twentieth century, of course, also saw changes that went well beyond just those associated with cotton and textiles. A few of them might be recalled here. The section of the Grand Canal north of the Yellow River and south of Linqing gradually fell into disuse after 1855, when the Yellow River changed to its present course into the Daqing in Shandong. At the same time, with the opening of Tianjin as a treaty port in 1860, the coastal shipping route from the lower Yangzi became the preferred means of transport over the Grand Canal. The completion of the Tianjin–Nanjing railroad in 1911, finally, removed any urgency for dredging and clearing the section of the Grand Canal between the Yellow River and Linqing. The impact on Linqing was devastating: from a city with a population of at least 100,000 in 1600, it dwindled to a mere town of 36,000 in the 1930's (Jing & Luo 1959: 5–6; Wilkinson 1978: 256). The broad social and economic consequences for the surrounding countryside, indeed for the areas all along this section of the Grand Canal, can only be detailed by painstaking inquiry into the local sources.

The northernmost section of the Grand Canal, between Tianjin and Tongxian, similarly, fell into disuse after the completion of the Beijing–Shanhaiguan railroad in 1901 (Sun Jingzhi 1957: 74). Again, the depressive impact on the area along the canal and the stimulative impact on the area along the new railroad can be told only by narrowly focused local studies of the affected zones. Among the Mantetsu-surveyed villages, for example, Michang village switched to cotton cultivation and became highly commercialized under the stimulus of the new commercial networks opened up by the railroads. Cotton grown in Michang was sold to merchants in

*Kathy Walker (dissertation in progress at the University of California, Los Angeles) explores these points in a study of Nantong county in southern Jiangsu.

Xugezhuang (just ten kilometers north of the village) and Tangshan, both on the railroad between Tianjin and Shanhaiguan, to be sent on to Tianjin and Manchuria by rail (MT, Kitō 1937b: 1, 4).

The overall impact of railroads on the economies of Hebei and Shandong is also beyond the compass of this study.* Let me only point here to the most obvious effect. Railroads made possible the commercialization and urbanization of areas not served by major navigable rivers, such as Weifang, on the trunk line between Qingdao and Jinan, and Tangshan, on the Tianjin–Shanhaiguan line. Elsewhere, in places like Baoding, Shijiazhuang, and Jinan, it augmented older river transport networks and stimulated further development and commercialization. The new cotton-growing area along the Xiaoqing River, we saw earlier, was based on river transport to Jinan and Zhangdian, and thence by rail to Qingdao.

Finally, railroads linked up the inland economies with ocean transport and the world economy, as exemplified by the rapid development of major treaty ports like Tianjin, which became a city of over 1,000,000 by the 1930's, and Qingdao, a mere fishing village in the nineteenth century, which became a city of 592,000 by 1938 (Sun Jingzhi 1957: 10–12, 75–85, 147–50; Perkins 1969: 293). In Shandong, as we have seen, the rise of the new industrial-transport network reoriented the entire cotton economy of the province toward Qingdao, replacing the older Grand Canal–linked system centered on Tianjin.

In time, the coming of modern transport and industrialization was to fundamentally alter the relationship of the North China plain to the national economy of China. The North China plain, along with the Guanzhong plain of northwest China, was of course the historical heartland of Chinese civilization down to the Tang. By Tang times, however, even though the political and administrative center of the empire remained in the northern regions, the economic center of gravity had shifted down to the more productive lower Yangzi valley. The capitals (Changan in the Sui–Tang, Kaifeng in the Northern Song, and Beijing in the Ming–Qing) had to be supplied from the south via the Grand Canal dug for that purpose. It was only with the coming of industrialization and modern transportation that the north was able to emerge once more as the major economic center of the country. This story, which takes us rather far afield from our concern with the commercialization of agriculture, has been made

---

*See Zhang Ruide 1979 for a useful study of the impact of the Beijing–Hankou railroad on the economy of North China.

graphically clear by Dwight Perkins (1969: 143, 156, 174–84; see also Sun 1957: 7–14).

Still, it is against the background of such changes that we must see the essential continuities in the small-peasant economy. Large parts of Hebei–northwest Shandong remained relatively unaffected by the cultivation of cotton, as Map 7.1 shows. The villages in the unshaded counties (where cotton occupied less than 10 percent of the cultivated area) remained to a considerable extent dispersed units, unintegrated into the larger economic system of the nation or the world. Dependency theory and world-system analysis have tended to place singular emphasis on and exaggerate the role of the market (and, in this respect, ironically resemble classical economics). It is useful to recall here the analyses of Chayanov, Polanyi, and Scott, emphasizing the subsistence producer–consumer face of the peasant.

Moreover, changes of the kind surveyed above occurred within the context of the small-peasant economy. As I showed in Chapter Four, more than 80 percent of the cultivated land in this area remained under small family farms in the 1930's. The world economy did not undermine the small peasant economy. It only pushed it further along the path of change it had been on. The patterns and principles of change in the twentieth century were essentially the same as those earlier: cash-cropping simultaneously increased the returns and the investments of the peasants, and thereby pushed forward their differentiation.

But we must not underestimate the scale and intensity of the changes either. After all, the agriculture of this area did commercialize at a hugely rapid pace in the first four decades of the century. The incorporation of Chinese agriculture into the world economy telescoped and greatly accelerated changes in the small peasant economy. That is the background to the managerial and family farming of the 1930's.

# CHAPTER 8

# Managerial Farming and Family Farming: Draft-Animal Use

Readers familiar with the orthodox Marxist analysis of the development of capitalism in a peasant economy will have by now noted the similarities between the patterns of change I have outlined so far and those outlined in Lenin's *The Development of Capitalism in Russia.* If the commercializing small-peasant economy was indeed changing in the direction of the development of large farms based on hired labor, was it not undergoing a transition to capitalism? Were not the managerial farmers described in the preceding chapters in fact protocapitalists? Were not the laborers they hired in fact a rural proletariat? Did not these production relations signal the arrival of a new capitalist mode of production?

Commercialization and the rise of wage-labor relations are in fact at the heart of the "incipient capitalism" argument in post-1949 Chinese scholarship. Scholars began with the amassing of evidence on commercialization and on the development of wage-labor relations in industrial and protoindustrial enterprises in China. More recently, important work has been done on the rise of wage-labor relations in agriculture.

My disagreement with this important body of scholarship has nothing to do with the insistence on the development of wage-labor-based farming. On the contrary, I believe all the available evidence points conclusively to an even greater growth of wage labor in the countryside than has commonly been assumed, as noted in the preceding chapters. My disagreement has instead to do with how we are to understand these production relations. In overpopulated China, in which millions of declassed and dispossessed people "floated" on the surface of society, the mere demonstration of the availability of a free wage-labor force is not enough to prove the sprouting of qualitative changes in the mode of production. The critical question is: was the rise of wage labor accompanied by the accumulation of capital that led also to qualitative breakthroughs in agricultural productivity?

Two studies from the "incipient capitalism" tradition have gone on from the evidence on production relations to argue that those changes represented qualitative changes in productivity as well. Jing Su and Luo Lun, in their pioneering study of "managerial landlords" in Shandong, argued that these farmers (1) possessed superior farm implements, farm animals, and fertilizer, (2) had access to more labor through hired labor, and (3) enjoyed economies of scale in production; and that for these reasons, they were able to increase farm productivity (1959: 130–41). Adachi Keiji (1981), building on this analysis to develop a full theory about managerial farming, holds that these farms were distinguished from small ones above all by their heavy reliance on draft animals. He points in particular to evidence from a number of agricultural treatises (*nongshu*) that it was quite common in the Ming and Qing to use teams of four oxen for plowing. In addition, much attention was paid to the accumulation of animal fertilizer. What this means, Adachi says, is that the managerial farms combined animal husbandry with farming. On the one hand, they were able to extend their scale of operation through the use of animal power. On the other hand, they were able to raise the degree of intensification of farming through the use of animal fertilizer. This was *dainōhō*, or large-scale farming based on draft-animal power and draft-animal fertilizer. It must be distinguished from *sho nōhō*, or small-scale farming with little or no use of draft animals, as exemplified by the rice growers of the lower Yangzi, who used only one ox for plowing. By linking their arguments on production relations with productivity, these scholars have in fact anticipated my criticism of studies that focus exclusively on production relations.

The question of the historical meaning of managerial farming turns critically on what we think of the validity of these arguments. If the managerial farms did represent major breakthroughs in productivity, then we can indeed say that the small-peasant economy itself generated qualitative changes toward a new kind of economy, whether or not we wish to label that economy "capitalist." On the other hand, if the managerial farms did not herald new levels of productivity in the farm economy, then they must be seen as part and parcel of an involuting but differentiated small-peasant economy, and they would not merit the label "capitalist sprouts." I therefore begin my comparative analysis of managerial and family farming with a detailed examination of Jing and Luo's and Adachi's arguments and their evidence.

The first crucial empirical question is: did the managerial farms in fact have a higher rate of productivity than the small family farms? The Mantetsu data suggest that they did not, indeed to my own initial surprise. As we see in Table 8.1, in the four villages in which the investigators compiled relatively detailed crop yield data on each household, there is no consistent pattern of either higher or lower yields on the managerial farms, as compared with the village averages. For cash crops and foodgrains alike, the managerial farms were just as likely to obtain higher-than-average yields as they were to obtain lower ones. This of course confirms the findings of John Lossing Buck, who paid a good deal of attention to the question of the relative productivity of different-sized farms (1937a: 273; 1937b: 295).

If managerial and family farms did not differ consistently in yields on the same crops, might they still have differed in total productivity based on the proportion of land they placed under cash crops or double-cropped? Judging by Table 8.2, we would have to say they did not. Once again, no consistent pattern of either greater or lesser farm productivity is discernible. Though the Dabeiguan figures might lead us to conclude that managerial farms cultivated a higher proportion of cash crops, the figures for Macun, Michang, and Xiaojie are utterly ambiguous: some managerial farms gave less land to cash crops, others more. When it comes to cropping frequency, the evidence again suggests no substantial difference between managerial and family farms: though the Macun data suggest that managerial farms did less double-cropping, the data for Xiaojie suggest the opposite, Dabeiguan shows no differences, and Lujiazhai and Michang show both patterns. There was no simple correlation between size of farm and cropping frequency. Once again, this conclusion confirms Buck's findings. When he recorded the index of double-cropping on different-sized farms, he found no correlation between farm size and intensity of land use in any of the cropping areas in China (1937b: 296).

The explanation, I suspect, is that cropping choices were dictated not so much by farm size as by other considerations. One major determining factor was ecology, which affected managerial and family farms equally. No managerial or family farm, for example, would have willingly risked growing cotton on low-lying, easily waterlogged land. The usual choice for such land was low-investment and water-resistant sorghum. That is why the villages in poorly drained northeastern Hebei, such as Dabeiguan, Lujiazhai, and Michang, de-

TABLE 8.1

Crop Yields of Managerial Farms in Four Hebei Villages, 1930's

| Managerial farmer | Size of farm (mu) | Cotton[a] (jin/mu) | Sorghum (dou/mu) | Maize (dou/mu) | Millet (dou/mu) |
|---|---|---|---|---|---|
| Dabeiguan (1936) | | *38.4* | *9.9* | *9.7* | *10.6* |
| Zhang Cailou | 211.5 | 39.3 | 9.3 | 13.2 | 13.4 |
| Zhang Chonglou | 188.5 | 40.0 | 8.3 | 13.2 | 11.7 |
| Zhang Deyuan | 124.0 | 20.0 | 9.3 | 8.0 | 10.0 |
| Xiaojie (1935) | | *115.0* | *12.6* | *10.8* | |
| Household 1 | 251.0 | 90.0 | 4.0 | 15.0 | |
| Household 112 | 127.0 | 94.6 | 12.5 | 12.5 | |
| Macun (1939) | | *92.0* | | | *9.5* |
| Household 1 | 101.0 | 82.0 | | | 7.0 |
| Michang (1936) | | *134.9* | *6.1* | *9.4* | *4.9* |
| Dong Dezhai | 183.0 | 158.0 | 8.3 | | 10.0 |
| Dong Tianwang | 120.2 | 126.2 | 6.0 | 8.9 | |
| Dong Jizhong | 109.0 | 135.0 | 6.0 | 9.9 | |

SOURCES: *Dabeiguan, Michang,* MT Kitō 1937a: Table 11, 1937b: Table 11; *Xiaojie,* MT, Tenshin jimusho chōsaka 1936b: 109–16; *Macun,* MT, Hokushi keizai chōsajo 1940d: Tables 3, 27, 31, 35.

NOTE: Village averages in italic. The only managerial farmer who grew wheat was the one in Macun. His yield was lower than the village average (5.3 dou per mu vs. 6.6).

[a]Unginned cotton; ginned cotton is usually 30% to 40% less in weight.

voted a considerable proportion of their land to sorghum, whereas well-drained Macun on the piedmont plain of west-central Hebei grew none at all. As for winter wheat, it was effectively precluded in cotton-growing villages like Michang and Dabeiguan in the northern part of northeastern Hebei, where the fall period was a busy race against the clock under the combined pressures of early frost and cotton harvesting—hence the very low double-cropping index for those two villages.

Access to the market was another major determining factor in cropping choices. Thus, the establishment of a railroad linking Michang to the Tianjin market was a great boost to the growth of cotton cultivation in the village in the Republican period. Similarly, Xiaojie's access to Tianjin via the Grand Canal, and in the twentieth century to Beijing by rail and truck, helped to stimulate cash-cropping in that village.

Beyond the dictates of natural environment and marketing, farmers and peasants generally tried to crop in such a way as to minimize their risks and to spread the work load as evenly as possible through the year. Table 8.3 shows the cropping schedules of Lujiazhai village in northeastern Hebei in 1936 and Qizhai village in northwest Shan-

TABLE 8.2

Cash-Cropping and Double-Cropping on Managerial Farms in Five Hebei Villages, 1930's

(Percentage of cropped area)

| Managerial farmer | Cash crops | | | Sorghum | Millet | Maize | Double-cropping [b] |
|---|---|---|---|---|---|---|---|
| | Cotton | Wheat | Other [a] | | | | |
| *Dabeiguan (1936)* | *10.5%* | | | *20.3%* | *36.0%* | *9.7%* | *100.0* |
| Zhang Cailou | 14.4 | | | 13.9 | 26.7 | 9.8 | 100.0 |
| Zhang Chonglou | 19.1 | | | 15.9 | 27.6 | 17.3 | 100.0 |
| Zhang Deyuan | 16.1 | | | 21.4 | 32.2 | 5.1 | 100.0 |
| *Lujiazhai (1936)* | | *8.8%* | *7.4%* | *32.6%* | *25.3%* | *10.8%* | *106.0* |
| Household 32 | | 20.0 | 15.0 | 30.0 | 20.0 | 10.0 | 106.5 |
| Household 33 | | 9.5 | 14.3 | 28.6 | 24.1 | 9.5 | 103.3 |
| *Xiaojie (1935)* | *26.5%* | *4.8%* | *3.7%* | *4.4%* | | *38.4%* | *105.3* |
| Household 1 | 22.1 | 7.4 | 12.2 | 7.4 | | 36.9 | 107.9 |
| Household 112 | 25.2 | 13.6 | | 5.4 | | 32.7 | 115.7 |
| *Macun (1939)* | *26.4%* | *23.0%* | *3.7%* | | *27.7%* | | *133.0* |
| Household 1 | 24.0 | 15.5 | 4.9 | | 32.5 | | 112.2 |
| *Michang (1936)* | *30.8%* | *1.0%* | *3.4%* | *43.7%* | *4.9%* | *14.7%* | *103.5* |
| Dong Dezhai | 27.6 | | 3.8 | 38.4 | 1.1 | 14.8 | 108.6 |
| Dong Tianwang | 51.4 | | 1.1 | 33.9 | | 11.7 | 101.1 |
| Dong Jizhong | 27.5 | | 1.4 | 37.6 | | 11.0 | 102.8 |

SOURCES: *Dabeiguan, Michang,* MT, Kitō 1937a: Table 11, 1937b: Table 11; *Lujiazhai, Xiaojie,* MT, Tenshin jimusho chōsaka 1936a: 92–99, 1936b: 44–52; *Macun,* MT, Hokushi keizai chōsajo 1940d: 86–87 and Table 3.

NOTE: Village averages in italic.
[a] Primarily fruits and vegetables.
[b] Ratio of cropped area to cultivated area.

dong in 1942. As can be seen, had a farmer or peasant grown only one crop, he would have found himself in the impossible position of having all the year's farmwork peak around the rush periods of that crop. In the case of cotton, that would mean the late-April planting period, the June/July weeding and cultivating period, and the September/October/November harvesting and plowing period. A diversified cropping pattern that mixed foodgrains with cotton permitted, first of all, a much more practical distribution of work: sorghum could be planted after the cotton, in May, followed by maize in late May, and late millet or maize in June or July. The harvests were similarly spread out across the year. Moreover, the risk of losing all of the year's work in a single natural disaster could be avoided. Winter wheat, for example, was substantially free from any threat of flood damage, since its growing season covered the relatively dry winter and spring (though it was still vulnerable to drought). Soybeans were

TABLE 8.3

Planting and Harvesting Schedules in Lujiazhai, Hebei, and Qizhai, Shandong, 1936 and 1942

| Crop | Lujiazhai | | Qizhai | |
|---|---|---|---|---|
| | Plant | Harvest | Plant | Harvest |
| Millet (early) | 4/20–5/4 | 8/23–9/6 | 5/1–5/15 | 9/1–9/15 |
| Cotton | 4/20–5/4 | 9/20–10/31 | 4/20–5/4 | 8/20–11/10 |
| Sorghum | 5/5–5/19 | 9/8–9/22 | — | — |
| Maize (early) | 5/21–6/4 | 9/15–9/29 | 6/1–6/15 | 9/1–9/15 |
| Millet (late) | 6/6–6/20 | 8/23–9/6 | — | — |
| Maize (late) | 7/7–7/21 | 9/15–9/29 | 7/1–7/15 | 9/10–9/24 |
| Soybeans | 7/7–7/21 [a] | 9/23–10/7 | 6/7–6/21 | 9/20–10/4 |
| Wheat | 9/23–10/7 | 6/21–7/5 | 9/20–10/4 | 6/1–6/15 |

SOURCES: *Lujiazhai*, MT, Tenshin jimusho chōsaka 1936a: 107–12; *Qizhai*, Kita Shina 1943b: 15.
NOTE: All beginning dates are approximate. Two weeks or thereabouts were scheduled for the planting of all crops and two weeks for the harvesting of most of them. Cotton harvesting covered a longer period, some six weeks in Lujiazhai and about twelve in Qizhai.
[a] Usually interplanted with maize at the same time.

of special value in part because of their short growing season: they could be planted in July after the winter wheat was harvested. At the same time, they helped to replenish the soil, since two-thirds of the nitrogen absorbed by the plant stayed in the roots and stem to be returned to the soil (Chen Wenhua 1981, 1:119). Soybeans were therefore a crucial link in the three-crops-in-two-years agrarian system.

When it came to cropping frequency, ecological considerations were again paramount. The long growing season of cotton, indicated in Table 8.3, effectively ruled out double-cropping. The peasant growing the usual combination of maize/sorghum/millet followed by winter wheat, on the other hand, had to harvest the spring-sown crops and complete the planting of his winter wheat before the first frost in the space of about six weeks. This time constraint limited the proportion of land that any farm, managerial or small, could plant under winter wheat, even assuming adequate fertilizer and favorable soil conditions. In Shajing village, for example, the fall rush was such that neither managerial nor family farms were able to plant more than one-third of their land under wheat. It was only with the coming of tractor plowing in 1959 that a higher index of double-cropping was attained (Shajing interviews, April 1980).

Cropping patterns, in short, were largely shaped by ecological and market considerations. That is why we find considerable variation from one area to another. But there was little differentiation in cropping patterns within a village between managerial and family farms.

If the above suggestions are substantially correct, it should not be surprising to find that the Mantetsu data also show little difference between managerial and family farms in their uses of animal power. Table 8.4 shows the number of draft animals on 12 managerial farms in five villages, converted into donkey equivalents, and the per-mu use of those animals. A single donkey, as can be seen, was made to cover as few as 17.6 mu and as many as 91.5 mu. The average was 36.4.

A comparison of the mu-per-donkey equivalent on the managerial farms with the village averages reveals no greater animal use on the managerial farms. On the contrary, in eight of the 12 cases, each ani-

TABLE 8.4

Draft Animals on Managerial Farms in Five Hebei and Shandong Villages, 1930's–1940's

(Land in mu)

| Managerial farmer | Land farmed | Horses | Mules | Oxen | Donkeys | Donkey equivalent[a] | Land farmed per donkey equivalent |
|---|---|---|---|---|---|---|---|
| Dabeiguan (1936) | | | | | | | 27.6 |
| Zhang Cailou | 211.5 | 1 | 2 | 4 | 0 | 12.0 | 17.6 |
| Zhang Chonglou | 188.5 | 0 | 3 | 0 | 0 | 6.0 | 31.4 |
| Zhang Deyuan | 124.0 | 2 | 0 | 0 | 0 | 4.0 | 31.0 |
| Lujiazhai (1936) | | | | | | | 21.8 |
| Household 32 | 100.0 | 0 | 1 | 0 | 1 | 3.0 | 33.3 |
| Household 33 | 105.0 | 1 | 0 | 0 | 1 | 3.0 | 35.0 |
| Xiaojie (1935) | | | | | | | 43.8 |
| Household 1 | 251.0 | 2 | 1 | 0 | 1 | 7.0 | 35.9 |
| Household 112 | 127.0 | 0 | 1 | 0 | 2 | 4.0 | 31.8 |
| Michang (1936) | | | | | | | 49.6 |
| Dong Dezhai | 183.0 | 0 | 1 | 0 | 0 | 2.0 | 91.5 |
| Dong Tianwang | 120.2 | 0 | 1 | 0 | 0 | 2.0 | 60.1 |
| Dong Jizhong | 109.0 | 0 | 1 | 0 | 0 | 2.0 | 54.5 |
| Qizhai (1941) | | | | | | | 34.9 |
| Household 111 | 165.0 | 0 | 3 | 1 | 0 | 7.5 | 22.0 |
| Household 112 | 102.0 | 0 | 1 | 1 | 0 | 3.5 | 29.1 |

SOURCES: Dabeiguan, Michang, MT, Kitō 1937a: Table 9, 1937b: Table 9; Lujiazhai, Xiaojie, MT, Tenshin jimusho chōsaka 1936a: 117, 1936b: 94, 97; Qizhai, Kita Shina 1943b: 67, Appendix Table 1.

NOTE: Village averages in italics.

[a]Donkey equivalents are calculated by the villagers' own rule of thumb as reported by the Michang investigators: 1 adult (more than 2 years old) horse or mule = 2 donkeys; 1 adult ox = 1.5 donkeys.

mal on the managerial farms worked a larger farm area than the village average. This finding is supported by Buck's data. In his "winter wheat–kaoliang area" as a whole, "small farms" (not precisely defined) averaged about 19 mu per "labor animal unit," and "large farms" about 38 mu (1937b: 299). Much of this difference can probably be explained by the inefficiencies involved in animal use on the smaller farms. Whereas the managerial farms generally had their own farm animals, several small family farms often shared a draft animal, a practice in which time was necessarily lost in the wait in line and the moving of the animal from one farm to another. Added to this was the fact that an animal would generally work best only for the owner who fed it.*

The Mantetsu data suggest, in short, that there was no greater use of animal power and no greater productivity on the managerial farms than on the small family farms, contrary to the arguments of Adachi and Jing and Luo. Before confronting the evidence they marshaled in support of their arguments, let us first take a closer look at the role animal power played in the agriculture of the North China plain and see why the 1930's managerial farms did not use more of it.

### THE ECONOMICS OF DRAFT-ANIMAL USE

Agriculture on the Hebei–northwest Shandong plain was such that a certain amount of draft-animal power was indispensable. The natural rhythms of farmwork in this ecosystem create two great rush periods: the spring and the fall. In the spring planting season, rains are sparse and the sun beats down strongly. This means that planting must be done within a day or two after a rain, in order to take full advantage of every drop of moisture in the soil before it evaporates. One Japanese field study estimated that one man working without an animal could plant less than one mu of cotton a day—far from sufficient to complete the job on an average sized family farm in a couple of days. A team of five men with a plow drawn by three oxen, by contrast, could plant 20 mu a day (Kita Shina 1943b: 68–72). The Shajing villagers figured that four or five men working with one horse or mule, or two donkeys, could plant ten mu of maize or wheat in a day (Shajing interviews, April 1980). Four- or five-men teams—in which one man plowed, one seeded, one or two fertilized, and one backfilled—were used for the same reason draft animals were used: to take advantage of the remaining moisture in the soil. To plow,

*I am grateful to Diana Lary for calling this point to my attention.

seed, fertilize, and backfill in one step was an organization of work adapted to the particular needs of unirrigated dry farming. The logic of this operation applied to the small family farms no less than to the large farms, though they often had to pool their draft animals, implements, and labor to this end. In general, all land was planted in this way (MT, Tenshin jimusho chōsaka 1936a: 107–12; Kita Shina 1943b: 69; Shajing interviews, April 1980).

For the three-crops-in-two-years farms of central and southern Hebei and northwest Shandong, the fall rush was especially difficult. The soil had to be turned (geng) right after the harvest—again in order to make use of the moisture in the soil (for soil after harvesting is particularly prone to moisture loss)—so the wheat could be planted. One man without a draft animal could plow only about a quarter of a mu to a depth of about four inches in one day, again far from sufficient for the average-sized family farm. A man using two oxen, on the other hand, could on relatively level land and not unusually difficult soil (such as that in Shajing or Qizhai) plow four and a half to five mu to a depth of five inches a day, and with two mules or horses he could do about ten (Kita Shina 1943a: 70; Shajing interviews, April 1980).* Again, managerial and family farms alike had to rely on animal power to meet the wheat-planting deadline. Where agriculture was under a one-crop-a-year regime, as it was in most of northeastern Hebei, the fall rush was less intense, but the soil still had to be turned after the harvest.

The third main part of the farm cycle that required animal power was cultivating (zhonggeng), generally done in July, after weeding in June and early July. Sorghum, millet, and maize all had to be weeded and then plowed. One man with one donkey could generally cover four or five mu in a day (MT, Tenshin jimusho chōsaka 1936a, 107–12; Shajing interviews, April 1980).

There is no question, then, that draft animals were indispensable to agriculture on the North China plain (and had been used since the Han).† But the degree to which they were relied on must not be exaggerated. For each mu of crops, the animal power required for plow-

---

*Where the land sloped or the soil was hard to plow, more animal power was used. In different parts of Shandong in the 1930's, three-animal teams were used: usually either three oxen or oxen and mules together, but sometimes even teams of three mules. Depending on the terrain, such teams could barely do three mu a day, and at best nine mu (Amano 1936: 53–54). For our purposes, the general rule of thumb used by villagers of Shajing and Qizhai will suffice.

†See Hsü 1980: Intro. and Chap. 4. The 5th-century agricultural treatise Qimin yaoshu documents the use of draft animals specifically in Shandong (Wang Yuhu 1979: 28; Adachi 1981: 539).

ing, planting, and cultivating adds up to just one donkey day (0.6 for plowing, 0.2 for planting, and 0.2 for cultivating).

We find a good example of the minimal reliance on animal power use on the managerial farms of Michang. The Chinese researcher the Mantetsu investigators posted in that village took great pains to record the numbers of days of animal power used each month by the different households. Two of the three managerial farmers, Dong Ji-zhong and Dong Tianwang, followed a virtually identical pattern. Each used his one mule for a total of about 75 days (74.6 days and 75.8 days, respectively) in 1937, or, in donkey equivalents, about 150 days. The peak times of use in this one-crop-a-year village were the spring planting, July cultivating, and October/November plowing periods. Take Dong Jizhong, for instance. He used his mule 14 days in March, 16.5 days in April, 11.5 days in July, 12 days in October, and 9 days in November. The animal was used only one or two days in each of the other months. On a per-mu basis, Dong Jizhong used 1.09 donkey days per cropped mu (1.12 donkey days per cultivated mu on his holding of 133 mu in 1937). Dong Tianwang used 1.16 donkey days per cropped mu (1.21 per cultivated mu). These two managerial farmers in fact used somewhat less animal power than did the average family farm in Michang (MT, Hokushi jimukyoku chōsabu 1938–41, 1: Table 50). For them and for the peasants alike, the fact that in a nearby marsh there was a kind of reed that could be used as fertilizer lessened the value of animal manure and helped tip the scale of animal use further toward the minimum level of necessity. Where the index of cropped to cultivated land was higher, as it was in two crops-in-three-years central and southern Hebei and northwestern Shandong, the minimum level of animal use would increase by about 50 percent, to an average of 1.5 donkey days per cultivated mu.

In considering the additional use of animals beyond the bare minimum, managerial farmers and peasants alike had to weigh the benefits against the cost. Animals saved human labor for such tasks as hauling fertilizer to the fields, transporting harvested crops, milling, and, in areas where irrigation was widely used, powering the waterwheels.

The other main benefit of maintaining more farm animals was the added fertilizer they produced. As is well known, dung was generally mixed with earth and garbage (in a ratio of about 3:7) to make compost. In Shajing and Lujiazhai, both in northeastern Hebei, peasants used about 1,800 to 2,000 catties (one large cart; *da che*) of this compost per cropped mu (MT, Tenshin jimusho chōsaka 1936a: 103,

107; Shajing interviews, April 1980). This compares with about 3,000 catties in more highly developed and irrigated Macun, in the piedmont plain area of west-central Hebei (MT, Hokushi keizai chōsajo 1940d: 89). One donkey provided fertilizer sufficient for about three mu of cropped area (5,400 catties), and one horse, mule, or ox, for about four mu (7,200 catties; MT, Tenshin jimusho chōsaka 1936a: 103).

But against these benefits were relatively high maintenance costs. A horse, mule, or ox required about ten catties of "coarse feed" a day (maize and millet stalks, sorghum leaves, and the like), or the equivalent of the "secondary produce" (fuchan) of about 15 to 20 mu of foodgrains. A donkey required about 50 percent to 60 percent of this amount. In addition, during periods of work, these daily rations had to be supplemented with "concentrated feed" of foodgrains (sorghum, maize, soybeans). A horse, mule, or ox needed about two catties a day, or roughly twice the amount consumed by an adult male; a donkey required about one cattie (Amano 1936: 52–54; MT, Tenshin jimusho chōsaka 1936b: 121; MT, Hokushi keizai chōsajo 1940d: 90; Kita Shina 1943b: 87).*

At the wage levels of the 1930's, a farmer could employ a day-laborer for roughly the cost of maintaining a donkey for a day's use. Indeed, in Shajing village, such an equation was explicitly made in practice: a man hiring out with a donkey for the day was generally paid at twice the usual rate. Zhang Shoujun, sixty-four years old in 1980, recalled that he had habitually taken his donkey to nearby Wangquansi and Renhezhen in the fall to hire out as a day-laborer, always for the double wage (shuang gongqian; interview, April 1980). From the point of view of the managerial farmer or the rich peasant, then, the choice was between using a donkey for one day and hiring an additional laborer for the day.

The extra animal power certainly made good sense where the animal could be set to the basic tasks of planting, cultivating, and plowing. After that, however, its marginal utility to a farm diminished. The transport of grain and fertilizer, flour milling, and the like could be done by men. And seeding, fertilizing, weeding, harvesting, and a multitude of the other chores involved in the highly intensive "traditional agriculture" of this region could be done only by humans. In

---

*The Mantetsu studies are pretty well agreed on these amounts. Investigators of Xiaojie village, Tongxian (just east of Beijing), reported a higher level of "concentrated feed" requirements—1,000 catties a year for a horse or mule, and 500 catties for a donkey—but these figures were probably calculated on the mistaken supposition that the animals were worked every day (MT, Tenshin jimusho chōsaka 1936b: 121).

deciding whether or not to use additional animal power, a farmer needed to take all this into account.

The benefit of added fertilizer from maintaining more animals likewise had to be weighed against costs. As we saw, in coarse feed alone, a work animal was maintained at the cost of the secondary produce (stalks, leaves, chaff, bran) of from 7.5 to 20 mu of foodgrain, material that would otherwise be used for fuel. The animal produced in return a relatively meager amount of fertilizer, sufficient for three to four mu of cropped area. No farmer could afford to maintain a work animal principally for its fertilizer contribution; its work contribution had to be the paramount consideration.

Of our villages, Macun made the greatest use of animals. The managerial farmer in this village used 4.1 donkey days per cultivated mu, and the family farmers averaged an even higher 4.6 days. The greater reliance on farm animals in this village, relative to Michang, was due in part to a somewhat longer growing season that favored double-cropping (see Tables 8.2 and 8.4), and in part to the good drainage in this piedmont plain area, which permitted a highly developed well-irrigation system. Macun had fully 185 wells capable of irrigating 20 mu each. (The village had a total cultivated area of 4,209.8 mu.) These two features created both the need for and the means to support numerous farm animals (6 oxen, 81 mules, and 4 donkeys in a village of 308 households; MT, Hokushi keizai chōsajo 1940d: 87–90 and Table 49).

The top limit of draft-animal maintenance appears closely correlated with the cropped area. It certainly made good economic sense to put the foodgrain stalks and leaves (beyond the household's fuel needs) to use as fodder. On the other hand, a farm that chose to maintain animals beyond the level of its own ability to produce fodder would have to purchase at least some feed. This meant increased marginal costs at the same time that marginal benefits declined. The usual "equilibrium" level that resulted from these considerations appears to have fallen in the range of one donkey equivalent for 20 to 50 mu of cultivated land, as we have seen in Table 8.4.

These economic considerations applied equally to managerial farms and family farms. For the heaviest of the farmwork—plowing—peasants sometimes had to use each other's animals to form an adequate team. The poor often split the costs of buying and maintaining a donkey among several households (so that sometimes each owned only the proverbial one leg of a draft animal). In Dabeiguan, for example, most of the households farming less than 15 mu owned a fraction of a donkey, usually one-half or one-third. In one case (household 71, a year-laborer who farmed 8.5 mu), the share was one-sixth (MT, Kitō 1937a: Table 9). But except for the inevitable inefficiencies that accompanied animal sharing, managerial and family farms employed the same methods of plowing, planting, and cultivating, with the same requirements for animal power, and made the same kinds of cost-benefit calculations.

Adachi's singular emphasis on the use of draft animals clearly exaggerates the contribution they made as a source of fertilizer. Draft animals, as we have seen, were maintained at a ratio of one donkey equivalent to 20 to 50 mu of cultivated area, but one donkey supplied only enough fertilizer for three mu of land, in the amounts used in unirrigated villages like Shajing and Lujiazhai. In other words, a donkey supplied power for seven to 17 times the amount of land that its excrement fertilized. At such a ratio, even if a farm had maintained several times the average number of animals, it would still have fallen well short of its fertilizer needs.

Ecological and historical constraints precluded reliance on grazing (as opposed to crop-consuming and scavenging) animals for fertilizer. The proportion of lowland plains in the total Chinese land mass was a low 10 percent, compared with better than 50 percent in Western Europe and the United States (Chen Ping 1979). The short frost-free season of the Hebei–northwest Shandong plain (six to seven and a half months a year) was an additional limiting factor on the development of a livestock industry. Most of all, high population density precluded the luxury of devoting large land spaces to animal husbandry, when the same land under foodgrains could support several times more people.

Under China's crops-only agrarian regime, the main source of animal fertilizer was the hog, not the draft animal. As Chinese villagers point out, the hog is the king of fertilizer production, both in terms of quantity and in terms of quality. A Shajing or Lujiazhai villager fortunate enough to own one got 9,000 catties of compost a year, capable of fertilizing five mu of land—and of a higher grade than the 7,200 catties from a horse, mule, or ox, or the 5,400 catties from a donkey (MT, Tenshin jimusho chōsaka 1936a: 103; Shajing interviews, Nov. 1980).

But as with all else in the agrarian economy, the decisions on whether or not to keep hogs, and how many, were determined by careful calculations of costs and benefits. In the 1930's and 1940's most Shajing households routinely raised one hog for market. About 20 households had none; a few raised two. Asked why he did not raise more, the managerial farmer Zhang Rui observed that "it did not pay." That is to say, even counting the benefits of fertilizer, the market prices were not high enough relative to feed costs to make the enterprise worthwhile. In Xiaojie village, for example, the Mantetsu investigators estimated that one hog alone consumed 336 catties of black soybeans and 840 catties of chaff a year (MT, Tenshin jimusho chōsaka 1936b: 121). In general, hog raising appears to have paid off only so long as the feed could be supplied on the farm itself; it did not pay to purchase feed.

## THE QING PERIOD

We are now ready to look backward at animal use during the Qing period and to examine more closely the evidence adduced by Adachi and Jing and Luo. The supporting data for Jing and Luo's case that the farms of managerial landlords were partly "capitalist" farms and were distinctive for their superior productivity come from oral history testimony collected in the 1950's about levels of productivity in the 1890's. The data center around three "model" farms, all from the piedmont plain area of northern Shandong. The data on one of these, that of the Li lineage (Taihetang Li) of Dongfanliu village in Zhangqiu county, are quite detailed (Jing & Luo 1959: 56–57, 138). Jing and Luo also collected testimony for a broader group of 41 villages, but these data are rough and ambiguous (*ibid.*, pp. 138–41). It is the Li material that is the heart of their case.

As for Adachi, he is able to show, on the basis of a number of agricultural treatises, that the farms of North and Northwest China quite commonly used teams of four oxen for plowing in the Ming–Qing period. He also shows that much attention was paid to the accumulation of the fertilizer from these animals (Adachi 1981: 539–42). As one of his three examples of large managerial farms, he points to a large farm of the Daoguang period (1821–50) in Sanyuan, Shaanxi, which used long-term workers and planted alfalfa as animal feed. But the source (Yang Xiuyuan, *Nongyan zhushi*) provides no details on the number of mu cultivated, the number of farm animals and laborers used, or the crop yields attained. The second of Adachi's examples is actually an eighteenth-century semi-leasing semi-managerial estate in Rizhao county, in southeastern Shandong, near the coast. The tenant-workers (*lihu*) on this estate had some semblance of tenants' rights: they had separate responsibility for different plots and could hire out to others as day-laborers. But they also worked under the close supervision and at the will of the estate owner. They were called together the night before a major task such as hoeing, and given instructions by the estate owner. The relations on this estate appear to have been transitional from a managerial to a leasing estate. But once again, Adachi's source (Ding Yizeng, *Xi shi-liang nongpu bianlan*; 1755) provides no specifics on size of farm, animal use, or productivity. Like Jing and Luo's, his case in fact turns mainly on the example of the Li lineage of Zhangqiu county, Shandong, in the 1890's. It is the one and only example that provides specific information on the scale of farming, the extent of animal use, the degree of fertilizer application, and productivity.

By Jing and Luo's account, the large Li lineage-operated managerial estate of 472 mu, worked by 13 year-laborers, three to five month-laborers (*yuegong*), and 20 to 40 day-laborers hired as needed, had 17 draft animals: nine oxen, four mules, and four donkeys. In addition, it maintained 40 hogs and 100 sheep. In consequence of this combined animal-raising and farming operation, according to Jing and Luo (1959: 54–56), the Lis were able to use 4,000 to 8,000 catties of compost fertilizer per mu, compared with only 1,200 to 4,000 catties on the small farms.

I believe the information on farm animals on the Li farm is precise and credible. It also makes sense in terms of the analysis I presented above about the nature of draft-animal use and hog raising in this area. In donkey equivalents, the farm had 25.5 animals, one for every 18.5 mu. Given that this piedmont plain area was comparable in irrigation and cropping frequency to Macun village, the 1930's example we looked at earlier, the 18.5 mu figure is reasonable. (Macun, it will be recalled, farmed 21.6 mu with each donkey equivalent.) The Lis probably used four to five days of animal power on each cultivated mu, as did the managerial and family farms of Macun in the 1930's.

The numbers on the hogs and sheep likewise seem plausible. On the first, take the example of Lujiazhai village: here managerial farmer 32 raised 11 hogs, or one for each 9.1 mu, and managerial farmer 33 raised 10 hogs, or one for each 10.5 mu. Compared with a village average of 23.6, this looks like a high ratio of hogs to farm area. But many of the poor villagers here had no hogs. If we eliminate those households and compare the managerial farmers with only the middle and rich peasants (those owning more than 15 mu in this case), we find an almost identical ratio of farm area to number of hogs: 9.8 mu per hog (MT, Tenshin jimusho chōsaka 1936a: 72–

82, 116–19). The Lis' estate raised one hog for every 11.8 mu of farmland.

There is nothing questionable about the size of the Lis' sheep flock. In Hebei–northwest Shandong sheep or goat raising appears to have been quite common in the foothill areas, where the animals could graze on the sparse stands of grass and shrubs. The managerial farmer Zhang Cailou of Dabeiguan, for example, had 58 sheep in 1936. This was not an important source of fertilizer, however. In Lujiazhai, the Japanese investigators reported that one sheep or goat produced waste enough for only about 1,800 catties of compost, just enough for one mu of crops.

I am suspicious, however, of the figures on the amount of fertilizer the Lis' animals produced: 5,000+ carts of 400 catties each of compost fertilizer a year (Jing & Luo 1959: 56). Applying the Japanese researchers' figures to the Li animals yields only 655,200 catties of compost, a far cry from the 2,000,000 figure, and 4,000 to 8,000 catties per mu, that Jing and Luo suggest.

My most important disagreement with Jing and Luo and Adachi, however, has to do with their claim for a distinctly higher productivity on the large managerial farms. As I have shown, managerial and family farms maintained essentially the same ratio of draft animals to cultivated area, because the cost-benefit considerations that determined their use were the same for both of them. Moreover, fertilizer from draft animals was in any case only a relatively small part of the total fertilizer used by both. That is one important reason why productivity on the two types of farms was essentially the same, as shown by the Mantetsu field research data. Adachi's logical chain—that large farms used more draft animals, hence had more fertilizer, hence obtained higher yields—simply does not hold up against the field research evidence and the logic of animal use in the agrarian system of the North China plain.

It is possible that under the frontier-like conditions of the depopulated parts of North China in the thirteenth and fourteenth centuries, and the seventeenth century, the ratio of animal power use to human power was considerably higher than in the twentieth century. That higher use of animal power might have stemmed from the comparatively large surpluses obtained under a more favorable land-to-population ratio, or it might have stemmed from the need for greater power to plow uncultivated land, or both. But we will need to have more evidence to speculate any further. In any case, I suspect that the different cost-to-benefit calculations of a frontier environment would have applied equally to large farms and to small ones.

For all this, Adachi, in particular, seems to me to have made an important contribution to our understanding of North China's agriculture by directing our attention to its requirement for animal power. He has shown us that the four-oxen plowing team dates back at least to the Yuan:

> According to the farming customs of the north, . . . the land being flat and unirrigated dry land, one plow is always pulled by two, three, or four oxen and wielded by one man. . . . In the south, plowing is of wet earth in irrigated fields, and the paddies are not on the same level and come in different widths and sizes; one plow is pulled by one ox. . . . This is suited to the different land conditions of the south. (*Wang Zhen nongshu* [1313], juan 2, "Kengeng," cited in Adachi 1981: 542)

The practice was common enough, moreover, for the seventeenth-century *Chibei outan* by Wang Shizhen to note that "north of the Yangzi and the Huai, a team of four oxen is called a 'set.'"

Yet these passages must be interpreted as applying to farming on the North China plain in general, not to large managerial farms alone. Adachi's own sources say as much. The Dengzhou prefecture gazetteer for the Shunzhi period (1644–61), for example, observed that "the poor team up in as many as three or four households to make up a [four-oxen] set" (Adachi 1981: 542). Such animal use did not alter the fundamental character of agriculture on the North China plain, whether on managerial or family farms: it was intensive farming based principally on human labor. Under that agrarian regime, the managerial farms did not differ significantly from the family farms in animal use or land productivity.

# CHAPTER 9

# Managerial Farming and Family Farming: Labor Use

If managerial and family farms did not differ in the use of technology, land, or "capital investment" (in animal power and fertilizer), did they differ at all in labor use? This chapter will show, first of all, that the managerial farms had a higher level of output per labor day than the family farms. Though their yields were much the same as those of the family farms, they were able to attain that level of output with substantially less labor input.

How are we to explain this difference in labor productivity between the two kinds of farms? I shall show that the most obvious explanation, that the managerial farms enjoyed certain economies because the farming could be done by work teams, is not in fact a satisfactory one, for the simple reason that family farms grouped together to form the same kinds of teams.

The explanation lies instead in the different ways in which the two kinds of farms responded to land scarcity and the presence of surplus labor. The managerial farms, operated with hired labor and oriented toward profits, did not tolerate excess labor, whereas family farms often had no other choice. Those peasants whose farms were undersized relative to their household labor supply, either because of population pressure or because of low economic position, or both, had to tolerate the existence of surplus labor on their farms.

Under those conditions, many of the farms responded by involuting—by applying more labor than was optimally necessary, at the cost of sharply diminished marginal returns, and at the cost of a certain unavoidable slackening of effort as a result of diminished marginal incentives. Poor peasant family farms demonstrate this pattern most clearly, both in the sense of excessive labor input per crop and in the sense of excessive reliance on a single cash crop.

But involution alone cannot explain the paradox that family farms put in more labor per unit of land than the managerial farms without any gain in yields. To complete the picture, we need to see that involution was only one of two main ways in which poor peasant farms responded to land scarcity. Many poor peasants found themselves compelled to hire out in the busy periods, at the cost of inadequate or untimely work on their own small farms in those crucial periods. Others lacked the requisite capital or quality of land to cultivate any cash crops at all. Thus poor peasant farms tended to deviate in both directions from the optimal patterns of cropping and of labor input, rather than only in the direction of involution. Since output dropped off more sharply at less-than-optimal levels of labor input than it increased at above-optimal levels, the lower output of poor peasants who did not put in enough labor could only be compensated for by the greater labor time of those who put in more than enough labor. As a group, then, poor peasants attained yields comparable to managerial farms only at the cost of more labor time.

The differential labor productivity of the two types of farms tells us something about certain basic characteristics of each. The managerial farms' higher labor productivity shows that their organizational logic permitted them to avoid the underemployment that characterized the family farms. But they remained tied to the small-peasant economy in technology, land use, and capital investment. The deviation of poor peasant farms from optimal cropping patterns reveals the two-sided way in which subsistence pressures related to commercialization: those pressures could propel as well as obstruct commercialization. The substantivist view of family farms as oriented above all toward subsistence tells only part of the story, for that orientation could drive poor peasant farms to a risky concentration on cash crops. Likewise, the formalist view of family farms as oriented above all toward entrepreneurial profit making tells only part of the story, mainly that of the managerial and rich peasant farms. Commercialization, in fact, was propelled by both subsistence-oriented poor family farms and profit-oriented managerial farms.

### THE CONTRAST IN LABOR PRODUCTIVITY

Table 9.1 shows the number of mu farmed by each adult male on the managerial farms of five villages compared with the village averages. Considering all the variations in local conditions, the pattern that emerges is surprisingly consistent: each adult male on the larger farms typically worked more mu than the average village farmworker. The difference was substantial, varying (with one exception) from 40 percent to 100 percent or more.

Once again, these data confirm John Lossing Buck's findings. In both of his surveys he found a similarly consistent and significant difference in the ratio of workers to farm area on large and small farms: an adult male laborer on a large farm cultivated two to two and a half times as much crop area as an adult male on a small farm (Buck 1930: 126, 129; 1937a: 283, 287; 1937b: 291, 302). Another 1937 study, of 4,312 farms in Jiaxing county in Anhui province, similarly found that on farms larger than 50 mu, a single laborer cultivated an average of 17.30 mu, compared with only 12.97 on farms of 20–50 mu and 8.28 on farms of less than 20 mu (Institute of Pacific Relations 1938: 77–78).

TABLE 9.1

Cultivated Land per Adult Male Farmworker on Managerial Farms in Five Hebei and Shandong Villages, 1930's–1940's

(Land in mu)

| Managerial farmer | Number of workers | | | Cultivated land per worker |
|---|---|---|---|---|
| | Household labor[a] | Hired[b] | Total | |
| Dabeiguan (1936) | | | | *16.0* |
| Zhang Cailou | 4.2 | 5.2 | 9.4 | 22.5 |
| Zhang Chonglou | 3.3 | 4.1 | 7.4 | 22.5 |
| Zhang Deyuan | 2.2 | 2.0 | 4.2 | 29.5 |
| Lujiazhai (1936)[c] | | | | *9.1* |
| Household 32 | 3.0 | 3.0 | 6.0 | 16.7 |
| Household 33 | 1.0 | 5.0 | 6.0 | 17.5 |
| Macun (1939)[d] | | | | *14.8* |
| Household 1 | 1.0 | 3.0 | 4.0 | 28.8 |
| Michang (1936) | | | | *12.3* |
| Dong Dezhai | 7.7 | 6.0 | 13.7 | 13.3 |
| Dong Tianwang | 2.0 | 4.0 | 6.0 | 20.0 |
| Dong Jizhong | 2.3 | 4.0 | 6.3 | 17.0 |
| Qizhai (1941) | | | | *17.7* |
| Household 111 | 1.0 | 3.0 | 4.0 | 41.3 |
| Household 112 | 1.0 | 2.0 | 3.0 | 34.0 |

SOURCES: *Dabeiguan, Michang,* MT, Kitō 1937a: Table 4, 1937b: Table 4; *Lujiazhai,* MT, Tenshin jimusho chōsaka 1936a: 67–71, 91–96; *Macun,* MT, Hokushi keizai chōsajo 1939: Tables 1, 3; *Qizhai,* MT, Kita Shina 1943b: Appendix Table 1.

NOTE: Village averages in italic.

[a]The figures for Dabeiguan and Michang take into account the work capacity of different age groups on the following formula: ages 13–14 = 0.2; 15–17 = 0.5; 18–19 = 0.8; 20–55 = 1.0; 56–60 = 0.5; over 61 = 0.2.

[b]The figures for Dabeiguan and Michang include the number of days of day-labor hired, computed as fractions of 200 days a year.

[c]The third managerial farmer shown in Tables 4.1 and A.2 was not interviewed in depth; hence this information is not available for that household.

[d]Only one of the four managerial farmers was interviewed in depth on this subject.

TABLE 9.2

Labor and Income per Mu by Household Type, Michang, 1937

| Household type and number | Farm size (mu) | Number of labor days per mu | Gross farm income per mu (yuan) | Gross farm income per labor day (yuan) |
|---|---|---|---|---|
| Managerial farmer | | | | |
| Household 1 | 133 | 10.8 | $16.5 | $1.53 |
| Household 2 | 125 | 11.1 | 15.3 | 1.38 |
| Average | 129 | 11.0 | $15.9 | $1.46 |
| Rich peasant | | | | |
| Household 3 | 65 | 13.5 | $15.8 | $1.17 |
| Household 5 | 60 | 15.5 | 18.6 | 1.20 |
| Household 6 | 47 | 20.9 | 19.4 | 0.93 |
| Average | 57 | 16.6 | $17.9 | $1.10 |
| Middle peasant | | | | |
| Household 4 | 62 | 16.9 | $12.7 | $0.75 |
| Household 7 | 17 | 16.2 | 15.0 | 0.93 |
| Household 8 | 34 | 14.7 | 15.1 | 1.03 |
| Household 9 | 32 | 19.5 | 10.4 | 0.53 |
| Average | 36 | 16.8 | $13.3 | $0.81 |
| Poor peasant | | | | |
| Household 10 | 13 | 28.3 | $18.0 | $0.64 |
| Household 11 | 21 | 9.9 | 4.9 | 0.50 |
| Household 12 | 15 | 16.9 | 13.0 | 0.70 |
| Household 13 | 10 | 21.2 | 11.0 | 0.52 |
| Household 14 | 6 | 20.3 | 14.8 | 0.73 |
| Average | 13 | 19.3 | $12.3 | $0.62 |

SOURCE: MT, Hokushi jimukyoku chōsabu 1938–41, 1: Tables 3, 13, 40.

NOTE: The peasant households are defined by the standards used in the Land Reform: rich peasants, those hiring more labor than their families put in; middle peasants, those who did most of the farmwork themselves; poor peasants, those who hired out to supplement the income from their farms, usually rented.

The detailed data on Michang village permit us to decompose the unit "farming adult male" into the more precise unit of labor days, and to compare the incomes per labor day for managerial farms and the different categories of family farms. Table 9.2 shows that the managerial farms were typically able to cultivate each mu with substantially fewer labor days than the smaller farms, without suffering any loss in average farm output. As a result, each labor day on the managerial farms accounted for average farm incomes substantially higher than those on the smaller farms.

Part of these differences can be explained by the fact that peasant operators of family farms tended to work fewer days a year on the farm than the hired farm laborer, so that the term "adult male farmworker" needs to be more closely defined. In Jiaxing, for example, the hired laborers of the large farms were employed an average of just under 200 days a year, compared with 153 days spent on the 20–50 mu farms, and 107 days on family farms of less than 20 mu. Buck likewise found just about twice as many labor days a year being spent on large farms as on the small ones. In Michang, the nine year-laborers employed on the two managerial farms worked an average of 252 days in 1937 (putting in only a few days in the first month, moving up to 10 to 20 days in months two and three, to an average of 24 days in months four–six, and finally to a full workload of 29–30 days in the next four busy months; the workload was reduced to less than 20 days in the eleventh month, and slacked off to four or five days in the last one.) This compared with an average of about 180 days a year for the middle peasant adult male (MT, Kitō 1937b: Tables 1, 40).*

The disparity of work "years" helps to explain why the hired year-laborers farmed more cultivated land on average, generally in the range of 15 to 30+ mu per worker, as opposed to about 10 to 17 mu on the small farms. But it cannot explain why, on the large farms, each mu of land could be farmed with fewer days of labor: about 11 days, as opposed to an average of 16 to 19 days, as shown in Table 9.2.†

### HIGHER EFFICIENCY OF TEAM-FARMING ON THE MANAGERIAL FARMS?

To explain this difference, I had speculated that there might have been certain advantages in using four- to eight-man teams for working a farm of a scale of 100 to 200 mu. Perhaps several men working together could more quickly accomplish a job than the same number of men working alone. This is one argument made in favor of collectivized farming, and it could explain why the larger farms required fewer labor days per mu to attain the same yields as the smaller farms.

Here I must call first on my extended conversations on this sub-

---

*As Peter Schran has shown (1969: Chap. 3), the expansion of agricultural production in the 1950's was helped mightily by increasing the average number of days peasants worked each year: from 119 in 1950 to 121 in 1955, 159.5 in 1957, and 189 in 1959 (see also Gurley 1976: 244).

†Yoshida 1975 and Kawachi 1963, 1964, explain the difference only in terms of the number of labor days worked by laborers on the two types of farms. But as I hope to show in what follows, such a view misses a crucial difference in labor use between the managerial farm operating under an optimal combination of land with labor and a family farm cultivating less than what its labor can optimally farm.

ject (in April and November, 1980) with six older peasants of Shajing village: eighty-year-old Zhang Rui, former managerial farmer and village head; fifty-four-year-old Zhang Linbing, Zhang Rui's year-laborer for three years from 1944 to 1946 and now brigade head of the village; seventy-year-old Li Guangzhi, former middle peasant with 27 mu of land (after the division of the family's property in the early 1940's); sixty-two-year-old Li Xiufang, another middle peasant who, with his brother, had owned 49.5 mu that they farmed with the help of a year-laborer; sixty-four-year-old Zhang Shoujun, a poor peasant who had rented 20 mu at the time of the Mantetsu investigation; and seventy-four-year-old Li Guangtai, who had worked as an apprentice in a noodle shop on the outskirts of Beijing and only returned to the village in 1944.

The best example of the advantages of teamwork, it seemed to me, would be found in the planting team: where four men were used, the top man (*da datou*) generally wielded the plow, a task that required the most experience and control; the others followed, planting the seed, spreading the fertilizer, and filling in the furrow. To my surprise, the Shajing villagers pointed out that this practice was standard among all village households. Friends or relatives pooled their labor, implements, and farm animals to reach the required level of equipment and manpower for the plowing-planting team (or *datao*). I have since confirmed this fact with other village survey material: Japanese field investigators reported the practice in Qizhai in northwest Shandong and Lujiazhai in northwestern Hebei, for example.

In that case, I wondered, could the difference in labor productivity between the managerial and the family farms be due to economies of scale in other kinds of farmwork? In the transport and application of fertilizer, for example, to which Jing and Luo referred? In team-hoeing or team-harvesting?

Though the Shajing peasants had no pat answer to offer, it was clear after several days of discussions that this particular hypothesis simply made no sense to them. As Zhang Linbing, the former year-laborer and current brigade head, pointed out, there was an unwritten but generally agreed-on set of expectations, known to all, of what a year-laborer was to accomplish in a day (called the *changgong huopu*, lit., work standards for year-laborers). According to these expectations, a four-man team with one mule or two donkeys was to plant ten mu a day; a laborer working alone was to hoe four mu a day, or to harvest two mu of sorghum, four mu of maize, or one mu of wheat a day. On each of these I asked the former middle peasant Li Guangzhi whether he was able to manage the same amount of work; on each he assured me that he was certainly able to do every bit as much as the best of the year-laborers. All the villagers agreed that a good man was able to accomplish as much on his own farm as a year-laborer.

These discussions suggested to me that team-farming with four to eight men had no intrinsic advantages over individualized family farming, so long as the small farmers could join forces when team-work was required. Under the technological constraints of traditional agriculture, the advantages of collectivized farming perhaps lie rather in cooperative labor on large-scale projects—such as re-grading and providing drainage for easily waterlogged land, dredging a river, and other kinds of water-control measures—that were beyond the capabilities of a managerial farm no less than a family farm.

POOR PEASANT DEVIATIONS FROM OPTIMAL PATTERNS

If a greater efficiency in team-farming cannot explain the managerial farms' superior labor productivity, might the explanation then lie in the small farms' overuse of labor? Whereas the managerial farms would stop further input of labor when the marginal product of labor sank below prevailing wages, some family farms were driven by the dictates of subsistence to increase labor input until the marginal product of labor approached zero (Georgescu-Roegen 1960; Chayanov 1966a: 7; 1966b: 113–36). In such circumstances we would expect the average product of labor to be higher on the managerial farms than on the smaller farms, hence the difference in the figures on unit labor productivity.

This line of analysis, however, immediately runs into a problem: these small farms should show higher yields than the larger farms, albeit not to the same proportion as the added labor input. Yet, as we saw in the preceding chapter, their average yields per crop or per unit of cultivated area did not differ significantly from those of the large farms.

To attempt to explain this paradox of apparently higher labor intensity but no higher land productivity on the small farms, I grouped the farms of Xiaojie and Michang into categories roughly approximating the economic characterizations we have been using to this point: less than 10 mu, poor peasants; 10–29 mu, middle peasants; 30–99 mu, rich peasants; 100 mu or more, managerial farmers. This breakdown is shown in Table 9.3. The proportion of land that each of these groups of farms placed under cotton and their cotton yields are also shown to test for possible correlations with farm size.

As can be seen, this finer breakdown of family farms does not alter the picture projected by the earlier comparisons between village averages and the managerial farms: there is no consistent pattern of either higher intensity in land use or higher yields per crop.

A further disaggregation of these figures, however, reveals a significant pattern. Table 9.4 shows the number of farms in each group that placed below-normal (less than 10 percent), normal (11–40 percent), above-normal (41–70 percent), and extremely high (71–100 percent) proportions of their cropped areas under cotton. As we see, both of the managerial farmers of Xiaojie chose to give about one-quarter of their cropped area to cotton, or very near to the village average; and more than half the rich peasants (54.1 percent) also cultivated cotton to an extent that fell within the normal range. But this was true of only 34 percent of the middle peasants and a mere 12 percent of the poor peasants. Two-thirds of the poor peasant farms grew no cotton at all, but 12 percent put most or all of their land under cotton. A similar pattern, though less graphic, obtained in Michang (MT, Kitō 1937b: Table 11).

The same contrast emerges with respect to cotton yields. Table 9.5 shows the number of Xiaojie farms in each group that attained yields at, below, or above the normal range of 81–100 catties per mu. Once again, both of the managerial farms and most of the rich peasant farms (72 percent) fell in the normal range, compared with less than half of the middle and poor peasant farms.

These data suggest the following hypothesis: the managerial and rich peasant farms generally adopted diversified cropping portfolios that spread their risk, rather than chancing disaster with exclusive dependence on a single crop. They also spaced out farmwork and staggered the rush periods with such diversified cropping portfolios, so that the most intense demands for labor would not all fall at the same time. In addition, they invested only normal amounts of labor in a given crop, for normal yields, and avoided the sharply diminished marginal returns that came with over-intensive labor input.

Poorer peasants, by contrast, were often compelled by circumstances to opt for less well-balanced cropping patterns. Some of them tended to rely heavily or exclusively on a single crop, at the cost of greater risks and unbalanced work schedules. Such peasants were being pressured by the dictates of subsistence to "gamble," one might say, for the possibility of higher short-term returns. Milton Friedman's classic analysis of consumer choice under conditions of risk well "rationalizes" such behavior: suppose a balanced and safer portfolio could bring an "actuarial return" (considering probabili-

TABLE 9.3

Cotton Cultivation and Yields on Different-Sized Farms in Two Hebei
Villages, 1935–1936

| Farm size (mu) | Number of households | Total cropped area (mu) | Cropped area under cotton | | Total yield (catties) | Yield per mu (catties) |
|---|---|---|---|---|---|---|
| | | | Total area (mu) | Percent of total cropped area | | |
| Michang (1936) | | | | | | |
| 100 or more | 4 | 537.2 | 176.3 | 32.8% | 23,782.9 | 134.9 |
| 30–99.9 | 17 | 833.1 | 241.8 | 29.0 | 31,893.4 | 131.9 |
| 10–29.9 | 53 | 992.7 | 291.2 | 29.3 | 39,359.0 | 135.2 |
| 0.1–9.9 | 21 | 142.8 | 36.8 | 25.8 | 5,114.8 | 139.0 |
| Xiaoje (1935) | | | | | | |
| 100 or more | 2 | 378.0 | 97.0 | 25.7% | 8,900.0 | 91.8 |
| 30–99.9 | 24 | 1,284.0 | 375.0 | 29.2 | 35,859.0 | 95.6 |
| 10–29.9 | 47 | 767.5 | 219.0 | 28.5 | 18,440.0 | 84.2 |
| 0.1–9.9 | 58 | 256.5 | 58.5 | 22.8 | 5,340.0 | 91.3 |

SOURCES: Michang, MT, Kitō 1937b: Table 11; Xiaojie, MT, Tenshin jimusho chōsaka 1936b: 46–52, 109–16.

TABLE 9.4

Extent of Cotton Cropping by Farm Size, Xiaojie, Hebei, 1935

| Farm size (mu) | No. of households | No. of cotton-growing households | Proportion of cropped area under cotton | | | |
|---|---|---|---|---|---|---|
| | | | Low (1–10%) | Normal (11–40%) | High (41–70%) | Very high (71–100%) |
| 100 or more | 2 | 2 | — | 2 | — | — |
| 30–99.9 | 24[a] | 18 | — | 13 | 3 | 2 |
| 10–29.9 | 47 | 34 | 3 | 16 | 13 | 2 |
| 0.1–9.9 | 58 | 19 | — | 7 | 5 | 7 |

SOURCE: See Table 9.3.
[a]No data on four households.

TABLE 9.5

Cotton Yields by Farm Size, Xiaojie, 1935

| Farm size (mu) | No. of cotton-growing households | Yield per mu (catties) | | | |
|---|---|---|---|---|---|
| | | Low (40–80) | Normal (81–100) | High (101–20) | Very high (121–30) |
| 100 or more | 2 | — | 2 | — | — |
| 30–99.9 | 18 | 3 | 13 | 1 | 1 |
| 10–29.9 | 34 | 15 | 14 | 5 | — |
| 0.1–9.9 | 19 | 5 | 9 | 4 | 1 |

SOURCE: See Table 9.3.

ties) of 70 yuan a year,* compared with 60 yuan for an unbalanced one. The peasant who opted nonetheless for an unbalanced portfolio can be seen as paying a 10-yuan premium a year in order to "gamble" for the possibility of a higher return in any given year (Friedman & Savage 1948).†

Let us take Household 12 in Michang in 1937 as an illustration of a peasant household pressured by the dictates of subsistence to adopt a high-risk cropping portfolio (see Table 9.2). The two men on this farm had only 15 mu to cultivate, or less than half as much land as they could farm. They apparently did not have the option of other employment. What they did was to push land use to the utmost intensity by placing all 15 mu under cotton. This single-crop portfolio gave them the fullest possible employment, as well as the possibility of the highest returns on their farm in any given year. But it was at the cost of higher risks, an unbalanced work schedule, and probably a lower average return over a period of years.

Another pattern was where poor peasants intensified labor input on a given crop to abnormal levels, substantially higher than the already highly intensive agrarian regime of the managerial farms, for sharply diminished marginal returns. Household 10 in Michang is a good illustration: this household invested fully 28.3 days of labor per cropped mu (compared with the managerial farmers' 11 days). The greater labor input accounted for the household's ability to obtain a higher gross income per mu (18 yuan as opposed to 15.9 yuan). But the gain was hardly commensurate with the 150 percent more labor that the household had to put in. The household chose nonetheless to put in that labor, presumably because it had surplus labor and because household consumption needs dictated that it increase its use of labor to that extent. Once again, such behavior can be readily "rationalized" in the terms of conventional microeconomic theory: the presence of surplus labor on the farm meant that there was little or no "opportunity cost" to the marginal inputs of labor. And the poverty of the household meant that the increased yields held very high "marginal utility" for this household struggling to subsist.

Other poor peasant farms were forced to deviate in the opposite direction from "normal" patterns. Some poor peasants could not gain access to the high-quality land that cotton required, or they

---

*A 40% chance for a return of 100 yuan and a 60% chance for a return of 50 yuan in any one year, for example, would make for an "actuarial return" of 40% x 100 yuan + 60% x 50 yuan, or 70 yuan, for that year.

†Just as a peasant who opted for the lower average return of a balanced portfolio can be seen as paying a ten-yuan premium for "insurance" on a safer return.

found the costs of fertilizer or draft animals prohibitive, or they had to hire out during the busy cotton period and therefore could not cultivate cotton themselves. Whether for reasons of land, capital, or labor, such poor peasants were unable to turn to cotton to take advantage of the higher returns offered by commercialized agriculture. The 39 poor peasant households in Xiaojie village that did not cultivate cotton illustrate this pattern.

The mixture of both higher and lower than "normal" levels of intensity of cultivation among poor farms helps explain the paradox with which this chapter began. The higher crop yields attained by the small farms that cultivated with greater intensity were offset by the lower yields of those that cultivated with less intensity, to result in an average not substantially different from that of the managerial farms. Since yields increased very little at above-normal levels of intensity of cultivation, but dropped off sharply at below-normal levels, the equality in average yields was obtained through greater labor input by the poorer farms as a group.

### UNDEREMPLOYMENT AND DIMINISHED INCENTIVES ON THE POOR FARMS

The above data carry a further implication. If it is true that the labor use on managerial farms approximates the optimal level under the existing technological and ecological conditions, then it is obvious that most family farms were undersized. My figures on managerial farms in this area suggest that a farmworker could farm 15 to 30+ mu. But according to the Guomindang Land Commission's survey of 1,500,000 households, 68.2 percent of the farm households in Hebei and 77.9 percent in Shandong cultivated less than 20 mu (including both land owned and land rented); moreover, some 40 percent of the households in Hebei and 49.7 percent in Shandong farmed less than 10 mu (Tudiweiyuanhui 1937: 26).

Oral testimony given to Japanese researchers in the 1930's shows that the workday of a year-laborer was pretty well fixed by custom, rather like the "standards of work for year-laborers." He generally began the day at the crack of dawn, putting in an hour of work before breakfast. He got 30 minutes of rest after breakfast, then worked till noon, with one more 20- to 30-minute rest period. After lunch, he got a 30-minute rest and generally did light chores until 3:00 P.M. (On very hot summer days, he would be permitted to nap instead.) He then worked from 3:00 to 7:00, getting two more breaks of 20 minutes each before supper. His only days off were generally the three-day *duanwu* holidays (the third to fifth days of the fifth month) and a ten-day vacation during the summer (KC, 2 : 35, 50–51; 3 : 195). It was a hard schedule by any standard.

The obvious question is whether peasants working on undersized farms drove themselves to this same level of effort. My conversations with the Shajing villagers suggest that they probably did not. The middle peasant Li Guangzhi recalls that he used to slack off quite a lot on his family's farm. He especially liked to go to market or to the local temple to join the crowd and watch the action. This was when his family had a total of five adult males (father, three sons, and a nephew) to cultivate a farm of 84 mu, or about 17 mu per man. Later, however, when the family property was divided up, each son received 27 mu (the nephew got only a small parcel). It was only then that Li worked as hard as he could. He recalls proudly that he was able to cultivate all 27 mu with only 20 days of hired labor a year and obtained a yield that was second to none in the village.

The middle peasant Li Xiufang similarly recalls that each male adult in his family farmed an average of 16.5 mu. Asked why he did not reach the scale of over 20 mu that each of the managerial farmer Zhang Rui's year-laborers could work, Li responded: "Because we were lazy. We liked to go to the market and watch the bustle and excitement [*kan renao*]."

Such testimony suggests that a peasant tended to put out significantly less effort when the farm was undersized. The Shajing villages of course did not furnish a theoretical explanation for this phenomenon, but I would hypothesize that inputs of labor above the normal ranges entailed both sharply diminished returns and sharply increased drudgery, thereby reducing the incentive to work at that level.*

Much confusion has surrounded the question of what overpopulation or underemployment might mean in the rural areas of Third World countries. One old idea is that under conditions of underdevelopment and overpopulation, part of the labor working in agriculture in fact has a "marginal productivity of zero." Theodore Schultz countered this argument by drawing on the example of India before and after the influenza epidemic of 1918–19. That epidemic reduced the working farm labor force by about 8 percent. If part of the pre-epidemic agricultural labor had indeed had "zero value,"

---

*I am of course drawing on Chayanov's classic model (1966) that the level of farming intensity is determined by the equilibrium point between the drudgery involved and the level of satisfaction of consumption needs brought by marginal inputs of labor.

Schultz reasoned, this abrupt decline in the size of the labor force should not marginally affect agricultural production. In fact, of course, the decline did have an adverse effect, reducing the area sown to crops by a measurable coefficient; hence Schultz concluded that the pre-epidemic labor could not have had a marginal productivity of zero (1964: Chap. 4).

Schultz's argument is of course flawed by its presumption that the epidemic affected all households equally, when it in fact probably wiped out some and left others untouched. But even if we allowed for the logical possibility that it might have affected all households equally, removing only the surplus labor in the households, we should still not conclude from Schultz's evidence that there had been no such thing as overpopulation or underemployment. Agricultural work is highly seasonal. A farm with a quarter of its workers idle much of the year might well have to use them to the full in peak periods. Indeed, it might even have to hire day-labor for the busiest days, especially the harvesting-planting rush period in the fall. Clearly, then, if one were to abruptly remove a quarter of the workers, and the supply of short-term day-labor, the farm would be hard hit by a labor shortage during the crucial planting periods, to the detriment of its sown area (and consequently its output). But this does not mean that there had not been underemployment on this farm for most of the year.

How might one measure or quantify such underemployment? If one cannot go by the peak periods alone, or by the slack periods, by what standard should overpopulation be measured? One common method in the past was to use some "average" farm-size figure as representing an adequate subsistence level and an "equilibrium" between the use of labor and other "factors." Farms falling below the figure might then be considered undersized and overpopulated or underemployed. (Kao et al. 1964 sum up some of the earlier literature.)

The difficulty with all such standards is that they do not take account of ecological variations from one locality to the next: a household too large for 15 mu of farmland in Hebei–northwest Shandong could be much too small for the same-sized farm in the rice-growing region of the Pearl River delta. Variations in technological levels pose additional problems for measurement: what is overpopulation for dry farming can easily be underpopulation for irrigated agriculture. The introduction of modern capital inputs further complicates the picture, for such inputs could be labor-saving (as tractors for plowing would be) or labor-intensifying (as the addition of chemical to organic fertilizer for a second application of fertilizer would be).

The advantage of a comparative analysis of managerial and family farming is that it furnishes an empirical standard for measuring optimal and underemployed labor use under the same technological and ecological conditions. This chapter has sought to supply a concrete demonstration of what the combined pressures of overpopulation and underemployment meant for the poor family farms: they were often driven to overintensify labor for diminished marginal returns and diminished marginal incentives or to underuse labor for lack of land, fertilizer, or time. For them, optimizing their chances of survival often meant less than optimal farming patterns. The economy of poor peasants was oriented toward survival, not toward profit making or maximum farm productivity as such.

# CHAPTER 10

# The Underdevelopment of Managerial Farming

It is easy to explain, in retrospect, how managerial agriculture became interlocked with both the small-peasant economy and the sociopolitical order built on that economy. In the absence of substantial breakthroughs in farm productivity, the managerial mode tended to work best at the scale of 100 to 200 mu, as will be seen. Beyond that size, managerial farming no longer paid, and at the same time the landowner found other options open to him. Those consisted chiefly of combining leasing-out with commerce or with education for a degree, both of which offered the possibility of moving into the upper tier of Chinese society, where the returns were of a much higher order than in the lower tier. Managerial agriculture, therefore, tended to return via landlordism to the same small farming from which it arose.

Such an analysis, however, cannot explain fully the underdevelopment of managerial agriculture. Why did the managerial farms of 100 to 200 mu not make innovative investments? What kinds of technological changes and capital investments were possible, and why did the managerial farms not make them? Was there indeed a "high-level equilibrium trap" against innovative investment, as Mark Elvin has suggested?

I shall call on the concrete example of postrevolutionary Shajing village to illustrate the kinds of productive improvements that might have been undertaken, and then return to the question of why such improvements were not made under the managerial agriculture of prerevolutionary China. Labor-saving technological innovations were indeed obstructed by population pressure. But the failure to draw on other kinds of capital inputs that were compatible with high labor intensity, and indeed even stimulative of a further intensification of labor, cannot be explained by population pressure. I contend that the roots for the underdevelopment of agriculture in this area

TABLE 10.1

Use of Farm Labor by Household Type, Michang, 1937

| Household type and number | Farm size (mu) | Percent of cropped area under cotton | Labor days | | | Percent household labor | Number of year-round workers | | Land worked per worker (mu) |
| | | | Household | Hired | | | Household | Hired | |
| | | | | Day-laborer | Year-laborer | | | | |
|---|---|---|---|---|---|---|---|---|---|
| Managerial farmer | | | | | | | | | |
| Household 1 | 133 | 42% | 149 | 45 | 1,245 | 10.4% | 1 | 5 | 22.2 |
| Household 2 | 125 | 50 | 193 | 176 | 1,022 | 13.9 | 1 | 4 | 25.0 |
| Rich peasant | | | | | | | | | |
| Household 3 | 65 | 51% | 39 | 73 | 763 | 4.5% | — | 4 | 16.3 |
| Household 5 | 60 | 64 | 297 | 75 | 555 | 32.0 | 1 | 3 | 15.0 |
| Household 6 | 47 | 81 | 188 | 81 | 717 | 19.1 | 1 | 2+ | 16.0 |
| Middle peasant | | | | | | | | | |
| Household 4 | 62 | 49% | 705 | 44 | 303 | 67.0% | 4 | 2 | 10.3 |
| Household 7 | 17 | 45 | 229 | 10 | 43 | 81.2 | 1 | 1 | 8.5 |
| Household 8 | 34 | 61 | 348 | — | 152 | 69.6 | 2 | 1 | 11.3 |
| Household 9 | 32 | 50 | 417 | 206 | — | 66.9 | 2 | — | 16.0 |
| Poor peasant | | | | | | | | | |
| Household 10 | 13 | 60% | 239 | 12 | 117 | 64.9% | 1 | 1 | 6.5 |
| Household 11 | 21 | 62 | 184 | 25 | — | 88.0 | 1 | — | 21.0 |
| Household 12 | 15 | 100 | 240 | 13 | — | 94.9 | 2 | — | 7.5 |
| Household 13 | 10 | 50 | 206 | 6 | — | 97.2 | 2 | — | 5.0 |
| Household 14 | 6 | 64 | 71 | 51 | — | 58.2 | — | — | 6.0 |

SOURCE: MT, Hokushi jimukyoku chōsabu 1938–41, I: Tables 1, 3, 40.
NOTE: Discrepancies between this table and Table 9.1 stem from changes between 1936 and 1937.

must finally be sought in an interlocked system comprising the natural environment, population, and the sociopolitical order. To isolate only one of these dimensions is to overlook the crucial interdependent relationships of the ecosystem as a whole.*

## WHY MANAGERIAL FARMS WERE USUALLY OVER 100 MU

In order for the organizational logic of wage labor–based farming to operate, a farm needed to be based mainly on hired labor. We cannot expect family farms using only limited amounts of hired labor to have operated according to a managerial logic. Since a male adult in this area could farm upwards of 15 mu, and since most of the more well-to-do peasant households contained more than one adult male, a farm clearly had to reach a certain minimum size before hired labor would predominate over the family's own labor.

At the same time, an optimal combination of labor with land could obtain only if the hired labor actually worked at the maximum level of effort. That, I suggest, is not something a worker would normally have done voluntarily and without close personal supervision from the employer, which is why most managerial farms were operated under the personal management of the farmer himself.

A farm that met these conditions could be expected to effect substantial savings in labor costs relative to farms on which labor was underemployed. Other things being equal, such farms would attain a higher rate of return after expenses than the other farms.

These expectations are borne out by the detailed statistical material on Michang village. As Table 9.2 showed, the two managerial farmers were able to obtain yields comparable to those of the smaller farms with a strikingly lower use of labor. Table 10.1 shows that these two farms were in fact the only ones to meet the triple qualification of (1) a high proportion of hired labor in the total labor expended on the farm; (2) a land-to-labor ratio that approximated the optimum in this village, thus reflecting the managerial expectation for labor to perform at an optimum; and (3) close personal supervi-

---

*The question of underdevelopment here is of course narrower than the question of underdevelopment in the economy as a whole. But a close look at the obstacles to modernization in agriculture can contribute much to our understanding of the larger question. There can be little doubt that agriculture, though not sufficient in itself to explain either development or underdevelopment, plays a crucial role in the transition to capitalist industrialization. A large surplus from agriculture can contribute powerfully to capital accumulation for industry and to a strong market for industrial goods. An underdeveloped agriculture, on the other hand, poses difficulties for capital accumulation and for the formation of a domestic market.

sion—in this case, Household 1 (Dong Jizhong) put in 149 days a year, and Household 2 (Dong Tianwang) 193 days. The result was the most efficient utilization of labor of any farms in the village: 10 to 11 days per mu, as opposed to 13 to 20 days per mu for the other farms. (The exception here, Household 11, used only 9.9 days of labor per mu, and suffered a drastically lower yield, only 4.9 yuan per mu compared with the 10.9 average for all farms.) The lower output per worker on the smaller farms is readily explained by the phenomena discussed in the preceding chapter: of either excessive labor coupled with slackened effort or too little labor for lack of time.

### WHY MANAGERIAL FARMS WERE USUALLY UNDER 200 MU

Managerial operations like the ones in Michang imposed their own limits on the farm size because the total landholdings were highly fragmented. Take the case of Dong Tianwang: his farm was divided into 17 parcels, or an average of seven mu per parcel (MT, Kitō 1937b: Table 6). On Dong's scale of farming, this fragmentation did not present difficult logistical problems. He could personally oversee the work of his four hired men and move with them from one parcel to the next as a team. However, if his scale of operation were doubled to 250 mu and eight hired workers with no change in the parcel size, he would clearly be faced with some severe problems of management. In planting, for example, his eight men could make up two four-men teams and do about 20 mu a day. If they were to stay together, they would finish a parcel in well under a day, and would then have to waste much time moving on to the next. If they split up and worked separate parcels, they could not all be closely supervised. The problem would be even worse, of course, in hoeing, where each of his eight men could cover about four mu a day.

But what kept these managerial farmers from hiring "foremen" to help them oversee farmwork, we might ask. The difficulty there is that this would have quickly eroded the thin margin of advantage the managerial farm enjoyed over the family farm. If the foreman was a year-laborer himself, he could not be expected always to demand the most of the workers. And if the foreman was someone divorced from production, who might identify more closely with the interests of the managerial farmer, the added costs of his supervisory work would more than eat up the narrow edge of labor savings that the managerial farms enjoyed.

Most managerial farms thus remained under 200 mu. In the sample of 40 farms that I took from the Mantetsu surveys, only three exceeded 200 mu, and even then not by a lot (211, 220, and 226 mu; see Table 4.1). More than two-thirds (69.8 percent) of Jing and Luo's sample of 331 "managerial landlords" in 1890's Shandong, similarly, managed farms of less than 200 mu, even when they owned much more land. The remainder was usually leased out in small parcels.*

MANAGERIAL FARMING VERSUS LEASING LANDLORDISM

For the landowner who held 100 to 200 mu, managerial farming was clearly more attractive than leasing landlordism. A closer look at two examples of how managerial farmers fared against leasing landlords will help to illustrate this point. Let us start once more with the Michang data, with a comparison between the rates of return for the two groups. As shown in Table 10.2, in 1937 the managerial farmer Dong Tianwang netted 1,032 yuan, or an average of 8.26 yuan per mu on his 125-mu farm. The managerial farmer Dong Jizhong netted 1,200 yuan, or 9.02 yuan per mu. At the average land price of 62.5 yuan per mu (the range from low-quality to high-quality land was 45 yuan to 100 yuan per mu), this was an annual return of about 13–14 percent of the land price (although it includes the imputed value of the farmer's household labor). The landlords who leased the 93 mu rented by the households surveyed, on the other hand, received an average rent of only 4.06 yuan per mu. Assuming that these landlords were taxed at the same rate as managerial farmers, 84 cents per mu, they netted only 3.22 yuan per mu, or less than half of the net income of the managerial farmers. It was an annual return on the land of only about 5 percent. This differential is explained in part by the managerial farms' savings in labor costs. In Michang's case, the disparity was still greater because the rental rate for land under cotton was relatively low: 30.9 percent of the crop, as compared with over 50 percent in Sibeichai (MT, Hokushi jimukyoku chōsahu 1938: Tables 3, 29, 32, 33).

A differential of this magnitude would have been difficult to resist for an owner of 100 to 200 mu of land. Table 10.3 shows the sizes of the households of the rich owners of more than 100 mu in six villages. The average works out to 14 members a household, substantially larger than the average of five members for rural China as a

---

*Their smaller sample of 131 managerial landlords, on which they base most of their observations, is skewed in favor of large landowners: in that sample, only 35% of the farms were under 200 mu. Their use of three wealthy lineage estates to illustrate managerial agriculture only skewed their data further. In my calculations, I have assumed that any farm hiring nine or more year-laborers had more than 200 mu.

TABLE 10.2

Net Farm Income of Two Managerial Farmers, Michang, 1937

| Item | Dong Tianwang | | Dong Jizhong | |
|---|---:|---:|---:|---:|
| Farm size (mu) | | 125 | | 133 |
| Gross farm income (yuan) | | $1,915 | | $2,192 |
| Expenses | | | | |
| Wages[a] | $569 | | $550 | |
| Fertilizer | 171 | | 152 | |
| Taxes | 104 | | 113 | |
| Miscellaneous | 39 | 883 | 177 | 992 |
| Net farm income[b] | | $1,032 | | $1,200 |
| Net farm income as percent of gross | | 53.8% | | 54.7% |

SOURCE: MT, Hokushi jimukyoku chōsabu 1938–41, 1: Tables 13, 14.
[a]Includes expenses of laborer's board computed at 22 cent per laborer per day.
[b]Includes the imputed value of the farmer's household labor.

whole (Tudiweiyuanhui 1937: 24). With a household of that size, a leasing landlord would have needed the rental income from 84 mu of land, assuming a rent rate of 50 percent of produce, in order to equal the standard of living of a middle peasant household of five working an average-size farm of 15 mu. And in Michang, with its relatively low rental rates for cotton land, a 14-member leasing household would have needed the income from 135.9 mu to meet that standard. Such a household would have been under great pressure to adopt the managerial mode of farming over the leasing mode.

Bigger landowners, however, were under less pressure to engage in farming themselves in order to make the most out of their land. Many had access to other sources of income, as for example, money-lending and commerce. This was especially true of the more highly commercialized areas.

Sibeichai village, in the heart of Luancheng county in the irrigated and cotton-growing zone of central Hebei, provides one particularly striking example of the alternatives open to the bigger landowner. This was one of the most highly commercialized villages in the North China plain. The villagers had grown cotton at least since the early Qing; by the 1930's cotton accounted for about 40 percent of the cropped area. Society in this area was more highly stratified than in the Michang area, and land concentration was much more highly advanced.

A single big landowner—Wang Zanzhou—dominated the village's economic life. Wang's father had been able to dictate a change in the terms of rent from the earlier sharecropping system to a fixed-rent-in-kind system that worked to his advantage. According to Zanzhou, the fixed rent had been instituted in part to save time and trouble: where his father used to have to go personally to the fields to collect the rent at harvest, the tenants could now deliver the rent to his storehouse in town. At the same time, Wang's father had set the fixed rent at 40 catties of cotton (unginned) per mu, one-half of the best of harvests. According to the villagers, yields of 80 catties were attained only "once or twice in ten years"; the normal yield was 60 catties or so. Over the long haul, therefore, the Wangs were in fact obtaining rents substantially higher than 50 percent of produce, compared with the 30.9 percent in Michang in 1937 (KC, 3: 218, 235, 241). Fixed rents had the further advantage of guaranteeing to

TABLE 10.3

Size of "Rich" Households in Six Hebei and Shandong Villages,
1930's–1940's

(Land in mu)

| Village and household | Household size | Number of adult males | Total land owned |
|---|---|---|---|
| Dabeiguan (1936) | | | |
| Zhang Deyuan | 17 | 3 | 145 |
| Zhang Cailou | 27 | 5 | 243 |
| Zhang Chonglou | 14 | 4 | 218 |
| Shajing (1942) | | | |
| Zhang Wentong | 18 | 3 | 110 |
| Sunjiamiao (1938) | | | |
| Zu Xiaojiang | 16 | ? | 176 |
| Michang (1936) | | | |
| Dong Tianwang | 8 | 3 | 130 |
| Dong Dezhai | 35 | 10 | 157 |
| Dong Jizhong | 9 | 3 | 109 |
| Qianlianggezhuang (1936) | | | |
| Bai Hongyi | 5 | 1 | 179 |
| Bai Boyi | 5 | 1 | 192 |
| Bai Heyi | 2 | 1 | 172 |
| Fu Shizhen | 12 | 4 | 118 |
| Wang Xizhen | 10 | 2 | 104 |
| Dongjiao (1943) | | | |
| Household 2 | 19 | 4 | 105 |
| Household 3 | 14 | 3 | 150 |

SOURCES: *Dabeiguan, Michang, Qianlianggezhuang*, MT, Kitō 1937a: Table 1, Kitō 1937b: Table 5, Kitō 1937c: Tables 1, 2; *Shajing*, KC, 1: Appendix; *Sunjiamiao*, Chūgoku nōson keizai kenkyūjo 1939: Appendix, p. 3; *Dongjiao*, Kahoku sōgō chōsa kenkyūjo 1944a: Appendix table 1.

NOTE: The land shown here is the property owned, as opposed to the land farmed or managed shown in Tables 4.1, 10.1, and 10.2.

the Wangs a certain income regardless of natural or man-made calamities. Sibeichai saw three major disasters in the Republican years:
in 1917 a flood, caused by torrential rains, inundated the village's
fields until the following winter, destroying the entire year's crop; in
1928 grasshoppers ate up the entire millet crop, though the sorghum
and cotton crops survived; and in 1937 the Japanese army imposed
labor drafts that caused a serious labor shortage with the consequent
loss of about one-third of the year's crop (KC, 3:218, 222–23, 237,
307). The Wangs had routinely collected their rents despite these
catastrophes.

Wang Zanzhou, moreover, had taken advantage of the impoverishment caused by these calamities to institute yet another system to
enrich himself. This was the land-pawning (dian) arrangement. Under this system, he lent a villager 60 percent to 70 percent of the
market price of a piece of land and held the title in pawn. This title
enabled him to lease out the land, usually to the man who pawned
it, and collect the customary rent on it in lieu of interest. If the bor-
rower failed to repay his loan within the agreed period (generally
three to five years), then Wang could acquire full title to the land by
paying the balance between the amount of the original loan and the
full purchase price of the land (KC, 3:199, 235, 244, 256, 307–8, 312).

What this system did, in effect, was to raise substantially the rates
of return on Wang's investments. The land-pawning arrangement
gave him the same returns in rent for two-thirds of the purchase
price of the land. He was thus able to raise the effective yield from
his investment from the usual annual rate of 7 percent or so of land
price to fully 10.5 percent. In addition, by holding only pawned title
to the land, he did not have to pay taxes on it, still the burden of the
owner, thereby improving his returns by another 1 percent or so
(KC, 3:35, 37).

Land-pawning was only one part of Wang's network of interlinked
activities. He held a virtual monopoly over moneylending in an entire marketing area that encompassed Sibeichai. On small loans, he
charged an interest of 2.5 percent to 3 percent a month, usually
under the arrangement of "borrow in the spring; return in the fall"
(chunjie qiuhuan); a loan of 20 yuan for millet in the spring required
a repayment of 25 yuan in the fall. The usual annual rate of interest
on a strictly cash arrangement was 30 percent. Larger loans were
made only against land, either under the land-pawning system or
under a straight collateral system. In the "point to the collateral land
and borrow money" (zhidi jieqian) arrangement, Wang loaned 30
percent of the land price at 3 percent interest and received a partial

lien over the land, so that the owner could not sell or pawn it without his permission (KC, 3 : 199, 235, 244, 256, 307, 309, 312).

On top of all this, Wang used the rents he collected in kind to manipulate the grain and cotton markets, hoarding at the bottom and selling at the top. Since prices varied as much as 25 percent between the fall harvest months and the hungry spring months, he profited considerably from these dealings. Wang thus combined in a single monopolistic and interlinked operation the roles of landlord, usurer, and merchant. It was an immensely lucrative operation. Wang had managed in a single generation to triple his landholdings: in July 1941 he owned outright 304.5 of the total 2,054 mu in the village and held pawned title to at least another 80. He alone controlled fully 28 percent of all the rented land in the village (KC, 3 : 177–78, 237, 525–33, and map on p. 536).

Wang's operation had simply suffocated the possibility of any managerial farms developing in the village. In the 1930's Sibeichai was made up almost entirely of tenants (22.7 percent), part-tenants (41.8 percent), and farm laborers (28.2 percent); there was not a single rich peasant in the village, let alone a managerial farmer (see Appendix A).

The Sibeichai case illustrates how landlordism combined with usury and commerce obstructed the development of large-scale managerial agriculture. One pattern was where successful managerial farmers were drawn into Wang's types of activities to increase their income, gain social status, and perhaps enjoy the leisure and comforts of urban living. This acted to siphon off the most successful managerial farms. We have seen how Jing and Luo's 331 managerial landlords tended to give up farming for leasing when their landholdings exceeded 200 mu. Another pattern was where men who made their wealth in commerce and/or office-holding chose to invest their money in land and to live as absentee landlords. When that happened they in fact took away land that might otherwise have been available for managerial agriculture. In either case, landlordism based on small-parcel farming acted powerfully to obstruct managerial farming: from the bottom by buttressing the small-parcel economy and from the top by reproducing itself through the most successful managerial farms.

## MANAGERIAL FARMING AND THE SOCIOPOLITICAL SYSTEM

Qing society consisted of two separate but interlocked social systems. At the base of the sociopolitical order was the farming world.

Stratification in this world was powered mainly by dynamics internal to agriculture. In Hebei–northwest Shandong, managerial farmers were at the top of the system; men like Dong Tianwang, after all, were the village rich. Superimposed on this farming world was another in which wealth and power derived from sources outside of agriculture. At the top of that world were the court and the imperial officials, the top of an elite that included a much larger group of degree-holding gentry and of merchants who could buy their way into elite status. In this system, upward movement was achieved largely by gaining some connection to the imperial state or through commercial success, or both.

Wealth in the upper tier of this social pyramid was of an entirely different order of magnitude from that in the bottom tier. Whereas a small landlord or a managerial farmer of the nineteenth century might have had an annual income of a couple of hundred taels (Chang Chung-li estimates rental income to have been about one tael per mu), a provincial governor averaged an estimated 180,000 taels a year, and a county magistrate 30,000 taels (including, besides regular salary and expenses, the normal "extra" fees and gifts). The formal garb of the magistrate alone cost 3,000 to 4,000 taels in the early twentieth century (Chang 1962: 11–14, 30–31). In this upper tier, a family needed to secure an office only once in several generations to be able to own land on a scale unthinkable for the average managerial farmer.

The two tiers were of course not closed castes, but rather interlocked, with frequent upward and downward movement. A gentry family or a successful merchant family might well slip downward after several subdivisions of family property—just as a successful managerial farmer might well become a landlord, enter commerce, or move into the bureaucracy through the imperial examinations.

It was the lower tier's relatively open access to the upper, in fact, that made this sociopolitical system so obstructive to the further development of managerial farming. Everyone could see plainly that the path to true wealth and status lay not in farming, but in entry into the world of commerce and officialdom. For those who could afford to consider other options, there was very good reason indeed to abandon agriculture for leasing or absentee landlordism, in order to have the time for commerce or for study and preparation for the examination system. It is not surprising, therefore, that the most successful managerial farmers turned into absentee landlords, and the most successful absentee landlords into successful merchants, degree-holding gentry, and office-holding bureaucrats.

In the Republican period, though this two-tiered structure changed in certain respects, it remained very much the same in its essentials. There was greater social fluidity as more commercial opportunities opened up, often linked to foreign trade, and as military careers became an increasingly important path upward. But the two-tier distinction remained: farming led at most to status as the village rich; true wealth and power came from careers outside of farming.

In the 1930's, as we have seen, the top of the lower tier of society in this area consisted mainly of the managerial farmers in the villages. Above them, in the upper tier of the social pyramid, were first of all the county-level rich. Like Wang Zanzhou, these men were usually owners of at least 300 mu. According to the Guomindang Land Commission's figures, there were 13 big landlords on average in each of the surveyed counties of Hebei and Shandong (242, owning 300–10,000 mu, in 18 counties of Hebei, and 49, owning 500–2,000 mu, in four counties in Shandong; Tudiweiyuanhui 1937: 32). Also like Wang Zanzhou, they were generally absentee landlords, who combined leasing landlordism with other activities. Few big landowners, as we have seen, engaged in farm management.

The state apparatus (and the sociopolitical system it engendered) thus lent powerful support to the circular pattern of rural socioeconomic change outlined in this chapter. The family farm economy did contain its own internal dynamic of differentiation and stratification; a small number of family farmers became rich peasants and managerial farmers. But then they came up against a sociopolitical system in which true wealth and power could only be derived from careers outside of agriculture. Managerial farming thus gave way unavoidably to landlordism, and to the sociopolitical system based on that landlordism.

INNOVATIVE POSSIBILITIES

In describing the links between managerial farming, landlordism, and the sociopolitical order, we look back at a system as it was. A retrospective view starts by accepting as given the fact that managerial agriculture did not generate any breakthroughs in farm productivity. It cannot answer the important question of what kinds of technological changes were possible in the 1930's and why those changes were not made.

Here I call on the concrete example of Shajing village to illustrate the kinds of changes that might have been possible. Agriculture in Shajing was already at a fairly high level of intensification in the twentieth century, powered by the population increase of the preceding centuries. In terms of cropping frequency, the means of intensification had been interplanting. In the 1930's, 20–25 percent of the cultivated area was interplanted, either in alternative rows of wheat and maize or millet (called *ailong*), or in a row of wheat for every two rows of maize or millet (called *danshan*). The maize or millet was planted in the spring (maize could also be planted in July) and harvested in September; the wheat was planted in the late fall and harvested in July. By this means, as has been seen, the villagers were able to double their yields from one crop of 100–150 catties per mu to two crops of that size. In terms of fertilizer input, the village had reached 2,000 catties of compost per mu (animal, mainly hog, and human manure mixed with soil) in the 1930's. Labor input had reached the levels expressed in the generally accepted work standards for year-laborers.

The direction in which Shajing's agriculture might have been further intensified is shown by developments since 1949. First of all, the proportion of the interplanted area has been raised: to 550 mu of the 983.2 mu of the village in 1979, or 56 percent of the cultivated area. In addition, fertilizer use has been increased to 8,000 catties of compost per mu as "base fertilizer" (*jifei*), with 100 catties of chemical fertilizer (or "chase fertilizer"; *zhuifei*) in a second application. The result has been to increase the per-mu yield to 900 catties: 400 of wheat and 500 of maize, or more than three times the level achieved with interplanting in the 1930's, and more than six times the level achieved with single-cropping.

But this intensification has been possible only through radical changes in the pre-Revolution mix of social and economic structure, technology, ecology, and state involvement—in the total ecosystem, to use my earlier term. The first and critical problem that had to be overcome was waterlogging, which dictated that a substantial proportion of the land be given to sorghum. That has required elaborate regrading of the land and an elaborate system of drainage ditches, which has been made possible only by a massive collective effort. The result has been a much-expanded area for the cultivation of maize.

A second major breakthrough has been irrigation. The huge Miyun Dam east of Beijing, built with state investment and coordination, has had a profound effect on Shajing. Today a concrete water canal runs right between the village's residential area and its fields, feeding a system of small irrigation canals that crisscross the entire cultivated area of the village. This has assured a water supply for crops that formerly had to rely solely on the summer rains. Winter wheat, which was not watered before the Revolution, is now irrigated three times a season. State investment in irrigation is also responsible for the turn to chemical fertilizer, which must be thoroughly watered into the soil.

It is the state's active encouragement of hog raising that has allowed the village to quadruple the amount of organic fertilizer applied per mu. In 1980 the village had 450 hogs, compared with fewer than 100 in the 1930's, by the villagers' estimate.* Hog manure (mixed in a roughly 3:7 ratio with earth) accounts for nearly 90 percent of the natural fertilizer used, human excrement only 2 to 3 percent.

Chemical fertilizer came to the village in the years 1958–61. According to the village's brigade head, Zhang Linbing, even with the much heavier use of compost, yields would not be nearly what they are if the base fertilizer was not supplemented with the chase fertilizer. Without it, he estimates they would get only a little over 200 catties of wheat per mu and 270–300 catties of maize. Chemical fertilizer made possible the breakthrough to 400 catties of wheat and 500 catties of maize.

Finally, interplanting in pre-Revolution Shajing had been limited by the great fall rush, when maize had to be harvested and wheat planted in the space of about six weeks. As Li Guangzhi noted, he simply could not interplant more than nine mu of wheat (or 18 mu total of wheat and maize) on his 27 mu of land. (Fertilizer, he pointed out, was an additional constraint: both crops required heavy inputs of compost, 2,000 catties per interplanted mu, or 1,000 catties for each crop; sorghum of course required little or none.) In 1958, after collectivization but before the coming of tractors, the Shajing villagers had been able to increase the interplanted area to 400 mu. However, it was only the introduction of tractors in 1959 (which the brigade rents from the commune), allowing wheat planting to be completed in the short space of two weeks, that brought the proportion of interplanted land up well past the 50 percent mark.

A "HIGH-LEVEL EQUILIBRIUM TRAP"?

We must now ask why a managerial farmer like Zhang Rui of Shajing did not make some of these kinds of innovative changes in his

---

*In China as a whole, the number of hogs has increased from 58,000,000 in 1949 to 238,000,000 in 1976 and 301,000,000 in 1979 (Liu & Zhang 1981: 105).

day. We return to Elvin's "high-level equilibrium trap" thesis. As we saw earlier, part of that thesis—that population increase in China eroded the surplus above subsistence and hence the wherewithal for innovative investment—cannot stand up to an analysis that takes account of unequal distribution and the existing production relations. As Victor Lippit has shown, the "potential surplus" in prerevolutionary rural China might have totaled as much as 30 percent of total agricultural output. When the question of the roots of the underdevelopment of Chinese agriculture is directed at a group like the managerial farmers, it obviously makes no sense to speak of population pressure having eroded the surplus above subsistence. Those farms certainly controlled a surplus that could have been used for innovative investment. The real question is why they did not use it for that purpose, not why they had no surplus.

The second part of Elvin's thesis merits more consideration. It suggests that in the Chinese case population pressure had driven agricultural intensification to such a high level that there was little room left for further advances in productivity. Obviously, where new capital inputs can significantly raise output, there would be both the incentive for and the means to finance such inputs. Where new capital inputs would merely replace labor inputs without any significant change in output, however, there would be little incentive to make innovative investments. Agriculture would thus be trapped at an equilibrium at a high level.

This analysis does have a certain relevance to the underdevelopment of managerial agriculture in the 1930's. Farm productivity had indeed been pushed to or near its limits within the existing ecosystem. The interplanting of maize and winter wheat to maximize cropping frequency, the use of 2,000 catties of organic fertilizer per mu, the method of planting in four-men teams in order to take advantage of the moisture in the soil, and so on, all attest to the high degree of development of the prerevolutionary agricultural system. The already very high level of labor intensification in this system certainly also precluded advances in the direction of American-style highly capital-intensive and non-labor-intensive agriculture. Even the expanded use of animal power, as has been seen in Chapter Eight, was blocked by the wide availability of cheap surplus labor from the small farming economy.

But this is not to say that population pressure obstructed all forms of further capital inputs, traditional or modern. Postrevolutionary Shajing's use of greater amounts of organic fertilizer along traditional lines, coupled with a second application of chemical fertilizer, for example, not only has not displaced labor, but has in fact increased the demand for it. Even the tractor, for all the work it has saved in plowing and planting, has contributed to this demand by permitting the villagers to interplant more acreage. Capital inputs such as these have by no means been prevented by high population density. And their effects have been dramatically demonstrated by the more than threefold increase in output in Shajing village since 1949. The Shajing brigade turned from grain growing to a concentration on vegetables in 1981. That will mean much greater labor as well as an increase in capital inputs (in fertilizer and irrigation, especially) per mu. It will greatly expand the farm employment opportunities for the villagers, multiply the value of their agricultural output, and substantially increase their income. If the village's population should remain constant or not increase more than the increased labor requirements, there will certainly be the opportunity for expanded accumulation and innovative investment. Shajing does not have to repeat the experience of the last 30 years, in which population increase ate up so much of the expanded productivity.

To explain why a modern input such as chemical fertilizer could not be incorporated into the pre-1949 agricultural system of Shajing, we need to turn from population pressure to look at the interdependent relationships between the natural environment and the sociopolitical order. Chemical fertilizer requires irrigation, and irrigation in Shajing has come only through state intervention. That intervention was not forthcoming from the prerevolutionary state. Moreover, chemical fertilizer is very effective for maize, but of little importance for sorghum, which means that its use is linked also to overcoming the problem of waterlogging. As we have seen, the proportion of land placed under maize has been increased in Shajing only with the dramatic regrading of land and construction of drainage ditches and canals. Those efforts were based on a collective village organization of a kind that is difficult to imagine under the prerevolutionary system of fragmented individual parcels.

Thus, even if a low-cost chemical fertilizer had been available in the 1930's, it alone could not have effectively altered the condition of agriculture in the village. An agricultural system is the result of the interaction of a human society with its natural environment; it can be expected to be interlinked with both the physical world and the sociopolitical order. To isolate the variable of population from the interdependent ecosystem, as the "trap" thesis does, is to overlook the crucial interconnections between society, polity, economy, and environment. And to equate all modern capital inputs with labor-saving inputs that are offset by population growth is to adopt too narrow a conception of modern agriculture.

If we look beyond agriculture to the economy as a whole, it is difficult to see precisely what the "trap" thesis suggests. The model is at bottom based on the interrelationships of population, farm output, and technological innovation. Such a model does not really begin to deal with the issues of development in the industrial or protoindustrial sector, or with the possible linkages between underdevelopment in agriculture and underdevelopment in other sectors. The focus of my discussion here is on agriculture; more general issues of development in the economy will be addressed in the concluding chapter.

# CHAPTER 11

# The Persistence of Small-Peasant Family Farming

In the absence of increased productivity, population growth and social stratification placed immense stresses on the lower strata of the peasantry. By the 1930's a majority of peasant farms on the North China plain had been driven well under the average subsistence size of 15 mu. Many of them were rented in whole or in part, and thus their operators had to bear the double burden of inadequate size and rent. Yet somehow the small-family-farm economy held on as the predominant form of agriculture, still accounting for more than 80 percent of the cultivated area at this late date.

To explain how and why small-parcel family farming proved to be so tenacious in spite of the immense pressures on the poorer half of the peasantry, we will need to look at the ways in which it came to be interlocked with other forms of production for support, especially commercialized handicraft production and wage labor. It was only with those dual crutches that poor peasant family farming managed to survive against the combined workings of involution and social stratification.

## PRESSURES ON THE LAND

Though the available data do not permit a precise demographic history of this area, there can be no doubt about the long-term trend of population growth and mounting pressures on the land. As noted earlier, Hebei and Shandong had a combined population of perhaps 7,000,000 in 1400, 50,000,000 in 1800, and 75–80,000,000 in the 1930's. The peak period of growth, to judge by the spread of cotton cultivation, was between 1550 and 1800, with a brief interruption during the wars of the Ming–Qing dynastic transition. The rate of increase might have leveled off in the nineteenth century, to judge by the prefectural data (see Appendix B), though the peripheral areas

TABLE II.I

Farm Income and Expenses by Household Type, Michang, 1937

(Yuan)

| Household type and number | Farm size (mu) | Number of adult male farm-workers in household | Land rented (mu) | Gross farm income | Fertilizer[a] | | Rent | | Wages | | | Tax | | Miscellaneous | |
|---|---|---|---|---|---|---|---|---|---|---|---|---|---|---|---|
| | | | | | Cost | Pct. of gross farm income | Cost | Pct. of gross farm income | Cash paid | Board cost | Pct. of gross farm income | Cost | Pct. of gross farm income | Cost | Pct. of gross farm income |
| Managerial farmer | | | | | | | | | | | | | | | |
| Household 1 | 133 | 2 | 0 | $2,192 | $152 | 6.9% | $0 | 0.0% | $298 | $252 | 25.1% | $113 | 5.2% | $177 | 8.1% |
| Household 2 | 125 | 2 | 0 | 1,915 | 171 | 8.9 | 0 | 0.0 | 307 | 262 | 29.7 | 104 | 5.4 | 39 | 2.0 |
| Rich peasant | | | | | | | | | | | | | | | |
| Household 3 | 65 | 1 | 0 | $1,029 | $250 | 24.3% | $0 | 0.0% | $224 | $197 | 40.9% | $43 | 4.2% | $57 | 5.5% |
| Household 5 | 60 | 3 | 8 | 1,117 | 161 | 14.4 | 14 | 1.3 | 144 | 115 | 23.2 | 41 | 3.7 | 128 | 11.5 |
| Household 6 | 47 | 2 | 7 | 912 | 253 | 27.7 | 48 | 5.3 | 200 | 148 | 38.2 | 32 | 3.5 | 75 | 8.2 |
| Middle peasant | | | | | | | | | | | | | | | |
| Household 4 | 62 | 5 | 0 | $790 | $136 | 17.2% | $0 | 0.0% | $77 | $61 | 17.5% | $53 | 6.7% | $62 | 7.8% |
| Household 7 | 17 | 1 | 0 | 255 | 21 | 8.2 | 0 | 0.0 | 10 | 9 | 7.5 | 13 | 5.1 | 65 | 25.5 |
| Household 8 | 34 | 2 | 7 | 514 | 114 | 22.2 | 35 | 6.8 | 36 | 44 | 15.6 | 22 | 4.3 | 16 | 3.1 |
| Household 9 | 32 | 2 | 13 | 332 | 83 | 25.0 | 67 | 20.2 | 57 | 7 | 19.3 | 15 | 4.5 | 44 | 13.3 |
| Poor peasant | | | | | | | | | | | | | | | |
| Household 10 | 13 | 2 | 7 | $234 | $53 | 22.6% | $38 | 16.2% | $29 | $37 | 28.2% | $6 | 2.6% | $15 | 6.4% |
| Household 11 | 21 | 1 | 21 | 104 | 36 | 34.6 | 52 | 50.0 | 9 | 5 | 13.5 | 2 | 1.9 | 7 | 6.7 |
| Household 12 | 15 | 2 | 15 | 196 | 69 | 35.2 | 46 | 23.5 | 4 | 1 | 2.3 | 0 | 0.0 | 4 | 2.0 |
| Household 13 | 10 | 3 | 10 | 110 | 0 | 0.0 | 37 | 33.6 | 0 | 1 | 0.9 | 2 | 1.4 | 28 | 25.5 |
| Household 14 | 6 | 1 | 6 | 89 | 17 | 19.1 | 41 | 46.1 | 7 | 6 | 14.6 | 1 | 0.9 | 3 | 3.4 |

SOURCE: MT, Hokushi jimukyoku chōsabu 1938–41, I: Tables 4, 10, 13, 14.

[a]Includes only fertilizer purchased; no attempt was made to assign a cash value to home-supplied fertilizer.

of Hebei (Yongping prefecture in northeastern Hebei and the eastern portions of Tianjin and Hejian prefectures of central Hebei) probably continued to grow at a fast pace. Population growth probably accelerated again in the twentieth century, along with industrial development, the rapid commercialization of agriculture, and urbanization.

The growth of cultivated acreage, on the other hand, had reached a standstill in the mid-eighteenth century (see Appendix C), pushing the per-capita figure down from five mu to three by the 1930's. Unequal distribution compounded the problem, with the result that nearly half the households in the North China plain were farming less than ten mu by 1934–35 (40 percent in Hebei, 49.7 percent in Shandong; Tudiweiyuanhui 1937: 26).

### POOR-PEASANT FARM INCOMES

We saw in Chapter Nine how survival considerations often compelled poor peasants either to adopt unbalanced cropping portfolios that relied excessively on a single cash crop or to ignore the advantages of cash cropping and to expend too much or too little labor on their fields, at a cost of diminished marginal returns or a serious falloff in output.

About one of every two of these peasants also had to bear the burden of rent, which tended to consume a huge proportion of their gross farm income: about one-third, on average, in the case of the five poor peasant households of Michang village shown in Table 11.1.

When we look at the farm budgets of the two managerial farmers in Tables 11.1 and 11.2, we find that capitalistic accounting principles work quite well for them. We can speak meaningfully about a net farm income (including the imputed value of the household's own labor) of about 13–14 percent of the value of the land (see also Table 10.2). And indeed we can even speak of a "net profit" to the farm operation after deducting all expenses and the imputed value of the family's own labor. These two managerial farms lend concrete substance to the formalist view of peasants as profit-maximizing entrepreneurs.

But if we try to apply the same principles to the farm budgets of the poor peasants, we immediately run into difficulties. As Chayanov has pointed out, it is difficult to disaggregate into units either the labor input or the total output of a family farm. Peasants tend to think of their household's total labor input for the year as a single unit, and of the year's harvest after production expenses as a single lump-sum labor product or net income. It is difficult to assign a

TABLE 11.2

Net Farm Income and "Net Profit" by Household Type, Michang, 1937

(Yuan)

| Household type and number | Net farm income[a] | Household labor days | Cash equivalent[b] | "Net profit" |
|---|---|---|---|---|
| Managerial farmer | | | | |
| Household 1 | $1,200 | 149 | $67 | $1,133 |
| Household 2 | 1,032 | 193 | 87 | 945 |
| Rich peasant | | | | |
| Household 3 | $258 | 39 | $18 | $240 |
| Household 5 | 514 | 297 | 134 | 380 |
| Household 6 | 156 | 188 | 85 | 71 |
| Middle peasant | | | | |
| Household 4 | $401 | 705 | $317 | $84 |
| Household 7 | 137 | 229 | 103 | 34 |
| Household 8 | 247 | 348 | 157 | 90 |
| Household 9 | 59 | 417 | 188 | −129 |
| Poor peasant | | | | |
| Household 10 | $56 | 239 | $108 | $−52 |
| Household 11 | −7 | 184 | 83 | −90 |
| Household 12 | 72 | 240 | 108 | −36 |
| Household 13 | 42 | 206 | 93 | −51 |
| Household 14 | 14 | 71 | 32 | −18 |

SOURCES: Tables 10.1, 11.1; MT, Hokushi jimukyoku chōsabu 1938–41, 1: Table 40.
[a]Net farm income is gross farm income minus the cost of fertilizer, rent, wages, tax, and miscellaneous expenses.
[b]Computed at the average daily wage (cash and board) of 45¢.

value to the family's own labor and to deduct that value from the year's net income to arrive at something akin to a net profit.

The best we can do here is to compute, rather arbitrarily, the family's labor at the prevailing wage rate for farm labor, including board. This procedure is followed in Table 11.2, using 45 cents—the amount the resident investigator in Michang village estimated as the going daily rate in 1937. That figure includes 22 cents for the worker's daily ration of foodgrains, or about the same amount as the cash wage. This estimate is borne out by the payment system used in Shajing village, called the *baogong* system, in which the employer did not supply board but simply paid twice the prevailing cash wage (KC, 2:51).* As for the fare the laborers received, one Shajing villager detailed for the Japanese investigators his customary board as

---

*These figures differ somewhat from the findings of a 1933 nationwide survey, which put the average daily cost of board in Hebei and Shandong at 25 cents and 28 cents, respectively. These amounts represented 44.2% of the worker's total "wages" in Hebei, 31.8% in Shandong. The national average for board was 22 cents, and the combined total wage 49 cents (Chen Zhengmo 1935: 6–7, 10–12).

follows: in the spring, gruel for breakfast, "dry" boiled millet for lunch, and gruel with vegetable for supper; in the summer, "watered" boiled millet for breakfast, "dry" boiled millet and bean-noodles in soup for lunch, and boiled millet and a vegetable for supper; in the fall, gruel for breakfast, "dry" boiled millet and bean-noodles in soup for lunch, and "watered" boiled millet for supper (*ibid.*). Note how the consistency of the boiled millet thickened with the needs of heavy labor; in less busy times, it was watered into a gruel to make the grain stretch farther.

Even assigning such a bare-bones value to the poor peasant families' own labor, however, leaves us with a negative figure for their "net farm profit," meaning simply that they worked for less than the market wage. This fact immediately raises a host of questions. Why did these families continue to put in labor even when the marginal product of that labor sank below market wages? Why did they not give up their farms and simply hire out? How did they manage to survive? Why was the family farm able to remain the dominant form of productive organization when the poorer farms worked under such pressures?

### USURY

A similar paradox obtained in the credit system that prevailed in this small-family-farm economy. In 1936 Japanese investigators gathered household-by-household lending and borrowing data, with a ten-year time depth, for each of three villages: moderately commercialized Dabeiguan, and highly commercialized Michang and Qianlianggezhuang. Interest rates in these villages generally varied from 1.2 percent a month to 3 percent a month, with most loans made at 2 percent. The lowest rates were generally obtained by the most well-to-do households, because they had the influence to procure them and were considered good credit risks; the highest rates were borne by the poorest households, considered the worst risks. This harsh money market logic could be exploited by the well-off households for gain: in Michang Households 23 and 36, for example, borrowed at less than 2 percent and loaned out at higher rates. In 1936, 44 of the 114 households in Michang (39 percent) had outstanding debts ranging from ten yuan to several hundred; and in Dabeiguan 36 of 98 households (37 percent) owed from five to 261 yuan (MT, Kitō 1937a: Table 15; Kitō 1937b: Table 15).

These interest rates had become so widely accepted by the 1930's that they were uniformly used for loans between relatives and friends. Usurious rates of 20 percent or more per year had become so common and so much an integral part of the farm economy that they were seen by all as the "fair" rates that anyone with that kind of money deserved to earn. The favor extended by a friend or relative consisted in the act of the loan itself, given the great demand for such loans, rather than in any discount in the interest rates.

We have seen that even the highest rates of return from farming—those obtained by the managerial farmers—were generally in the range of 13 to 14 percent. Since the returns to poor peasant farms, if we can indeed speak in such terms, were so much lower, how was it possible for a poor-peasant economy surviving at or below the margins of subsistence to sustain a money market operating at such high rates?

An answer to that question needs to begin with an analysis of the distinctive characteristics of the family farm as a unit not only of production, but of production and consumption merged into one. The production decisions of such a unit were shaped at once by the family's own consumption needs and by calculations of returns from producing for the market. In the case of the poorer family farms, consumption to meet survival needs could not help being paramount. Such a family farm did not operate according to the logic governing the behavior of a capitalist enterprise. For a capitalist enterprise, it could make no sense to continue investing in labor past the break-even point, resulting therefore in a negative return. For a poor peasant family farm with surplus labor and struggling on the margins of hunger, however, it made sense to continue using that labor as long as the marginal product of labor remained above zero. A person nose deep in water, we might say, would do almost anything to rise above the surface.

The same logic applied to usurious interest rates. Though a capitalist enterprise would not normally tolerate interest rates higher than the prospective returns to invested capital, a hungry family can be made to bear almost any interest rate.

To see the poor peasant family farm as a unit concerned above all with survival can explain why these families tolerated net farm incomes below wage levels and bore interest rates higher than any returns they might achieve. But it cannot explain how they were able to maintain and reproduce themselves. For that, we need to turn to the ways in which poor peasants combined family farming with other kinds of activities for support.

## THE SMALL FAMILY FARM AND HOUSEHOLD
### HANDICRAFT PRODUCTION

One obvious prop for the small family farm was household handicraft production. It was made necessary, on the one hand, by the inability of the household to maintain itself by farming alone. It was made possible, on the other hand, by the availability of surplus labor on most farms. Because of the seasonal nature of farmwork, there was always some surplus labor in the slack season. The family, moreover, was a highly elastic unit of production—the women and children could be mobilized for subsidiary production. Where the farm was undersized for the available household labor, there was surplus labor even in the farming seasons.

Marx saw the combination of home industry with small farming in China and India as the very basis of a "natural economy" of largely self-sufficient households operating outside of the cash economy. This was responsible for the stagnation of society and explained why those countries proved so resistant to the intrusion of the products of British industry: "The broad basis of the mode of production here is formed by the unity of small-scale agriculture and home industry. . . . The substantial economy and saving in time afforded by the association of agriculture with manufacture put in a stubborn resistance to the products of big industries" (Marx 1967, 3: 333). Mao and most contemporary Chinese historians have followed Marx's lead, depicting China's premodern economy as mainly a "natural" one in which "the men farm and the women weave" (*nangeng nüzhi*; Xu Dixin 1980: 57–58).

However, as I showed in Chapter Six (and as many Chinese historians working on the "sprouts of capitalism" have shown), the notion of a natural economy is a misleading one. By the eighteenth century even the relatively underdeveloped (as compared with the lower Yangzi, for example) North China plain had become fairly commercialized. Wheat was a highly commercialized crop, and cotton was widely cultivated. In handicrafts many areas had long passed the "natural economy" stage of producing for household consumption to become part of the market economy.*

That such commercialized household handicraft production was a crucial prop for the small-family-farm economy can readily be seen

*G. William Skinner's work on marketing systems and urbanization (1964–65; 1977a, b) has probably done more than anything else to show the inadequacy of the natural economy model.

in my sample of villages with developed handicraft industries (Type IV, Appendix A). Consider, first of all, the example of Qizhai, in Gaotang county, northwest Shandong. Fully 60 percent of its cropped area was under cotton, the highest proportion of any of my 33 villages. Yet unlike the other important cotton-growing villages, Qizhai was inhabited mainly by owner-cultivators (94.8 percent of the households); only 3.4 percent of its cultivated area was rented. Although the survey data do not permit a conclusive demonstration of how this anomalous combination came to be, the most plausible explanation is that the small family farms that might have otherwise slid down to tenancy had been able to maintain their owner-peasant mode of operation through the supplementary income derived from cotton spinning and weaving. Though the village's upper-income women either did not spin and weave or did so only for home use, most of the others spun and wove year-round, producing several times what they needed themselves to help support the family (Kita Shina 1943b: 12, 93).

Lengshuigou, also in northwest Shandong, is another example. Like Qizhai, it shows the anomalous combination of a fairly high degree of commercialization (33 percent of the cropped area was under rice, sold mainly in nearby Jinan) with a low incidence of tenancy (only 28 of the 360 farm households in this village rented some land; almost all the rest were owner-cultivators). Once again, the most plausible explanation is the village's highly developed strawbraids industry. Subsidiary income from this activity gave the small-owner family farms here a cushion against the stratifying effects of commercialized agriculture.

Duyake, in Zaoqiang county, southern Hebei, tells a similar story. Here the owner-cultivator households had been propped up by a developed cotton-weaving and sheepskin-processing industry. Although the village was moderately commercialized (with 33 percent of its cropped area under winter wheat), tenancy had been kept to a minimum: less than 10 percent of the cultivated area in 1937.

Additional evidence of the support that commercialized handicraft production lent the small-family-farm economy can be seen in the villages of Xiaowangzhuang and Zhimafeng, both in Yutian county in northeastern Hebei. Both villages had an exceptionally low land-to-population ratio: only 1.2 mu and 1.4 mu per capita, respectively, compared with an average of 4.2 mu in the province as a whole. The problems posed by this scarcity were compounded by a harsh natural environment: much of the land in both villages was susceptible to waterlogging, evidenced by the high proportion of cropped area given to sorghum (50 percent and 66 percent, respectively). These villages simply could not have supported their populations on farming alone. The key to the villagers' survival had been their production of cloth, sent mainly to the Manchurian market. Xiaowangzhuang's 155 farm households had at one time owned no fewer than 142 looms, and Zhimafeng's 76 farm households some 50. The closing of the Manchurian market under the Japanese occupation dealt a disastrous blow to both villages. By 1936 only 34 of the 142 looms in Xiaowangzhuang and only 25 of the 50 in Zhimafeng were still operating. Many of the villagers had had to turn to hiring out in other villages, as evidenced by the unusually high proportion of year-laborers in these two Type IV villages at that date: 25.8 percent in Xiaowangzhuang and 28.9 percent in Zhimafeng. The withdrawal of the supportive role of handicraft industry quickly devastated the village economies (MT, Kitō 1936a, 1.2: 42).

The general pattern of poor peasant farms deriving supplementary support from commercialized handicraft production of course obtained very much earlier. The Leting county gazetteer of the Qianlong period noted, for example, that "trading cloth for millet was actually one way the poor people manage to keep themselves fed" (cited in Kataoba Shibako 1959: 93).

### WAGE LEVELS IN THE HANDICRAFT INDUSTRY

To be sure, the relationship between these two activities can be seen also from the opposite vantage point. Just as the handicraft industry might be seen as having propped up an otherwise tottering family-farm economy, so family farming might be seen as lending support to handicraft industry. Just as subsidiary income from handicrafts could help sustain a family farm producing a net income below the subsistence level, so too family farming could sustain weavers receiving a cash income below the subsistence level.

The weavers of Xiaowangzhuang village, Hebei, earned 30 to 40 cents a day after expenses in 1936; and the daily rate in Shandong at that time was 25 to 50 cents (MT, Kitō 1936a, 1.2 : 41, 43, 44; Amano 1936: 219). At 40 to 50 cents a day, a weaver earned roughly the same amount as an agricultural laborer, or about two days' worth of foodgrains for an adult male. At 25 cents, he or she earned only food for the day.

Such wages were really below the level of subsistence in the sense that Marx intended the word. The subsistence Marx had in mind was not just that of the laborer himself, but also that of his household; subsistence required that the worker be able to reproduce. It was a conception that might be more precisely called "subsistence for the household," whereas a wage of 25 to 50 cents a day was really closer to subsistence for the laborer alone. (In Marxist terms, this was a level of exploitation that extracted not only the surplus value of labor, but also part of the "necessary labor," necessary for the reproduction of the laborer.)

These hunger-level wages could be sustained for the same reasons that hunger-level farm incomes could be sustained by the poor-peasant family farms. The absence of alternative employment opportunities and the dictates of subsistence combined to compel poor peasants to accept employment at less-than-subsistence wages. And the interlocking of handicraft labor with family farming enabled them to derive a partial and incomplete subsistence from each.

These low wages, on the other hand, enabled a rural weaving industry equipped with the iron-gear loom to stay within competitive range of the modern textile mills. As late as 1932–36, if we use Chao Kang's (1977) figures, handwoven cloth still accounted for 66 percent of the total output in China. In the North China plain, as we have seen, areas like Gaoyang and Baodi even emerged as important new handicraft weaving centers during the period in which China's modern textile industry experienced its most dynamic growth.

Thus, contrary to Marx's original analysis, it was not the self-sufficient "natural economy," but rather commercialized handicraft production and protoindustry that proved to be resistant to the penetration of modern industry. And imperialism's effects did not consist so much in shattering the supposed natural economy as in changing a handicraft industry based on domestic markets into one that was incorporated into the world economy and influenced by its market.

In China commercialized handicraft production proved in the end to be more of an obstruction than the springboard to capitalist industry that some have argued it was in Western Europe. Franklin Mendels (1972), for example, suggests that the combination of merchant capital with home industry set the stage for industrial capitalism: the merchant capital and marketing networks of this "proto-industrialization" were the basis for industrial capital; the later industrial areas were generally the earlier protoindustrial areas. Hans Medick (1976) further suggests that protoindustrialization heralded certain long-term social changes often associated with industrialization: that the shift from a society based on landed property and inheritance to a society based on work altered the status of the family patriarch and the relationship between the sexes. But in Hebei—northwest Shandong no such qualitative changes seem to have accompanied what Mendels and Medick call protoindustrialization. Instead, the old family-farm economy simply absorbed market-oriented handicraft production as an added prop. Old-style merchant capital took advantage of the low opportunity costs of farm household labor to compete with the new modern textile mills. In the process, the merchants drained away both major portions of the limited amount of available capital that might have found its way into industry and major portions of the market that might have supported modern industry.

This is not to say that handicraft production could not have followed a protoindustrial route. There were indeed the glimmerings of such a possibility. We will recall, for example, the case of Bi Fenglian, who started with 30 mu and who, at the time of his death in 1840, had parlayed his profits from silk weaving into a large estate of over 300 mu and a workshop of over 20 looms (Jing & Luo 1959: 68—72). Had there been a greater incidence of this type of development and had such development led to capitalist industrialization, the Mendels-Medick hypothesis might be more applicable to China. We might also want to analyze the family farm cum household industry production unit in terms of an analytical model such as that developed by Stephen Hymer and Stephen Resinick (1969), in which household handicraft production is seen as part of a farm enterprise that optimizes the allocation of scarce labor between food production and "Z" activities in response to changing market conditions.

The problem facing the poor peasants of the North China plain in the twentieth century, however, was not a scarcity of labor relative to employment opportunities, but the reverse: underemployment and an overabundance of labor. Under those conditions, it makes little sense to think in terms of the formalist logic of "optimizing" the allocation of scarce resources to maximize profits. The poor peasant farm under the twin pressures of underemployment and extractive social relations was oriented above all toward the struggle for survival. Handicraft production for below-subsistence wages was a part of that struggle.

FAMILY FARMS AND DAY-LABOR

Though the handicraft industry certainly helped to sustain the small-peasant economy, we must not exaggerate its role. The fact that only five of my 33 villages had a developed handicraft industry cautions against imagining an economy in which almost all poor family farms drew on home industry for support.* Furthermore, the fact that a certain number of farm households turned to home industry for support cannot explain a question posed earlier in this chapter: if many poor peasants earned less from their farms than they could earn by working the land of others, why did they not give up their farms to become year-laborers? After all, their women and children could still work at weaving as before, as indeed they themselves could presumably do during idle periods. They would thus have been better paid for their farmwork, and could still have supplemented their income with whatever home industry they had been engaged in. In short, there was no reason why a household could not have combined hiring out with home industry just as well as family farming with home industry.

I estimated in Chapter Four that short-term labor accounted for perhaps 6 percent of total farm labor, or a little under a third of all hired labor, and that just over a third of all farm households hired out as day-laborers in Hebei–northwest Shandong in the 1930's. Most of these households were poor peasants: the owner of a few mu, the tenant or part-tenant working a plot too minuscule to support a family.

Table 11.3 shows the number and type of households that hired out as day-laborers in moderately commercialized Shajing (in 1941) and highly commercialized Michang (in 1936). As we see, 33 of the 40 households in Michang owned ten mu or less, and fully 31 of them owned five mu or less. Similarly, the majority of day-laborers in Shajing (15 of 21) owned ten mu or less. The data on day-laborers in Shandong in the 1890's reveal the same picture: in 86 percent of the 141 villages surveyed, the short-term laborers owned less than ten mu; and in only 6 percent of the villages were there men who hired out from households with more than ten mu (Jing & Luo 1957: 126–28, and App. Table 3). Households owning so little land often could not sustain farms of a size adequate for the full employment and subsistence of their available labor; they therefore had to hire out to supplement their farm income. The head of Household 88 in Michang might be considered representative: he farmed 9.5 mu of rented land and hired out his own excess labor for a total of 35 days in 1936, earning a cash income of 8.75 yuan to help support his

---

*The natural economy model conjures up such a picture.

TABLE 11.3

Households Hiring Out as Day-Laborers by Size of Holding and Type of Tenure in Two Hebei Villages, 1936–1941

| Land owned (mu) | Michang | Shajing | Type of tenure | Michang | Shajing |
|---|---|---|---|---|---|
| 0 | 21 | 8 | Landless | 4 | 2 |
| 1–5 | 10 | 2 | Tenant | 17 | 6 |
| 6–10 | 2 | 5 | Part-tenant | 16 | 5 |
| 11–15 | 3 | 1 | Owner | 3 | 8 |
| 16–20 | 4 | 3 | TOTAL | 40 | 21 |
| >20 | 0 | 2 | | | |
| TOTAL | 40 | 21 | | | |

SOURCES: *Michang*, MT, Kitō 1937b: 5–10, 25–28; *Shajing*, KC, 1: Appended chart.

TABLE 11.4

Daily Cash Wage of Day-Laborers in Four Hebei and Shandong Villages, 1939–1942

(Yuan)

| Year | High (7th–9th months) | Low (winter) | Average | Village |
|---|---|---|---|---|
| 1939 | — | — | $.50 | Lengshuigou |
| 1940 | — | — | .50–.60 | Lengshuigou |
| Early 1941 | $.80 | $.30 | .50 | Sibeichai |
| Late 1941 | 1.00 | .50 | .70–.80 | Shajing |
| Late 1942 | 2.00 | 1.00 | 1.50 | Houjiaying |

SOURCES: *Lengshuigou*, KC, 4: 152–53; *Sibeichai*, KC, 3: 194; *Shajing*, KC, 2: 32, 50–51, 87–88; *Houjiaying*, KC, 5: 292.

TABLE 11.5

Total Net Income of Poor Peasant Households, Michang, 1937

(Yuan)

| Household number | Wages | Net farm income | Total net income |
|---|---|---|---|
| Household 10 | $117 | $56 | $173 |
| Household 11 | 73 | −7 | 66 |
| Household 12 | — | 72 | 72 |
| Household 13 | 54 | 42 | 96 |
| Household 14 | 72 | 14 | 86 |

SOURCES: Table 11.2; MT, Hokushi jimukyoku chōsabu 1938–41, 1: Table 13.

household of three (MT, Kitō 1937b: 9–10, 27–28). Hao Xiaowu in Sibeichai village, to give another illustration, farmed four mu of rented land (which he had owned but which was now held in pawn by his landlord) and supplemented his meager farm income by hiring out for 50 days in 1941 (KC, 3:528–29).

The usual pattern of day-labor hiring went like this: in the busy agricultural seasons, the men who wished to work gathered in a certain place before sunrise, between 3:00 and 4:00 in the morning, awaiting their prospective employers. The Sibeichai villagers gathered in front of an old willow tree just east of the "south gate" of the county seat. As many as 300 laborers could be in the crowd at the peak of the cotton harvest. Each man brought the appropriate tools for the season: small hoes in the early spring, larger hoes in the late spring, sickles in the summer, and so on (KC, 2:50–51; KC, 3:194–95, 223, 272). In Lengshuigou, Shandong, the workers gathered on the temple grounds at the nearby market town—some 20 to 80 at a time, depending on the season (KC, 4:152–53). The employers came around 4:00 A.M. Most were managerial farmers or their head laborers, rich peasants, and middle peasants. The hiring was done between 4:00 and 5:00, seldom past 6:00. The terms of employment were generally settled verbally directly between the employer and the laborer. The employers would vie for the men who had reputations as the best workers (KC, 3:194–95).

The hired hand then went promptly to the farm to begin work, usually before the crack of dawn. The schedule was like that of the year-laborer: an hour's work was generally done before breakfast; the workday then went on to sundown, with breaks after meals and three others in the course of the day, more or less fixed by customary practice. Most employers supplied food, usually no more than three meals of coarse grains—one of gruel and two of more solid food, as detailed earlier, plus a cash payment at the end of the workday. The cash wage, according to the testimony of villagers, varied considerably from the offseasons, when demand for labor was low, to the busy seasons; the difference sometimes was more than 100 percent, as shown in Table 11.4. As wartime inflation set in, wages began to rise to keep up with the rising prices of foodgrains.

A day-laborer, if we add the cash equivalent for board, averaged perhaps 50 percent more a day than a year-laborer and thus could theoretically match his annual earnings in a matter of 100 to 150 days. But few day-laborers were able to find that much work in a year. In Michang, for example, the 54 men who hired out worked only an average of 54.8 days in 1936 (MT, Kitō 1937b: 25–26). In less commercialized Dabeiguan 64 men hired out for an average of 41 days in 1936 (MT, Kitō 1937a: 26–29). Even so, this supplementary income was crucial to the poor peasant household, as can be seen in Table 11.5. The year-laborers of Michang earned from 70 yuan to 110 yuan, counting their board (MT, Hokushi jimukyoku chōsabu, 1938–41, 1: Tables 1, 14, 40), well above the net farm income of four of the five poor peasant households. But with their added wages, those households were able to equal or exceed that amount. The poor peasant mode of operation was thus in reality family farming *plus* wage work.* If we add to the purely economic benefit of this cash income the fact that these peasants could still retain the sense of being their own bosses on their family farms, and that their social status in the village community was generally higher than that of the year-laborers (a point to which we will return), it becomes perfectly understandable why poor peasants should have chosen to cling to their undersized farms.

### FAMILY FARMS AND YEAR-LABOR

Even year-laborers were inextricably tied to the small family farm economy. In Table 11.6 I have compiled data on the landownership and inheritances of 23 year-laborer heads of household in four Hebei villages. As can be seen, in the 1930's ten of these men still owned and operated tiny farms of one to six mu (usually with the help of the women and children of their household). Of the remaining 13, five had inherited some land and had only recently sold it to become completely "proletarianized" agricultural wage workers. Two other households had come from families that had owned some land. Only four of the 23 were clearly landless for the second generation in a row. (The landownership status of the fathers of the remaining two is not recorded.)

That the majority of year-laborers still relied partly on their tiny plots of land for a living should not really be surprising. At wages that amounted only to the equivalent of the foodgrain consumption needs of one adult male (above and beyond his own board), the completely proletarianized agricultural worker could not really afford to maintain a family. Had women been able to work as agricultural workers or in other jobs, these men might have been able to form

---

*The Land Reform Law of 1950 in fact used hiring out as one of the defining characteristics of the poor peasant (*Tudigaige shouce* 1951: 56).

## TABLE 11.6
## Landholdings of Year-Laborer Heads of Household in Four Hebei Villages, 1936–1942
(Land in mu)

| Village and household | Age | Household size | Land owned | Land inherited | Land owned by father | Land owned by grandfather | Number of generations resident in village |
|---|---|---|---|---|---|---|---|
| Shajing (1942) | | | | | | | |
| Li Zhuyuan | 47 | 2 | 4 | 20 | | | Old family |
| Zhao Wensheng | ? | 4 | 0 | 10 | | | Old family |
| Liu Tanlin | ? | 4 | 6 | 6 | | | Old family |
| Yang Yongyuan | 41 | 7 | 3 | 20 | | | Old family |
| Yang Yongrui | 46 | 4 | 3 | 20 | | | Old family |
| Li Guangxiang | ? | 3 | 0 | 0 | | | Old family |
| Yang Mingwang | 43 | 6 | 3 | 6 | | | Old family |
| Michang (1936) | | | | | | | |
| Household 102 | ? | 4 | 0 | 9 | 9 | 39 | 13 |
| Household 103 | ? | 4 | 0 | 0 | 0 | ? | 5 |
| Household 104 | ? | 4 | 0 | 3 | 3 | 6 | 14 |
| Household 105 | ? | 6 | 0 | 0 | 0 | 0 | 14 |
| Household 106 | ? | 2 | 0 | 0 | 0 | 0 | 1 |
| Sibeichai (1942) | | | | | | | |
| Zhao Xiaoxin | 38 | 2(U) | 4 | 12 | | | Old family |
| Wang Gouyin | 54 | 2 | 1 | 20 | | | ? |
| Hao Geban | 38 | 6 | 4 | ? | | | Old family |
| Xu Jinzhu | 39 | 4 | 5 | ? | | | Old family |
| Zhang Luolin | 43 | 3 | 3 | 3 | | | Old family |
| Hao Changming | 41 | 2(U) | 0 | ? | | | Old family |
| Qianlianggezhuang (1936) | | | | | | | |
| Wang Fulai | 31–45 | 4 | 0 | 0 | 5 | 15 | 2 |
| Hou Junde | 20–30 | 5 | 0 | 0 | 0 | 0 | 3 |
| Fu Long | 46–50 | 1(U) | 0 | 0 | 2 | ? | Since Ming |
| Zhang Keshun | 56–60 | 2 | 0 | 11 | 22 | ? | ? |
| Fu Yunxing | 46–50 | 5 | 0 | 17 | 51 | ? | Since Ming |

SOURCES: *Shajing*, KC, 1: Appended chart; *Michang*, MT, Kitō 1937b: 7–10, 25–28; *Sibeichai*, KC, 3: 524–32; *Qianlianggezhuang*, MT, Kitō 1937c: 10–11, 20–23, 26–27.

NOTE: (U) indicates unmarried worker.

families and reproduce. As things were, however, the overabundance of surplus labor in a stagnant economy ruled out such employment opportunities for women. The result was that the completely proletarianized male agricultural workers tended to remain an unmarried "bare stick" (*guanggun*) and become the last generation of their families. That is why we find that the majority of these men were landless only in their own generation, just recently pressed down from the ranks of poor peasants, and still clinging for as long as they could to their land to supplement their inadequate wages. These were not individuals joining a group engaged in a new and dynamic form of production, but people about to fall to the bottom of the social heap, their ranks to be replenished by other poor peasants on the downward slide.* That is the difference between a society undergoing capitalist development and one merely undergoing social differentiation with little or no economic growth.

The combined workings of population pressure and social stratification on a stagnant peasant economy thus resulted in a tenacious system that was particularly vicious in human terms. Poor peasants came to be locked into a dual dependence on family farming and hiring out, unable to do one without the other, and compelled to accept below-subsistence incomes from both. Their cheap labor, in turn, propped up a nonproductive landlordism and a stagnant managerial agriculture. Poor peasants, more than anyone else in the rural society, had to labor under the mutually reinforcing pressures of overpopulation and unequal social relations.

---

*Moise 1977 uses scale analysis to show how the removal of a portion of the rural population from the bottom of society lowered the relative position of others even if nothing else was changed.

# CHAPTER 12

# The Commercialization of
# Production Relations

Social differentiation along the axes of rent and wage labor was joined in the twentieth century by substantial changes in the nature of those production relations. Accelerated commercialization resulted in an overall trend toward the replacement of personalized and relatively durable relationships by impersonal and short-term arrangements based wholly on supply and demand.

Conventional Marxist analysis has generally equated the depersonalization of production relations with progressive developments: greater personal independence for tenants and laborers, the waning of feudalism, the spread of a commodity economy, and the development of capitalism (see, for example, Liu Yongcheng 1979a). Substantivists take the opposite view: the precapitalist peasant society has a moral economy in which patron-client relations and reciprocity obtain, and in which landlords observe the tenants' right to subsistence and reduce or waive rents when that right is threatened. The coming of impersonal capitalist market relations does not make things better for tenants and laborers. Instead, it breaks down the moral economy and makes class relations harsher than before (Scott 1966: Chaps. 1, 2, 6).

Though such an analysis projects a somewhat romanticized view of class relations in a precapitalist peasant society, it has the virtue of directing our attention to ways in which production relations might have become harsher with commercialization. This chapter will show that in Hebei–northwest Shandong the process did lead, as Marxist analysis suggests, to the increased independence of tenants and laborers from personalized ties to their landlords and employers. That aspect of the change needs to be understood as part of the larger process of the partial proletarianization of increasing numbers of the peasantry. The tenant paying a fixed rent on a year-to-year contract was more like the proletarian of the modern age than the long-term sharecropper with a strongly proprietary attitude toward "his farm." But the changes in production relations need to be considered also in light of the constant threats of floods and other disasters in this area: in such an unstable environment, fixed rents (whether in kind or in cash) were much harsher than sharecropping, putting the burden of crop failures entirely on the tenants. In addition, the end of ceremonial patterns of reciprocity that had helped cloak the harshness of the class relationship probably aggravated the tensions in the landlord-tenant and employer–wage worker relationship. In these respects, the substantivist analysis is correct in emphasis if not in specifics.

### FROM SHARECROPPING TO FIXED RENTS

As we saw in Chapter Five, in eighteenth-century Hebei–northwest Shandong possibly two-thirds of the rental agreements were based on sharecropping. This appears to have remained the preferred arrangement down to the eve of the twentieth century. Table 12.1 shows the rental arrangements that prevailed in six villages at the

TABLE 12.1

Rental Forms in Six Hebei and Shandong Villages, 1890's and 1940's

| Village | Form of rental, 1890's | 1940's, tenants and part-tenants | | |
|---------|------------------------|------------|------------|-------------|
| | | No. of house-holds | % of all farming house-holds | Form of rental |
| Houxiazhai (1942) | Mainly share of crop (*fenzhong*) | 13 | 10.5% | 50% share of crop; 50% fixed rent-in-kind |
| Shajing (1942) | Mainly share of crop (*huozhong*) | 13 | 22.4 | 80% fixed cash rent |
| Sibeichai (1942) | Mainly share of crop (*shaozhong*) | 71 | 64.5 | Mainly fixed rent-in-kind (*baozhong*) |
| Lengshuigou (1941) | Part share of crop (*fenzhong*); part fixed rent-in-kind (*nazu*) | 25 | 7.9 | Mainly fixed rent-in-kind |
| Houjiaying (1942) | Part share of crop; part cash rent (*diandi*) | 48 | 46.6 | All fixed cash rent |
| Wudian (1942) | Mainly share of crop (*fenzhong*) | 52 | 91.2 | 90% fixed rent-in-kind (*siliang*) |

SOURCES: Houxiazhai, KC, 4: 462–63, 475; Shajing, KC, 2: 81; Sibeichai, KC, 3: 217, 235, 241; Lengshuigou, KC, 4: 9, 147, 154, 174–75; Houjiaying, KC, 5: 5, 159, 163, 182; Wudian, KC, 5: 518, 537–38.

NOTE: The local term used for the rental form is given in parentheses.

TABLE 12.2

National Survey Data on Rental Forms in Hebei and Shandong, 1935–1936

| | Hebei | | Shandong | |
|---|---|---|---|---|
| Rental form | Land Commission (9,752 hsehlds.) | Ministry of Industry (107 counties) | Land Commission (12,084 hsehlds.) | Ministry of Industry (83 counties) |
| Fixed: cash | 62.6% | 52.3% | 22.1% | 30.4% |
| Fixed: in kind | 17.6 | 21.6 | 36.6 | 30.5 |
| Total fixed | 80.2 | 73.9 | 58.7 | 60.9 |
| Share of crop | 16.7 | 26.1 | 40.3 | 39.1 |
| Other | 3.1 | — | 1.0 | — |
| TOTAL | 100.0% | 100.0% | 100.0% | 100.0% |

SOURCES: Tudiweiyuanhui 1937: 43; *Nongqing baogao*, 3.4 (April 1935), cited in Yagi 1943: 17–18.

time they were surveyed by the Japanese and in the 1890's. Five of the seven categories of villages in my typology are represented in this group (uncommercialized villages and suburban villages are not included). Though the shift to fixed rents was already well in evidence in two of the villages by the 1890's—Lengshuigou, a village with developed rural industry, and Houjiaying, a home village of emigrants to Manchuria—sharecropping was clearly still the conventional arrangement. But sharecropping gave way to fixed rents so rapidly under the impact of the accelerated commercialization of agriculture that by the early 1940's the shift was not only in evidence everywhere, but virtually complete. Only in the moderately commercialized village of Houxiazhai was sharecropping still relatively common, but even there fixed rents had made considerable inroads since the turn of the century.

This fact is confirmed by the national surveys of the time. Table 12.2 shows two sets of figures for 1935–36, one collected by the Guomindang and the other by the Ministry of Industry. According to these figures, about four-fifths of all rentals in Hebei and three-fifths in Shandong were based on fixed rents by this time.

SHARECROPPING

Sharecropping was predicated on resident landlordism and generally involved a considerable amount of personal contact between landlord and tenant. It typically took place between kin or close friends, usually resident in the same village, and was based solely on a verbal agreement. Asked why no written contract was drawn up, a Lengshuigou villager replied: "Because the agreement is generally between kin or people who are close. Moreover, since the rent is collected by the landlord himself at the field, there is really no need to worry about nonpayment" (KC, 4:464; see also Yagi 1943: 117). Wang Zanzhou, the absentee landlord of Sibeichai, pointed out, similarly, that he did not require an intermediary or guarantor for the few sharecropping agreements he had (almost all his rental contracts involved fixed rents-in-kind), because he reserved these for only the "most trustworthy" tenants (KC, 3:241).

Sharecrop rent was generally collected in two ways. In the *fenlong* system, the landlord and the tenant divided up the crop before harvest by counting the furrows, and the landlord or his hired hand then came to the fields and harvested his rows.* In the *fengu* system, the landlord came to the fields after the harvest, and the two men divided up the grain peck by peck (KC, 2:80–81). Because of the personalized nature of this relationship, tenants usually had certain other obligations to their landlords. In Houxiazhai, for example, a sharecropper was expected as a matter of custom to pay his respects to his landlord on holidays, to give token wedding and funeral gifts to members of his family, and to help with their house construction and repairs. In the most dependent form of sharecropping, where the tenant's only contribution was labor, he got two shares of the crop to the landlord's eight, as indicated in the term *erbafenzi*. Such a "two-eight tenant" was expected to do additional work for the landlord, such as helping him move soil and manure, and making small household repairs (KC, 4:465). Marxist analysis has emphasized the exploitative character of these extra-economic obligations.

On the other hand, the fact that landlord and tenant were generally relatives or friends made for a high degree of stability in the sharecropping relationship. An uncle leasing to his nephew in the same village was unlikely to change tenants from year to year. And stability, in turn, made it possible for the sharecropper to think of the plot he worked as "his farm." Moreover, the harshness of an economic relationship in which the landlord usually extracted one-half of the produce was cloaked by the ties of kinship or friendship. In these respects, the substantivists' analysis seems to me essentially correct.

But James Scott's suggestion that landlords were morally bound to reduce or waive rents when their tenants' "moral claim" to a "right to subsistence" was threatened, as for example by natural disaster,

---

*This system permitted the landlord to pick the better furrows, as one Shajing tenant pointed out (Yagi 1943: 104).

seems to me unlikely to have obtained in this area. The typical land-lord here was the small landlord, a man whose standard of living was not separated from that of his sharecropper by as wide a gulf as that between the large gentry landlord and his sharecropper. For such landlords, a natural disaster that reduced the harvest by half, and therefore cut his expected rental income in half, might threaten his accustomed standard of living. A further reduction might well have meant, from his point of view, real hardship and a threat to his "sub-sistence." For the poor peasant sharecropper struggling to survive in the zone between meeting just his own foodgrain requirements and meeting those of his entire household, subsistence could mean as little as two meals of coarse grain gruel a day, and wheat-flour buns without meat at New Year's. To the small landlord, however, cus-tomary subsistence often included refined flour, polished rice, and meat. To expect him to willingly absorb a reduction in his subsis-tence level in order to honor some nebulous "moral claim" to a nebulous "right to subsistence" at some indeterminate level seems to me an excessively sanguine expectation. Such a landlord could not be expected to act according to a moral code that might have fig-ured among the very rich, who could more easily afford charity. Rent relations for such landlords after all basically concerned a zero-sum situation in which the gain of the tenant was a substantial loss for the landlord. I do not think they should be equated with patron-client relations between, say, an official and the degree candidate he sponsored, in which the gain of one was also the gain of the other.

In fact, this was a question that the Mantetsu investigators ex-plored. A Shajing villager was asked: "In sharecropping, when the harvest is bad, does the landlord ever let the tenant take all of the produce?" "No," the informant replied. "Does the landlord ever re-duce the proportion due him to allow the tenant a larger share?" "No." Likewise, in Huzhuang village, Ninghe county, northeastern Hebei, investigators were told that landlords always insisted on the agreed-on rent. Only in Sunjiamiao village, in Huimin county, Shan-dong, were rents sometimes waived when the harvest was less than one-tenth of the usual level. Otherwise, even if the harvest was barely over that level, there was no reduction (Yagi 1943: 124–25).

The fact that sharecropping was often between kin and friends, that it involved considerable personal contact, clearly did not alter the harsh realities of a zero-sum situation. In sharecropping, as in loans, the prevailing rates seem to have been accepted by all parties as the appropriate ones. Given the very keen competition for rentals and for loans in the small-parcel economy, the special consideration given friends and kin often consisted in the very act of leasing or lending to the person, and did not extend to special considerations in the terms of tenure or rent. As one villager observed, when a poor kinsman seeks to rent your land, he receives priority because he is a relative, but that tie does not make the rent any cheaper or its collection any less important (KC, 5 : 143–44). When sharecropping terms were extended in the face of the preponderance of harsher fixed rents, this logic applied all the more. In Lengshuigou, as has been seen, such arrangements were made only between relatives or very close friends. In Sibeichai Wang Zanzhou reserved his few sharecropping rentals for the most trusted tenants. That was favor enough.

### FIXED RENTS

The impersonal, fixed-rent system emerged in part as a result of the urbanization of landlords, who became involved in nonfarm pursuits and sought to minimize the time and work required in rent collection. Asked why he preferred fixed rents, a Houjiaying landlord replied: "It is simpler" (KC, 5 : 194). In sharecropping the landlord had to be physically present to make sure that he was actually getting his proportion of the crops. It was also a time-consuming arrangement, whether he collected his rent by doing the harvesting himself or by measuring out the grain after the harvest. Fixed rents made things a lot easier. The reason why Wang Zanzhou's father had introduced the practice in Sibeichai, according to one villager, was that "he had so much land and couldn't attend to everything" (KC, 3 : 235). Zanzhou himself also put the matter very clearly: he used fixed rents "for convenience and because sharecropping was cumbersome" (KC, 3 : 241). In part also, as we will see in the next section, fixed rents were the landlords' response to heightened instability in the Hebei–northwest Shandong countryside.

Not surprisingly, fixed-rent agreements often took place between landlords and tenants not previously known to each other. One consequence was the need for intermediaries—go-betweens who could bring together prospective landlord and tenant, and serve as a conduit for working out the terms of the agreement. Variously called the *zhongjianren* (middleman), the *jieshaoren* (person making the introduction), or the *shuoheren* (person talking [the two parties] into an agreement), the intermediary was typically someone well known to both parties who would move back and forth between them, holding one or two discussions with each as he nailed down the terms of tenure and payment.* If the agreement was a written one, the inter-

---

*This was the pattern in Shajing, Sibeichai, Houjiaying, Wudian, and Lengshuigou alike (see KC, 2 : 73–74; 3 : 161–63, 188; 4 : 147, 177; 5 : 156, 178, 182, 436).

mediary's name might be included in the contract (as in Lengshui-gou and Sibeichai).

Though these men acted as brokers, they were not paid for their services. In rare cases, an intermediary would be treated to a meal by the landlord (KC, 5 : 156), but usually he got no remuneration of any kind, not even a token gift from the landlord or the tenant. There was thus no such thing as a professional rental broker in the countryside despite the increasing reliance on this brokering system as fixed rents became the established practice.

If a tenant failed to pay rent, the landlord would approach the intermediary to press the man for the money, but the middleman had no legal obligation to the landlord and was not liable for the tenant's rent. He was thus not a guarantor or sponsor, even though in undertaking this role he was often in some sense vouching for the tenant's reliability to the landlord.

When the rental contracts involved in-kind payments, there was sometimes personal contact between the tenant and the landlord at the time the rent was due. Some Lengshuigou landlords, for example, either collected the rent themselves or had the tenant bring the crop to their homes or storehouses (Yagi 1943: 171−72). Occasionally, a fixed rent-in-kind agreement retained certain other features of the older sharecropping arrangement. In Lengshuigou, for instance, the terms were sometimes converted to a share of the crop if the yield fell below 60 percent of the usual harvest. A few rental agreements in Sibeichai made similar provision for a harvest that fell below 50 percent. But such practices were merely vestiges of the old system that lingered on in the transition to the new one. In most fixed-rent arrangements the relationship was an inflexible one, in which tenants were required to pay the full amount due regardless of the harvest (*ibid.*, pp. 167−70).

The final stage in this development was of course the payment of cash rents, generally in advance of cultivation. By the late 1930's this was the predominant or exclusive form in two of the six villages in Table 12.1, Shajing and Houjiaying. The usual practice was for the tenant to make a deposit as soon as agreement was reached, and to pay the balance by the fifteenth of the tenth month in the year before he used the land. In no case was the deposit or the rent payment ever returned, according to the villagers' testimony (Yagi 1943: 225−26). Such arrangements were so completely depersonalized that the tenant generally never met the landlord, making the agreement and paying the rent entirely through the intermediary (KC, 2 : 73−74).

Commercialization paralleled depersonalization. Cash rents were tied to price movements and the dictates of supply and demand in ways that sharecropping was not. When prices rose, landlords found themselves under great pressure to raise rents to keep up. And when the demand for rentals exceeded the supply, some landlords were tempted to bump one tenant for another willing to pay a higher rent.

One result was an increasingly rapid turnover in land rentals. Table 12.3 shows how long each rental relationship in three Hebei villages had been in effect without a change in landlord, tenant, or land at the time of the Mantetsu survey—1936 in all three cases. As we see, fully two-thirds of the arrangements had existed for only five years or less. Moreover, 87 of the 301 tenants, or almost 30 percent, were farming a new plot under a new agreement. The picture one gets is of a fairly high rate of turnover in rent relationships, a far cry from the permanent tenure that had generally characterized share-cropping and that was still relatively common in the lower Yangzi valley. (Permanent tenure agreements accounted for 41 percent, 31 percent, and 44 percent, respectively, of all rentals in Jiangsu, Zhe-jiang, and Anhui, in the mid-1930's, as compared with a mere 4 percent in Hebei and Shandong; Tudiweiyuanhui 1937: 45–46.)

Wartime inflation brought still more rapid turnovers. As shown in Table 12.4, by the late 1930's most rentals in one-crop-a-year north-eastern Hebei were made on a year-to-year basis. (A Shajing ten-ant duly noted how quickly the situation had changed: "In the past rental tenures usually continued for three, five years, or even longer, but recently rentals usually change every year"; KC, 2:74.) In north-west Shandong the contracts usually ran for two years, to allow for the completion of the three-crops-in-two-years planting cycle. Where

TABLE 12.3
Rental Tenure in Three Hebei Villages, 1936

| Number of years tenure | Dabeiguan | | Michang | | Qianlianggezhuang | | | |
|---|---|---|---|---|---|---|---|---|
| | Number of contracts | Percent of total | Number of contracts | Percent of total | Number of contracts | Percent of total | Total | Percent |
| 1 | 34 | 59.6% | 21 | 17.2% | 32 | 26.2% | 87 | 28.9% |
| 2–5 | 18 | 31.6 | 20 | 16.4 | 74 | 60.7 | 112 | 37.2 |
| 6–10 | 4 | 7.0 | 14 | 11.5 | 13 | 10.7 | 31 | 10.3 |
| >10 | 1 | 1.8 | 67 | 54.9 | 3 | 2.5 | 71 | 23.6 |
| TOTAL | 57 | 100.0% | 122 | 100.0% | 122 | 100.1% | 301 | 100.0% |

SOURCES: *Dabeiguan*, MT, Kitō 1937a: 40–43; *Michang*, MT, Kitō 1937b: 39–50; *Qianliangge-zhuang*, MT, Kitō 1937c: 36–45.

TABLE 12.4

Predominant Rental Arrangements in 15 Hebei and Shandong Villages, 1936–1942

| Rental form | Village | Duration of agreement (years) |
|---|---|---|
| | HEBEI | |
| Fixed cash rent | Asuwei, Dabeiguan, Houyansi, Jigezhuang, Shajing, Xiaoying, Longwo, Michang, Qianlianggezhuang, each | 1 |
| | Houjiaying | Indef.[a] |
| Fixed rent-in-kind | Sibeichai | Indef.[a] |
| | Wudian | 1 |
| | SHANDONG | |
| Fixed cash rent | Sunjiamiao | 2 |
| Fixed rent-in-kind | Houxiazhai,[b] Lengshuigou | 3–5 |

SOURCES: *Dabeiguan, Michang, Qianlianggezhuang,* MT, Kitō 1937a: 40–43, Kitō 1937b: 39–50, Kitō 1937c: 36–45; *Sibeichai, Lengshuigou, Houxiazhai, Wudian, Houjiaying,* KC, 3: 187, 4: 147, 4: 461, 5: 511, 5: 158; all others, Yagi 1943: 207–10.
[a] The written contracts did not specify a time period but were understood to require verbal renewal every year.
[b] Most of the fixed-rent agreements required payment in kind, but half of the renters in this village were still sharecroppers (see Table 12.1).

fixed rents were paid in kind, tenants were often given longer contracts, because the landlords were not under the same pressure to adjust rents for price movements.

Villagers found the rapid turnover easy to explain. Year-to-year contracts worked to the advantage of the landlords because "they can raise the rent" (Yagi 1943: 232–33). As one Shajing peasant put it:

> The most common reason for terminating a rental is an increase in rent. On occasion, a rental is terminated because of the partition of family property. It is seldom because of selling or pawning land. It is almost never caused by disputes. The practice of one tenant bumping another surreptitiously by offering a higher rent has become common last year and this year. (KC, 2:75)

So common had this practice become in fact that villagers had developed a special term for it: *duanqian* (lit., pulling or dragging by gripping one tip of a string or rope). Tenant bumping was considered unethical and had to be done "in the secret of the night" (KC, 2:75).

By the end of the 1930's, in sum, the renting of land had come to be highly commercialized, subject to the play of an impersonal market. Tenant and landlord seldom knew each other. The harshness of the economic relationship was no longer cloaked under personal relations involving kin, friends, or neighbors. Land had to a large extent become a highly liquid asset whose interest rates, much like those of other forms of capital, were pegged to market conditions. Tenants renting land under these circumstances were essentially partially proletarianized peasants, a quite different breed from the proprietor-like long-term sharecropping tenants of an earlier day.

RELATIVE RENTAL BURDEN

The change from sharecropping to fixed rents did not in itself necessarily render the burden of rent either more or less harsh. Sharecropping meant that landlord and tenant shared in the gains as well as the losses in the harvests. Fixed rents, however, separated the rent from the harvest, and the fortunes of the landlord from those of the tenant. Whether it worked to the advantage of the landlord or the tenant depended on how it was adjusted to farm yields. In villages like Sibeichai, the landlords were able to impose fixed rents that amounted in effect to a larger proportion of the produce than before. In villages like Michang, on the other hand, tenants benefited from fixed rents in the switchover to cotton cultivation after the 1910's. Here there were no landlords like Wang Zanzhou and his father in Sibeichai to dictate terms that benefited the landlord. On land under cotton, rents actually shrank as a proportion of produce—from the old fifty percent of the harvest on land cropped under sorghum to about one-third of the harvest.

In most of the North China plain, however, returns on the land in the twentieth century remained close to earlier levels. The switch to commercial crops, after all, involved only a relatively small part of the total cultivated land. The same relatively noninflatable foodgrains continued to be grown on most of the land, with little increase in yields to redistribute between landlords and tenants. Actual rents collected thus remained at the level of about 50 percent of the crop into the last years before the war (53.7 percent in Hebei in 1936, and 49.8 percent in Shandong; Tudiweiyuanhui 1937: 44).

For this area, the real significance of the change to fixed rents needs to be understood instead against the background of the political and environmental instabilities of the twentieth century. This period saw the addition of a multitude of man-made disasters to the chronic instabilities of the natural environment. Neglect of flood control by the rapidly changing warlord and local governments; banditry, which became endemic with the civil wars of the 1920's; the disruptions of the civil wars themselves; and Japanese invasion all combined to place vast areas of the countryside under permanent siege and predation. Table 12.5 brings these disasters down to the level of individual villages. It is hardly surprising that the three villages that were relatively less hard hit by disasters—Houxiazhai an Lengshuigou, in northwest Shandong, and Sibeichai, in souther Hebei—were relatively more prosperous than the other village shown. Shajing and Houjiaying, in northeastern Hebei, and Wudian in central Hebei on the main road to Beijing, barely had time to re cover from one major disaster, from flood, drought, or warlord requi sitions, before suffering another.

Such instabilities meant that, over time, total returns from the land declined, even if agricultural productivity remained at a relatively constant level in the normal years. That lent new urgency to the question of which party—the landlord or the tenant—was to absorb the losses from such disasters.

This was precisely how the villagers perceived the situation. Asked by Japanese investigators, "Generally speaking, what arrangement does the tenant prefer?," Zhang Yueqing (who had been the village head of Sibeichai for 12 years) replied, "Sharecropping." "And the landlord?" "Fixed rent" (KC, 3:201). As one Shajing tenant put it:

> From the standpoint of the tenant, sharecropping is a better arrangement than cash rent. In our locality, which often has natural disasters, cash rent, since it is paid in advance, means that all is lost in a disaster year. Sharecropping, on the other hand, means that rent is paid after the harvest, and that rent is based on one-half of the actual produce. It is therefore safer. For this reason, it is better for the tenant. (KC, 2:42)

As for landlords, to the question "Why have landlords changed from sharecropping to fixed rents?," one leasing landowner replied, "Because [in sharecropping] I had no fixed income" (KC, 2:235).

Fixed rents, in other words, were the landlords' response to declining returns due to the twentieth-century instabilities in this area, a way to make the tenant shoulder all the risks and losses from natural and man-made disasters instead of having to accept them along with the sharecropper. Where, as in Sibeichai, population pressure put rental land in short supply, landlords were of course easily able to arrange things to their liking.

The predominance of one or another institutional form in a village usually meant also the predominance of a certain set of expectations about what was just in the allocating of the burdens from

TABLE 12.5

Natural and Man-Made Disasters in Six Hebei and Shandong Villages, 1917–1941

| Year | Houxiazhai | Shajing | Sibeichai | Lengshuigou | Houjiaying | Wudian |
|---|---|---|---|---|---|---|
| '917 | | | Flood[a] | | *Average* | |
| 918 | Bandits | | | | *of one* | |
| 919 | | Flood[b] | | | *major* | |
| 920 | | | | | *flood* | |
| 1921 | | | | | *every* | |
| 1922 | | | | | *four* | |
| 1923 | | Drought | | | *years* | |
| 1924 | | | | | | Warlord war |
| 1925 | | | | | | Flood[b] |
| 1926 | | Warlord war | | | | |
| 1927 | | | | | | |
| 1928 | | Warlord war; frost | Locusts[b] | | | Flood[b] |
| 1929 | | Flood[c] | | | | Flood[b] |
| 1930 | | | | | | |
| 1931 | | | | Locusts[c] | | |
| 1932 | | | | | | |
| 1933 | | | | | | |
| 1934 | Locusts | | | | | |
| 1935 | | | | | | |
| 1936 | | | | | | |
| 1937 | Flood | | Japanese | Flood | | |
| 1938 | | Flood[c] | war | | | |
| 1939 | | Flood[c] | | | | |
| 1940 | Hail; boll-worms | | | | | Drought[c] |
| 1941 | Hail | | | | Bandits | Drought[c] |

SOURCES: *Houxiazhai*, KC, 4: 397; *Shajing*, KC, 1: 91, 2: 160, 181, 268, 293, 499; *Sibeichai*, KC, 3: 222, 223, 237, 307; *Lengshuigou*, KC, 4: 40, 48, 162; *Houjiaying*, KC, 5: 147, 180; *Wudian*, KC, 5: 420, 576.

[a]More than ¾ of the crop destroyed.
[b]¼ to ½ of the crop destroyed.
[c]½ to ¾ of the crop destroyed.

disasters. In a community dominated by sharecropping rentals, a "sharecropping ethic," we might say, generally prevailed. Landlords were expected to share in the loss. Where fixed rents prevailed, disasters were assumed to be matters of no concern to the landlords. As has been seen, some of the landlords of Lengshuigou and other villages under fixed rents in the 1930's still made some concession to the old sharecropping ethic by settling for a share of the harvest in case of severe crop losses. Those arrangements, which were not the rule even in those villages, were merely transitional in the broad trend toward the use of fixed rents in this area.

WAGE LABOR

In the course of the Ming–Qing transition, as has been seen, worker-serfs personally bound to their estate masters gave way to free wage laborers employed mainly by commoners. My sample of those rural wage laborers shows that a large proportion of them were not locals, but in-migrants from other counties and provinces (Tables 5.1–5.3). Early Qing society was a highly fluid one that saw much migration from one area to another.

Still, when we compare the employer-worker relations of that time to those of the twentieth century, we can see a trend similar to that observed for rent relations. The pre-twentieth-century agricultural wage laborer tended to be a long-term employee, as indicated by the very term *changgong* (lit., "long-term laborer"). He also tended to have strong personal ties to his employer, often practically becoming a member of his household. As the Board of Punishment noted in its ruling on a case in 1760, relatives often employed each other; and employer and wage laborer, as the 1788 code noted, normally "sit and eat together and are not differentiated from each other like serfs from masters." The harshness of the economic relationship, moreover, tended to be cloaked, for both employer and worker, by a variety of ceremonial relationships. Traces of those ceremonials remained down to the 1930's. At the beginning of the year's work, for example, it was customary for the employer to provide a special meal with such treats as rice or wheat-flour buns, and sometimes even a little wine. A similar treat was often given after harvest (KC, 2:54; 5:172). In certain places the employer gave the laborer a "red envelope" containing three to five yuan at New Year's (KC, 4:172; Kita Shina 1943b: 57; but this practice had already been abandoned in Shajing, for example; KC, 2:52–54). In the summer employers were sometimes expected to supply their laborers with a straw hat or a hand towel (KC, 4:172; Kita Shina 1943b: 57). They might even give them tobacco and matches, as the employers in Lengshuigou did (KC, 4:3). On the occasion of a wedding or funeral in the laborer's family, his employer might contribute a token 50 cents or one yuan for snacks (KC, 2:54).

The twentieth century, however, saw great fluidity in employer–wage laborer relationships, much greater even than in the highly fluid early Qing society. Increased employment opportunities with further commercialization, disruptions caused by man-made and natural disasters, the attractions of urban and frontier employment, and so on, all contributed to increased movement in rural society. Though we do not have data on this development of the same degree of detail as on the change in rent relations, some indication of its extent is provided by evidence from individual villages. In Houjia-ying, for example, the twentieth century saw a constant flow of villagers on the move to Manchuria to take advantage of the employment opportunities offered by the new frontier. Such movement turned rent relations wholly into fixed cash-rent arrangements, as shown in Table 12.1. A similar development occurred in wage-labor relations. As one employer in the village noted for the Japanese investigators, employment in the village had come to be usually for periods of only one year at a time (KC, 5:172).

In Shajing, similarly, the twentieth century saw an outflow of workers to take up jobs in the cities. In 1942, 34 villagers were working more or less permanently in urban enterprises, mainly in Beijing, this in addition to the 50 to 60 who went to Beijing each winter for seasonal employment in the manufacture of candied religious offerings (KC, 1:Appended chart; 2:23). The frequent disasters that struck this village (see Table 12.5) only added to its progressive atomization. The result, in rent relations, was a dramatic shift from long-term sharecropping to year-to-year rentals that required cash payments in advance. The shift to short-term wage-labor relations was no less dramatic. Take the managerial farmer Zhang Wentong (and his son Rui) for example. In the late 1930's Zhang had in his employ two Shajing villagers and another laborer from a neighboring village, all of whom had worked for him five or six years. In 1941, however, the two village laborers moved away, and the third laborer turned to other work. Zhang had to hire three new laborers from outside the village. Two of these men left at the end of 1941, so that Zhang was again in search of laborers at the time of his interview with Japanese investigators (KC, 2:52–53). As with rental agreements, by the 1930's and early 1940's wage-laborer contracts were generally for only one year and were reached verbally through a middleman. (See, for example, MT, Tenshin jimusho chōsaka 1936a: 165–66; Kita Shina 1943b: 54–57.) This trend was in fact reflected in the rise of another term for agricultural wage laborers: *niangong* (lit., "year-laborers").

Under these conditions, many of the earlier customary ceremonials in employer–wage laborer relations fell into disuse. The employers of Shajing, as we saw, no longer observed the custom of giving their wage laborers red envelopes at New Year's; nor did they supply them with straw hats and hand towels in the summer months or give them tobacco and matches as small, ingratiating gestures. The relationship between them was becoming a much more purely economic one, stripped of the former mitigating ceremonial cloak.

The accclerated commercialization of the twentieth century thus substantially altered the lives of tenants and laborers in Hebei– northwest Shandong. Where once the typical tenant had share-cropped on a long-term basis with a landlord whom he knew person-ally, the typical tenant of the 1930's paid a fixed rent, generally in advance and usually on a year-to-year contract, to a landlord whom he often did not know or even see. And where once the typical wage worker had worked for a kinsman who maintained a ceremonial re-lationship of reciprocity with him, the typical wage worker of the 1930's worked for a single wage without any ceremonial niceties on his part or his employer's. Tenants and agricultural laborers alike had taken on more of the characteristics of the free "proletarian" selling his labor for a wage.

These changes were part of the three-centuries-long process of agrarian change in North China that involved the combined work-ings of involution, social differentiation, and semiproletarianiza-tion. The heart of that process was the formation of an involuted-differentiated peasant economy and society in which one-half of the peasants were partly proletarianized, locked into a dependence on both family farming and wage labor for survival. Compared with the smallholder of the early Qing, these poor peasants led a different and more precarious existence: their family farms were involved in market-oriented production to a much greater degree; their farms were also generally undersized relative to their labor supply, a result both of population pressure and of unequal distribution; their farm-ing income was generally too small to live on, so that household members had to hire out to supplement that income; and wages, like net income after rent payments, were driven to bare-bones levels, a result of the combined workings of unequal production relations with population pressure. The burden of rent, meanwhile, had also become heavier with the switch away from sharecropping; and rent and wage labor alike had come to operate more and more by the im-personal logic of the market, without the ceremonial niceties of an earlier age. By the 1930's, in short, the peasants of the North China plain were coping with social and economic conditions very differ-ent from those that their early Qing predecessors faced.

# 3

# THE VILLAGE
# AND THE STATE

# CHAPTER 13

# Villages
# Under the Qing State

Villages in prerevolutionary China were neither the wholly market-oriented entities of the formalist conception nor yet simply the stratified societies of the Marxists. Villages were at once atomized neighborhoods, stratified societies, and insular communities. It is this last, substantivist perception of the village as an isolated unit that has been too often overlooked.

This chapter will show that even in the 1930's, all but the most highly commercialized villages of the North China plain were still relatively insular communities. Villagers had minimal social intercourse with outsiders, and village affairs were governed largely by endogenous leaders, despite the state's repeated attempts to bring the countryside under its administrative control. All the evidence that I have come across strongly suggests that before the accelerated commercialization and political modernization of the twentieth century, most villages of the Hebei–northwest Shandong plain were only integrated into larger trading and political systems to a very limited extent.

To see the village as relatively insular units of commoners with their own political structures is to substantially revise the prevailing American and Chinese conceptions of the sociopolitical structure of Qing China. Instead of a dualistic structure shaped mainly by alternating shifts of power between state and gentry, we need to think in terms of a triangular structure involving three-way relations among state, gentry, and village. And instead of conceiving of an all-intrusive state, we need to think in terms of a two-tiered structure in which the state wielded direct power in the upper tier alone. It controlled the lower tier only indirectly through the gentry and by attracting the upwardly mobile members of the rural society into the upper tier. The sociopolitical changes of the twentieth century must be understood against this baseline.

## THE INSULARITY OF THE VILLAGES
### OF THE NORTH CHINA PLAIN

Let us begin by reviewing the differences between the villages of the North China plain and those of the Chengdu plain (where Skinner did his research on marketing structures). The distinctive residential patterns are the most immediately obvious difference between the two areas, the one marked by communities consisting of single large clusters of houses, the other by loosely grouped communities of scattered *ba* (or *yuanba*, or *yuanzi*) of a few houses each, usually defined by a bamboo grove.

It is a difference that accounts for important differences in the degree of community solidarity. In illustration, let us take the customs surrounding the building of a new house. On the North China plain, it was (and generally still is) the custom for an entire village to turn out to help. In Shajing the community typically contributed about 100 man-days for a five-room house (the usual size). On the first day, when the foundation was laid and the posts and beams put in, 20 to 30 men helped; on the second day, when the walls and the roof were built, 70 to 80 men helped. All members of the community were expected to lend a hand; and the owner of the house, in his turn, was expected to serve three meals a day to all helpers. According to my informants in 1980, even the kind of food one was expected to serve was pretty much set by custom: "coarse at the two ends, fine in the middle" (*liangtou cu, zhongjian xi*). In other words, coarse grains were adequate for breakfast and supper, but a fine grain (usually wheat-flour noodles) was expected at the main midday meal. In Xinyan village, south of Chengdu, by contrast, only neighbors of the same ba were expected to help.* But the fact that less manpower was needed for Chengdu area homes, which were built of relatively light and easy-to-carry bamboo, no doubt had something to do with the limited community participation there.

The other most striking difference between the two areas was in the degree of commercialization. Fertile and stable West Sichuan was long one of the most advanced parts of China. The completion of the Dujiang weir on the Min River in the third century B.C. brought flood control and irrigation to the Chengdu plain; and this, together with the mild climate, made possible two or even three crops a year of high yields. With three navigable rivers to form a network of trans-

---

*Xinyan village together with neighboring Shunjiang today forms the Ninth Brigade of the Cuqiao Commune, embracing 97 yuanba (interviews, brigade members, Nov. 1980).

port routes—the Yangzi, Jialing, and Min—crops were easily brought to market, with the result that peasants of this area spent as many as 72 days a year marketing their produce, compared with a mere 23 days in Hebei–northwest Shandong (Buck 1937b: 343).

The sharp differences between these two areas—particularly in residential patterns and degree of commercialization—suggest that though the market may have figured more importantly than the village community in the lives of the Chengdu peasants, this was not the case on the North China plain.

It was only after many hours of conversation with the seventy-year-old former middle peasant Li Guangzhi of Shajing village (a mere 45 kilometers northeast of Beijing, and only two kilometers from the county seat of Shunyi) that I realized how very different his social life had been from the one I had imagined with Skinner's marketing model. True, Li had gone to market often, whenever he could in fact. He tended to go more often before he and his brothers divided up the family's land (in 1944) than after, for he had a little more time to spare then. His reason for going was "*kan renao*," mainly, or "to watch the hustle and bustle," Li indicated. It was just more fun than working on the farm. And that was a much more important reason than selling or buying things. He had not really had that much to sell or that much to buy, for he grew mainly foodgrains on his farm. Beyond this point, reality diverged from the Skinner model. Li *never* went to a teahouse to chat; he found the idea a strange one. Nor, as I eventually realized, did he chat with anyone when at the market. Of course he would recognize some people, and he would "nod and break at the waist" (*diantou hayao*) in a kind of equivalent to tipping his hat. But according to him, he *never* stopped to chat. To talk with someone outside the village struck him as quite unthinkable.

But did he not at least chat with the villagers of neighboring Shimen, which was only about 30 yards or so up the path from the last Shajing house? Besides, that village had shared a school with Shajing (along with Wangquansi and Meigouying, one and two kilometers south, respectively) since around 1910 (KC, 1:79; see also pp. 89, 120). About a third of the village's boys, including Li himself, had attended that school, usually from age eight or nine to about thirteen. If the children of these villages went to school together for four or five years, surely friendships were formed that lasted beyond school—at least among the residents of the two adjoining villages. But again I was in for a surprise. Li had never in his adult life chatted with any Shimen villager. To be sure, he knew a few people in that village by sight, but when he met up with them on the road or at the market, he would not stop, just nod and break at the waist (*bu guo diantou ha yao er yi*). Once again, Li thought it strange that I should assume he would have any social relationship with people from Shimen village.

It was not long before I confirmed that most of the other elderly men in the village were of the same mind. It was in fact part of their worldview—something taken for granted, so obvious that it needed no articulation. Of course one chats only with one's fellow villagers! Shimen? Wangquan? Classmates? But they are from another village!

I later had occasion to verify this point at one of the other Mantetsu-studied villages—Dabeiguan in Pinggu county, another moderately commercialized village. The older peasants there— Zhang Yuming, sixty-eight; Hao Yonghai, fifty-nine; Liu Shuchen, seventy-three; Guo Zhishan, sixty-three; and Li Yuan, about sixty-five—confirmed that when they went to the market, it was much like our going downtown to windowshop; one did not expect to meet up with or chat with anyone, or to visit a teashop to catch up on the latest gossip, as the Skinner model would predict.

This village-bound view of social intercourse was in many ways institutionalized in custom. Communal house-building, for example, was a purely Shajing affair; aid was never extended to residents of Shimen village up the path. In wedding banquets, the order of priority in inviting guests was the members of one's own lineage in the village and relatives from outside the village, then other villagers; the guests *never* included a friend from another village. Not one of the old men I interviewed in Shajing and Dabeiguan had invited someone from outside the village to attend his wedding just as a friend. The fictive kinship operative in the village—by which every villager knew his or her precise generational standing relative to every other villager—was also limited to the village.

### INSULARITY AND DIFFERENT VILLAGE SOCIAL STRATA

The degree of insularity in the social lives of villagers tended to vary from one stratum to another within a given village.* Middle peasants like Li Guangzhi led the most insulated life of any group: all of Li's property and all of his work were within the village; none of his

---

*It also varied with sex. Village wives of course generally came from outside the village and remained close to their natal families and villages. In this respect, they were less tied in outlook to a single village than the men. On the other hand, they were even more limited by social custom in their contacts with outsiders than the men were, especially in this area.

production activities brought him into contact with anyone from outside the village. This was not true either of the village's elite members or of its poor. Take Zhang Rui, for one example, the only managerial farmer in Shajing and the village head for several years after 1942 (KC, 1: 182). He had inherited from his father, Wentong, a tie with the operators of a candied offering shop near Tiantan in Beijing and went there every winter, taking along a group of villagers to work in the shop. His social world was not limited to the village. Or take Yang Yuan, who was village head before Zhang Rui and owned a handicraft shop (for making women's hair clasps) in the county seat. Yang went into the town almost every day. Yang's world too was larger than the village.

At the other end of the social spectrum, the poor peasant Zhang Shoujun rented 12.6 mu from a landlord in the county seat, who required him to come to town periodically with his rent payments. To supplement his income from this and another small plot of some seven mu he rented, Zhang worked as a peddler in the winter, going from village to village in the surrounding area. At harvest times he would take his donkey with him to the market town, and there seek employment as a day-laborer in nearby villages. In marked contrast to an owner-cultivator like Li Guangzhi, Zhang had a whole array of activities that brought him into contact with the outside world. Consider finally the case of a worker-peasant, Li Guangtai. Guangtai had left the village at the age of seventeen to work as an apprentice in a general store in Beijing. There he stayed for eight years, before returning to the village in 1944. Since he owned a mere 6.5 mu of land, he periodically took employment in the county seat, in a flour mill and noodle shop. He too was not nearly so firmly and exclusively rooted in the village as Li Guangzhi. (Interviews with Zhang Rui, Zhang Shoujun, and Li Guangtai, April 1980.)

Other villages had greater or less contact with outsiders than Shajing, of course, depending on how commercialized they were. Cash-cropping meant much broader outside exchanges. It also meant, as has been seen, greater social stratification. This in turn meant larger proportions of both rich and poor peasants, the groups that tended to be most integrated into the outside world.

As we have seen, Hebei–northwest Shandong was so uncommercialized and unstratified even in the 1930's that in fully 25 of the 33 Mantetsu-surveyed villages there was not a single resident landlord with more than 100 mu. The villages of North China tended to be communities of cultivators; some, perhaps 32 percent, were exclusively made up of poor, middle, and rich peasants; the rest, perhaps

60 percent, included one or more managerial farmers of over 100 mu.* But even those men, as has been seen, generally got their hands dirty in the fields alongside their hired laborers. The social distance between peasants and managerial farmers was not nearly so great as that between peasants and landlords completely divorced from the soil. Most of the villages of the Hebei–northwest Shandong plain, in other words, were relatively unstratified communities, just as most of the cultivators owned at least some land.

## VILLAGE AND STATE BEFORE THE TWENTIETH CENTURY

These characteristics were of course even more prominent in earlier centuries. We have seen that in the early Qing this area was a land of predominantly small owner-cultivators (outside of the court-created estate economy). We have also seen that eighteenth-century cadastres of Huailu county document a landholding pattern substantially the same in its broad outlines as in the twentieth century. These considerations should alert us to be on the lookout for inward-looking communities such as Shajing and Dabeiguan.

The relative social and economic isolation of these villages should lead us to be on the lookout also for political insularity. We need to look first at the extent to which bureaucratic power actually succeeded in intruding into the villages. We can then turn, in the next section, to look at the role the gentry played in village and supravillage political structures.

The archives of the Baodi county Punishment Office afford us a view of the actual working relationships between the state and the village communities in the nineteenth century. The formal institutional framework was the result of the merging of three organizational systems that had been intended to operate separately: the *lijia* system, for tax registration, the *baojia* system, for police control, and the *xiangyue* system, for ideological indoctrination.† In the nineteenth century, Baodi county had 19 *li*, 46 *bao*, and 900 villages,

---

*These figures are based on only the dominant types of villages, I–IV, as shown in Appendix A.

† The tendency for separate, bureaucratically created artificial systems to merge over time is discussed and demonstrated in Hsiao 1960: 6–7, 201–5. There we see how the tax functions of the lijia were absorbed into the baojia structure by the mid-18th century, and how the xiangyue evolved into a police control system and was likewise merged with the baojia. In the Baodi system, the term xiangbao was a combination of the terms *xiangyue* and *dibao*, as shown by frequent official references to the xiangbao as the xiangyue dibao (Shuntian fu archive, 87, 1820, n.d.; 87, 1832, 4.13). All the subsequent citations of this form are from this archive, part of the Ming–Qing Archives in Beijing; the order is bundle (*bao*) number, year, month, and day (or month only if the document is not identified by the day).

which were theoretically divided into *jia* of 100 households and 10 *pai* each. The corresponding "officials" in this institutional hierarchy were the *shushou*, the *xiangbao*, the *jiazhang*, and the *paitou* (*Shuntian fu zhi: dili, cunzhen*, 2, *juan* 28). In theory, the county government appointed subcounty officials all the way down to the paitou, the man responsible for ten households. But in practice, it did not try to extend its influence down the hierarchy farther than the xiangbao, who oversaw a group of 20-odd villages. A xiangbao was required to appear before the county yamen to take an oath of office, but there was no such requirement for the village-level posts. The selection of these officeholders was left entirely to the xiangbao. An incoming xiangbao normally just named a slate of men as paitou and jiazhang, and that was it. The yamen did not go through any ceremonial gestures of confirmation.*

The reality was that the xiangbao, as the lowest level quasi-bureaucratic agent, had to work with the community leaders in the villages. We have the telling example of an 1879 case in which such a group of leaders, the *shoushi* of the village, brought suit in the county yamen against a xiangbao for trying to impose the paijia organization on them. Their complaint stated, in part: "Our community never had pai or jia. The business of aiding the xiangbao in various tax chores had always been carried out by us, without error or failure." The yamen ruled in favor of the village leaders, noting that the old practice should be continued (93, 1879, 3.15). In another file of the same year, we find the xiangbao of Xingbao li reporting that none of the 26 villages under his charge had any paitou at all. He did not give any indication that he intended to correct the situation, nor do we find the yamen instructing him to do so (94, 1879, 4.11).

By the middle of the nineteenth century, this working relationship was so widely recognized that we find it confirmed in the language of bureaucratic communications. For a good illustration of the earlier language, we can take this instruction from the yamen to a shushou in 1824. The matter at hand was finding a replacement for a xiangbao who had reportedly run away, to which end the shushou was directed to "meet with the elders, the gentry, the paitou, the jiazhang, the *cheling*, and others of the villages to select from the villages of the li someone of substance, experience, and honesty" (94, 1824, 4.9).† The gap in this instance between official perception and reality is revealed in the runner's report back to the yamen. The

---

*87, 1811, 3.24; 87, 1813, 2; 87, 1818, 2.13; 88, 1827, 6.12; 90, 1834, 7.6; 88, 1846, 9.4; 91, 1861, 2.1; and 92, 1870, 9.13.

†The cheling was a quasi-military figure responsible for military levies. He was of lower official status than the shushou, but higher in the hierarchy than the xiangbao.

shushou of this li, it turned out, had been dismissed quite some time before and had not been replaced. Moreover, the runner reported, he could not locate the cheling or any local leader who would accept responsibility for selecting a new xiangbao. The formal institutional structure turned out to be a phantom of no real substance. By the 1850's, however, the yamen was ready to acknowledge the real situation in its formal communications, so that now we find it issuing a quite different order: "According to established practice, the selection of a xiangbao must be done by the shushou together with the village leaders [shoushi], local gentry, and commoners, to nominate and guarantee by public consensus" (91, 1854, 11.18). This pat wording about meeting with village leaders came to be widely used from this time on. It no longer even paid lip service to the existence of the paitou and the jiazhang.

The xiangbao was therefore the lowest-level quasi-official, and as such the crucial locus of the intersection between state power and the village leadership. But even at this level, the state did not exert full control. The xiangbao was not designated directly by the county yamen, and the post was not a salaried one. The fact was that the formal apparatus of the imperial bureaucracy largely stopped at the level of the county yamen. The government was aware that an official at the subcounty level would likely have found his job quite unmanageable, for he did not have the coercive machinery with which to impose his will on the village leaders. Official practice therefore recognized that the state's ends could best be served by acknowledging the limitations of official power below the county level. That is why the xiangbao were not simply appointed by administrative fiat, but were always *nominated* by the local and village leaders, and then given official sanction through the ceremonial confirmation of office at the county yamen. The standard procedure was for the nominee, if he agreed to serve, to travel to the county yamen and file a document acknowledging the responsibilities he was to assume. (The term for this procedure was *renzhuang*.)

The state's chief concern in all this was the collection of taxes. Ideally, a local leader of real substance would serve as xiangbao, so that the state could act through his connections for maximum leverage. At the same time, in theory local leaders assumed collective responsibility for the xiangbao's actions by "guaranteeing" (*jubao*) him. From the state's point of view, these guarantors were collectively liable if the man they nominated failed to fulfill his responsibilities or embezzled tax monies. When tax quotas were not met, the state, again in theory, required that the xiangbao and his sponsors pay the balance due and get their money back as best they could from delinquent taxpayers. (Making such a payment was called *dianfeng.*) In short, the state chose to extend its reach by trying to bend the power of community leaders to its service.

In practice, things seldom worked according to these designs. We do find some instances in the first half of the nineteenth century when the xiangbao turned out to be the real leaders the state intended them to be. Their status buoyed by official recognition, such men were willing to shoulder responsibility for more than the mere collection of taxes. In Xingbao li in 1834, for example, we find a xiangbao strong enough to coordinate the defense of the 18 villages under his charge. On instructions from the county yamen, he had convened all of the leaders of these villages, and together they had agreed to organize a force to stand watch against bandits. Each of the villages agreed to contribute four men (or six for the larger villages) and undertook to ensure that the burden for this service was equitably distributed by means of a household-to-household rotation system (88, 1834, 10. n.d.). Ten years later, another set of villages was mobilized to build guard stations along the main highway to assist government troops in dealing with bandits in the area (88, 1844, 10.28). In this same li in 1824 the xiangbao Ma Wantong led the village leaders in a round-the-clock watch against flooding from the area's rain-swollen river. The Punishment Office's connection with this case is particularly interesting. Ma had had to put off his tax collection work in this emergency, and for this delinquency, the Punishment Office had ordered him dismissed from his post. But it rescinded the order when the local leaders appealed the decision, explaining that Ma had devoted all his time to leading the villages' efforts against flooding (89, 1824, 2.27).

The men in these examples, however, were unusually strong xiangbao. More often, the xiangbao was one of the locality's lesser lights, propped up by the real leaders to serve as a buffer between themselves and state power.* To most of those leaders, the post of xiangbao could only have seemed a thankless burden. There was no salary attached to the "office." And one was caught in the middle between the local powers and the state. The burdens of the post became particularly onerous when additional government impositions met with local and/or village resistance, or when the villages were

---

*In all the Baodi cases, I found not one example of a xiangbao who held a degree. Typically, the local powers tried to install a middle peasant or some other stable resident of the locality who could be trusted to stay put (as opposed to a landless poor peasant or year-laborer, for example).

hard pressed to meet their tax quota because of poor harvests. Under such conditions, the xiangbao had to attempt to enforce tax collection without much in the way of state help to back him up. His chief hope for effective enforcement rested on his ability to enlist the cooperation of village leaders to pressure a delinquent taxpayer into payment. Where they were unable or unwilling to cooperate, the xiangbao was the one who would be held accountable by the state.

It was no wonder, in these circumstances, that most village and supra-village leaders refused to serve. We have the telling case of a shushou named Wang Dianyuan who was charged by the county government with the task of naming a new xiangbao. Wang used this order as a threat against Guo Xujiu, who paid him 25,000 copper *cash* (*wen*) to avoid the honor. Another man was named and confirmed. But that man was quickly found to be not up to the task, and once again Wang threatened Guo with a nomination. This time Guo paid 6,000 copper *cash*. When Wang repeated his threat yet a third time, this time extorting 35,000 copper *cash*, Guo had no choice but to go into hiding. The case came to the attention of the Punishment Office when Guo's wife brought suit against Wang (155, 1832, 12.7). We also have numerous examples of nominated xiangbao who refused to serve, of shushou reporting that they could find no one to serve, and of xiangbao who ran away when they could not make good on a tax shortage.*

The balance of power between the state and the village in nineteenth-century Baodi was such that the state managed to hold only the xiangbao accountable, not the supra-village and village notables who nominated and sponsored him. When a xiangbao ran away, all the county authorities could do was to press for another nomination. We do not have a single documented instance in which the state managed to make the sponsors behind a failed xiangbao pay up.

There were of course exceptions to this general picture of the xiangbao post as being a thankless and unwanted "office." For those without the purest of intentions, the position could provide some rewards. Two of the Baodi cases concern xiangbao who absconded with the tax monies they had collected (91, 1861, 1; 94, 1874, 8.23). There are also cases in which "local bully and evil gentry" types saw in the xiangbao post opportunities for tax abuse. In Shangjie li in

---

*This last was a not uncommon occurrence. In a total of 73 cases pertaining to Xingbao li between 1810 and 1910, 18 concerned runaway xiangbao (87, 1810, 3.25; 87, 1818, 5.24; 90, 1823, 3; 94, 1824, 9; 90, 1828, 7.26; 89, 1832, 3.17; 90, 1833, 10.27; 90, 1839, 6.6; 89, 1848, 9.10; 90, 1850, 2.7; 91, 1852, 7.2; 91, 1852, 9.29; 91, 1855, 2.19; 91, 1860, 2.13; 91, 1860, 3.6; 91, 1861, 1; 94, 1874, 8.23; 93, 1883, 9.4).

1897, for example, a degree holder named Wang Guoxiang was found to have insinuated his nephew, Wang Shunqing, as xiangbao. Together they had extracted 140,000 copper *cash* from the eight villages under their charge, ostensibly to meet tax arrears demanded by the county authorities. The Wangs' abuse came to the attention of the Punishment Office when the local leaders joined together to bring suit against them. The Wangs defended themselves by claiming they had collected 50,000 of the 140,000 *cash* to cover interest and expenses for their tax-collection work and 30,000 to cover expenses incurred in providing a banquet for official purposes; the other 60,000 was passed off as a temporary loan the villages had made to them. The evidence was so overwhelmingly against the Wangs that the county authorities ordered them relieved of their duties (93, 1897, 4).

In another case of the abuse of office, we find the xiangbao of Juren li arrogating to himself certain police powers. As the "official" of the locality, Zhang Yangwu took it upon himself to confiscate the cart of a widow on the grounds that one of her relatives had used it in a theft. When the widow sought to get her cart back, Zhang promised to return it for a fee of 25,000 copper *cash*. But he did not come up with the cart when she paid him, and the widow brought suit. (The county government ruled in her favor and ordered the xiangbao to repay the money; 154, 1839, 5.) Another xiangbao was found to have bullied a newcomer to a village into paying him 50,000 *cash* on the threat of reporting him to authorities as a bandit in hiding (159, 1903, 6).

Such money-making possibilities explain the anomaly of a few instances in which men competed and maneuvered for a position that was dreaded by most. For example, several years after the xiangbao Tian Kui was dismissed from his post when local leaders complained to county authorities that he had abused his authority, he sought reinstatement, charging his accusers with fabricating evidence against him. The Punishment Office conducted an investigation, calling various concerned parties to the yamen for questioning, and was able to ascertain that Tian had been guilty as charged—that he had embezzled funds and used the money to keep a woman of ill-repute. Tian's plea for reinstatement was rejected, and the local leaders were ordered to nominate someone for the job (87, 1814, 12.4).

In these few exceptions to the rule, actually, we find good evidence of the checks on the xiangbao's power. After all, there were 20-odd separate villages under his purview, each with its own interests and interest groups. As long as aggrieved parties could avail themselves of the judicial system and bring suit at the yamen, it was not that easy for a man or group of men to flagrantly abuse the xiangbao position. We have seen that the Wangs' misuse of tax monies was checked by such a suit, as was Zhang Yangwu's chicanery—by the complaint of a widow whom he had no doubt considered helpless.

The one instance in the Baodi archives of a xiangbao who was largely beyond the control of the law crops up in a relatively lengthy case in Xingbao li in the late 1890's. The xiangbao in this case was the creature of a member of the gentry, an exceptionally large landlord named Dong Weizeng, who towered over the area with a landholding of 20,000 mu. Dong had put his man into the position of xiangbao, only to see him dismissed for irregularities. He had then simply put the man back in under a different name. Again the xiangbao was dismissed, and again Dong brought him back, this time under yet another name.

Control over the post was particularly important to Dong because by this means he had long evaded paying taxes on his land. But this meant that other landholders in the locality had to bear his share of the tax quota. It was they who brought suit against Dong's man, and they had managed twice to have him removed from the post. In between, they had even succeeded in having their own nominee, Yin Xueqin, installed as xiangbao. But Yin had not been able to keep the post, for he and his supporters simply lacked the power to make Dong pay up. Yin had accordingly been dismissed for failing to meet the tax quota.

The third time Dong installed his xiangbao, these community leaders managed to find themselves a "big name"—a military officer above the fifth rank by the name of Wang Kunbi—to stand as the complainant. Complex negotiations followed, involving Wang, Dong, the county government, and various local leaders who were called on to participate. A compromise was reached that saw Yin Heli installed as the new xiangbao. But the fundamental source of the conflict remained: Dong would not pay his land taxes, and neither the county government nor the local leaders had the power to make him do so. Yin, the pawn in this power struggle, could not enforce payment from either side; he resigned in short order, only five months after his appointment. The records do not disclose the end of the story. The situation remained stalemated when the file was closed (94, 1896, 5; 1898, 2; 1898, 7.15).

Given the complex balance of power between state and local society, and given the complex configuration of interests within any given locality, such protracted abuse of the xiangbao position must be considered the exception rather than the rule. Powerful gentry-landlords like Dong were relatively rare in this area, as has been seen. Most localities had a more balanced mix of lesser elites, among whom any one man or group would have found it difficult to engage in such flagrant and sustained abuse of the tax structure as in Dong's case.

The problem of tax collection exposed in these cases suggest that state power penetrated local societies to only a limited degree. In nineteenth-century Baodi, at least, official power certainly came nowhere near to the abstract bureaucratic ideal embodied in the paochia and lichia systems. Nor, for that matter, did it approximate the fall-back position of making the local leaders collectively responsible for tax collection. Instead, the Baodi example suggests a kind of equilibrium in power between state and local society, in which taxes could generally only be levied to the extent that local leaders and village communities considered tolerable.

### VILLAGE AND GENTRY IN THE NINETEENTH CENTURY

We are now in a position to take a closer look at the relationship between villages and the gentry in their locality. The Baodi materials suggest that at the supra-village level of the xiangbao, the lower gentry played a substantial role. The lists nominating xiangbao were generally headed by one or two men specifically identified by their degrees, usually a shengyuan or jiansheng, followed by a much longer string of commoners (89, 1824, 2.27; 89, 1826, 12.8; 91, 1857, 6.9; etc.). Whether or not these degree-holding gentry were actually the acknowledged "natural" leaders among the elite at this level, they were treated as such as a matter of convention and form. In this respect, the Baodi archives largely confirm the picture we get from earlier research that the nonofficial gentry performed important leadership functions below the county level.

It is at the level of the village community that we need to question the findings and assumptions of earlier research. Of the hundreds of paitou, jiazhang, and shoushi identified in the Baodi documents, almost all were commoners. I found only four instances of degree-holders: a shengyuan, a lingsheng (or shengyuan on stipend), a military shengyuan, and (in a major market town, Bamencheng zhen) a ranking officer (*dusi*) of the green camp (93, 1898, 12.13; 92, 1864, 3.9; 93, 1883, 11.13; 94, 1898, 7.15).

It is possible, of course, that paitou and jiazhang were chosen pretty much as the xiangbao were: men of stability but little standing who were put forward by the real village leaders to serve as buffers between them and the bureaucracy. But this seems to me unlikely for two reasons. For one thing, as will be seen in the next section, we have abundant evidence to show that when, in the twentieth century, county governments sought systematically to identify the head and deputy head of every village, the village communities invariably just named their own leaders. This suggests to me that earlier villagers would have likely responded the same way. Furthermore, since bureaucratic power in nineteenth-century Baodi did not reach below the level of the xiangbao, village leaders were already buffered from the bureaucratic apparatus by this "office"; there was no need to create another buffer between themselves and the county governments. For these reasons, the paitou and jiazhang who were named by the xiangbao in the first half of the century were probably the actual leaders of their communities.

As K. C. Hsiao has pointed out (1960: 271–72), nineteenth-century Western observers, from a writer for the *Chinese Repository* in 1836 to Francis H. Nichols in the 1900's, repeatedly noted that the village "head man" was usually the acknowledged "natural" leader of the community, often from the most powerful family in the village. In any event, by the second half of the nineteenth century, village leaders came to be referred to simply by their community title of shoushi in the Baodi documents. And those shoushi, as has been seen, were almost all commoners.

This should not be surprising. It is entirely consistent with what we found in our consideration of the socioeconomic structure of these villages in Part Two: degree-holders were exceedingly rare among their residents (rarer, I suspect, even than college graduates in today's villages in China); their elites tended to be mainly or wholly cultivators—middle peasants, rich peasants, and managerial farmers.

In the rare instances where a villager's son succeeded in obtaining a degree, the young man was generally drawn toward "central places" higher up the hierarchy of local society, to major market towns and county seats. That was where the action was—the gentry circles, the government offices, the big merchants and shops, the luxury goods, and so on. A degree-holder with an eye out for the main chance, "lower gentry" though he might be, usually set his sights upward and outward from the village. Few among the ambitious would have remained inside a village to concern themselves with the details of its governance.

This picture is confirmed by the joint Mantetsu–Tokyo University six-village survey, which looked at village community structure in detail. Researchers identified only one degree-holder within the villagers' memory: Wang Baojun of Houxiazhai village. Wang had obtained the lowest degree of *xiucai*, probably just before the examinations were terminated in 1905; he was fifty-nine years old in 1942, when the survey was taken. Wang had reportedly lived outside the village until 1932, when he finally gave up on the possibility of an official career and returned to the village to become a teacher and a doctor. At the time of the survey he owned 35 mu of land and was widely respected in the village for his learning, not his rather modest economic standing (KC, 4: 401).

## LINEAGES

If it is true that villages on the North China plain in the nineteenth century were mainly communities of commoner cultivators, and if it is true that those communities were generally rather insular, we need to question just what roles degree-holding gentry might have played in their internal power structures. There is no doubt, as has been seen, that lower gentry in nineteenth-century Baodi often figured importantly in affairs at the bao level, which embraced 20 villages or so. But does this mean that gentry power and leadership actually dominated those villages? Should we think of the power structures at the county and subcounty level simply in terms of a duality between state and gentry? Or do we need to think in terms of a triangular power relationship involving the county government, the bao elite, and dispersed village communities with their own power structures?

The answer to these questions seems to me to turn critically on the role of lineages. If lineage organizations were highly developed and powerful, and generally crossed the boundaries between villages and their central places (whether administrative or commercial), then the village as a possibly inward-looking collectivity is not of very large concern. On the other hand, if lineage organizations generally stayed within village boundaries, then this would tend to reinforce the picture being projected here of relatively insular village communities.

In many areas of the south, as K. C. Hsiao and others have pointed out, single-surname villages were common. In Gao'an county in Jiangxi, for example, 87 percent of the villages (1,121 of 1,291) were "monoclan" villages. And this was true of 40 percent of the villages in Huaxian, Guangdong (157 of 398; Hsiao 1960: 327). But the single-surname village was very rare on the Hebei–northwest Shandong plain. In our group of villages, for example, Shajing had 8 different surnames, Sibeichai 13, Wudian 13, Houjiaying 7, Houxiazhai 11, and Lengshuigou 10. In Dingxian, Li Jinghan and Sidney Gamble found three or more surnames in 59 villages in a sample of 62; only one of the 62 was a single-surname village (Gamble 1963: 315). In short, few villages of the area were of the lineage-community type in which kinship ties were reinforced by community bonds.

More important, perhaps, these villages were on the whole also much less socially stratified than those of the south. As we have seen, in the Mantetsu-surveyed villages, households owning more than 200 mu were very rare indeed (see Table 4.2, for example). The majority of the "rich" villagers owned between 100 and 200 mu, and in perhaps one-third of all villages in the Hebei–northwest Shandong plain there was no "rich" household at all.

As Hu Hsien-chin (1948), K. C. Hsiao (1960: esp. Chap. 8), Maurice Freedman (1966: esp. Chaps. 3, 5), and others have shown, the strength of lineages tended to be proportional to the wealth and prominence of their leaders; the most-developed lineage organizations were those headed by powerful and wealthy gentry who could afford to "endow" the lineage with substantial corporate landholdings—who might maintain schools, granaries, and the like for it. Such corporate activities and properties helped to ensure the power of the lineage organization.

I would add here the further consideration of another difference between the North China plain and the delta areas, noted in Chapter Three. Most of the North China plain either was not irrigated at all or was irrigated by wells owned by individual households, in contrast to the lower Yangzi and Pearl River delta areas, where canal irrigation and land reclamation typically required coordination among substantial numbers of people and households. This difference might be thought of as an ecological basis for the contrast in the roles played by lineage organizations in the two areas.

Other ecological factors that should be considered are the practice of planting in four-men teams in Hebei–northwest Shandong and the relatively greater use of animal power in plowing. On the surface, these agricultural practices seem to suggest an economic basis for close lineage ties: brothers and cousins make natural cooperative teams for these purposes. However, as I have shown in Chapters Eight and Nine, these requirements occupied only a few days of the entire agricultural cycle. Though some peasants did indeed engage in the necessary animal and labor pooling with relatives, others just as easily did so with friends or neighbors. This was not reason enough to keep married brothers together in joint families, if the brothers did not otherwise get along. Nor was it of sufficient economic importance to form a basis for strong lineage organizations.

Whatever the reasons, lineage organization was comparatively undeveloped in Hebei–northwest Shandong. The only form of corporate lineage property was typically a few mu of arable land around the lineage's common gravesite. As we see in Table 13.1, even the 84-household Hou lineage of Houjiaying held only a couple of mu in common. When asked to name the lineage that had the largest amount of corporate property, Zhang Yueqing, the village head of Sibeichai, in cotton-growing and highly commercialized Luancheng county, cited the example of a nearby lineage named Guo, with some 40 to 50 mu of common land; the land had long been left uncultivated (KC, 3: 91). It was an exceptional case that only helps to prove the rule that the peasant lineages in this area were quite unlike the highly developed organizations we associate with upper-class families.

Typically, these small plots of lineage land were rented out, usually to one of the lineage's poor members, and the rent was used to defray the expenses for the Qingming ceremony, when the members paid their respects to their ancestors. Usually, the prevailing rate of rent was charged, which was paid either in cash to the heads of the lineage's Qingming association (Qingming hui; KC, 3: 91; KC, 5: 81–82) or in the form of the paper money and incense the tenant was obliged to furnish for the Qingming rituals (KC, 1: 276–78). In rare instances, the rent was reduced, thereby giving some substance to the ceremonial of a lineage taking care of its poor. (The Wei lineage of Houxiazhai charged only one yuan on a gross yield of five to six yuan on its one mu; KC, 4: 447.) All the members of the more well-off and solidary lineages would gather for a meal at Qingming; the less well-off lineages limited participation in the meal to a few representatives. Many of the lineages, especially during the war years immediately before the field surveys, had done away with the ceremonial meal completely and made only minimal offerings to the ancestors beyond the requisite ceremonial burning of paper money and incense.*

*The tendency to downplay the ceremony is well documented. It is mentioned in KC, 1: 262–63; KC, 3: 91; KC, 4: 440, 447; KC, 5: 81–82, 452, 487; etc. There were minor variations on this pattern. In Lengshuigou, for example, ancestral ceremonials were also observed on *guijie*, the first day of the tenth lunar month, in a manner similar to Qingming—that is to say, the members would go to the gravesite to make offerings and burn paper money and incense (KC, 4: 19, 86). And in Houxiazhai the ancestral ceremonials were observed also at New Year's; this was when the Ma and Wang lineages gathered for their meal (KC, 4: 438–40; compare KC, 4: 416, which notes that only the Mas observed the ceremonial at New Year's).

TABLE 13.1

Amount of Arable Land Held in Common by the Lineages with the Largest
Property Holdings in Six Hebei and Shandong Villages, 1940's

(Land in mu)

| Village | Lineage | Number of households | Arable land owned |
|---------|---------|----------------------|-------------------|
| Houxiazhai (1942) | Wang | 51 | 1 |
| | Ma | 30 | 3–4 |
| | Wu | 18 | 3 |
| | Li | 9 | 1 |
| Shajing (1941) | Yang | 14 | 4[a] |
| | Li | 14 | 8 |
| Sibeichai (1941) | Hao | 40 | 3+ |
| Lengshuigou (1941) | Wang | ? | 2–3 |
| Houjiaying (1942) | Hou | 84 | 2 |
| Wudian (1942) | Yu | 12 | 6 |

SOURCES: *Houxiazhai*, KC, 4: 10, 435; *Shajing*, KC, 1: 251, 260, 262–63; *Sibeichai*, KC, 3: 91;
*Lengshuigou*, KC, 4: 86; *Houjiaying*, KC, 5: 81–82, 116; *Wudian*, KC, 5: 452, 487.
NOTE: Most of these holdings were ancestral gravesites.
[a]The Yangs held 20 mu in common, but this was all that was arable.

The Qingming ceremony was, in this world where lineage activities played a relatively minor role, one of the few occasions on which
lineage members got together. Lineage members typically also paid
their respects to each other at the lunar New Year. This could take
the form of a ceremonial visit to each member's home (followed by
ceremonial visits to the neighbors' homes), as the Yangs of Shajing
did, for example (KC, 1: 261). Or all members would gather at the
home of the senior member, when everyone *koutou*-ed before all
their lineage seniors; this was the practice of the Haos of Sibeichai
(KC, 3: 90). The Mas and the Wangs of Houxiazhai, as noted, chose
to celebrate the occasion with a collective meal at the house of a
member. (The burden of hosting this gathering was rotated, and the
costs borne by collections from the members.) Outside of the ancestral and the New Year observances, lineages typically gathered together only for the weddings and funerals of their members.

But this was about as far as the lineage activities went. There was
not one lineage in any of the six villages that maintained a granary,
school, or temple. There is no evidence of any lineage organization
playing some kind of relief role on the many occasions when drought
and flood struck these villages. Nor is there any evidence of lineage
aid to a member in need. The only evidence of special consideration

to lineage members was in the choice of tenants for the land around the lineage graves. But the rent, as has been seen, was usually set at the prevailing rate. In cases where the tenant supplied offerings for the Qingming rituals, there was the appearance of a free rental—which was of course more show than real.

## THE ENDOGENOUS VILLAGE POLITICAL STRUCTURE

The reach of all the lineages described above was limited to the village community itself. Thus the absence of well-elaborated lineage organizations also meant the absence of a critical integrative unit that might have cut across the boundaries between town and country, and between the gentry and the village commoners. We should not be surprised, then, to find that the villages of this area generally contained political structures that were endogenous to the community, with only minimal influence from the outside. We have abundant evidence for this in the Mantctsu field surveys.

Zhang Yueqing, the long-time head of Sibeichai, best outlined the principles of village political structure for the Mantetsu investigators. It was a structure embedded in the village's lineages. Disputes among lineage members—over the division of family property, say—were generally settled within the lineage by its leaders. Those leaders were in theory the oldest (in generational rank and age) lineage members, but in practice they were often the most well-to-do, respected, and able men. Matters that could not be settled within the lineages—such as disputes between different lineages or the community's dealings with the outside world (especially taxcs)—were handled by a kind of informal council of 12 lineage leaders, who were called *dongshi*. Each of the village's seven multi-household lineages was represented on this body (by two members in the case of the larger lineages; KC, 3: 41–44).

The accuracy of this picture of village governance can be seen in the system's tenacity in the face of repeated efforts to supplant it. Consider the example of Houxiazhai. Here the village was grouped by kinship into three *pai* (neighborhoods): the Mas in the east, the Wangs in the middle, and the Weis (plus other minor lineages) in the west. When the Japanese studied it, in 1942, the villagers could not remember a time when these lineages had not supplied the heads of their pai. In 1928, when the Nanjing government called for village elections, Houxiazhai had simply declared the old leaders "elected" heads. And in 1931, when the government called for the imposition of the five-household linlü system, the villagers had just ignored the order and gone on as they always had. The villagers even managed to resist the Japanese occupation authorities' attempts to impose a baojia system on them. The Mantetsu investigators found this a closed and uncooperative village (KC, 4: 404–5, 424, 450).

Houxiazhai, to be sure, was a relatively solidary community of mainly owner-cultivators well into the twentieth century. But even in Shajing, where the peasants were well on the road to semiproletarianization and the bonds of the community had weakened, the legacy of a political structure embedded in the lineage organizations held on. In the 1910's there were seven "heads of associations" (huishou) in this village.* When outside authorities tried to impose the linlü system in the late 1920's, Shajing went along, but only in form: the old huishou simply renamed themselves the neighborhood heads (lüzhang) for outside consumption. To the villagers they remained the huishou. In 1939, when the Japanese occupation authorities ordered the village to organize itself into decimal household groupings, the huishou again simply went along in form, now calling themselves jiazhang. In reality, each group of supposedly ten households actually remained groupings of five to ten households, mostly of the same lineage, and headed by a lineage member as before (KC, 1: 100–101, 116–18, 124).

These lineage leaders and village "councilmen" were generally also the village rich. Table 13.2 shows the village leaders of Shajing (the huishou) and Lengshuigou (the shoushi) and their landholdings. Shajing village, it will be recalled, had only one managerial farmer and no rich peasants employing more labor than they put in themselves. It was a village of mainly poor peasants: 51 percent of the households in the village cultivated less than ten mu. These "natural" leaders, therefore, were the richest men in the village. The only exception was Du Xiang. But Du had his education to recommend him; his calligraphy apparently was very good, and he was always relied on to copy village documents. In addition, his grandfather had been the village's biggest landowner in his day. The list of Lengshuigou leaders speaks for itself: these were the economic elite of the village. When asked, "Are the leaders the powerful men of the village?," a Lengshuigou villager replied: "They are individuals who have a lot of land. Also ability. They are all long-time residents of the village" (KC, 4: 25).

---

*Village leaders in Hebei–northwest Shandong were called variously dongshi or shoushi (lit., "directors" or "leaders of affairs") and, more commonly, huishou, as in Shajing. The use of the word hui, "association" or "society," suggests that the term huishou might have been linked originally to village "temple associations" (miaohui) or "crop-watching associations" (kanqing hui).

TABLE 13.2

Landholdings of Village Leaders of Lengshuigou, Shandong, and Shajing, Hebei, 1935 and 1942

(Land in mu)

| Lengshuigou (shoushi) | Land owned | Shajing (huishou) | Land owned | Land cultivated |
|---|---|---|---|---|
| Li Fenggui | 40.0 | Du Xiang[a] | 11.5 | 18.5 |
| Li Fengjie | 140.0 | Li Ruyuan | 76.0 | 76.0 |
| Li Wenhan | 100.0 | Li Xiufang[b] | 49.5 | 54.5 |
| Li Xiangling | 160.0 | Yang Run[c] | 11.0 | 11.0 |
| Ren Dexuan | 100.0 | Yang Yuan[b] | 40.0 | 40.0 |
| Wang Weishan | 80.0 | Yang Ze | 35.0 | 35.0 |
| Yang Hanqing | 160.0 | Yang Zheng[b] | 40.0 | 40.0 |
| Yang Lide | 60.0 | Zhang Rui[d] | 110.0 | 110.0 |
| | | Zhang Yongren | 46.2 | 57.2 |
| | | Zhao Tingkui | 14.0 | 34.0 |

SOURCES: Lengshuigou, KC, 4:25; Shajing, KC, 1: 100, 124, appended chart.
NOTE: Local terms for village leaders are shown in parentheses.
[a] Village status established by his calligraphy and role as village "notary."
[b] Recent addition to the village leadership.
[c] Had just sold 22 mu, retaining 11 for his own use.
[d] Son of Wentong.

This overlap between property and leadership, between a village's economic elite and its political elite, is confirmed in Sidney Gamble's research on villages in the 1930's:

Property ownership was a qualification [for status as a village elder] in a great many villages. Sometimes the amount was indefinite, and the heads of the richest families were the ones chosen. Sometimes the family had to own a fixed amount of land or number of oxen before the head could serve as elder. . . . In some villages a poor man never was appointed, partly because of his small landholdings, but also because village service took a considerable amount of time and a man needed at least some leisure if he were to serve. (Gamble 1963: 50–51)

As Gamble goes on to show, this was also to some extent a self-perpetuating elite. Thirty-seven of 48 leaders in five villages were at least the second generation of their families to have served, and fully 33 were serving for at least the third generation. In another sample, of 141 leaders in 12 villages, Gamble found that 55 had inherited (or been appointed to) their positions before they reached the age of thirty (making the term elders for these village leaders not entirely appropriate). Most of the leaders, moreover, had served for stretches of more than ten years (Gamble 1963: 323). These men were clearly not democratically elected representatives presiding over communities of equals. Though commoners, the village leaders generally formed a distinct political and economic elite, whose positions, like landed property, usually passed from generation to generation.

But this does not mean that village leaders constituted a closed caste. After all, 11 of the 48 leaders in Gamble's survey were serving for the first time. Gamble also supplies fragmentary evidence reaching back a century before the 1930's on the elites in one village, which shows much fluctuation in the number of village leaders over the years, from four to as many as 11 and back down to three and then up again to eight (Gamble 1963: 62–63). This suggests considerable movement in and out of these ranks. The village elite, in other words, was by no means a hereditary aristocracy.

There were of course villages in which a single family or group of families, especially if they happened to be gentry, towered above the rest of the villagers generation after generation. But in the majority of villages the evidence suggests a very much narrower distance between village leaders and their lineage constituents. Some were managerial farmers, small landlords, or rich peasants. Many were well-to-do middle peasants. Almost all were commoners. Their positions were hereditary only to the extent that landed wealth could be maintained from generation to generation in this small-family-farm economy with its partible inheritance system. A small landlord could easily slip down to middle-peasant status after only one division of family property among several sons. And another division could drive most of the third generation down to poor-peasant status and out of the ranks of the village leadership. Meanwhile, the middle peasant who managed to accumulate enough land to become a rich peasant or a managerial farmer or a small landlord would move into the ranks of the community's elite. Village political structure, in short, very much reflected the social and economic structure I have outlined in Part Two of this book. Continuity as well as change in political leadership paralleled to a great extent the continuity as well as the fluidity of social and economic status on the Hebei–northwest Shandong plain.

### COMMUNITY LEADERS OR AGENTS OF THE STATE?

Under these circumstances, we would expect that village leaders would tend to identify more with the interests of their community than with the interests of outside political or parapolitical authorities. Once again, we can find substantial evidence for this hypothesis in the Japanese field research data.

One of the first steps taken by twentieth-century county governments to modify village political structures was to institute a system of village heads (*cunzhang* or *cunzheng*) and deputy village heads (*cunfu*). In theory, these men were to be appointed by the county governments and were to act as agents of the bureaucracy. They were to be responsible for tax collection, police control, schools, road repairs, collective security, and the like. In practice, however, most of these early efforts at bureaucratizing the villages failed to change the old order. In Houjiaying, for example, the nine huishou had customarily selected one of their number as the village head, called the *dazonghuitou*. When the county government tried to install the village-head system, all that changed was the title. In carrying out his duties, the "new" village head always consulted with all the other huishou on matters of importance, as he had done before (KC, 5: 47). This system held until 1939, when the county government appointed a gambler and opium addict as the head of the administrative village (*xiang*) over Houjiaying, and he installed his own agent as head of Houjiaying.

In Shajing, similarly, the huishou simply named one of their own to the new county-imposed position and announced their decision at a purely ceremonial meeting to which 20 or 30 "knowledgeable" villagers were invited. Informants recalled for the Mantetsu researchers as specific examples of this practice the selections of Li Zhenzong, who served as village head in the 1900's, and Du Ruhai, who served in the 1920's. When, in 1927, the county government instructed that the villages were henceforth to elect their heads by written ballot, Shajing once more went along only in form. The village elite selected the one and only candidate, who was then ceremonially "elected" at a meeting of some 30 or 40 villagers (KC, 1: 123, 146). The old elite retained control over the village government until 1939, when they finally refused to participate in the face of intolerable intrusions and exactions.

The elite of Wudian withdrew from village government earlier, in the 1920's, in the face of warlord and bandit requisitions. In Sibeichai the old elite tried to withdraw in the early 1930's, only to be forced back into concerted action against the flagrant abuses of a thug who insinuated himself into the position of village head in 1933. But in Houxiazhai and Lengshuigou, both highly solidary village communities, the old political structure remained intact to deal collectively with successive intrusions and exactions from the outside (KC, 4: 406, 408, 424, on Houxiazhai; KC, 4: 18 on Lengshuigou).

As long as a village's political structure remained intact, its elites continued to perceive themselves primarily as leaders of their own community, not as agents of the state. For one thing, the position of village head remained unsalaried down to the 1930's. County government budgets made no allowances for the staffing of village-level functionaries. Villages were left to decide for themselves, as always, whether or not to pay their heads. Usually, the position was treated as essentially a voluntary service. When this position became an onerous and dreaded burden, the elites of some villages simply refused to serve.

Even under the best of circumstances, in fact, the position tended to entail more work than reward. In Shajing the village head apparently received neither salary nor gifts for his service, despite the many demands on his time in acting as middleman in land rentals or labor hiring or matchmaking (functions that fell to the village head there because he was usually a man with wider outside contacts than the average villager). His one significant source of remuneration was from a fee that he charged for writing up new property deeds to document the sale and purchase of land (KC, 1: 96). The village head of Sibeichai fared a little better. He received some gifts of eggs, meat, mooncakes, and the like from the other members of the village elite and was also paid a fee of one-half of 1 percent of the sale price for validating land sales. Since about 300 mu changed hands between 1910 and 1940, and the land prices ran around 50 yuan per mu until 1937 and 100–150 yuan per mu in 1940–41, this activity earned him about 2.5 yuan a year before 1937, and perhaps double that amount in the early 1940's (KC, 3: 38, 66, 251–52, 331).

That service as village head was not normally all that lucrative can be seen from the record of the financial fortunes of Zhang Yueqing, who served as head of Sibeichai for a total of 16 years (1919–30 and 1934–39). During that period he had suffered a series of economic reverses, to the point where he had had to pawn 63 of his 83 mu between 1932 and 1937. His downfall resulted largely from certain business ventures. Some years before, in 1924, he had unsuccessfully attempted to establish a wine shop and restaurant. Then, in 1936, he had been equally unsuccessful in trying to raise 90 head of sheep, almost all of which became diseased and died. On top of this, funeral expenses for his brother, an alcoholic, and sister-in-law and nephew in 1937 had cost him about 500 yuan. Zhang's service as village head did not cause these losses, to be sure, but the position was certainly not lucrative enough to keep him from having to pawn off most of his land, for a total of about 2,000 yuan (KC, 3: 347–48).

Indeed, judging by the histories of the heads of Houjiaying village, these men did not usually profit from their position. Table 13.3

TABLE 13.3

Landholdings of Village Heads of Houjiaying, Hebei, at Time of Service and in 1942

| Name | Term of office | Land owned At time of service | Land owned In 1942 |
|---|---|---|---|
| Hou Changzan | 1915–17 | 80 | 60 |
| Hou Xianyang | 1917–22 | 150 | —[a] |
| Hou Enrong | 1922–26 | 70 | 37 |
| Hou Baotian | 1926–28 | 70 | 35 |
| Hou Baochen | 1928–32 | 60 | —[a] |
| Hou Dasheng | 1932–36 | 80 | 40 |
| Hou Quanwu | 1936–39 | 160 | 160 |
| Liu Zixiang | 1939–41 | 170 | 170 |
| Hou Yuanguang | 1942– | 97 | 97 |

SOURCE: KC, 5: 42.     [a] No longer alive.

shows the successive heads of the village, from 1915 to 1942, and the amount of land each owned at the time he served and at the time of the survey. In no case had a man managed to expand his landholdings as a result of his service as village head, and four of the seven living heads had lost some land. We do know from the Mantetsu surveys that the village head Hou Yuanguang, who took over in 1942, was engaging in a variety of abuses in collusion with the administrative village head Qi in Nijingzhen town (KC, 5: 50–51). But until that time, the record certainly indicates that there was no great reward in this service.

Gamble found much the same pattern in the 11 villages he studied: "According to our records, all village elders and officers gave their services without pay. . . . Most of the elders belonged to the wealthier village families and had leisure time that they could devote to community service. . . . There ordinarily was little opportunity for personal gain" (1963: 60).

Even under the impositions of outside political authority in the twentieth century, therefore, villages in this area retained for a time their own political structures, headed by members of the "natural" elite of their lineages, who tended to identify with the community rather than with the state. "Exploitation" went on, but generally under the accepted norms of rent, wage labor, and moneylending. Abuse in the form of the arbitrary use of heteronomously derived political power, soon to become so widespread as to bring the term evil tyrants (*eba*) into common parlance, was the exception, not the rule. The village, by and large, dealt with the outside world through its own leaders. Compared with villages in more highly commercialized areas, those in Hebei–northwest Shandong were relatively insular communities, economically, socially, and politically.

All this is not to deny that villagers were part and parcel of larger trading and power systems. Even the most uncommercialized villages in the North China plain had some measure of contact with the outside world long before the coming of world capitalism. Those who would project onto the precapitalist village a "natural economy" devoid of market influences must confront the power of Skinner's model of marketing structures. The precapitalist–natural economy model must also deal with the reality of a highly centralized imperial state and a highly integrated gentry elite whose influence as intermediaries between state and village certainly left few villages untouched.

But it is important to restore to our image of villages their other dimension as dispersed entities rather than as units totally integrated into larger systems. For it is only from this standpoint, from the view of villages as collectivities, that we can understand some of the popular movements that shook North China in the twentieth century. Roxann Prazniak (1980) has shown how villages led by commoners formed the backbone of the tax-resistance movement in Laiyang, on the Shandong peninsula, in 1910, when the Qing state attempted to finance its "New Policy" modernizing reforms through special tax levies on the villages. The peasants' grievance was directed especially against powerful merchant tax-farmers, who took advantage of the situation by manipulating the exchange rates between silver and copper and imposing additional surcharges. The resistance movement was led mainly by village-level cunzhang and supra-village shezhang, commoners all, and looked down on by the gentry elite of the county seat. At its height, it encompassed virtually all of the northern half of the county and engaged some 50,000 people.

Elizabeth Perry, looking into resistance of another type, has shown well how the Red Spears movement of the 1920's and the Sino-Japanese War years was above all a community self-defense movement. That movement, which at its height included possibly 3,000,000 members on the North China plain, began with the efforts of the established leadership and property owners of individual villages to organize their communities against the predations of bandit gangs. When the warlord Wu Peifu and then the Guomindang government tried to increase their exactions from the villages, these organizations turned readily into units of a tax-resistance movement. And again when Japanese forces invaded, they became units of defensive resistance. In all these instances, the villages showed that they could act in concert for short periods of time in response to an external threat. Once the crisis passed, however, they quickly returned to their original dispersed state (Perry 1980: 152–207).

Liu Shaoqi's 1938 report on the Communists' efforts in North China pointed out very clearly how this insularity affected the revolutionary movement:

> Militarized organizations such as the Red Spears, the Heavenly Gate Society [Tianmen hui] and the Association of Villages [Lianzhuang hui] pose a very serious problem in the resistance war in North China.
>
> Many localities in North China have this kind of organization, whether Red Spears or the Association of Villages. Most recently, because of the invasion of the Japanese bandits and the harassment of defeated armies and local bandits, these organizations have developed even further. These are military organizations with deep roots among the people. They are spontaneous in origin and have no basis in the laws of the state. But they have a long history. Their principal purpose is to oppose excessive exactions and various kinds of taxes, and the harassment of armies and bandits. They are purely self-defense military organizations. If the Japanese armies, defeated soldiers, and local bandits do not go to harass them in their home territory, they will not come out to engage actively in resistance, to attack bandits, or to fight as guerrillas. Most of their leaders are tyrants or gentry, but they are especially attuned to the backward and narrow self-interest of the peasantry. That is why they are able to unite them so solidly. Superstition is one of their methods for uniting the peasants (the Association of Villages has no superstitions and is better). They deal with all problems affecting their interests. They oppose whoever harasses and robs them, whether it is the Japanese, the puppet army, the resistance army, bandits, or some political party. Their political stance is neutral. Under normal conditions, they do not have standing fighting units, but when the time comes to fight, they can marshal a very large fighting force. . . . They have time and again demonstrated great power in fighting for the defense of their own locales. . . . It is difficult to mobilize such organizations to participate actively in the resistance, to fight as guerrillas, to sacrifice their self-interest and fight for the collective interest of the nation. (Liu 1938: 51)

As Perry has shown so well (1980: Chap. 6), after a rather tortuous relationship with these organizations, the Chinese Communist Party was in the end to part company with them.

As if to encompass such phenomena as the Red Spears, and as if to correct his own earlier overemphasis on the "standard marketing community," G. William Skinner supplied an analytical model in 1971 that returned the village to center stage. In that model, villages undergo cycles of "opening" and "closure." Dynasties reestablish order, more trade follows, and then more mobility up the administrative and commercial channels of society. This is the pattern of the "opening" of village communities, a process that proceeds, in Skinner's terminology, from the coercive, to the economic, and finally to the normative. With the onset of dynastic decline, however, opportunities to move up become limited, disorder mounts and breaks down trade systems, and the rise of banditry and rebellion leads to village crop-watching and self-defense, ending finally in walled, armed communities—the ultimate closed community. Thus the process of closure proceeds from the normative to the economic to the coercive (Skinner 1971: 270–81). In such a scheme, the village as a collectivity returns to demand our attention, at least for the periods of dynastic decline.

I shall show in the next chapter that closure was only one of two important patterns of community response to the changes of the twentieth century. The other was the progressive loosening of community bonds in the face of the long-term process of partial proletarianization discussed in Part Two of this book. When communities of partly proletarianized peasants were confronted with increasingly intrusive outside power, the result was not closure, but the collapse of their political structures and a power vacuum that permitted the rise of village bullies and tyrants.

That process needs to be understood from a baseline picture of the village as a collectivity. It needs also to be analyzed from the perspective of a three-way relationship between the village, the state, and the gentry. A dualistic model of state and gentry will not do, especially not for relatively uncommercialized and unstratified Hebei–northwest Shandong. In this area, the village as a relatively insular community needs to be placed at the starting point of our efforts to understand the patterns of community change in the twentieth century.

### SOCIOECONOMIC AND SOCIOPOLITICAL
### STRUCTURE IN THE QING

The political economy of the Qing embodied three interdependent components: small farming, landlordism, and a centralized imperial state. From the point of view of the state and its official apparatus,

smallholders were the ideal subjects for tax revenue and military re-
cruits; they were far less threatening to state power than large estates. Like other dynasties before it, the Qing therefore encouraged
the expansion of the smallholder economy. It also sought to close
tax loopholes for the large estates. From the small peasants' point of
view, the Qing state (after the forcible "enclosure," or *quandi*, practices of its early, land-granting years) in general guaranteed and protected their claims to private property. Though the Qing legal code
confirmed them in their status as commoners, below the gentry
elite, it also protected that status, for tenants as well as smallholders. In the eighteenth and nineteenth centuries, as has been
seen, provincial officials and the court acted to forbid large estates
from treating their tenants as sub-commoner tenant-bondservants.
For the small peasants in our area, the managerial function of the
state loomed particularly large because of the scale of the projects
that were required for flood control.

The imperial state and landlordism were similarly interdependent. From the point of view of the imperial state, an institutional
system in which landownership was divorced from administrative,
judicial, and military power was far preferable to the parcelization of
power under European manorialism. The fully elaborated late imperial state, moreover, came to rely mainly on the landlord class for its
officials, recruited principally through the examination system. Below the level of the official apparatus, landlords were indispensable
intermediaries in the state's dealings with the peasants. The imperial state, we might say, walked on the two legs of small farming and
landlordism, taking care to balance the interests of one against the
other.

From the point of view of the landlord class, the state protected its
claims to land rents and therefore to much of the surplus produced
in the small peasant economy. It was this surplus that permitted
members of that class the luxury of careers divorced from farming.
The state, moreover, held before the landlords the lure of elite legal
status via the examination system. Entry into upper gentry status
and officialdom, finally, promised financial rewards beyond the reach
of the commoner. The average income of a county magistrate in the
nineteenth century was about 30,000 taels, and of a provincial governor about 180,000 taels, compared with about 100 taels in rent receipts for a small landlord of 100 mu. The truly successful landlord
was one who became a member of the gentry, and the truly successful degree-holder was one who became an official.

Landlordism and small farming, finally, were also interdependent.

There could be no landlordism without the tenants on whose surplus the landlords relied for support. From the smallholder's point of view, he was dependent on the distinctive system of private landownership and the private buying and selling of land to the same extent as the landlord. As for the tenant, former smallholder as well as aspiring smallholder that he generally was, he had little reason to question the landownership system on which landlordism was based. Although landownership was far less concentrated in the North China plain than in the lower Yangzi or the Pearl River delta, the principles remained much the same.

Keeping these three parts together turned crucially on the state's ability to control the vast numbers of relatively insular village communities. Direct administrative control of possibly as many as a million villages would have required an apparatus well beyond the capacity of any premodern state. What the late imperial Chinese state did was to resort in the main to an indirect means of control, attempting to secure the loyalty of the village elites by holding before them the possibility of entering the upper tier through the well-controlled examination system. In short, what connected and held together the two tiers of this sociopolitical system were the avenues of mobility that gave commoner elites access to the gentry elites, that allowed rich peasants, managerial farmers, and landlords to become gentry landlords and officials. Those avenues lent flexibility and vitality to the Qing system. It was only when all three of these components underwent fundamental changes that the entire structure fell apart to give way to a totally new system. Until then, most villages of the North China plain remained relatively insulated socially and politically from the outside world.

# CHAPTER 14

# Changes in
# the Village Community

The accelerated commercialization of the twentieth century and the partial proletarianization of increasing numbers of peasants had profound effects on the villages of the North China plain. We need not dwell here on the obvious: that they became less insular as a result of these trends. What is less obvious is how these trends affected village solidarity.

This chapter will draw on the Mantetsu–Tokyo University six-village survey to show that the social composition of a village's population shaped the way in which the community responded to external threats. The villages of mainly owner-cultivators tended to remain solidary units; those of mainly partly proletarianized poor peasants tended to be less tightly knit. Whereas the solidary villages sometimes responded to external threat with "closure," becoming armed communities turned in on themselves, the others sometimes simply disintegrated into atomized neighborhoods, highly vulnerable to arbitrary abuse by agents of outside powers.

## ISSUES SEPARATING THE OWNER-CULTIVATOR FROM
## THE AGRICULTURAL WORKER

As we saw in Chapter Ten, middle peasants often hired labor to supplement their own household labor (see Table 10.1 for the use of labor in Michang). Quite a number of them employed year-laborers: Table 14.1 shows 28 such middle peasant employers in four villages (of a total of 43 employers of year-laborers). Together they accounted for 29 of the 72 year-laborers employed in these villages. Not surprisingly, they relied especially on short-term help and were by far the greatest employers of day-laborers. They accounted for fully 27 of the 32 employers shown in Table 14.2, and for 1,773 of the 2,457 labor-days hired on a short-term basis in these villages.

TABLE 14.1

Classification by Household Type of Employers of Year-Laborers in Four Hebei Villages, 1936–1942

(Land in mu)

| Village and household | Household size | Number of adult males | Number of year-laborers | Land owned | Land rented | Total land farmed | Household type |
|---|---|---|---|---|---|---|---|
| Dabeiguan (1936) | | | | | | | |
| Household 1 | 27 | 5 | 5 | 243 | 0 | 212 | Managerial farmer |
| Household 2 | 14 | 4 | 4 | 218 | 0 | 189 | Managerial farmer |
| Household 3 | 17 | 3 | 2 | 145 | 0 | 124 | Managerial farmer |
| Household 6 | 3 | 1 | 2 | 63 | 0 | 63 | Rich peasant |
| Household 7 | 7 | 2 | 1 | 59 | 0 | 59 | Middle peasant |
| Household 11 | 4 | 1 | 1 | 48 | 0 | 48 | Middle peasant |
| Household 13 | 3 | 1 | 1 | 40 | 0 | 40 | Middle peasant |
| Household 31 | 3 | 1 | 1 | 20 | 5 | 25 | Rich peasant[a] |
| Shajing (1942) | | | | | | | |
| Household 1 | 17 | 4 | ½ | 76 | 0 | 76 | Middle peasant |
| Household 6 | 9 | 3 | ½ | 31 | 0 | 31 | Middle peasant |
| Household 7 | 9 | ? | 1 | 50 | 5 | 55 | Middle peasant |
| Household 19 | 3 | 1 | 1 | 25 | 0 | 25 | Middle peasant |
| Household 35 | 5 | 1 | 1 | 17 | 0 | 17 | Middle peasant |
| Household 36 | 8 | 2 | 1 | 16 | 30 | 46 | Middle peasant |
| Household 49 | 5 | 1 | 1 | 40 | 0 | 40 | Middle peasant |
| Household 59 | 5 | 1 | 1 | 19 | 5 | 24 | Middle peasant |
| Household 61 | 18 | 3 | 3 | 110 | 0 | 110 | Managerial farmer |
| Michang (1936) | | | | | | | |
| Household 3 | 9 | 2 | 1 | 61 | 0 | 37 | Rich peasant |
| Household 5 | 8 | 1 | 2 | 51 | 0 | 32 | Rich peasant |
| Household 7 | 12 | 3 | 3 | 81 | 22 | 103 | Rich peasant |
| Household 8 | 8 | 3 | 2 | 130 | 0 | 120 | Managerial farmer |
| Household 9 | 12 | 3 | 3 | 109 | 0 | 109 | Managerial farmer |
| Household 11 | 8 | 3 | 1 | 51 | 5 | 56 | Middle peasant |
| Household 13 | 4 | 2 | 1 | 41 | 0 | 41 | Middle peasant |
| Household 17 | 8 | 3 | 2 | 18 | 0 | 18 | Middle peasant |

| | | | | | | |
|---|---|---|---|---|---|---|
| Household 22 | 35 | 10 | 6 | 157 | 26 | 183 | Managerial farmer |
| Household 23 | 9 | 3 | 2 | 58 | 14 | 72 | Middle peasant |
| Household 25 | 5 | 2 | 5 | 57 | 8 | 65 | Rich peasant |
| Household 32 | 2 | 1 | 2 | 21 | 2 | 23 | Rich peasant |
| Household 34 | 22 | 3 | 1 | 26 | 12 | 38 | Middle peasant |
| Household 59 | 4 | 1 | 2 | 5 | 20 | 25 | Rich peasant |
| **Sibeichai (1942)** | | | | | | | |
| Household 2 | 3 | 1 | 1 | 2 | 30 | 32 | Middle peasant |
| Household 34 | 5 | 3 | 1 | 18 | 23 | 41 | Middle peasant |
| Household 44 | 15 | 4 | 1 | 0 | 60 | 60 | Middle peasant |
| Household 48 | 11 | 3 | 1 | 25 | 51 | 76 | Middle peasant |
| Household 55 | 4 | 2 | 1 | 13 | 34 | 47 | Middle peasant |
| Household 64 | 9 | 1 | 1 | 35 | 4 | 39 | Middle peasant |
| Household 72 | 14 | 2 | 1 | 26 | 32 | 58 | Middle peasant |
| Household 82 | 6 | 3 | 1 | 20 | 63 | 83 | Middle peasant |
| Household 89 | 14 | 3 | 1 | 39 | 50 | 89 | Middle peasant |
| Household 119 | 14 | 2 | 1 | 23 | 14 | 37 | Middle peasant |
| Household 132 | 6 | 3 | 1 | 8 | 50 | 58 | Middle peasant |
| Household 138 | 6 | 2 | 1 | 24 | 15 | 39 | Middle peasant |

SOURCES: *Dabeiguan*, MT, Kitō 193 a: 30–39; *Shajing*, KC, 1: Appended chart; *Michang*, MT, Kitō 1937b: 29–38; *Sibeichai*, KC, 3: 524–33.

[a] Also employed 90 days of short-term labor and did not do much farmwork himself.

TABLE 14.2

Classification by Household Type of Employers Hiring More Than Ten Days of Short-Term Labor in Four Hebei Villages, 1936–1942

(Land in mu)

| Village and household | Household size | Number of adult males | Number of hired labor days | Land owned | Land rented | Total land farmed | Household type |
|---|---|---|---|---|---|---|---|
| Dabeiguan (1936) | | | | | | | |
| Household 1 | 27 | 5 | 40 | 243 | 0 | 211 | Managerial farmer |
| Household 2 | 14 | 4 | 18 | 218 | 0 | 188 | Managerial farmer |
| Household 9 | 6 | 2 | 200 | 48 | 2 | 50 | Middle peasant |
| Household 31 | 3 | 1 | 90 | 20 | 5 | 25 | Rich peasant |
| Household 33 | 4 | 2 | 200+ | 20 | 4 | 24 | Middle peasant |
| Household 63[a] | 4 | 1 | 70 | 11 | 0 | 11 | Middle peasant |
| Shajing (1942) | | | | | | | |
| Household 47 | 5 | 1 | 60–70 | 35 | 0 | 35 | Middle peasant |
| Household 50 | 10 | 2 | 50 | 14 | 20 | 34 | Middle peasant |
| Household 54 | 6 | 1 | ? | 20 | 0 | 20 | Middle peasant |
| Household 68[b] | 4 | 1 | 25 | 0 | 4 | 4 | Unknown |
| Michang (1936) | | | | | | | |
| Household 6 | 3 | 2 | 33 | 24 | 0 | 19[c] | Middle peasant |
| Household 7 | 12 | 3 | 92 | 81 | 22 | 103 | Rich peasant |
| Household 8 | 8 | 3 | 400 | 130 | 0 | 120 | Managerial farmer |
| Household 12 | 8 | 3 | 90 | 42 | 0 | 42 | Middle peasant |
| Household 15 | 6 | 2 | 65 | 20 | 5 | 25 | Middle peasant |
| Household 17 | 8 | 3 | 50 | 18 | 0 | 18 | Middle peasant |
| Sibeichai (1942) | | | | | | | |
| Household 62 | 7 | 2 | ? | 3 | 62 | 65 | Middle peasant |
| Household 69 | 9 | 1 | ? | 3 | 28 | 31 | Middle peasant |
| Household 70 | 7 | 2 | ? | 19 | 14 | 33 | Middle peasant |
| Household 78 | 5 | 2 | ? | 10 | 10 | 20 | Middle peasant |
| Household 79 | 5 | 2 | ? | 10 | 10 | 20 | Middle peasant |
| Household 80 | ? | ? | ? | 17 | 1 | 18 | Middle peasant |

| Household 93[d] | 3 | 2 | 150 | 7 | 8 | 15 | Middle peasant |
|---|---|---|---|---|---|---|---|
| Household 94 | 8 | 4 | 50 | 6 | 35 | 41 | Middle peasant |
| Household 95 | 8 | 1 | 50 | 20 | 0 | 20 | Middle peasant |
| Household 96 | 7 | 1 | 25 | 15 | 7 | 22 | Middle peasant |
| Household 105 | 7 | 3 | 30 | 10 | 50 | 60 | Middle peasant |
| Household 111 | 7 | 2 | 50 | 18 | 10 | 28 | Middle peasant |
| Household 121 | 4 | 1 | −100 | 19 | 3 | 22 | Middle peasant |
| Household 135 | 2 | 1 | 90 | 8 | 7 | 15 | Middle peasant |
| Household 138 | 6 | 2 | 40 | 24 | 15 | 39 | Middle peasant |

SOURCE: See Table 14.1.

NOTE: Assigning 65 to the figure 60–70 and 50 to each unknown amount yields a total of 2,457 short-term worker days. 1,773 of these were worked for middle peasants, 226 for rich peasants, and 458 for managerial farmers.

[a] Household head was a weaver.
[b] Household head worked outside.
[c] Household leased out 5 mu.
[d] Household head was a 65-year-old man.

Proprietary farms like these benefited substantially from hiring labor. Yang Yuan of Shajing village (Household 49), for example, worked his 40 mu together with one year-laborer. If he had had to rely entirely on his own labor (there were no other adult males in the household), his income would have been limited to the produce from 20 mu, the approximate amount of land one man could farm. My work with the Michang data suggests that year-laborers were generally paid only about a quarter to a third of the gross produce of their labor, and that production expenses—fertilizer, taxes, seed— accounted for about another third. The added increment in net income to a labor-employing middle peasant proprietor like Yang thus amounted to about a third of the laborer's produce.

The same principle applied in the use of day-laborers. Household 47 in Shajing (shown in Table 14.2), for example, was able to farm more land than its lone adult male could have cultivated with just his own labor, by hiring 60–70 days of labor. This family was thereby able to increase its income by the added increment of the net farm income generated by its hired labor, minus wages.

The fact that most of the middle peasants were frequent employers of day-labor, and that many were also employers of year-labor, meant that they were more likely to identify their interests with those of the labor-employing rich peasant and managerial farmer elite of the village than with the labor-selling agricultural workers.

This was perhaps even more true of them in their role as tax-payers. In the second quarter of the eighteenth century, as we have seen, the Qing state formally merged the head tax into the land tax. Since that tax and its associated surcharges constituted by far the major portion of the total tax burden rural dwellers bore, the change in effect virtually exempted landless year-laborers and tenants from state taxation (there were of course certain commodity and exchange taxes but these were relatively insignificant; see Table 15.5). This principle was not called into question until the imposition of special levies to support the twentieth-century modernizing reforms.

Taxation, accordingly, was seen as an issue only by the landowners as a rule. And the stake they had in taxes made them more likely as a group to be involved in the business of village government, whose main concern after all was taxation. They were also more likely as a group to be involved in tax resistance. Even where entire villages were mobilized behind tax resistance through the bonds of kinship, community, or ideology, or just through the charismatic qualities of a leader, the fact remained that the interests of the tax-paying landowners were more vitally at stake than those of the landless.

As might be expected, one of the most obvious distinctions between the landed and the landless was in social standing. Year-laborers were generally considered by villagers to be at the very bottom of village society (excepting of course vagabonds, beggars, prostitutes, and the like). In Houxiazhai, for example, the villagers thought themselves above such a lowly occupation; only in the last few years before the field surveys had three of them been forced to start working as year-laborers. Before that, the ten long-term laborers who had worked in the village had all been outside "mountain people" hired from nearby Taian county (KC, 4: 178).

There was still considerable social distance between employer and year-laborer in the 1930's, even though year-laborers had long since been recognized as legally of commoner status. In most villages the year-laborer could not use familiar forms of address with his employer, but was expected to address him as "boss" (*zhanggui*) and his adult sons as "young boss" (*xiao zhanggui*). The employer and his family, on the other hand, addressed the laborer as "worker" (*huoji*), sometimes combined with his surname or some other distinguishing label, such as "big" (*da huoji*, for the head worker) or "number two worker," "number three worker" (*erhuoji, sanhuoji*). Sometimes the workers were simply called by their given names (KC, 3: 145; KC, 4: 94, 402; Jing & Luo 1957: 120–22).

The laborers' lowly status in the eyes of the village community stemmed of course in part from their poverty. They seemed to other villagers the dreaded examples of failure in the intense struggle to cling to one's land, to survive, and to maintain one's lineage. Theirs was the lot and the fate that all villagers wished to avoid. But their lowly status was due also to the fact that many were outsiders and often transients. Of the 52 wage workers of the eighteenth century profiled in Tables 5.1–5.3, only seven were specifically identified as local men, and even when we put all the questionable cases in that category, about two-thirds of all the workers were in-migrants. By the twentieth century, larger numbers and proportions of local men had become partly proletarianized, but outsiders still accounted for a large proportion of the year-laborers working in most villages. villages.

We can get some indication of the actual proportions from a few of the Japanese surveys that are detailed enough to show us which year-laborers were local and which were not. (Most of the household surveys included only those people whose long-term residence was in the village and give us no information on outsiders who only worked in the village.) These reveal that 17 of the 34 year-laborers employed in Michang, 11 of the 18 in Dabeiguan, and 17 of the 21 in Lengshuigou were outsiders (MT, Kitō 1937b: 25–28; MT, Kitō 1937a: 27–33; KC, 4: 4, 178).

Year-laborers, then, were generally marginal members of the village community. To most of the villagers where they worked, they were mere sojourners who returned to their homes for the holidays. To those in their home villages, they were absentee members of the community who worked outside, returning home for only a few weeks or less a year. In neither workplace nor home village were they full-fledged members of the community.

Owner-cultivators, by contrast, tended to be the most stalwart members of the community, forming a sort of village "middle class" and "upper middle class." Where the community contained in its midst elite members—big landlords or managerial farmers—these "middle-class" peasants constituted the main base of support for the "establishment." More typically, from their very ranks came the dongshi or huishou, the community's "natural" leaders.

### CLASS DIFFERENCES IN MARRIAGE PRACTICES

One of the most graphic ways to illustrate the social differences between owner-cultivators and year-laborers is to look at their respective marriage practices. Propertied families generally followed accepted and standard practices in marriage. Their sons would pay a substantial bride-price; their daughters would have a respectable dowry. The sons- or daughters-in-law they chose were likely to be members of families of comparable station, under the principle of *mendanghudui* (lit., properly matched-up gates and households). The ceremony would be proper and presentable, with the proper celebrations and gifts. All of this gave the bride marrying into a new family and community legitimacy and acceptability.

By contrast, year-laborers often simply could not afford to get married or had to resort to the frowned-on practice of taking a child bride. In "Ten Mile Inn," in southern Hebei at the foot of the Taihang mountains, taking a child bride appears to have been a common resort among the poorest members of the community (Crook & Crook 1959: 101, 104–6). But it was seemingly not considered an acceptable alternative in Hebei–northwest Shandong as a whole. The Mantetsu–Tokyo University surveys turned up only two instances of such arrangements: one in Houjiaying and one in Zugezhuang (KC, 5: 61; KC, 6: 90). Lengshuigou and Wudian villagers reported that there were no child brides in their communities, though there had been "a long time ago" (KC, 5: 110, 488). In general, the poorest villagers seem far more likely to have remained single than to have taken a child bride.*

The considerations that gave rise to child brides were well explained to Japanese investigators by a Wudian villager: "[A daughter is given as a child bride] when the family is poor and finds it easier to have her eat in another's house. From the point of view of the prospective groom's family, this is a cheap way to get a bride compared with what it would cost to get a grown one." But, as the villager went on to note, the family that took in a child bride was socially stigmatized, for such brides "were not considered to be high class" (KC, 5: 488–89). Still, Jiao Yu of Zuge village in Anci county acquired a bride for his son this way because "we would not be able to afford a bride when our son is grown . . . since the [grown] bride's family would ask for money" (KC, 6: 90).

As the Wudian villager suggested and as the Crooks observed in Ten Mile Inn, such a suspect marriage set the tone for the girl's status in her new village. Like her husband, she would remain only a semilegitimate member of the community. Moreover, in Ten Mile Inn, at least, the poor formed something of a subcommunity in the village, set apart by sexual mores unlike those of the "puritanical" middle peasants. Stamped as these women usually were with a certain illegitimacy, and married to men who often had to be away from home for extended periods, they may well have tended to be relatively free in their sexual associations (Crook & Crook 1959: 106; see also Nee 1979). Mao Zedong (1927: 237) had made a similar observation in his report on the peasant movement in Hunan: "Since for economic reasons the poor peasant women had to participate in production much more than the women of the wealthier classes, they enjoy relatively more power to speak up and to make decisions. They had relatively more sexual freedom, too; in the countryside triangular and multi-angular affairs were quite pervasive among the poor peasant class." (The second sentence was deleted in the edited version of this essay in the official *Selected Works*, perhaps on the advice of people more sensitive to possible sexist and classist connotations.)

*When I asked about this in Shajing in 1980, I was told that there had been one case—of Yang Baosen, the son of Yang Mingwang, a poor peasant who had owned 3.5 mu of land. The very fact that the villagers could name the one child bride in the village of course attests to both the relative rarity of the practice in the area and the stigma attached to it. (Wolf & Huang 1980: 326–29 sums up the available evidence on different regional patterns in China as a whole.)

Between the two poles of a well-to-do owner-cultivator who gave celebrative feasts for the entire village and the year-laborer who could not afford to get married or married a child bride was an entire spectrum of subtle but real shades of difference in status. In Shajing, for example, wedding banquets were graded very clearly on two scales: the quality of the food and the number of guests. On the food scale, the rankings in descending order of prestige were the "two eights" (er ba or ba die ba wan), eight plates of vegetable dishes and eight bowls of meat dishes; the "eight plates and four bowls" (ba die si wan); and the meatless "eight plates and eat noodles" (ba die chi mian). Among my informants, the former managerial farmer (and village head) Zhang Rui and the former middle peasant Li Guangzhi recalled that they had the best: eight plates and eight bowls. But the current brigade head, Zhang Linbing, who had worked for three years as a year-laborer before the Revolution, had had "eight plates, four little bowls, and noodles."

The guest list was likewise ranked in three grades. "Doing it big" (daban) meant inviting as many as 30 tables of six guests each, including not just relatives and lineage members, but also fellow villagers. Zhang Rui had put on such a banquet for his eldest son in 1940, at a cost of roughly two times a year-laborer's annual wage. The second grade was "doing it modestly" (xiaoban), inviting only relatives and the other members of the lineage in the village. This usually came to some ten tables. The middle peasant Li Guangzhi had had such a wedding. In the lowest grade, called "not doing it" (buban), there were just three or four tables of close relatives. Zhang Linbing had had something in between the middle and lowest grade: eight tables.

This custom, as well as the status consciousness that goes with it, persists to this day. Zhang Linbing, who now does well as brigade head, was quite proud to announce that he had given his eldest son 12 to 13 tables of a "two eights" banquet in 1974, at a cost of more than 100 yuan. Zhang Rui, by contrast, had been able to give his third son only five tables of eight plates and noodles, without meat dishes. The Revolution had thus turned things around for nephew and uncle, former wage worker and his employer.

### THE DUAL CHARACTER OF POOR PEASANTS

The contrast between owner-cultivators and year-laborers is of course a sharper one than that between middle and poor peasants. Year-laborers were only about 10 percent of the rural population and a minority of the rural poor. The majority of the poor only hired out part-time and still operated a small family farm. They combined the characteristics of both the proprietary peasant and the year-laborer.

One-half or more of the poor peasants in Hebei–northwest Shandong in the 1930's rented at least part of their farm. In an earlier day, when tenants had enjoyed secure long-term tenure, they were closer in character to owner-cultivators, using their own tools, making their own production decisions, and looking on the land they worked as "their farms." But the shift to short-term contracts, resulting in frequent turnovers in rental properties, and to fixed rents (in cash or in kind) sent tenants one step farther down the road of partial proletarianization. They were unlikely to develop strong proprietary attitudes toward the farms they cultivated and could be expected to carry some of the attitudes of a laborer working another's land, even though they made their own production decisions.

The great majority of poor peasants, tenants and landowners alike, hired out as day-laborers. Thus, in addition to being "their own boss" on the family farms they operated, they also had the experience of working for another for a wage. Such work experience gave them wider contact with the world outside their own village than most owner-cultivators had, if only with other laborers and employers in nearby villages. Day-labor also brought them very close in social status to year-laborers. As one Shajing villager pointed out, when year-laborers and day-laborers worked together in the same field, it was the day-laborer who was expected to take orders from the year-laborer (KC, 2: 86). For reasons of both status and economic interest, therefore, poor peasants were less bound up in the village community than their more well-off fellows.

## TWO SOLIDARY VILLAGES AND COMMUNITY "CLOSURE"

Houxiazhai village, near the periphery of the Shandong plain, was a relatively solidary community. Despite a moderately high degree of agricultural commercialization by the 1930's (20 percent of the cropped land under peanuts and 5–10 percent under cotton), only a minimal amount of social stratification had taken place. The village's owner-cultivators had been favored by a relatively stable environment and the absence of an infusion of commercial capital into land. In the late 1930's fully 107 of its 124 farming households owned all the land they farmed. There were only 13 farming households that rented part of their land, and only four whose members hired out as long-term agricultural workers. (Six households relied mainly on nonagricultural sources of income.) Houxiazhai had no "rich" households by the villagers' standards—there was not a single resident who owned over 100 mu (KC, 4: 10, 399, 402, 459, 464, 475). This was, in other words, a community of relatively undifferentiated owner-peasants.

Not surprisingly, lineage organizations here were relatively stable, even if not particularly imposing or powerful. All the major lineages, the Wangs, Mas, and Lis, retained their common gravesites into the years of Japanese occupation. They all rented the few mu of arable of these gravesites to a poor member of the lineage, in accordance with long-standing practice, thereby maintaining the ceremonial of a lineage giving aid to its poorest members. Ceremonial gestures to honor the ancestors were maintained at New Year's and at Qingming. The Mas and the Wangs continued to gather for a meal at New Year's even during the lean war years (KC, 4: 438–40). In addition, the lineages gathered for the weddings and funerals of their members, as was the general custom in our area.

As we saw earlier, political leadership remained closely bound to lineage organization. Of the three neighborhood clusters in this village (called pai here in deference to official nomenclature in Qing times), the Mas (30 households) were grouped in the east, and the head of the pai had to everyone's memory always been a Ma, just as the head of the middle neighborhood, where the Wangs (51 households) lived, had always been a Wang (KC, 4: 424). This structure held on even against twentieth-century efforts to impose other groupings on the village.

The relative solidity of lineages in this village is evidenced also in their close observance of the custom of giving priority to lineage members in any buying or selling of land. This custom was intended to keep landed property inside a lineage and prevent fragmentation beyond that caused by partible inheritance. As long as the tradition held, the cultivated land, as well as the residences, of lineage members tended to remain clustered, so that the custom also served a very practical purpose: when an impoverished member of a lineage was forced into selling land, his neighboring kinsmen had first claim on buying land that was near to or contiguous to their own. In Houxiazhai this custom still held such force even in the late 1930's that, according to the testimony of one villager, a violation of the practice would have constituted grounds for a lawsuit against the offending party (KC, 4: 401).

Lineage ties also held considerable sway in production relations. Of the 13 rental arrangements, seven were between kin (and all the rest between good friends). Five of the seven were personalized share-cropping arrangements, and all seven were for fairly long periods, commonly from three to five years (KC, 4: 461, 475). Here landlord-tenant relations remained generally a many-stranded relationship involving personal ties of kinship or friendship. In a community such as this, one would be foolish to look only at class as the critical axis of village social relations.

The bonds of fictive kinship that went beyond lineages helped re-inforce the sense of community among villagers. In almost all of the North China countryside, the ceremonial of fictive kinship was maintained by the villagers. That this ceremonial held particular force in Houxiazhai was demonstrated to the Japanese investigators when they asked one informant about his standing relative to four other lineages. He was able to tabulate and match all members of each of the four lineages in generational sequence. Though he would call his juniors by their names alone, he habitually deferred to a se-nior by addressing him with some appellation like "grand uncle" (*yeye*) or "uncle" (*bofu, shufu*). The rigidity of this ceremonial can be illustrated with a single example: after Ma Fengwu married a daugh-ter of his former classmate, he had to address his former classmate as uncle and refer to himself as nephew (KC, 4: 436, 439–40, 447).

Newcomers to the village, who were described as "lodging" (*jizhu*) there, were not incorporated into this fictive kinship structure. But every one of the "old" villagers (or *laozhuang*, as they referred to themselves) knew exactly where he stood in relation to each of the others; all were socialized from early childhood to observe the proper forms of address.

Communal solidarity was further expressed in various village-wide organizations. One was mentioned earlier: the wheat-flour buns club (*bobo she*), which collected 20 cents each month from its members to purchase wheat flour in bulk so that they would be as-sured of this special treat at New Year's. Sometimes the club also made loans to members (KC, 4: 428–29).

Another important community organization was the Village Reli-gious Club (Xiang she; also called the Mount Tai Club, Taishan she). This group, organized for the worship of the so-called Old Mother of Taishan (Taishan Laomu), met on the seventh day of the month; generally some 70 people would attend these monthly meetings, held at the house of the head of the club. The members paid monthly dues of 10 cents. The club sometimes used these funds for loans to the needy (at 3 percent interest a month). But they were mainly de-voted to a once-in-three-years outing (*fajia*), when villagers mounted the sand hill east of the village, accompanied by a hired Daoist priest, to burn a picture of the Old Mother of Taishan as an offering to her. A banquet followed, with wheat buns, meat, and cabbage. It was a major festival for the entire village. The association that organized it was headed by the representatives of the village's three large lineages (KC, 4: 415–16).

Houxiazhai's response to twentieth-century intrusions was mainly one of community "closure." Harassed by bandits in the 1920's, the village welcomed the advent of Liu Wenxin, a teacher of Red Spears skills, who came to the village from nearby Deping county in 1925 and struck an immediate chord in a village sorely in need of self-defense. Some 70 men in Houxiazhai and adjoining Qianxiazhai quickly joined the new organization. Liu taught the villagers a few of the Red Spears rituals, instructing them to "sit" (dazuo) three hours a day so that they would be invulnerable in battle; to renounce cursing, seeking after wealth, and banditry; and to refrain from having sexual intercourse with their wives on the 1st, 3rd, 6th, 9th, and 15th days of the month. Members armed themselves with swords and spears to protect their property and their community (KC, 4: 417–18).

Elizabeth Perry has made crystal clear the connection between the phenomenon of banditry (which she calls "predatory") and that of community self-defense (which she characterizes as "protective"). More specifically, she shows that the Red Spears drew most of their members from the middle peasantry (and even in some instances required property ownership for membership; Perry 1980: 198). She also shows that the typical Red Spears community, under the leadership of the old propertied village elite, tended to be politically conservative and to resist the Communists' efforts to organize for a class struggle (ibid., esp. Chaps. 5, 6). This is not particularly surprising. And Houxiazhai might be considered something of a prototypical Red Spears village.*

When, in 1930–31, county authorities tried to impose the linlü system on the village, Houxiazhai did not even pay lip service to the new nomenclature, but simply went on as before, continuing to refer to its east, middle, and west pai; the lineage representatives in those neighborhoods remained the village leaders. And when, in 1938, the villagers were apparently dissatisfied with their village head, Wang

---

*This is of course not to say that all Red Spears villages were like this; some were certainly under the control of big powerful landlords or were anchored in market towns. It is only to suggest, as Perry does (p. 199), that these were relatively uncommon patterns.

Qinglong, they were able to settle the problem without taking the matter up with the county authorities, by forcing Wang to resign (KC, 4: 407, 450). This fact itself attests to the strength of the community's political structure.

Lengshuigou village—25 kilometers east of Jinan city—is our other example of a solidary community that responded to twentieth-century pressures with "closure." Like Houxiazhai, it was a community of mainly owner-cultivators. Only 25 of its 316 farming households rented land, and only three belonged to year-laborers. Here the small peasant economy had benefited both from a relatively stable environment and from a fairly well-developed handicraft industry in straw-braid making. Unlike Houxiazhai, however, the community did include three "rich" households of managerial farmers, a consequence both of its proximity to a major urban center and of a highly developed well-irrigation system that permitted one-third of the cropped area to be devoted to wet-rice (KC, 4: 175–76, 178–79).

Still, this was a relatively unstratified community of mainly middle peasants, and again this homogeneity resulted in a high degree of communal solidarity. In addition to activities similar to Houxiazhai's, this community participated in an elaborate religious ceremony related to droughts. The preparations for the one the Japanese investigators observed, held in the sixth month of 1941, evinced a complex organization: a total of 99 people were organized into 19 sections, each responsible for one aspect of the ceremony, ranging from collecting money (50 cents per household), to preparing the statue (*shenxiang*) and the required palanquin, to boiling water for those in the procession. The village also had a well-organized communal burial society (*wangshehui*), which collected one yuan a year from its elderly members (some 70 in 1941) toward the purchase of coffins (KC, 4: 30–33, 41).

When, in 1941, the village was attacked by six or seven bandits (who extorted 1,000 yuan from the village head), the community responded by organizing a highly elaborate defense system: for every five mu of land owned, a household had to contribute one adult male to serve in the defense watch for one day and night every tenth day. The village had about 4,200 mu, so that this produced a force of some 80 men to stand duty at a time. This daily group was further divided into ten-man units, posted at eight positions around the village to stand a split watch, with five on duty and five sleeping. In this way, the community was able to provide round-the-clock security for itself (KC, 4: 36).

It is not surprising, therefore, to find great continuity and stability in the village government of Lengshuigou: Du Fengshan, its head in 1941, had been serving in that position since 1927 (KC, 4: 6–8, 28). It is also not surprising to find Japanese investigators complaining that they found the village turned in on itself and singularly uncooperative with a survey sponsored by the conquerors (KC, 4: 9, 11, 55). Lengshuigou's response to outside intrusion, like Houxiazhai's, was basically that of community "closure." Its solidarity gave no opening to opportunistic individuals to insinuate themselves into a position of power in the village.

### PARTIAL PROLETARIANIZATION AND COMMUNITY DISSOLUTION

Communities of owner-cultivators like Houxiazhai and Lengshuigou were most likely to be found in the peripheral or ecologically stable areas of the Hebei–northwest Shandong plain. The other four communities in the six-village Mantetsu–Tokyo University survey, in the highly commercialized core areas or the disaster-prone areas, all evinced less solidarity and a quite different pattern of change in the 1920's and after.

Shajing is one good example of a village that underwent a high degree of partial proletarianization in the twentieth century. Located near a major urban center, it was, as we know, a moderately commercialized village, with about 28 percent of its cropped area under wheat and soybeans. What set Shajing apart from Houxiazhai, a village that falls into the same category in my typology, was, first of all, a relatively unstable natural environment. The Xiaozhong River just west of the village had flooded five times between 1913 and 1941, to the ruin of many small peasants. In addition, given the harsh environment and relatively infertile soil, managerial farming had probably developed here only because of the village's proximity to Beijing, which had allowed one household to make the most of the opportunities for urban employment. Zhang Wentong and after him, his son Rui, had risen and retained managerial status thanks to the income from their connection with the candied offering shop in Beijing.

The combined effects of population pressure, commercialization, natural disasters, and urban employment produced a considerably higher degree of social stratification and semiproletarianization in this village than in Houxiazhai or Lengshuigou. The Mantetsu investigators asked their informants to reconstruct the record of tenancy and wage labor in Shajing during the Republican period. The result, like so much of oral history, is not wholly reliable, but the rough estimates the villagers provided on the social composition of the community in the period 1912–40 do give a good indication of the overall process.

As we see in Table 14.3, those estimates are very rough indeed, inconsistent on their face even if we total each column using the lower ranges. Accordingly, I have included another set of figures in the table—from a household-by-household survey made in March 1942. Here the household's classification was based on the source of its income: a household deriving more than half its income from hiring out, for example, fell into the category agricultural worker, even if it owned or rented a tiny plot of land. And the same was true of households engaged in urban or nonagricultural employment. In the oral history data, it is clear, the informants grouped all who owned some land as owner or part-tenants even if they derived the bulk of their income from hiring out. The two sets of data are thus not fully comparable. Nevertheless, the thrust of the oral history material is unmistakable, showing the dramatic increase in part-tenants and short-term laborers between 1912 and 1940.*

In short, Shajing entered the Republican period as a community of mainly owner-cultivators or long-term tenants, and in less than 30 years became a community in which the majority of villagers were partly proletarianized. There was a contraction in the numbers and proportion of those whose property ownership, and the social and economic status that went with it, made them likely to be stalwart members of the community. And there was a corresponding increase in the numbers and proportion of those who had few or no property ties to the village, and whose work—whether as hired laborers or as tenants of absentee landlords—placed them in more contact with people outside the village. There was, finally, a breakdown of the village as an integral and solidary community. More and more outsiders came to hold property in the village as increased numbers of villagers were forced to sell their land to any available buyer. As we have seen, by the 1930's, 14 percent of the village's 1,182 mu were owned by outsiders (87 mu by absentee urban landlords living in the county seat and 78 mu by residents of other villages). Compare this state of affairs with that in Houxiazhai, for example, where every bit of the village land was owned by residents—where land was not in fact likely to be sold outside the lineage, let alone outside the village.

---

*The sharp drop in owner-cultivators and increase in short-term laborers in 1921–26 might have been due to the flood that wiped out from ½ to ¾ of the crop in 1919, followed by a year of drought in 1923 and a warlord war in 1926.

TABLE 14.3

Social Composition of Shajing Village, 1912–1942

| Category | Interview data, 1941 | | | | | | | House-hold survey, 1942 |
|---|---|---|---|---|---|---|---|---|
| | 1912 | 1916 | 1921 | 1926 | 1931 | 1936 | 1940 | |
| Number of households | 50 | 56 | 60 | 63 | 65 | 67 | 69 | 67 |
| Owner-cultivator | 30 | 36 | 38 | 28 | 28 | 29 | 31 | 26 |
| Part-tenant | 10–12 | 10 | 11 | 11 | 24 | 30 | 30 | 8 |
| Tenant | 8–10 | 10 | 11 | 11 | 11 | 7–8 | 7–8 | 5 |
| Agricultural worker | — | 3–4 | 10 | 6–7 | 5–6 | 3–4 | 3–4 | 19 |
| Nonagricultural worker | | | | | | | | 9 |
| Households hiring out as day-laborers | 7–8 | 7–8 | 10 | 20 | 15–16 | 13–14 | 15–16 | 32 |

SOURCES: *Interview data*, KC, 2: 72, 87; household survey, KC, 1: Appended chart.

NOTE: The Japanese researchers made no attempt to account for the obvious inconsistency in the interview data between the total number of households and the informants' estimates on the numbers of households falling in each category.

The sale of land to outsiders reflects not only the breakdown of community ties in Shajing, but more deeply, the breakdown of kinship bonds. In pre-Republican times here too kin, neighbors, and fellow villagers had customarily been given priority in the purchase of land. But in the course of the years impoverishment drove peasants to look to their own needs first. One detailed example will serve to illustrate the extent to which the old ethic had given way to an outlook in which land was a commodity to be sold at the highest possible price. The impoverished Li Zhuyuan, who owned one mu of land contiguous to the plots of four brothers and cousins, found that a man named Zhao Wenyou was bent on building his home on the land and, for that reason, was prepared to pay him 100 yuan for a plot that would otherwise have fetched only 70–80 yuan. Li knew that if he consulted with his relatives they would object to the sale, so he went ahead and sold the land to Zhao without informing them. The problem was that the only access Zhuyuan's cousin Guangen had to his plot was through Zhuyuan's, and the new owner, Zhao, had built his house on the access path. Guangen desperately tried to get Zhuyuan to rescind the sale or Zhao to sell the land back to the Lis, pleading with each in turn and enlisting the help of the village head and other community notables to exert what moral suasion they could, but it was all to no avail; Zhuyuan and Zhao refused to budge. Custom proved unable to overcome the contractual relations of the marketplace. Nor could Guangen go to court to claim easement rights, for no such provision had been entered in Zhuyuan's land deed (KC, 1: 289–90).

The dissolution of the Lis' kinship bonds is further shown in the fate of the lineage's shared ancestral burial grounds. The ancestral gravesite, as noted earlier, was the only collective property that most North China lineages possessed. It was the main concrete expression of the lineage as a collectivity. Shajing's impoverished Li lineage, however, had gone so far as to divide up this land. Continued economic pressures had then forced Guangen's father to pawn his share of the land (ancestral graveland could apparently still not be sold in deference to customary law; KC, 1: 258–60). This was a lineage on the verge of complete dissolution.

Under such pressures, little remained of the sort of lineage ceremonial observed in Houxiazhai in which the poorest members of a lineage were allowed to farm the couple of mu of arable at the gravesite ostensibly without rent (though actually bearing the burden of providing offerings at Qingming, which generally cost as much as half of the gross produce, a kind of transformed rent). Only three of the seven multi-household lineages in Shajing still rented this land out to needy kin at the time of the Mantetsu investigations (KC, 1: 262–63, 283–84, 303).

By then, few other ceremonials remained in this village to cloak the gap that separated the more well-to-do from the poorest members of the community. The villagers still observed the custom of permitting the very poor to pluck the leaves from the sorghum plants for a fixed period of days in the summer, just before the crop was harvested. Still, this long-standing custom had its basis in more than ceremonial charity. There was also a very real production need to remove the leaves at the right time to ensure proper ripening. In 1941 the poor could sell the leaves they gathered for 1.5 yuan per 100 catties—about the selling price of one cattie of cotton or half a peck (*dou*) of millet. The custom of "gleaning rights" for the poor was also observed in Shajing, in which people from outside the village were permitted to participate (whereas only fellow villagers were allowed to pluck sorghum leaves; KC, 1: 75, 186–87; KC, 5: 30, 53, 415). Such customs, however, could do little to alleviate the lot of those reduced to scavenging.

The general breakdown of the village's social fabric was evidenced in the absence of community-wide associations to meet specific civic needs. Crop-watching, for example, was carried out by an impoverished man in the village's employ. (The crop-watcher was paid about 60 yuan a year in 1940, or roughly the annual wage of an agricultural worker excluding board, and he had to guarantee with his own earnings the safety of the villagers' crops; KC, 1: 103, 119. It was a tough job.) The village had no self-defense organization of any kind.

Even the community religious association had given way to the atomization and partial proletarianization of the village. The New Year's offerings at the village's three temples, which had once been an organized community activity involving all of the villagers, were now a personal matter. By 1940 individuals worshipped "if they wanted to," and the annual banquet was attended only by those few villagers who paid a fee (KC, 1: 78, 143).

Under such circumstances, it is no surprise that the community should have been vulnerable to outside intrusion. When Japanese authorities in 1939 sought to impose the baojia system and to tighten their control over villages by subordinating them to the newly created administrative villages (xiang), none of Shajing's established leaders would agree to take on the position of xiang head. (The new unit included adjoining Shimen village as well as Shajing.) The result of this power vacuum, as we have seen, was a reign of terror under Fan Baoshan of Shimen, who was able to get himself installed in the position. Fan, apparently, was quite the stereotypical village bully. He had come from a fairly well-to-do family, his grandfather having owned over 100 mu of land, but he had squandered all of the family's funds and holdings. According to his fellow villagers, Fan always walked with a swagger and would beat up people if they so much as looked at him the wrong way. As the xiang head, Fan abused his power in many ways. One of his stunts was to steal for his personal use the railroad ties that had been sent down by the county authorities. When the authorities investigated, Fan tried to pin the theft on another villager, but the entire village turned out to testify in the man's defense, and Fan was convicted and sent to prison for two years. In 1942, however, he managed to get himself released from prison, returned to Shimen village and, at the time of the Mantetsu investigations, was once more stalking the streets to the terror of both communities. His scheme to swallow up the village's temple land, it will be recalled, was thwarted only through the intercession of the Japanese investigators (KC, 1: 197–98, 200–201).

Sibeichai, in the heart of the cotton-growing area of southern

Hebei, was even farther advanced on the road of semiproletarianization than Shajing. Since I have already discussed this village in some detail, I will merely briefly recapitulate here. Because of the lucrative cotton market, urban investors had bought up much of the village's land, and these outsiders had managed to install a highly profitable interlocked system. Tenants were required to pay them fixed rents-in-kind, thereby both protecting the landlords against the vagaries of weather and flood, and enabling them to take full advantage of price swings in the cotton market. Their monopoly on money-lending allowed them to develop a pawn-rent system that had the twofold advantage of hugely raising the returns on invested capital while freeing them of the tax obligation on the land, which still fell on the peasant who held full title. This system had enabled absentee landlords like the all-powerful Wang Zanzhou to double or triple their landholdings in a single generation. In the process, it had reduced 65 percent of the village's farm households to tenancy or part-tenancy, and 28 percent now belonged to agricultural laborers who relied on hiring out for more than half of their income.

Under such conditions, the community had become even more socially disorganized than Shajing. To continue with our ancestral graveland example, here even the fiction of charity to the poorest lineage members was no longer maintained. Some of the arable ancestral graveland in the village was handled like any other commodity: it was simply rented to whoever offered the highest rate, regardless (KC, 3: 91–92). We find no evidence of any of the kind of community associations that characterized the solidary community of Houxiazhai.

In the 1930's even the village head Zhang Yueqing, who prided himself on conforming to the gentry ideal in his 12 years of service to his community (Zhang told investigators a rather entertaining *High Noon* type of story in which he, his son, and his year-laborer had fought off a gang of 15 bandits by themselves, on May 18, 1940; KC, 3: 48–50), resigned under the twin pressures of intolerable exactions by bandits and the enforced reorganization of village government, with further exactions by the county authorities. No other member of the village elite would take Zhang's place. When, in 1933, the county authorities attempted to impose the artificial linlü system, a local ne'er-do-well named Li Yanlin seized the opportunity to represent himself to county authorities as the elected village head. Armed with official recognition, Li was able to extort money from villagers over the next two years. His hold on office came to an end only when the village leaders joined forces to file a formal complaint against him with county authorities. After an investigation in which the villagers unanimously testified to Li's extortions, he was found guilty of abusing his position and was sentenced to three months' imprisonment. Zhang Yueqing returned to serve once more as village head with the support of the community, but he was doing so under the increasingly onerous pressures of community dissolution and expanding external impositions (KC, 3: 50–51).

Wudian was located on the strategic highway approaching Beijing from the south. In Qing times, there had been a designated overnight stop nearby for the imperial party on its annual trips to the western tombs. For reasons of traffic more than productive agriculture, outsiders had been led to invest in land here, and as a result, this mainly subsistence-farming village was as socially stratified as any of the highly commercialized villages. In the 1930's all but five of its 57 households rented some land. A good part of this rented land (200 of a total of 600 mu of land rented in the village) was owned by three big absentee landlords: Wu Fengxin, Jian (given name unknown), and Qin Runtian. Wu owned at least 3,000 mu in Liangxiang county, and his was considered the county's "number one household." The son of a merchant, he had served for several years in the late Qing and early Republic as a county magistrate in Henan, and now ran a silk shop in Beijing. He owned 70 mu in Wudian. Jian, who had inherited a great deal of money from his father, had been a teacher, then became the principal of a school in the county seat. He owned 30+ mu in the village. The third landlord, Qin, had made good by serving a big official "in the south" and now lived in Beijing. He owned 100 mu in the village (KC, 5: 515, 519, 584).

Wudian's strategic location placed it in the path of the wars of the twentieth century. It was subjected to harsh requisitions by warlord armies in 1924, during the Zhili-Fengtian wars, then looted by them as they fell back in defeat. (The process was repeated during the resistance to the Japanese occupation.) The constant threat of further ravages by warlord armies drove most of those who could afford it to move away, leaving the village without its "natural" leaders. From 1920 on, the turnover in village heads was fairly rapid. In the next 22 years nine different men were induced to serve in the position. All were younger peasants and relatively poor; none owned more than 30 mu. This was in sharp contrast to the past, when the village head had generally been a man of some substance—like Guo Kuan, who owned 70 mu in the village and another 200 or so nearby, or Yu Xinsan, who owned 100 mu in the village (KC, 5: 418, 429–30).

Among other things, the withdrawal of the village elite from village government resulted in more and more abuses, a tendency that became particularly acute when the pressure of Japanese occupation was added to an already shaky relationship between village and state. In 1941 the village head, Zhao Fenglin, was found by county authorities to have embezzled some 90 yuan of village taxes a year earlier, and was removed from his post and jailed for a week. His successor, Zhang Qilun, a young middle peasant with 20 mu of land, turned out to be the puppet of a man who lived in the county seat and curried favor with the occupation authorities. Together Zhang and his sponsor, Zhao Quan, superimposed a 15-cent surcharge for their own pockets on the 35-cents-per-household levy imposed by the Japanese authorities. When county authorities discovered this, they called Zhang in for questioning, but Zhao managed to get Zhang released. At the time of the Mantetsu investigations, the two were once more imposing their personal surcharges on the villagers (KC, 5: 408, 421).

In the circumstances, it is not surprising to find that there was no observance here at all of the custom of giving priority to kinsmen in the selling of land (KC, 5: 473). In the 1890's almost all of the village's rentals had been of the personalized, risk-sharing sharecropping type; by the late 1930's depersonalized fixed rents were universal. The atomization of the community had advanced so far that the village could not boast of a single communal organization.

Houjiaying village was similarly atomized, though from different causes. As in Wudian, agriculture in this village was mainly subsistence grain farming, with a minimum of cash-cropping. Half of the farmland was poor sandy land or low-lying, easily waterlogged land, with the result that the average yield of sorghum or wheat here was only two dou per mu, compared with four dou for wheat and six for sorghum in nearby Michang (KC, 5: 144–45, 147–48, 180; MT Kitō 1937b: Table 11).

Pressured by low agricultural productivity, Houjiaying villagers looked northward to the expanding frontier economy of Manchuria for supplementary income. It was through the process of migration, from a village located about 70 kilometers south of the Shanhaiguan pass, the gateway into Manchuria, that this community had become socially stratified. Some villagers, like Hou Qingchang, had been able to make it to the top of village society. Hou had started working in a foreign goods store in Shenyang in 1901 and had eventually become the manager. In his 41 years at the store, he had been able to save up enough to acquire 153 mu of land to add to the 16 mu he had inherited from his father. His had become one of the leading households in the village (KC, 5: 288). Another success story was that of Hou Baolian. Baolian had worked from 1901 until 1931 in a flour mill in Ningan, Heilongjiang, and had done well enough to add 50 mu to his family's original 40. Meanwhile, his brother, who worked in an oil shop in Mudanjiang, also in Heilongjiang, managed to save enough to buy 20 more. The two brothers did not divide up their households, so that by the 1930's they jointly owned 110 mu (KC, 5: 175–76). Of the nine leading households in the village, five had attained their status in their own generation through employment in Manchuria (KC, 5: 151).

More often, though, the emigrants managed to earn only enough to help sustain the household, working variously as clerks, apprentices, or coolies. Most remained in Manchuria for stretches of three years at a time. As the villagers pointed out, the frequency of home visits was directly related to the cost of travel. For this reason, migrants from Shandong and Shanxi were able to go home only once in five years. No one could go for just one season, given the modest level of earnings. (See KC, 5: 94, 95, 175, 193, 250, 252–53, 284, 291, 295, 296, for examples.)

Not surprisingly, we find the villagers voicing different reasons for going to Manchuria. For one man, Hou Changyong, the reason was pure economic need. Emigration was something to be avoided if at all possible: "If you can afford to rent or sharecrop at home, it beats working in Manchuria." "What about someone like Hou Qingchang [who got rich]?" "Well, then, there are those who do not manage to make money." "Are there a lot of people who became rich from working in Manchuria?" "No, not necessarily. Few." (KC, 5: 193.) But another villager, Kong Ziming, noted: "Everyone goes in order to save money to buy land." He himself had managed to add six mu to the 10.5 he had, after 15 years in Shenyang (KC, 5: 283–84).

Frontier migration contributed to the growth of tenancy in the village because migrants whose households could not themselves cultivate the family's land often leased it to tenants. Liu Wanchen, for example, owned 17 mu but was the only adult male in his household. During the time he worked in Manchuria, he kept four mu to be farmed by his wife and children, and leased out the rest to four different parties (KC, 5: 97).

With the Japanese occupation of Manchuria in 1931, the flow of migrants from Houjiaying all but ceased. The occupation authorities severely restricted access to Manchuria as part of a conscious policy aimed at severing the economy of the northeastern provinces from China proper and linking it to metropolitan Japan. New permits for employment in commerce became almost impossible to obtain, although the authorities still granted passes for coolies. And remittances from the frontier back to the home community were forbidden. Only eight old-timers and seven coolies from Houjiaying were still working in Manchuria in 1942 (KC, 5: 144).

The village thus suffered the shock of losing a major source of income, similar to the whiplash effects that the closing of the Manchurian market had on cotton handicraft–dependent villages. By 1942 fully 47 percent of the households rented land, an unusually high proportion in a subsistence-farming community that might otherwise have remained relatively unstratified.

The combination of semiproletarianization with frequent movement in and out of the village during the years of migration had resulted in a highly atomized village. Even though this was essentially a single-lineage village (84 of the 116 households were Hous), lineage ties meant little. Land was usually sold and rented for whatever the market would bear (KC, 5: 67, 143, 197). As in Wudian, there was not a single community-wide service organization like the ones in Houxiazhai and Lengshuigou.

And also as in Wudian, the village government crumbled when the occupation authorities brought the village under their administrative control. A villager named Qi moved in to exploit the situation for his personal gain. Qi had been born into a troubled family: there had been difficulties between his father, who had been a soldier before he settled in Houjiaying, and his brother, a criminal; somehow, the brother had died at the hands of the old man. Qi himself was an opium addict and a gambler. In 1940 he managed to get himself appointed head of the administrative village responsible for Houjiaying, based at the town of Nijingzhen. At first, one of the members of the village elite, Liu Zixiang, a landlord and principal of the elementary school, served under Qi as the village head. But in 1942 he was succeeded by a yes man, Hou Yuanguang, who did whatever Qi asked of him. According to the villagers, Qi and Hou had collected 900 yuan from them, ostensibly to repair the village head's office, when 600 yuan would have sufficed to build the structure from the ground up. The village schoolteacher, apparently a young and idealistic man (and nephew of Liu Zixiang), decided to challenge Qi. He joined with two other men to file a formal complaint with the county government. But Qi managed to terrify all of the local and village leaders into silence. None dared come forward to testify against him; and in the end young Liu was given 50 lashes for bringing false charges. In 1942 Qi converted the temple in Nijing town (*zhen*) into a restaurant for his personal profit. He was said to have influential friends in the county government, and his power was apparently simply too great to be challenged (KC, 5: 48, 50–51).

The six villages surveyed by the Mantetsu–Tokyo University investigators thus showed two broad patterns of community change in the twentieth century. The villages that were relatively stable communities of mainly owner-cultivators tended to deal with external threat as solidary units. The villages in which a large proportion of the peasants had become partly proletarianized tended to fall apart in the face of external threat and to become vulnerable to abuse by aberrant elements. It is not enough to look at village change simply from inside the village, however. In the next chapter, we will look at how the other two components of the three-way sociopolitical structure—the state and the gentry—changed in the twentieth century to result in local governments that impinged much more heavily than ever before on the villagers' lives.

# CHAPTER 15

# Village and State in the Twentieth Century

The power and apparatus of county governments in China expanded enormously in the late Qing and Republican periods as they came to assume responsibility for maintaining military units at the ward (*qu*) level, as well as modern police forces and schools. It was a change that fundamentally altered the relationship between state and village. This alteration can be most clearly seen by looking at what happened to taxation, the crucial locus of the intersection of state authority with community organization. The expansion of county governments led to increased tax demands on villages and to new machinery to collect those taxes. I shall show how the 1920's and after saw the spread and increase of special levies to fund these new services and led to the institution of a new administrative apparatus to augment the feeble fiscal apparatus of old. When those new efforts at state intrusion into the village met a community in decline, the way was open to political abuse by local and village "bullies" and "tyrants."

## THE MILITARIZATION AND MODERNIZATION OF LOCAL GOVERNMENT

The expanding scope of local government in the twentieth century can be most clearly seen, perhaps, in its acquisition of land tax revenues that had for centuries gone to the central government. In 1753 about 73 percent of the total central government revenues derived from these taxes, and as late as 1908 they still accounted for about 35 percent of the total, even with the vastly expanded receipts from commercial taxes (Wang 1973a: Chap. 4). In the Nanjing decade (1928–37), all of this revenue, however, went to provincial and county governments, to fund their expanded activities.

It was under the "new policies" (*xinzheng*) of the last decade of the

Qing period that local governments first established modern police forces and public schools. Yuan Shikai, then governor-general of Zhili, was among the pacesetters of these efforts. He pushed for the institution of county police forces throughout the province, modeled on the one he had built in Tianjin in 1902–3. This model called for one policeman for every 50 households in the wealthier areas, and one for every 100 in the poorer areas. By 1907 the new county police forces in the province had an average strength of 270 men. Yuan's intent was explicitly to develop a coercive apparatus to supersede ad hoc local armed units under parapolitical leadership. These new police forces were meant to buttress the administrative power of county governments (MacKinnon 1980: 139–43, 150–63).

On the educational front, Yuan's reforms resulted in a tremendous expansion in primary education after 1902, to the point where the province had 8,723 schools by 1907. Almost all of these were newly established; only a few were converted from old-style schools (shuyuan). The number of primary-school students grew dramatically, from a mere 1,000 in 1902 to 148,399 in 1907 (MacKinnon 1980: 139–43, 145).

Official initiative of course played a larger role in Zhili than in most other provinces. Elsewhere, the gentry often led the push for educational and police reforms as part of the "self-government" movement of the time. In those instances, the reforms need to be understood not merely as efforts in the direction of modernizing bureaucratization, but also as a part of the process of the devolution of state power to the local gentry.

However it was brought about, local political modernization proceeded apace. By the time the Nanjing government undertook to rationalize local administration, it was forced to deal with powerful apparatuses that had developed out of the militarization and modernization of the preceding decades. Standing military guards, often incorporating the armed forces organized under warlords of the earlier years, came to be a standard feature of county governments, as did modern public schools and modern police forces.

The county government of Shunyi, Hebei, is a good example. As shown in Table 15.1, by 1931 almost half its expenditures went to the support of the police and military guards units. Its police force, started in 1905 at the initiative of local gentry and merchants, had swelled to a total of 102 men by 1928, deployed in each of the county's eight wards. This growth reflected both the widespread civil disorder of the period and the expectations of a modernizing government. The military guards units had been established and grew at a similar

TABLE 15.1

Expenditures of Shunyi County, Hebei, 1931 and 1940

| | 1931 | | 1940 | |
|---|---|---|---|---|
| Item | Amount spent (yuan) | Percent of total expenditures | Amount spent (yuan) | Percent of total expenditures |
| Police | $15,748 | 27.7% | $42,927 | 21.1% |
| Education | 13,686 | 24.0 | 14,358 | 7.1 |
| Military guards | 11,647 | 20.5 | 87,121 | 42.8 |
| Ward administration | 9,600 | 16.9 | ? | ? |
| Other | 6,227 | 10.9 | | |
| TOTAL | $56,908 | 100.0% | $203,632 | 100.0% |

SOURCES: *Shunyi xianzhi* 1933: 374–79; KC, 2: 327.
NOTE: "Other" includes administrative salaries, expenses in connection with tax collection and the administration of justice, and the like. The 1931 and 1940 budgetary records used different breakdowns; I have not tried to reconcile the two and detail the other categories of expense.

pace for the same reasons. By the 1920's the permanent military guards, who drew regular salaries, totaled 114 men, with 13 to 17 stationed in each ward (*Shunyi xianzhi* 1933: 318–24). The military forces in other places were often even more substantial. In Henan, for example, the strength of the county military guards ranged from 80 men to 700 in 1933 (Xingzhengyuan 1934a: 74). In Hebei the range was 30 to 1,113 (in 1932), and in Shandong 50 to 1,174. There were counties in South China and the lower Yangzi area with as many as 30,000 armed guards (Peng 1945: 50).

The Shunyi county's largest budget item after the police and armed forces in 1931 was education, accounting for almost a quarter of the total expenditures. The county's first public primary school had been established in 1904, at the urging of the county magistrate and with money raised from the local elite, again a part of the modernization movement of the last years of the dynasty. A second primary school was established in 1915 and a third in 1927, followed by a rural girls' school in 1930. Each class in these schools had an enrollment of from 20 to 40 students. More than half of the total education budget in 1931 (8,724 yuan of 13,686) went to pay the operating costs of these four schools (*Shunyi xianzhi* 1933: 377–78, 400–403). There were also some 200 village-financed primary schools in operation in the 1930's. Established during the last years of the Qing and the early years of the Republic,* they served some 6,125 students

*The Shajing village school had been started in 1910 (KC, 1: 79).

(*ibid.*, pp. 405–27). This was by no means universal education, in a county with a population of 165,521 in 1931. But it distinguished the partly modernized Republican county government quite clearly from county governments in imperial times.

The administration of the ward offices (*qu gongsuo*) was the fourth-largest budget item in 1931. The figure in the table, 9,600 yuan, or 16.9 percent of the total expenses, excludes expenditures for the military guards and police units that were attached to those offices.

As the 1940 figures show plainly, the twin processes of militarization and modernization became skewed grossly under Japanese occupation. Shunyi's military expenditures increased enormously, both absolutely and relatively. More money was spent on the military guards alone than was spent on all items in 1931, and those units and the police forces disposed between them a whopping 64 percent of the budget.

COUNTY GOVERNMENT FINANCE

During Qing times county governments met their expenses mainly through surcharges attached to the land tax. In the second quarter of the eighteenth century the imperial government legalized a fixed surcharge, called the *haoxian* (lit., "meltage fee"), for this purpose. But a fixed surcharge on a land tax that was likewise essentially fixed after 1750 could not meet the expanding needs of county governments. By the late Qing, as Wang Yeh-chien (1973a: Chap. 3; 1973b: Table 3) points out, this allowance contributed only fractionally to the expenses of at least two counties: one-sixth for Xiangtan county, Hunan, in the 1880's and one-tenth for Chuansha county, Jiangsu, in 1908. The difference was made up by "nonstatutory" surcharges (the *mujuan*). Wang estimates that by the early twentieth century taxes were actually collected at twice the statutory rate, and sometimes, as in certain parts of Zhili, at three times the rate.

County governments of the Republican period met their expanded revenue needs by essentially the same method: continually increasing the surcharges. In the early years these were frequently exacted on an ad-hoc basis, often by nonofficial local elites, whether militarists or reform-minded gentry and merchants. In 1928 and after, the new national government in Nanjing sought to formalize these taxes and to place them under the control of the bureaucracy. It gave legal sanction to the practice of making land taxes the revenue of the provincial governments. Though no statutory provision was made for the counties' share of these taxes, county governments were gen-

TABLE 15.2

Tax Revenues of Shunyi County, 1932 and 1940

| Source | 1932 | | 1940 | |
|---|---|---|---|---|
| | Amount received (yuan) | Percent of total revenues | Amount received (yuan) | Percent of total revenues |
| Surcharges on land tax (*tianfu fujia*) | $21,599 | 31.9% | $20,328 | 9.9% |
| Special levies (*tankuan*) | 21,068 | 31.1 | 58,959 | 28.8 |
| Surcharges on brokerage taxes (*yashui fujia*) | 14,679 | 21.7 | 41,344 | 20.2 |
| Surcharges on property deed taxes (*qishui fujia*) | 562 | 0.8 | 14,982 | 7.3 |
| Other | 9,786 | 14.5 | 69,165[a] | 33.8 |
| TOTAL | $67,694 | 100.0% | $204,778 | 100.0% |

SOURCES: *Shunyi xianzhi* 1933: 372–74; KC, 2: 295, 327.

[a]The largest item here was the special levies on merchants for police forces and police bonuses—a total of $22,195. Another large amount—$18,744—came from reserves of unidentified origin. Miscellaneous taxes accounted for the remainder.

erally expected to rely principally on the land tax surcharges to meet their expenses. These surcharges had increased to such an extent by 1928 that when the Nanjing government took power, it found it necessary to decree that they were not to exceed the land tax proper (Ishida 1944: 12–13, 67–78; Peng 1945: 2–3; Li Hongyi 1977: 6339–46).

But this regulation, like the one limiting the surcharge to the authorized haoxian, was unrealistic. A fixed land tax with a fixed surcharge could not even keep up with the rate of inflation, let alone pay for new services.* A relatively urbanized and commercialized county like Shunyi got some help from surcharges on business taxes —specifically, in this case, as shown in Table 15.2, on brokerage taxes.† But even so, the county government there had to do what other county governments did to meet their needs: impose new, special (nonstatutory) taxes on the villages. These levies had various names in different localities. In Hebei they were usually known as *tankuan* (lit., "shared-out fund," as in *cuntan jingkuan*, "police funds shared out to villages," or *cuntan xuekuan*, "education funds

*Wang Yeh-chien (1973a: Chap. 6) points out that even though taxes were collected at twice the authorized rate, prices tripled over the period 1750–1911.

†Jones 1979 begins to explore this subject. Note, however, that the brokerage tax itself, called *yashui* and collected by all licensed brokerage houses (*yahang*), went to the provincial government, not the county government.

shared out to villages"); in Shandong, they were called *tianfu fujuan* (lit., "contributions attached to the land tax"). In Shunyi county these special levies had already come to equal the statutory land-tax surcharges by 1932 (and those surcharges in turn roughly equaled the land tax proper). Under the Japanese occupation, as we see in the table, they became the county's single-most-important source of revenue, bringing in three times as much money as the land-tax surcharges.*

Yet important as these land-based taxes still were to the Shunyi treasury, by 1940 the county was managing to get more than half its revenues from other sources. Many other counties had nowhere else to go but to the peasants. In Luancheng county, Hebei, for example, the land-tax surcharges and special levies together supplied some 72 percent of the taxes collected, and the special levies alone some 51 percent—about 90,000 yuan in a total of 177,150. (Surcharges on brokerage taxes, at 5.1 percent, were not all that important in making up the difference; KC, 3: 379–80, 416, 444, 460–62.) And in relatively uncommercialized Enxian, Shandong, peasants were for all practical purposes the county government's only tax resource, supplying fully 97.8 percent of its total revenues of 195,600 yuan (KC, 4: 529).

### THE TAX BURDEN

There is no question that peasants were increasingly made to bear the burden for the added expenditures of county governments. Some indication of the scale of that burden in the 1930's is seen in Table 15.3, which shows the actual tax rates paid in 1937–39 by 14 households in Michang village. (As an aside, let me just say that these are the most credible data of this kind that I have seen, compiled by a resident Chinese researcher who helped these selected households to record detailed budgetary information over a three-year period.) In the pre-inflation and pre-occupation days of 1937, middle and rich peasants and managerial farmers paid roughly the same rate, in the general range of 3 percent to 5 percent of gross income. (When the rates are computed as a percent of gross farm income only, they climb somewhat—by perhaps a percentage point; see Table 11.1.) The 1938 figures reflect the added levies imposed by the occupation authorities, raising the effective rates to the neighborhood of 5–5.5

*Li Hongyi 1977: 6538–44 tabulates the land-tax surcharges as a percent of the total tax revenues for Hebei counties but unfortunately does not include figures on the all-important tankuan.

percent. Inflated farm prices, not a reduction of the village's tax quota, accounts for the lower rates in 1939. We do not have data of comparable quality for later years of the occupation. The 1941 Shajing figures shown in Table 15.4 are based wholly on oral testimony and can only be taken as an indication of renewed tax demands that outpaced inflation: the effective tax rate on the more well-to-do households of the village now hovered in the 6–8 percent range. In the last years of the war, taxes appear to have mounted drastically in the Guomindang-controlled areas as well as in the occupied areas.* All these figures would of course double or triple if we were to think in terms of net income rather than gross income.

Still, the pre-1941 figures would for good reason strike those of us accustomed to much higher income tax rates as surprisingly low. Wang Yeh-chien (1973a: 128) has made this point forcefully in his study of land taxation in the Qing dynasty. In the year 1908, for instance, he estimates that the land tax (and associated surcharges) equaled 2 percent to 4 percent of total agricultural produce. It was a relatively low rate in comparison with contemporary Meiji Japan, where the land tax has been estimated to have equaled about 10 percent of the total agricultural produce.

But the point, really, is not the absolute scale of the tax burden in twentieth-century rural China, which was certainly dwarfed by the 50-percent rent rate, for example. It is rather the weight of that burden relative to what peasants had long been accustomed to. There can be no doubt that the militarization and modernization programs of local governments in the twentieth century substantially increased the tax burden on the peasants, and that the peasants resented the new levies as increases over rates that they had long been used to.

We should not be misled by the existing scholarship on this subject. John Lossing Buck shows us, correctly, that the land tax and the statutory surcharges remained relatively fixed in the period 1906–33. By the index 1926 = 100, for example, these taxes only totaled 93 in 1907. By comparison, grain prices more than doubled in this period—from 46 in 1907 to 100 in 1926 (1937a: 319, 324–31). But Buck is dealing only with statutory taxes and did not consider the nonstatutory special levies. To ignore those is to be misled into concluding that the tax burden on peasants actually shrank in this period, a conclusion that Richard A. Kraus has in fact drawn on the

---

*The subject of wartime taxation requires a separate study in itself. Eastman 1981 shows convincingly that after 1941 the effective tax burden in the Guomindang areas increased to a whopping 20% of total agricultural produce.

TABLE 15.3

Tax Rates as Percent of Gross Income by Household Type, Michang, 1937–1939

(Yuan)

| Household type and number | 1937 | | | 1938 | | | 1939 | | |
|---|---|---|---|---|---|---|---|---|---|
| | Gross income | Tax rate | Gross farm income | Gross income | Tax rate | Gross farm income | Gross income | Tax rate | Gross farm income |
| Managerial farmer | | | | | | | | | |
| Household 1 | $2,291 | 4.9% | $2,192 | — | — | — | — | — | — |
| Household 2 | 2,030 | 5.1 | 1,915 | $2,469 | 5.3% | $2,329 | $7,487 | 3.3% | $7,369 |
| Rich peasant | | | | | | | | | |
| Household 3 | $1,169 | 3.7% | $1,029 | $1,313 | 5.8% | $1,161 | $3,671 | 2.6% | $3,332 |
| Household 5 | 1,519 | 2.7 | 1,117 | 1,749 | 4.1 | 1,410 | 5,484 | 2.1 | 5,121 |
| Household 6 | 1,117 | 2.9 | 912 | 1,174 | 4.9 | 1,055 | 2,743 | 2.7 | 2,558 |
| Middle peasant | | | | | | | | | |
| Household 4 | $898 | 5.9% | $790 | $1,421 | 6.5% | $1,287 | $3,908 | 3.1% | $3,796 |
| Household 7 | 359 | 3.6 | 255 | 454 | 5.7 | 250 | 1,115 | 3.0 | 871 |
| Household 8 | 621 | 3.5 | 514 | 789 | 4.8 | 745 | 1,703 | 3.5 | 1,668 |
| Household 9 | 388 | 3.7 | 332 | 821 | 3.2 | 733 | 2,032 | 1.1 | 1,951 |
| Poor peasant | | | | | | | | | |
| Household 10 | $389 | 1.5% | $234 | $536 | 1.9% | $306 | $959 | 1.4% | $757 |
| Household 11 | 217 | 0.9 | 104 | 305 | 1.1 | 206 | 633 | 0.4 | 393 |
| Household 12 | 228 | 0.9 | 196 | 506 | 0.8 | 469 | 962 | 0.3 | 772 |
| Household 13 | 282 | 0.3 | 110 | 439 | 0.6 | 206 | 691 | 0.3 | 279 |
| Household 14 | 195 | 0.5 | 89 | 291 | 0.4 | 137 | 728 | 0.3 | 469 |

SOURCES: MT, Hokushi jimukyoku chōsabu 1938–41: Tables 13 and 14 in all 3 vols.

TABLE 15.4

Tax Rates as Percent of Gross Income by Land Tenure Type, Shajing, 1941

(Yuan)

| Category | Gross income | Tax rate | Category | Gross income | Tax rate |
|---|---|---|---|---|---|
| Owner-cultivator | | | Part-tenant | | |
| Household 1 | $2,085 | 6.2% | Household 37 | $802 | 4.7% |
| Household 17 | 570 | 15.8[a] | Household 39 | 832 | 4.1 |
| Household 18 | 417 | 6.0 | Household 52 | 683 | 4.8 |
| Household 32 | 1,208 | 6.7 | Household 53 | 1,399 | 2.9 |
| Household 42 | 924 | 16.8 | Household 59 | 563 | 11.5[b] |
| Household 47 | 980 | 8.0 | Tenant | | |
| Household 48 | 542 | 7.7 | Household 9 | $405 | 0.2% |
| Household 66 | 676 | 8.6 | Household 10 | 745 | 2.7 |
| | | | Household 57 | 587 | 2.4 |

SOURCE: KC, 2: 270–91.

[a]Interviewer noted probable underreporting of income.

[b]Interviewer noted substantial outside income not reported.

basis of Buck's data (1968: 48). We are then left with the hopeless contradiction of a shrinking tax burden in the face of rising county government expenditures. What actually happened, as we have seen, is that county governments simply kept upping the special levies to meet their expenses.

From the peasants' point of view, and seen in the larger context of their relationship with outside political authority in the twentieth century, these taxes were quite intolerable. For one thing, they were imposed in a period of pervasive semiproletarianization, when many owner-cultivators were already under severe downward pressures. For another thing, they were frequently imposed by governments that seemed of questionable legitimacy to the peasant taxpayers. County governments came and went in the warlord period, and the lines between legitimate authority and illegitimate military power frequently blurred. Some county governments made their peace with local militarists or bandits; some were actually under bandit control (Billingsley 1981). In the Nanjing decade some semblance of order and legitimacy returned, but the demands made by county governments frequently also increased. Finally, Japanese invasion and occupation carried the long-term crisis in legitimacy to its extreme conclusion: added exactions by such authority, even if slight as a proportion of total produce, could easily seem unbearable.

Equally important, perhaps, was the violation of a long-established principle of tax allocation. Some readers might have been surprised by the clearly "progressive" character of the allocation of the tax burden shown in Tables 15.3 and 15.4, at least as regards the poor peasants. Seen in broad historical context, however, the fact that the landless poor paid any taxes at all was a departure from long-standing tradition, for after the head tax was merged into the land tax in the second quarter of the eighteenth century, only landowners in China had been liable for the land tax and its associated surcharges. The landless had not had to pay any land taxes at all for some two centuries.

The counties did not clearly specify whether these taxes were to be levied on land or on individual households. Much was left to the discretion of village authorities. In tightly knit communities like Houxiazhai, the old principles held. These levies were treated just like land-tax surcharges: the landowner paid, the landless laborer did not; the landlord paid, the tenant did not; the man holding pawned title to the land paid, the pawner did not (KC, 4: 468, 475). In more highly stratified and disintegrated Sibeichai, however, the centuries-old principle gave way to a considerable extent before the interests of the powerful absentee landlords. Here tenants were required to shoulder one-fifth of these levies against the landlords' four-fifths. Moreover, the landlords managed to institute the outrageous practice (or so it must have seemed to the man who pawned his land) of making the pawner pay half of the assessed tax. It was a practice that required influence in high places to maintain, along with a complete disregard for the sentiments of those already so desperately impoverished as to have to pawn their land (KC, 3: 11, 57). In totally atomized Wudian the old notions of fair practice broke down altogether; here the special levies were simply imposed on the cultivators, rather than the owners (KC, 5: 418).

We have excellent data for three northeastern Hebei villages for the year 1936. Investigators recorded the amount each household paid in land tax, in surcharges on the land tax, and in special levies for that year. In all three villages the land tax and surcharges were clearly assessed according to established principle—by landownership. Only those who owned land paid. But all, or very nearly all, of the households, including landless tenants and agricultural laborers, were required to "contribute" to the special levies. In Qianlianggezhuang, each of the nine agricultural year-laborers had to pay 10 to 25 cents that year, and each of the 12 landless tenants 10 cents to 3 yuan (MT, Kitō 1937c: 59–65). Similar assessments were made in Dabeiguan (MT, Kitō 1937a: 56–59). In Michang the

TABLE 15.5

Taxes Paid by Peasants of Three Hebei Villages, 1936

(Yuan)

| Category | Dabeiguan | Michang | Qianliangge-zhuang |
|---|---|---|---|
| Land taxes, including surcharges (*tianfu fujia*) | $181 | $24 | $185 |
| Special levies (*tankuan*) | 231 | 1,043 | 356 |
| Property deed taxes (*qishui*) | 15 | 35 | ? |
| Livestock taxes (*shengxu shui*) | 24 | 12 | 9 |
| Brokerage taxes (*yashui*) | ? | ? | 34 |

SOURCES: Table 10 in MT, Kitō 1937a, b, c, respectively.

agricultural laborers were exempted, but the slightly better-off landless tenants were made to pay (MT, Kitō 1937b: 61–65).

However slight these amounts, they must have seemed quite outrageous to the landless. After all, up till now they had only to pay taxes on a few commercial transactions such as the selling of hogs and certain cash crops. And as Table 15.5 shows, such taxes were in any case trifling relative to the main taxes, a fact also evidenced in the records of the tax revenues of the county governments, discussed earlier.

Given the abrupt break with long-established practice, the new tax assessments could not help becoming a divisive factor in the village community. From the point of view of the landowning peasants, their interests were best served if the special levies were borne by all households rather than only the propertied. And to them assessment by household could easily have seemed the just way: after all, there were no real precedents for such levies, and the government *had* allocated them by village. The new levies thus pitched property owners against the landless and helped to deepen cleavages within village communities.

As the tax burden increased with the further exactions imposed by occupation authorities, still greater inroads were made into the old principle of taxing only the landowners. In 1941 the Japanese sought to strengthen and bureaucratize the ground-level administrative units of the township (*daxiang*) and the village. The township administrative offices were empowered to collect their own "donations by the mu" (*mujuan*, under which rubric occupation authorities placed all land-tax surcharges *and* special levies). And village governments were instructed, probably for the first time in Chinese history, to pay the village head and develop an operating budget (KC, 3: 38; KC, 5: 418, 608). These additional pressures led, in some villages, to the practice of having all households equally shoulder these new "donations" for township and village administrative expenses. Japanese occupation policies thus brought to an extreme conclusion the trends evident earlier.

TAX COLLECTION

### The Old Fiscal Apparatus

To collect the various taxes levied, county governments of the Republican period came to rely on two mechanisms, one built on the old fiscal apparatus of the Qing and another created under the new efforts at bureaucratization. The old fiscal apparatus was one that fell considerably short not only of modern practice, but of the ideal of the imperial state, as has been seen in the case of Baodi county. And with the decline and disintegration of the state apparatus in the late Qing and early Republic, it eroded badly in many cases. In Licheng county, Shandong, and Luancheng county, Hebei, for example, the task of tax registration came to be farmed out to members of the county elites, private individuals with no official status (here called the *sheshu*). These men supposedly made the rounds of the villages once or twice a year to update tax records and record land purchases and sales. The governments based their tax notices on the records maintained by these private tax "assessors" (Ishida 1944: 17, 42–45). In Shunyi county the devolution of government fiscal power to the local elites had gone even further: here both registration and collection had long been farmed out to a number of private tax agencies, called the *lianggui* or *liangfang*, each headed by a "secretary" (*shuji*). These were lucrative posts from which the tax farmer could derive an income of 200 to 500 yuan annually. They tended to be hereditary, passed on from one generation to another (KC, 2: 381–83; Ishida 1944: 14, 38–40). Abuses by such tax farmers sometimes became issues for local armed resistance, as Roxann Prazniak (1980) has shown in the case of Laiyang county, Shandong, in 1910.

In the late 1920's many local governments—whether or not closely identified with the loose conglomerate that now constituted the Nanjing government—set out to modernize their creaking governmental machinery. In Shunyi a new tax bureau—the *jingzhengchu* —was created in 1928 to replace the private tax agencies, but bureaucratization in this instance simply took the form of incorporating the tax farmers into the new bureau, turning them into salaried official employees. At the same time, the county government enlarged the tax-collection apparatus by installing a collection agent (*baozheng*) in each of the eight new administrative wards. In turn, these ward-level tax agents oversaw a total of 53 "constables" (*difang*), each responsible for five or six villages (KC, 2: 297, 339–40, 341–42). In places like Sibeichai and Lengshuigou these constables were village-level agents.

Like the xiangbao of nineteenth-century Baodi, these ward-level tax agents and lower-level constables of the 1930's tended to be rather lowly figures. As one Shajing villager told the Mantetsu investigators, the constables were usually illiterate and poor, often without other employment (KC, 2: 400, 424). In Sibeichai the constable earned less than a year-laborer; in Lengshuigou he was not salaried at all, but went around twice a year to ask, almost beg, for some gifts in return for his services (KC, 3: 8, 48). The constable's job usually amounted to little more than an errand boy for the village head and village elite. He passed around notices and carried messages (KC, 3: 48; KC, 4: 436). The ward tax agent was similarly usually a man of fairly low status. In the description of a Shajing villager, he was "usually someone with not too much property, but had wide contacts" (KC, 2: 373). He was paid 20 to 100 yuan, about equal to the wages of a year-laborer (KC, 2: 373).

To this rather feeble, re-bureaucratized old fiscal apparatus was entrusted the task of collecting the old land tax and statutory surcharges. Those taxes, after all, had not grown very much more onerous in the twentieth century. They were also levied on landowning households according to well-established practices and principles. Their collection could be expected to be relatively easy and therefore did not seem to require added coercive muscle.

## The New Administrative Apparatus

It was apparent to Nanjing from the start that the more controversial special levies would require a more powerful administrative apparatus. The government thus chose to entrust the collection of the new taxes to the ward office, which had a full complement of police and military guards units to back up its control.

Under the ward came the administrative village (*xiang*) and the natural villages (*cun*). The administrative village was a nebulous unit, created to group together small villages into a complex of more than 100 households (*Shunyi xianzhi* 1933: 303). Until Japanese authorities sought in 1941 to strengthen bureaucratic control over the natural villages, the administrative villages were not provided for in the county government budget and had no revenue of their own. They existed mainly on paper, like the pentamerous groupings of households under the linlü system. The real units of importance were the wards and the natural villages. In Shunyi each of the eight wards oversaw about 40 villages of an average population of 500.

The ward and village heads were the crucial figures in the collection of the special levies. The county tax bureau assigned quotas to the ward heads, who then called together the village heads under their jurisdiction and allocated the taxes among them. The village heads were responsible for meeting the quotas assigned to their communities. The payments when collected went back up this administrative track: the village heads delivered the taxes to the ward heads (via the township heads if they existed), who issued receipts for the funds and delivered them to the county treasury (KC, 2: 339–42).

This new administrative apparatus quickly came to overshadow the old fiscal apparatus. Backed up by police and troops down to the ward level, it was far the more powerful, and hence prestigious, of the two systems. For that reason, it was generally staffed by men of greater substance and stature than the lowly ward agent and village constables of the fiscal apparatus. As has been seen, until widespread abuse set in in the 1920's and after, most of the new village heads were members of the village elites. This was even more true of the ward head, a position of considerable power and prestige that was filled and indeed often coveted by the well-to-do. The eight ward heads in Shunyi in 1931, for example, were all sons of families of some substance, for they had a middle school or higher educational background (*Shunyi xianzhi* 1933: 329–30). Similarly, the majority of a group of 44 ward heads in Henan province in 1933, according to a survey conducted by investigators sent by the Nanjing government, owned somewhere between 100 and 300 mu of land; six owned more than 300, and only 12 less than 100 (Xingzhengyuan 1934: 76; see also Kuhn 1975: 290).

As the special levies steadily expanded, first to equal the statutory land tax and surcharges and then to exceed them, the new administrative apparatus came to supersede completely the old fiscal structure. In Shunyi the ward agent became little more than a messenger boy for the ward head, just as the constable was for the village head and the village elite who wielded the real power. At both levels, the tax agents came in practice to be selected and appointed by the heads they served (KC, 2: 341–42). In Licheng and Luancheng counties, the old fiscal apparatus was never drawn into the bureaucracy and simply faded away (Ishida 1944: 46–50; KC, 3: 33; KC, 4: 20).

## THE RISE OF LOCAL TYRANTS AND VILLAGE BULLIES

Had the Republican government developed a truly modern administrative apparatus, had the Guomindang actually possessed the machinery with which to implement its ideal of a modern party, then the story of local political change would have been simply one of modern bureaucratization. Agents of the state would have penetrated deeply into local society and village communities, in the fashion of the People's Republic. At the other extreme, had the Republican authorities merely contented themselves with an apparatus similar to that of the imperial state, then local political change would have amounted to little more than an official rubber-stamping of the leadership roles of the local and village elites. What actually happened, however, fell somewhere between these two poles. The Republican political authorities failed to expand the bureaucracy to the point where they could administer affairs at the subcounty level through their own agents. They thus had to work through village and supra-village elites. At the same time, however, their power was sufficient to make their intrusions into subcounty administration more than merely nominal, as had been the case in nineteenth-century Baodi. They had both the wish and the ability to make their power felt to a greater extent than the late imperial state.

Under these conditions, the new position of ward head became a critical point of intersection between state and community, the locus of the tensions between heteronomous state power and community resistance to it. In some instances, elites descended from the old gentry, especially the lower gentry, who had led in militarization and then continued in their positions of leadership, took office to mediate between the demands of the new county governments and local communities. A few of these became "local bullies and evil gentry" who abused their new powers. This is the pattern suggested by Philip Kuhn (1975). In other instances, the ward heads were newcomers to the elite ranks, beneficiaries of the increased social mobility in Republican China. This group also supplied its share of bullies and tyrants. This is the pattern suggested by Guy Alitto (1979: 239–62). Future research will no doubt provide further substantiation of these patterns and uncover others.

What we do know with relative certainty is that there was widespread abuse at this level. In 1933 the magistrate of Huixian, in northernmost Henan, proudly reported to a team of Nanjing investigators that the county had replaced most of its ward heads to get rid of those who had imposed intolerable exactions on the people (Xingzhengyuan 1934: 90, 92, 94). The Guomindang party branch of Shunyi county similarly boasted of having effected, in 1928, the ouster of a particularly abusive ward head—Wang Guangxin of the 4th ward—who had enriched himself by imposing levies ostensibly intended for the national army; this was followed, in 1930 and 1931, by a major overhaul in the ward offices' personnel, including the replacement of each and every one of the heads (*Shunyi xianzhi* 1933: 329–30, 390–91). The extent to which such efforts did manage to correct abuses at this level in the 1930's will have to be determined by future research.

But my main concern in any case is with the lower point of intersection between state and society, at the level of village government. This was in many ways the more important of the two tension points, for it was here that the state came into direct contact with the village community and the bulk of the rural population. As I have indicated, the Mantetsu-surveyed villages responded to these heightened tensions in many ways, falling broadly, however, into two patterns. In one pattern, represented by Houxiazhai and Lengshuigou, the solidarity of the communities was such that the local political structure remained intact despite the increased pressures from the state. The villages resisted bureaucratic intrusion, and the villagers coped as best they could with the new impositions, under their old leaders and as a community. Where the tensions between state and village reached breaking points, armed resistance sometimes resulted. That was the background to the widespread community-based tax resistance movements of the 1920's, from the Red Spears to other splinter groups such as the Tianmen hui, the Dadao hui, and the Huang Sha hui (Zhang Youyi 1957, 2: 695–99; Perry 1980: Chap. 5).

The other pattern saw the dissolution, to one degree or another, of village community structure under the combined pressures of semi-proletarianization and state intrusion. In Shajing and Sibeichai, community solidarity weakened with the alienation of a majority of the villagers from landed property and with their increased involvement in wage work outside the village. New tax levies increased the tax burden of the villagers and aggravated fissures between the landed and the landless. Under those pressures, old community leaders refused to serve, opening the way for the rise to power of political "bosses" like Li Yanlin in Sibeichai and Fan Baoshan in Shajing. In Wudian and Houjiaying, community dissolution went further still. There semiproletarianization joined respectively with shell-shock and frontier migration to erode even more the bonds of kinship and community. Outside powers met little collective resistance in those highly atomized villages, resulting in unmitigated abuses in both.

Local and village bullies, however, were but the most visible manifestations of a deeper crisis in the entire sociopolitical structure. Twentieth-century changes in the nature of local government and in the nature of the peasant and the village placed immense and in the end intolerable stresses on the delicate three-way relations among state, gentry, and village that had underlain the imperial order. The tensions born of those changing relations were to result in a wholly new sociopolitical structure with a different sense of the proper relationship between state and society.

# CHAPTER 16

# Conclusion

## THE PATTERNS OF AGRARIAN CHANGE

While the peasant economies of Western Europe underwent capitalist development and transformation, China's involuted. While the peasant societies of Western Europe underwent social differentiation until they became completely transformed, China underwent only partial social differentiation and remained a peasant society. While increasing proportions of peasants in Western Europe became "proletarianized," those in China remained peasants, only partly proletarianized. These contrasts set the socioeconomic background for the imbalance in wealth and power that made China a victim of imperialism, as well as for the agrarian crisis that underlay the massive peasant upheavals of the nineteenth and twentieth centuries, from the Taiping and Nian to the Boxers and the Communist Revolution.

The process of change that led to the agrarian crisis can be seen in especially sharp relief on the North China plain. The Hebei–northwest Shandong area began the Qing period with a relatively sparse population and uncommercialized economy, and, outside the court created estates, a basically unstratified society composed in the main of owner-cultivators. By the 1930's, it was a densely populated area whose owner-cultivator economy had long since become sharply differentiated between landlords and tenants and between employers and wage workers. Three centuries of population increase had placed severe pressures on the land. And three centuries of agricultural commercialization, primarily in the form of cotton cultivation, had brought social divisions between those who profited from the higher returns of cash-cropping (about twice the return of foodgrains in the case of cotton) and those who suffered losses from the higher risks of cash-cropping. The combined pressures of population and social stratification had reduced some 45 percent of the farms in this area to a size of less than ten mu, when 15 mu was the average minimum required for sustaining a household. The intrusion of the world economy had not created this basic economic and social structure; it had only accelerated the earlier patterns of change.

The managerial agriculture of this area tells the story of social change without economic growth. The managerial farms had arisen mainly from small family farms that profited from commercialized agriculture after the sixteenth century and, by the 1930's, had come to account for about 10 percent of the cultivated area in Hebei–northwest Shandong and a majority of the "rich" farm households. They were the biggest and most successful of farms. Yet these managerial farms remained tied to the economy of the small family farm: they used "capital" (e.g., farm animals, fertilizer, and irrigation) only to the same extent and in the same ways as the small family farms did, and their productivity per mu was not significantly greater. Moreover, once they reached the scale of over 200 mu, they tended to give way to small farming as their owner-operators turned to landlordism, attracted by the higher returns promised by commerce and office-holding.

Past scholarship of the "incipient capitalism" school has tended to equate the development of free wage labor with "the sprouting of capitalism." In relatively labor-scarce Europe, such development was indeed one crucial part of the transition to the capitalist mode of production. In overpopulated China, however, in which millions "floated" on the surface of the countryside, a simple equation of wage labor with capitalism without the concomitant developments of a capital-accumulating class and qualitatively new developments in the productive forces amounts to a rather one-sided application of the mode-of-production analysis.

Rural wage labor in Hebei–northwest Shandong differed qualitatively from that of a society in the process of making a transition to capitalism. Here the combined pressures of population with social differentiation had driven wages so low that agricultural workers simply could not support their households on wage income alone. Those who were completely severed from family farming thus generally could not afford to marry and reproduce, and tended to become terminal members of their families. The agricultural workers who did have families, it turns out, were generally those still transitional between the poor peasant and the completely proletarianized worker. Most of them still clung to a small farm, whose produce was indispensable to the household's subsistence. In this economy, the main content of social change was toward increased numbers and proportions of part-peasant, part-workers tied at once to family farming and to wage labor, not of proletarians completely severed from family farming.

The Revolution called such partly proletarianized peasants "poor peasants." As the Land Reform Law put it:

> Some poor peasants own a little land and insufficient farm implements; others have no land at all and only have insufficient implements. Generally they have to rent land to cultivate, and are exploited by rent and by interest, and, in small part, by wage labor. These are all poor peasants.
>
> Middle peasants generally do not need to sell their labor, whereas poor peasants generally need to sell some portion of their labor. This is the main standard for differentiating middle and poor peasants. (*Tudigaige shouce* 1951: 56)

By the 1930's, about one-half of all rural households in this area fitted this description, hiring out to supplement the inadequate incomes from their undersized farms. Of those about one-half rented their farms in whole or in part. It was these poor peasants, more than other strata of the peasantry, that had to bear the double burden of population pressure and harsh production relations, without the outlet and relief provided by industrialization.

The differentiation of owner-cultivators into managerial farmers, rich, middle, and poor peasants altered the character of the family-farm economy. Though for relatively uncommercialized middle peasant owner-cultivators, "rational" economic behavior continued to mean seeking the best balance between the drudgery of work and the satisfaction of the family's consumption wants (as Chayanov pointed out), for the cash-cropping rich peasant and managerial farmer, it came to mean optimizing the use of scarce resources in order to maximize returns, in the manner that formalists have stressed. And for the partly proletarianized peasant, it meant above all the optimizing of his chances for survival, under the combined pressures of population and of exploitative rent and wage labor relations.

Semiproletarianization itself altered the relationship of many peasants to the state and to their communities. The owner-cultivator was taxed directly by the state, whereas the landless poor peasant was not. The landless peasant's surplus was extracted in the form of rent to the landlord, who then paid a portion of that rent to the state as tax. We will return below to the implications that such changes carried for the peasant's relationship to his village community and to a revolutionary movement.

A comparative analysis of managerial and family farming demonstrates, first of all, the fact of overpopulation and agricultural involution in modern China's peasant economy. There has been much dispute over the question of whether and when a family-farm economy might be considered overpopulated. Since farmwork is highly seasonal, all farms have some surplus labor in the offseason, and even the best manned of farms can be short-handed in the busy harvesting and planting periods. In addition, the labor requirements of a farm vary with technology and with ecological circumstance: what is an overabundance of labor for dry farming can be a shortage of labor for irrigated farming. Farm yields, moreover, are highly inflatable with increased labor input. Such facts make overpopulation exceedingly difficult to determine and to measure. The comparison of labor use on managerial and family farms operating under the same ecological and technological constraints supplies a concrete standard against which to measure overpopulation. Since the managerial farms could adjust their labor supply to the needs of the farm, they tended to approximate an optimal combination of labor and land under the existing ecosystem. The fact that the land-to-labor ratio of many poor peasant farms was much lower than that of the managerial farms attests to the fact of population pressure on them.

Farms that were too small relative to the household's labor supply and subsistence needs dictated involution. Many poor peasant farms applied as much as twice the amount of labor per crop as the managerial farms, for only sharply diminished returns. Others involuted in the form of excessive concentration on cash crops, often at the cost of lower long-term returns. Managerial farms generally maintained balanced cropping portfolios, mixing cash crops with varieties of cereals to attain optimal results in labor schedules, land use, and long-term returns against the risks of calamities. Many poor peasant farms could not afford to maintain similar cropping patterns, and placed abnormally high proportions of their farms under cash crops, in order to try to maximize short-term returns to cope with severe subsistence pressures.

Involuted farming, a result of both population pressure and unequal distribution, forced down farm incomes. When those pressures were further combined with rent payments totaling one-half of the farm's produce, net farm incomes often fell below the minimum subsistence needs of the farm household. Such a low level of farm income, in turn, drove poor peasants to hire out for additional income. The demand for such labor, finally, was furnished by upwardly mobile farms that were profiting from the cash-cropping that came with agricultural commercialization.

Hiring out, however, often interfered with the poor peasant's work on his own farm. The demand for hired labor was of course highest during the busy planting and harvesting seasons. Hiring out at those times prevented some poor peasants from putting in sufficient labor on their own farms, or kept them from putting in labor at optimal times, or made it impossible for them to take advantage of cash-cropping. As a result, the average yields per mu on these farms fell below those of the average family farm. In this respect, it is important to distinguish the poor peasant mode of operation—which merged family farming with wage labor—from the merging of family farming with handicraft production. Handicraft spinning and weaving could be done in the agricultural offseason and did not conflict with farm schedules. It could in fact prevent peasants from sliding down the road of partial proletarianization and might even allow semi-proletarianized peasants to become proprietors once more. Hiring out in agriculture, however, often clashed directly with family farming. Although the poor peasant in theory hired out only his surplus labor, in practice he often had to give up optimal periods, and sometimes even necessary labor, on his own farm in order to hire out.

When we lump all poor peasant farms together, we nevertheless get average productivity figures that are comparable to those of the managerial farms. This is because the somewhat higher output per mu on the involuted poor peasant farms made up for the lower output on the poor peasant farms that put in insufficient labor. But that comparable productivity was achieved at the cost of greater average labor time, because farm output fell off more dramatically at less-than-optimal levels of labor use than it increased at above-optimal levels. The crucial point here is that poor peasant farms were characterized neither simply by involution nor simply by its opposite, but by the fact of forced deviation in both directions from optimal patterns.

Continual increase in the supply of surplus poor-peasant farm labor for hire drove wages down to about one-third of the laborer's produce—an income sufficient only for the subsistence of the laborer's person, and not of his household. The result was a particularly vicious and tenacious structure, in which the poor peasant was forced to cling both to his family farm and to hiring out even when neither by itself supplied him with adequate subsistence. He came to be locked into a simultaneous dependence on both, unable to do one without the other.

This structure of semiproletarianization, while predicated on a substantial spread of wage labor, also precluded a complete transition to wage-labor-based farming. The fact that farm wages were sufficient only for the laborer himself meant that wage laborers could not become an independent and self-sustaining group separated from the family-farm economy. They could only reproduce if they remained attached to the family-farm economy. This poor-peasant economy defies simple profit- or production-optimizing analysis. The severe involution it tolerated needs to be understood in terms of a family farm that was a unit not only of production, but also of consumption, so that it could be forced by consumption needs to add labor even when its marginal product fell well below market wages. At the same time, the poor peasant was often compelled by poverty and the demands of hiring out to farm in ways that ran counter to the logic of optimizing productivity, whether in the form of excessive reliance on cash crops, inability to take advantage of cash-cropping, or inadequate labor input. His behavior at such times is "rational" from the standpoint of survival, even if not from that of farm productivity.

"Class exploitation" weighed much more heavily on people in such an economy than in one undergoing dynamic development. Fixed rents can become relatively insignificant in the budget of a farm with expanding productivity. On an involuted farm, however, rents amounting to one-half of produce were indeed a heavily exploitative burden that often drove net farm incomes below the household's subsistence needs. And, given low labor productivity, wages amounting to one-third of the laborer's produce similarly left the worker with only hunger-level income.

In thinking about these production relations, however, it is important to emphasize the systemic nature of the exploitation rather than the evil intent of individuals. Revolutionary rhetoric has often ascribed to landlords and employers vicious intentions. We have seen that small landlords not engaged in usury or commerce obtained only low rates of return from leasing out their land. Managerial farmers, similarly, held only a thin margin over family farms, a margin that was easily eroded when the managerial farmer himself ceased to go into the fields. Both had to face the tremendous pressures of partible inheritance. Both typically slid down the socio-economic ladder within a few generations. To attribute to them inhuman intentions of exploitation, while useful for the purposes of revolutionary mobilization, obscures the systemic roots of a problem born of the conjunction of involution with unequal production relations.

These characteristics of the poor-peasant economy caution against a simple equation of modern China's agrarian crisis with natural or man-made calamities. In an economy in which peasants enjoyed more of a margin above subsistence and worked under less harsh production relations, short-term disruptions would not have been nearly as devastating. It was the combination of long-term semi-proletarianization with short-term disasters that made the condition of the poor peasants in China so desperate. A poor peasant already at the margins of subsistence was easily forced into debt or even into pawning part of his land when he lost his crops on account of drought or flood. Once he did so, his already meager prospective income was further reduced by the new interest and rent obligations. Under those conditions, few could hope to recover and redeem their land. As one villager put it: "One drought year means that life cannot be good for three years afterward. Two drought years in a row means a bitter life on account of rent payments" (KC, 5: 442). A poor peasant, indeed, was like a man already standing neck-deep in water, so that even small ripples threatened to drown him (Tawney 1932).

These characteristics also argue against any simple equation of the development of a commodity economy with the transition to a capitalist mode of production. This book has outlined three major patterns of agricultural commercialization: first, where it was accompanied by increased accumulation leading to an expansion in the scale of production of the farm, as with the upwardly mobile farms leading to managerial farming. Such entrepreneurial commercialization is closest to our standard conception of the phenomenon. But we have also seen agricultural commercialization powered by poor peasants who were forced by subsistence pressures to cash-crop to an abnormal and counterproductive extent. That kind of subsistent commercialization should be distinguished from the first type. Finally, there was the dependent commercialization that was artificially stimulated by external intrusion and dependent on foreign capital, as with twentieth-century tobacco and cotton growing in Shandong. We should not indiscriminately equate all these types of commercialization with a transition to capitalism.

Most important, they suggest that it was the combination of population pressure with unequal class relations, not just one or the other, that formed the basic structural background to this economy and society. Rents that totaled one-half of produce were high, to be sure, but this by itself would not necessarily have made the tenant peasant's life difficult. It was the dual burden of rent payments and inadequate farm size that made the poor peasant's life so precarious.

And it was the huge supply of surplus labor that drove wages down below household subsistence levels. Conversely, the effects of population were mediated by class relations. Population pressure affected managerial farms and family farms very differently, and would not have been nearly as burdensome without unequal distribution. The poor-peasant society and economy was born of the interaction between the two, in the absence of economic growth.

## THE ROOTS OF UNDERDEVELOPMENT

Past scholarship has sought to explain modern China's underdevelopment by isolating a single factor as the independent and causal variable, be it Confucian values or imperialism, population or class structure, or the role of the state. Such efforts to isolate one among several interacting factors seem to me fundamentally misguided. The poor peasant economy, as we have just seen, was born of the interaction of population and class structure. It was, moreover, only one of several factors that together shaped the ways in which surplus was used in the economy, a fact that can be readily seen if we focus briefly on the crucial problem of capital formation.

The obstacles to capital formation in agriculture can be well illustrated by the story of managerial agriculture, which was caught between the poor-peasant economy and the existing sociopolitical system. The availability of cheap labor acted as a powerful disincentive to labor-saving capital investments by managerial farmers. Most of them chose to use no more animal power than the family farms, because the costs of using farm animals were so high relative to human labor that it was simply uneconomical to use them beyond the minimum required levels. At the same time, because the existing sociopolitical system offered much higher rewards for other pursuits, managerial agriculture tended to remain within the scale of 100 to 200 mu, unable to reach the size that might have permitted the kind of large-scale investments needed to alter the existing terms of land, capital, or labor use (by canal irrigation and drainage systems against waterlogging, for example). Managerial agriculture thus never took on the truly essential characteristic of a capitalist enterprise: of an entity bent on the accumulation of capital for its own sake, thereby powering new breakthroughs in both productive forces and production relations. It remained tied to the small-peasant economy—a part of a system in which landlordism was continually reproduced through managerial farming and in which the surplus produced in agriculture was continually siphoned off into investments in non-productive landed property.

Capital formation in the industrial sector faced similar problems. Cheap surplus labor in the countryside furnished the basis for a handicraft industry that proved to be powerfully resistant to modern industry. Merchants could compete against modern textile mills by a putting-out system in which they supplied cotton yarn to household weavers working for less-than-subsistence wages. In the process, capital that might otherwise have found its way into productive investment remained in circulation, and markets that might otherwise have been open to the new cotton cloth mills remained tied to the handwoven cloth of the peasant weavers.

The new enterprises were also hamstrung by a money market whose interest rates were shaped to some extent by the terms of credit in the countryside. Poor peasants, borrowing for survival, sustained interest rates at a level that capitalist enterprises, borrowing for profit, could not tolerate. The relatively high rates that new industries had to pay for capital forced many of them to undercapitalize—a critical weakness of many textile mills, as Chao Kang (1977) has shown. Furthermore, these modern industries tended to rely on the vast pool of unemployed and underemployed workers willing to accept below-subsistence wages, rather than to make labor-saving capital investments.

Modern Chinese capitalism was of course up against more than merely the poor-peasant economy; it had also to confront an obstructive state and imperialist competition. Fan Baichuan's (1983) important work demonstrates how critically important the role of the state was: significant industrial development in the first decade of the twentieth century was triggered only when the state turned from the position of forbidding Chinese entrepreneurs to engage in mechanized production to the policy of actively encouraging private industry through a modern Ministry of Commerce (later of Agriculture, Industry, and Commerce), a business code, and chambers of commerce. Sherman Cochran (1980) details how a Chinese company like the Nanyang Brothers had to compete against the British-American Tobacco Company, which used Chinese peasant labor of low opportunity cost and resorted to price wars to force out its competitor. Foreign enterprises were often favored not only with access to cheaper credit, but also with more favorable tax treatment by the Chinese state. Chao Kang (1977: 146) shows, for example, that Chinese textile mills of the 1920's and 1930's had to pay 15 yuan in interest and taxes per bale of yarn, whereas the Japanese mills needed to pay only 2.7 yuan.

A complete analysis of capital formation in modern China would of course also have to take into account the state as a potential agent for capital accumulation. Here again one suspects that the poor-peasant economy played an important role. A stagnating agricultural economy, coupled with the limited fiscal apparatus of the state, precluded substantial increases in tax revenues from the land, and helps to explain the financial weakness of modern Chinese governments. The state, aside from its own lack of will and organization for modernization, was of course faced also with the obstructive pressures of imperialism. Foreign powers imposed absolute limits on the customs duties that could be collected, and foreign invasion dictated a high level of military expenditures. Astronomical indemnity payments, finally, crippled an already weak late Qing government. Feuerwerker (1980: 58–69) notes that indemnity payments (interest and principal) on the Sino-Japanese War and the Boxer War totaled 476,982,000 taels between 1895 and 1911, or more than two times the estimated total capitalization of foreign and Chinese modern enterprises between 1895 and 1913. Like modern Chinese capitalists, the Chinese state was caught between an involuting peasant economy and imperialism.

We may not be far from the day when it will be possible to develop a complete analysis of the hows and whys of capital formation in modern China. The focus of current research in China, such as that by the Institute of Economics in Shanghai, is on the private sector,* whereas the focus in the West is on the role of the state in the economy. The synthesizing of these two sets of research findings with an analysis of the agricultural sector might enable us to show how the poor-peasant economy, imperialism, and the state together formed the structural context for the underdevelopment of Chinese capitalism. And, to the extent that the poor-peasant economy shaped capital formation in the economy, we might see it as not only an effect, but also a cause of underdevelopment.

---

*Under Professor Xu Xinwu and with the participation of Chang Chung-li, the Institute of Economics of the Shanghai Academy of Sciences has amassed materials on individual companies like the Nanyang Brothers and the British-American Tobacco Company, and on key industries like the cotton handicraft, cotton textile, silk spinning, silk weaving, and flour industries. The strategy is to move from "points" (*dian*) to "lines" (*xian*), and then to an overview study of the "surface" (*mian*) of modern Chinese capitalism, centering on the Shanghai area. Judging from the materials that have already been published, this project will fundamentally reshape our understanding of the subject.

SEMIPROLETARIANIZATION AND DEMOGRAPHIC TRENDS

The currently available demographic data, summarized in Appendix B, do not permit systematic analyses of possible interconnections between demographic trends and the patterns of agrarian change studied in this book.[†] I can only offer a few tentative observations here.

To begin with, wage-labor income expanded the subsistence possibilities of peasants and, to that extent, might have supported an expansion in population. Poor peasants derived crucial supplementary income from hiring out, while their labor made possible the cultivation of more labor-intensive cash crops. Where hiring out involved nonagricultural activities, as for example in rural industry, commodity transport, or urban employment, it also expanded the sources of subsistence support beyond agricultural production. Wage labor might thus have encouraged young peasant men into earlier economic independence, marriage, and child-rearing, thereby raising the fertility rates of a population otherwise constrained by fixed landed property. In this respect, semiproletarianization might initially have affected population in ways similar to protoindustrialization and proletarianization in the early modern West (Levine 1977; Tilly 1978).

But the formation of an economy and society of poor peasants also carried with it built-in checks on population growth. We have seen that the completely landless agricultural laborer often could not afford to get married. As a group, the rural poor probably had the lowest nuptiality rates in the countryside. Their mortality rates were also likely to be high, considering the pressures on their livelihood. As the proportion of poor peasants in rural society increased and subsistence pressures on them mounted, therefore, we would expect population growth to level off—an expectaion that is consistent with the slowing-down of growth rates in our area after about 1800. Rapid growth resumed only after the Revolution, when rural employment opportunities increased as a result of state investment in agriculture and the mobilization of rural labor. As the pressures on subsistence mount, however, we might expect a repeat of the curvilinear pattern evidenced earlier in the relationship between semiproletarianization and fertility.

*The Utah Genealogical Society is in the process of microfilming massive quantities (an estimated 1.5 million pages) of demographic materials (census rosters, genealogies, and birth and death records) kept at the Ming–Qing Archives in Beijing. These new data might well make possible the systematic testing of this and other hypotheses.

Substantiation for this hypothesis cannot be sought simply in the fact that poor peasant families tended to be smaller than those of other rural strata. The 1930's data showing that tendency (Malone & Taylor 1924: 22; Buck 1937b: 300) did not control for the differences between stem families (parents living with one married child) and joint families (with more than one married child). The Mantetsu studies demonstrate an unequivocal correlation between poverty and the incidence of family divisions. Severe subsistence pressures lowered the tolerance of one brother for another less diligent, and declining family fortunes lent special urgency to the desire for family division. For these and other reasons (to be detailed in a later study), stem and nuclear families were more common among the peasant poor, and joint families more common among the peasant rich. The discrepancy in family size between the two groups, therefore, does not say anything about their possible differential fertility. Real empirical support for the hypothesis here will have to come from reconstitutions of family histories over time. And finer points about the relationship that partial proletarianization bore to family structure and demographic behavior must await data and studies of a different kind from those of this book.

### THE PARTLY PROLETARIANIZED VILLAGE AND TWENTIETH-CENTURY GOVERNMENT

The process of semiproletarianization brought into being many villages that were part-solidary community and part-atomized neighborhood. The continued importance of community bonds in many of those villages can be seen in the persistence into the 1930's of the old village council made up of the most influential members of the community's lineages, of other community organizations such as temple societies and burial clubs, and of lineage and community gatherings for weddings and funerals. Moreover, the outlook of most villagers of Hebei–northwest Shandong remained inward-oriented, expressed for example by a shared assumption that one normally chatted only with one's fellow villagers, and by a well-articulated fictive kinship network that encompassed all long-term members of the village. Solidarity was also evidenced in some cases in the rise of new community organizations like crop-watching societies to cope with the disorders of the late Qing and Republican periods.

On the other hand, there is also evidence of the dissolution of community bonds as more and more of a village's residents became semiproletarianized. Poor peasants who had lost their land generally dropped in community standing and often also lost interest in the affairs of a village government whose principal concern was government taxation, which affected mainly landowners. Those who worked for a wage outside the village, especially the year-laborers who were away for long periods, tended to become less intimately bound to the village. The worst-off among the poor peasants often found it difficult to pay dues for temple societies or burial clubs, or to bear the cost of wedding and funeral ceremonies on a customary scale. Some lineages composed only of poor peasants ceased to sustain conventional lineage activities, first by doing away with the Qingming meals, and, in more extreme cases, by partitioning and even selling the common burial ground.

The Mantetsu materials show that middle peasant owner-cultivators were the mainstay of community activities. In contrast to the partly proletarianized poor, their production activities generally took place entirely at their own landholdings within the village. Landownership, moreover, lent them not only respectability in the eyes of the community, but also a vital stake in the affairs of village government. They thus tended to be the most actively involved in village government. Whereas many landlords, managerial farmers, and rich peasants were involved in economic activities outside the village (in commerce, moneylending, and the like) and were often tied into larger supra-village elite networks, the economic interests and social world of middle peasants tended to be confined to the village. When this group gave way through social differentiation to landlords, managerial farmers, and rich peasants at the top and to poor peasants and agricultural workers at the bottom, community bonds tended to weaken, and the insular-solidary community tended to give way to the part-atomized, part-solidary village.

This process coincided with the expansion of the state's power over villages. The politicization of local elites in modern China led in the beginning, to be sure, to a devolution of formal state power to informal gentry power. But that change soon gave way to bureaucratization, whether through the local elites arrogating to themselves official roles, or through the state's efforts to incorporate them or counter their growing power. In the end, the politicization of local elites acted as a crucial vehicle for the expansion of governmental power into villages.

Bureaucratic intrusion strained the old relationship between state and village, especially at the critical point of village government. The state in the Republican period could make its power felt in villages but did not have the apparatus to place its own salaried agents into villages, and had to work with unsalaried men drawn from the communities themselves. These men were now placed in the position of having to answer to the state's demands for new taxes at a time when government was seen as illegitimate by many villagers. To collect those taxes, they had also to cope with the new conflicts of interest between landowners, who wanted the village levies apportioned by head, and the landless, who wanted them based on the long-standing principle of landownership.

The response of individual villages to these pressures varied with the internal structures of the communities. Solidary communities of mainly owner-cultivators tended to present a united community front and, in some situations, even collective resistance; completely atomized villages tended to end up being totally at the mercy of opportunists working for outside powers; and partly proletarianized villages tended to bend under the simultaneous tugs of bureaucratization and community. At the close of our period, village and state remained in an uneasy relationship fraught with tension and abuse, or the potential for abuse.

### POOR PEASANTS AND THE REVOLUTION

Revolutionary rhetoric has sometimes portrayed the poor peasants as simply an exploited "class" whose collective struggle against the landlords who oppressed them powered the coming of the Communist-led Revolution.* The actual record of revolutionary actions, however, reveals a more complex reality and a recognition of the profound ambiguities of this group. Though the "New Democratic Revolution" was ostensibly an anti-feudal struggle against "feudal" relations of rent, the Land Reform Law in fact recognized the coexistence of wage labor and rent relations, even if it did in the end simply erase the earlier distinctions between "managerial landlords" and leasing landlords. Under the Land Reform itself, moreover, the appeal was to the poor peasant not only as exploited cultivator, but also as would-be proprietor. And "develop family fortunes" (fajia zhifu) of the early 1950's spoke even more directly to the peasant as an individualistic entrepreneur in search of upward mobility. The subsequent mutual-aid program built on the poor peasant's labor-sharing experiences; and collectivization appealed to him as a hired laborer, by promising to erase the differences between employer and wage

---

*William Hinton's classic and important *Fanshen* (1966) was influenced by this oversimplified formula: landlordism is somehow made out to be the central issue in the revolutionary process in a village with only one tenant household.

worker. But despite the supposedly collectivist tendencies of poor peasants, collectivization has left problems and tensions, acknowledged in periodic shifts of government policy toward greater emphases on private plots, free markets, and household responsibility, as in the early 1960's and again after the end of the Cultural Revolution. Finally, the state's unwavering insistence on grain storage against famine and war attests to the precariousness of the poor peasant's life before the Revolution, and the high priority attached to guaranteeing the basic subsistence of the population. Such actions confirm the multiple characteristics of the peasant analyzed in this book.

The tremendous importance of population pressure in shaping this poor-peasant society and economy has also been recognized in action. We can see in hindsight that one powerful imperative for the collectivization of agriculture was the very fact of population pressure itself. The collectivized production team or brigade shares a fundamental feature with the family farm: it is a unit of both production and consumption, which under severe subsistence pressures will tolerate agricultural involution to an extent unthinkable for a capitalist enterprise. Like the family farm, the collective does not fire its surplus labor. If managerial farming had become the dominant agricultural system, it would have left very large numbers of peasants unemployed. In the late 1970's, of course, we have seen the Chinese government adopt some of the most radical policies of birth control ever witnessed in human history, even if it has yet to incorporate the issue of population into official Marxist theory and interpretations of the Revolution.

The question of how poor peasants might have made the transition from a rather awkward and ambiguous "class in itself" (an economic category) into a "class for itself" (a political category) is a more difficult one. The oversimplified rhetoric of revolution would have us believe that poor peasants became a "class for itself" once the Chinese Communist Party gave expression to their class interests and leadership for their class action. The role of the poor peasants in the Chinese Revolution, in this view, is much like that of the proletariat's projected role in a socialist revolution (Mao 1927).

In its actions, however, the state has acknowledged the crucial importance of the village community, a vertical and segmented grouping as opposed to the horizontal and integrated grouping of class. The artificial units of the production team and brigade, like the imperial baojia and lijia units before them, have been imposed with the recognition of the village as a natural socioeconomic unit. Attempts during the Great Leap Forward to shift ownership and accounting to the supra-village level had to give way before this reality.

The village is in fact in many ways more encapsulated and seg-mented today than in the past. The village community now has a stronger basis in property than ever before because of collectiviza-tion, and is also a more precisely articulated unit because of the clear delineation of village boundaries. At the same time, government control of commerce has reduced the integrative role of markets, and stringent registration policies (Potter 1983) have bound peasants to their home communities more than in the past. The diminished role of lineages, moreover, may well have reduced interlineage conflict and increased the solidarity of multiple-lineage communities (Parish & Whyte 1978: Chap. 15). (Such developments, of course, need to be seen in the context of a pervasive state presence in the natural vil-lage. The removal of the supra-village gentry and the village no-tables of old has brought state power much more deeply into the village, buttressed by the apparatus of the Party. At the same time, the scope of the state's power over the village, and of the village col-lectivity's power over the individual peasant, has expanded enor-mously through the collectivization of production, the imposition of a planned economy, and the politicization of the population.)

Solid observations about how the "class" interests of the poor peasants might have translated into collective action in the Revolu-tion must await materials of a sort that have not been available to historians (such as archives of the Communist Party and oral history research with peasants). This book, however, has suggested some ten-tative ideas in that direction. As people who were exploited by rent and by wages, but did not pay much tax, the poor peasants were in greater economic conflict with landlords and rural employers than with the state. The interests of middle peasant owner-cultivators, by contrast, conflicted more with those of the state than with those of landlords or rural employers. In that respect, poor peasants made more likely allies for a revolutionary party that would do away with rent and wage labor. As people who were less intimately tied to lin-eages and villages than middle peasants, they were possibly also more open to trans-village organizing by outside revolutionaries. Those among them who became completely severed from family farming and had to hire out away from home as year-laborers might well have made up some of the most combustible kindling for revo-lution. On the other hand, most poor peasants were undeniably still very much proprietors or would-be proprietors in their outlook, as well as members of vertical lineages and communities that cut across class lines. Any effort to study their political action will no doubt have to consider the complex criss-crossings of those multiple loyalties and tendencies.

Seen in such a perspective, neither the substantivist, nor the formalist, nor even the Marxist analysis seems adequate for an understanding of poor peasant political action. Poor peasants, it seems to me, are unlikely to act only out of an impulse to defend and restore their threatened moral communities and subsistence, or only out of their desire to maximize their own interests in the sociopolitical marketplace, or only out of outrage at their exploitation as a class. A study of their role in the Revolution, I would speculate, needs to consider how these tendencies came together in different ways, depending on the kind of village and the nature of the outside political forces involved. The village-state relations studied in this book were shaped by both the internal structure of villages and the character of state power.

Comparative theorists have given us some useful hints for thinking about how poor peasants might have related to the Revolution as a whole. Barrington Moore (1966) urges that social revolution be analyzed not simply in terms of the overturning of one class by another, but in terms of an evolving coalition of a multitude of classes. This seems a particularly pertinent observation for a revolution based on so ambiguous and awkward a "class" as the poor peasants. Jeffery Paige (1975) urges that sets of class relations be differentiated according to how each of the two parties to the relationship changed or did not change. I have suggested that the combination in China of a noncapitalizing elite with a semiproletarianizing peasantry created a more revolutionary situation than the combination, in Western Europe, of a capitalizing elite with a proletarianizing rural population. Theda Skocpol (1977), finally, argues well for the potentially semiautonomous nature of the state and for the role that the transnational state system can play in shaping the character of the revolutionary state. It is a theme for which we can find ready and exaggerated echoes in the past Western scholarship on the Chinese Revolution, given its preoccupation with ideology (Schwartz 1953), international influence (Johnson 1962), and organization (Hofheinz 1977). Historians of China have yet to develop an analytical framework that would take account of all these themes.

Such observations aside, however, it is important not to lose sight of the basic socioeconomic background to the Revolution: the formation over several centuries of a poor-peasant economy and society under the twin pressures of involution and social stratification, without the relief of dynamic economic growth. Class differentiation and intense population pressure each made the other more unbearable. In our area, a man could not support a household on the wage he earned by hiring out, and wage work was foreclosed to

women. Under those conditions, losing one's family farm and becoming a full-time agricultural worker meant the dreaded prospect
of the extinction of one's family line. The poor peasant thus clung
fiercely to his undersized family farm, however little income it produced after rents or taxes. He tried as best he could to stave off becoming a full-time laborer by combining family farming with part-
time hiring out, depending on both for the subsistence of his family.
It was a precarious mode of survival that could easily be upset by any
further pressures, whether in the form of increased taxation, adverse
market swings, abusive government, war and banditry, or natural
disaster. This structural change to a semiproletarianized peasantry
underlay the massive upheavals of rural China in recent centuries.

# APPENDIXES

# Socioeconomic Profiles of the 33 Mantetsu-Surveyed Villages

The socioeconomic profiles of the 33 villages presented below are grouped according to the typology used for this study: I, relatively uncommercialized villages with less than 10 percent of their cropped area under cash crops; II, moderately commercialized villages with 10–30 percent of their cropped area under cash crops; III, relatively highly commercialized villages with more than 30 percent of their cropped area under cash crops; IV, villages with developed handicraft industries; V, suburban villages; VI, home villages of emigrants; and VII, shell-shocked villages that had continually suffered the ravages of war.

As noted in the text, we can expect some correlations between the degree of commercialization and the incidence of managerial farming and tenancy in a village. But no simple correlation should be expected with wage labor. Day-labor and year-labor often involved work outside the village. The laborer for hire could travel quite a distance from his home village; he was less tied to the immediate area of his house than a tenant who had to go to his fields every day from home. A highly commercialized village might have a low incidence of wage labor because its labor-employing farms hired mostly outsiders (e.g., Donghongyapo, Longwo, Zhongliangshan), and an uncommercialized village might have a high incidence of wage labor because its impoverished residents hired out to employers in other villages (e.g., Huzhuang).

The stratifying effects of commercialization are also often countered by the downward pressures of population, as has been seen with managerial farmers in Table 4.2, or by the development of rural industry, as in Qizhai and Lengshuigou. Natural disasters might be either positively or negatively associated with social stratification. In places like Sibeichai the rich were able to take advantage of natural disasters to accumulate land. But the most disaster-prone areas (e.g., Shajing and Wudian) tended to remain under subsistence crops, and hence to be negatively associated with cash-cropping and its stratifying effects.

This typology and the socioeconomic profiles tabulated, in short, are intended merely to convey the multiple forces that shaped village society, not to suggest any simple correlation between one factor and another.

In the tables that follow the bracketed figures are my estimates. However, I have not attempted to estimate the amounts of land given to subsistence crops where these were the village's main crops and the sources did not provide a breakdown. A question mark always indicates a lack of data.

Households or unmarried male adults deriving more than one-half of their income from hiring out long-term are counted as year-laborers, even though they often also owned or rented a small farm. Households earning more than half their income from nonfarm sources are categorized as nonagricultural. Those that also owned or rented a farm are re-counted under the farm households.

The sources for the village data are listed, by village number, below the last table, p. 320.

TABLE A.1

Type I: Relatively Uncommercialized Villages

| Category | 1<br>Asuwei,<br>Changping | 2<br>Huzhuang,<br>Pinggu | 3<br>Jiaojiazhuang,<br>Fengrun |
|---|---|---|---|
| Main crops (pct. cropped area) | Maize 34%<br>Millet 22%<br>Sorghum 19% | Sorghum 25%<br>Millet 25%<br>Maize 17%<br>Soybeans 8% | Sorghum 45%<br>Maize 30%<br>Millet 12% |
| No. of households | 102 | 218 | 196 |
| Pct. nonfarm households | 2.9% | 0.0% | 9.2% |
| Total cultivated mu | 1,527 | 2,400 | 2,502 |
| No. of cultivated mu per capita | 2.5 | 2.3 | 2.1 |
| Km from county seat | 15.0 | 12.5 | 15.0 |
| No. of resident landlords | 0 | 0 | 0 |
| No. of managerial farmers | 0 | 0 | 0 |
| Pct. cultivated land rented | ? | < 10.0% | 9.2% |
| Composition of farm households (pct.) | | | |
| Owners | 63.6% | 89.0% | 79.8% |
| Tenants, part-tenants | 27.3% | 6.4% | 14.6% |
| Year-laborers | 9.1% | 4.6% | 5.6% |
| Pct. farm households hiring out as day-laborers | 30.3 | 45.9 | ? |

Type II: Moderately Commercialized Villages

| Category | 4 Labeiguan, Pinggu | 5 Houxiazhai, Enxian | 6 Houyansi, Xianghe | 7 Jigezhuang, Jixian | 8 Lujiazhai, Zunhua |
|---|---|---|---|---|---|
| Main crops [pct. cropped area] | Millet 36% Sorghum 20% Maize 10% Cotton 11% | Millet [30%] Sorghum [30%] Peanuts [20%] Cotton [5–10%] | Maize 50% Millet 15% Soybeans 15% Wheat 10% | Sorghum 49% Wheat 16% Maize 13% | Sorghum 33% Millet 25% Maize 11% Wheat 10% Fruit 7% |
| No. of households | 98 | 130 | 320 | 128 | 195[a] |
| Pct. nonfarm households | 0.0% | 4.6% | 8.4% | 0.0% | 9.7% |
| Total cultivated mu | 2,438 | 2,530 | 5,012 | 1,575 | 2,497 |
| No. of cultivated mu per capita | 4.0 | 3.6 | 2.7 | 2.4 | 2.1 |
| Km from county seat | 5.0 | 2.5 | 4.0 | 14.0 | 28.0 |
| No. of resident landlords | 0 | 0 | 0 | 0 | 0 |
| No. of managerial farmers | 3 | 0 | 3 | 2 | 3 |
| Pct. cultivated land rented | 8.2% | 3.6% | ? | 0.0% | <10.0% |
| Composition of farm households (pct.) | | | | | |
| Owners | 49.0% | 86.3% | 51.0% | 65.6% | 69.3% |
| Tenants, part-tenants | 40.8% | 10.5% | 38.2% | 0.0% | 22.2% |
| Year-laborers | 10.2% | 3.2% | 10.8% | 34.4% | 8.5% |
| Pct. farm households hiring out as day-laborers | 41.8% | "Many" | ? | ? | 33.7% |

*Table continues overleaf*

TABLE A.2 continued

| Category | 9 Shajing, Shunyi | 10 Sunjiamiao, Huimin | 11 Tiaoshanying, Mancheng | 12 Xiaojie, Tongxian | 13 Xiaoying, Miyun |
|---|---|---|---|---|---|
| Main crops (pct. cropped area) | Maize 36% Sorghum 20% Soybeans 16% Wheat 12% | Wheat 24% Sweet potatoes 28% Soybeans 14% Millet 12% | Millet 32% Maize 28% Wheat 28% | Maize 38% Cotton 27% Millet 6% Sorghum 4% | Millet 30% Sorghum 20% Peanuts 10% Maize 10% |
| No. of households | 67[b] | 101 | 144 | 164 | 195 |
| Pct. nonfarm households | 13.4% | [5.0%] | ? | 20.7% | 21.0% |
| Total cultivated mu | 1,182 | 1,037 | 1,230 | 2,692 | 3,025 |
| No. of cultivated mu per capita | 2.5 | 2.1 | 1.4 | 2.7 | 3.3 |
| Km from county seat | 2.0 | ? | 2.5 | 3.0 | 17.5 |
| No. of resident landlords | 0 | 1 | 0 | 1 | 3 |
| No. of managerial farmers | 1 | 0 | 0 | 2 | 2 |
| Pct. cultivated land rented | 17.2% | 24.4% | 5.5% | 41.2% | 34.5% |
| Composition of farm households (pct.) | | | | | |
| Owners | 44.8% | 66.7% | 79.2% | 30.4% | 45.0% |
| Tenants, part-tenants | 22.4% | 25.0% | 15.3% | 62.2% | 55.0% |
| Year-laborers | 32.8% | 8.3% | 5.6% | 7.4% | ? |
| Pct. farm households hiring out as day-laborers | 55.2% | 53.1% | 61.1% | 19.3% | ? |

[a] Excludes 7 households on which there is no information.
[b] Excludes 5 households on which there is no information.

TABLE A.3

Type III: Highly Commercialized Villages

| Category | 14 Donghong-yapo, Fengrun | 15 Longwo, Yutian | 16 Macun, Huailu | 17 Michang, Fengrun | 18 Qianliang-gezhuang, Changli | 19 Sibeichai, Luancheng | 20 Zhongliangshan, Changli |
|---|---|---|---|---|---|---|---|
| Main crops (pct. cropped area) | Cotton 40% Maize 15% Cabbage 12% Sorghum 10% | Cotton 54% Sorghum 29% Soybeans 8% | Millet 30% Cotton 26% Wheat 23% | Sorghum 44% Cotton 31% Maize 15% | Sorghum 38% Fruit 28% Peanuts 7% | Cotton 40% Millet 30% Wheat 10% Sorghum 10% | Fruit 30% Sorghum ? Maize ? Millet ? |
| No. of households | 89 | 29 | 308 | 114 | 95 | 132[a] | 130 |
| Pct. nonfarm households | 16.9% | 3.4% | 21.8% | 3.5% | 7.4% | 16.7% | 26.9% |
| Total cultivated mu | 1,145 | 524 | 4,209 | 2,237 | 1,564 | 2,053 | 2,000 |
| No. of cultivated mu per capita | 1.2 | 2.3 | 2.5 | 3.3 | 2.7 | 2.9 | 3.0 |
| Km from county seat | 1.0 | 20.0 | 8.0 | 40.0 | 7.5 | 1.5 | 4.0 |
| No. of resident landlords | 1 | 0 | 0 | 0 | 5 | 0 | 1 |
| No. of managerial farmers | 1 | 1 | 4 | 3 | 0 | 0 | 2 |
| Pct. cultivated land rented | 19.5% | 10.5% | 24.2% | 34.6% | 36.0% | 66.8% | 18.5% |
| Composition of farm households (pct.) | | | | | | | |
| Owners | 39.2% | 75.0% | 49.4% | 14.9% | 39.3% | 7.3% | 69.1% |
| Tenants, part-tenants | 48.5% | 21.4% | 39.5% | 71.5% | 43.8% | 64.5% | 26.4% |
| Year-laborers | 12.2% | 3.6% | 11.1% | 13.6% | 16.9% | 28.2% | 4.5% |
| Pct. farm households hiring out as day laborers | —[b] | —[b] | ? | 33.7% | 30.3% | 34.0% | —[b] |

[a] Excludes 8 households on which there is no information.
[b] All day-workers in the village were from the outside.

TABLE A.4

Type IV: Villages with Developed Rural Industries

| Category | 21 Duyake, Zaoqiang | 22 Lengshuigou, Licheng | 23 Qizhai, Gaotang | 24 Xiaowangzhuang, Yutian | 25 Zhimafeng, Yutian |
|---|---|---|---|---|---|
| Main crops (pct. cropped area) | Wheat 33% Maize 33% Millet 25% | Rice 33% Wheat ? Sorghum ? Millet ? | Cotton 60% Millet 20% Wheat 10% Maize; soybeans 10% | Sorghum 50% Cotton 15% Millet 10% Soybeans 10% | Sorghum 66% Wheat 16% Maize 10% Soybeans 8% |
| No. of households | 98 | 331[a] | 115 | 174[b] | 86[c] |
| Pct. nonfarm households | ? | 4.5% | ? | 10.9% | 11.6% |
| Households participating in rural industry | Most; weaving, sheepskin | Most; straw braid | Most, poor, middle; spinning, weaving | Most; weaving | 55% in weaving till 1930's |
| Total cultivated mu | 1,558 | 4,200 | 2,245 | 1,036 | 676 |
| No. of cultivated mu per capita | [3.2] | [2.3] | 3.9 | 1.2 | 1.4 |
| Km from county seat | ? | 3.0[d] | 1.5 | 15.0 | 16.0 |
| No. of resident landlords | 0 | 0 | 0 | 0 | 0 |
| No. of managerial farmers | 2 | 3 | 2 | 0 | 0 |
| Pct. cultivated land rented | <10.0% | <5.0% | 3.4% | 20.0% | 5.3% |
| Composition of farm households (pct.) | | | | | |
| Owners | 91.6% | 91.4% | 93.1% | 41.3% | 67.1% |
| Tenants, part-tenants | 8.4% | 7.9% | 5.2% | 32.9% | 3.9% |
| Year-laborers | ? | 0.9%[e] | 1.7% | 25.8% | 28.9% |
| Pct. farm households hiring out as day-laborers | ? | 10.0% | "Most" | 22.6% | ? |

[a]Excludes 39 households on which there is no information.
[b]Excludes 13 households on which there is no information.
[c]Excludes 4 households on which there is no information.
[d]From Wangsherenzhuang.
[e]17 outsiders work in village as year-laborers.

## Type V: Suburban Villages

| Category | 26<br>Dongjiao,<br>Shijiazhuang | 27<br>Nanquanfuzhuang,<br>Jinan |
|---|---|---|
| Main crops (percent cropped area) | Millet 38%<br>Wheat 36% | Wheat 45%<br>Millet 36%<br>Soybeans 11% |
| Number of households | 203 | 222 |
| Percent nonfarm households | 46.8% | 74.3% |
| Percent in urban day labor | 28.1% | ? |
| Total cultivated mu | 1,459 | 279 |
| Number of cultivated mu per capita | 1.2 | 0.3 |
| Kilometers from city | 2.5 | 6.0 |
| Number of resident landlords | 0 | 0 |
| Number of managerial farmers | 2 | 0 |
| Percent cultivated land rented | 30.0% | 15.0% |
| Composition of farm households (percent) | | |
| Owners | 67.6% | 34.0% |
| Tenants, part-tenants | 32.4% | 26.6% |
| Year-laborers | ? | 39.4% |

## Type VI. Home Villages of Emigrants

| Category | 28<br>Binggezhuang,<br>Funing | 29<br>Baizhuang,<br>Leting | 30<br>Houjiaying,<br>Changli | 31<br>Huzhuang,<br>Ninghe |
|---|---|---|---|---|
| Main crops (pct. cropped area) | Sorghum 50%<br>Millet 25%<br>Cotton 10% | Wheat 20%<br>Sorghum ?<br>Millet ?<br>Maize ? | Sorghum ?<br>Soybeans ?<br>Rye ? | Sorghum 90%<br>Wheat 6% |
| No. of households[a] | 98 | 112 | 116 | 78 |
| Pct. nonfarm households | 9.2% | 22.3% | 11.2%[b] | 31.2%[c] |
| Pct. emigrant households | 60% to 1931;<br>then 20% | 80% to 1931;<br>then 20% | Many before<br>1931[d] | 70% |
| Total cultivated mu | 1,200 | 1,860 | 2,979 | 1,943 |
| Cultivated mu per capita | 2.2 | 2.6 | 4.4 | 5.1 |
| Km from county seat | 4.0 | 7.0 | 10.0 | 2.5 |
| No. of resident landlords | 2 | 0 | 1 | 0 |
| No. of managerial farmers | 0 | 0 | 4 | 0 |
| Pct. cultivated land rented | 45.0% | 30.0% | 12.1% | 47.5% |
| Farm households (pct.) | | | | |
| Owners | 29.2% | 59.8% | 53.4% | 25.9% |
| Tenants, part-tenants | 70.8% | 40.2% | 46.6% | 61.1% |
| Year-laborers | ? | ? | 0.0%[e] | 13.0% |
| Hiring out as day-laborers | 22.5% | 0.0%[f] | ? | ? |

[a]Columns 28, 29, 30 exclude respectively 14, 12, and 5 households on which there is no information.
[b]Beggars.
[c]6 beggars; 15 unemployed.
[d]10% in commerce in 1942.
[e]Year-laborers were hired from outside.
[f]Day-laborers were hired from outside.

TABLE A.7

Type VII: Shell-Shocked Villages

| Category | 32<br>Heitingzhuang,<br>Linyu | 33<br>Wudian,<br>Liangxiang |
|---|---|---|
| Main crops (percent cropped area) | Sorghum 30%<br>Millet 25%<br>Peanuts 23%<br>Maize 20% | Maize ?<br>Millet ?<br>Sweet<br>potatoes ? |
| Number of households | 89 | 57 |
| Percent nonfarm households | 14.6%[a] | ? |
| Total cultivated mu | 1,799 | 1,100 |
| Number of cultivated mu per capita | 4.2 | 3.9 |
| Kilometers from county seat | 7.0 | 1.5 |
| Number of resident landlords | 0 | 0 |
| Number of managerial farmers | 0 | 0 |
| Percent cultivated land rented | 72.7% | 54.5% |
| Composition of farm households (percent) | | |
| Owners | 13.2% | 8.8% |
| Tenants, part-tenants | 76.3% | 91.2% |
| Year-laborers | 10.5% | ? |
| Percent farm households hiring out as day-laborers | 23.7% | ? |

[a]About 50% of the households had members who worked across the frontier in the northeast before 1931, compared with only 2 households in 1936.

SOURCES

1. MT, Kitō 1936a, part 1: 7–9, 12–13.
2. Ibid., pp. 137–39.
3. Ibid., part 2: 148–72.
4. MT, Kitō 1937a: 2–5.
5. KC, 4: 7–9, 10, 399, 402, 459, 464, 497, 509.
6. MT, Kitō 1936a, part 1: 156–59.
7. Ibid., pp. 202–9.
8. MT, Tenshin 1936a: 72–83, 96, 136–39.
9. KC, 1: appended chart; KC, 2: 273–89.
10. Chūgoku nōson 1939: Appendix, pp. 2–15.
11. Kita Shina 1943a: 18–20, 41.
12. MT, Tenshin 1936b: 33–41, 69, 116–17.
13. MT, Kitō 1936a, part 1: 64–75.
14. Ibid., part 2: 132–47.
15. Ibid., pp. 12, 18, 22, 24.
16. MT, Hokushi keizai chōsajo 1940d: 81–82, 85–87.
17. MT, Kitō 1937b: 1, 5–12, 25, 69–88; MT, Hokushi jimukyoku chōsabu 1938–41, 1: 73–77.
18. MT, Kitō 1937c: 1–12, 24, 70–93.
19. KC, 3: 5–6, 197–98, 524–33.
20. MT, Kitō 1936a, part 2: 264–75.
21. MT, Tenshin 1937: 45–67.
22. KC, 4: 2, 4, 6, 9, 168, 175–76, 178, 240.
23. Kita Shina 1943b: 1, 13, 67, 93, 98, Appendix Table 1.
24. MT, Kitō 1936a, part 2: 10, 12, 16, 24, 27, 42.
25. Ibid., pp. 12, 15, 24, 42.
26. Kahoku sōgō 1944a: 26–30, 128–29.
27. Kahoku kōtsū 1940: 15, 16–17, 34, 41, 101.
28. MT, Kitō 1936a, part 2: 288–95, 298, 311, 313, 320.
29. Ibid., pp. 232–38, 240.
30. KC, 5: 5, 151, 179, 193, 275–78.
31. MT, Kitō 1936a, part 2: 91, 93–94, 115, 120.
32. Ibid., pp. 352, 357, 359–60, 387–88, 396.
33. KC, 5: 6–7, 412.

# The Population of
# Hebei and Shandong,
# 1393-1953

The data presented in the following tables have all the problems that have encumbered demographic research on China: the aggregate figures, though plentiful and of a substantial time depth, are highly questionable, and we have yet to find any data that would allow the "reconstitution" of the demographic histories of microsocietal units, which has done so much to advance demographic research on Western Europe and Japan.

Table B.1 gives the available provincial totals. The Ming data are of mixed utility. The 1393 figures are probably fairly good indications of actual population, as Ho Ping-ti (1959) and Dwight Perkins (1969) have argued. The later Ming figures, however, are of little use, as can readily be seen: a mere 38 percent increase in the 185 years between 1393 and 1578 seems highly implausible. Despite Robert Hartwell's (1982) important efforts to develop plausible figures for the period 750–1550 (by working from a careful sampling of prefectural and county data), we still lack the wherewithal to come closer to a reliable count for the later Ming, and so are left with just the figures on the start of the period.

The early Qing figures are low, perhaps because of the state's inadequate recording machinery or perhaps because, as Ho Ping-ti (1959) suggested, these figures were generally cadastral enumerations rather than actual population counts, or were some mixture of the two. The figures from 1776 to 1850 are reasonably good, reflecting the government's efforts to keep better track of the population. Most of the figures shown are from the Board of Revenue and Population (Hu bu), which issued annual tallies—*fensheng minshu gushu qingce*—based on reports from the provinces. The Ming-Qing Archives in Beijing have a substantially complete set of these qingce for the years 1787–1898, so that I am able to show the data at ten-year intervals (based on the compilation of the Institute of Econom-

TABLE B.1

## Reported Population of Hebei and Shandong, 1393–1953

(1,000's of people)

| Year | Hebei | Shandong | Total | Source |
|------|-------|----------|-------|--------|
| **Ming Dynasty** | | | | |
| 1393 | 1,927 | 5,256 | 7,183 | Liang 1980: 203–4 |
| 1491 | [3,431] | [6,760] | | |
| 1578 | [4,265] | [5,664] | | |
| | | | | |
| **Qing Dynasty** | | | | |
| 1661 | [2,858] | [1,760] | | Liang 1980: 258 |
| 1685 | [3,197] | [2,111] | | |
| 1724 | [3,407] | [2,278] | | |
| 1749 | 13,933 | 24,012 | | |
| 1753 | [9,374] | [12,770] | | |
| 1757 | 14,377 | 24,746 | | |
| 1762 | 16,132 | 25,293 | | |
| 1767 | 16,691 | 25,635 | | |
| | | | | |
| 1776 | 20,291 | 26,019[a] | | Provincial memorials, Ming- |
| 1779 | 20,708 | — | | Qing Archives |
| 1784 | 22,302 | 22,109 | | |
| | | | | |
| 1790 | 23,497 | 23,359 | 46,856 | Yan 1963: 362–74 |
| 1820 | — | 29,522 | | |
| 1830 | 22,063 | 30,874 | 52,937 | |
| 1840 | 22,646 | 31,876 | 54,522 | |
| 1850 | 23,401 | 33,127 | 56,528 | |
| 1860 | — | 34,346 | | |
| 1870 | — | 34,890 | | |
| 1880 | — | 35,998 | | |
| 1890 | — | 36,984 | | |
| 1898 | — | 37,789 | | |
| | | | | |
| **Republic of China** | | | | |
| 1912 | 26,721 | [29,556] | | Liang 1980: 268 |
| 1913 | 29,600 | 38,400 | 68,000 | Perkins 1969: 209 |
| 1933 | 38,400 | 40,300 | 78,700 | Liu & Yeh 1965 (adjusted),[b] |
| | | | | cited in Perkins 1969: 212 |
| 1948 | 39,000[c] | 39,300 | | Guan 1956: 1–3 (adjusted) |
| | | | | |
| **People's Republic** | | | | |
| 1953 | 46,600[d] | 48,900 | 95,500 | 1953 census, cited in |
| | | | | Perkins 1969: 212 |

NOTE: Brackets indicate figures of questionable utility.

[a]1773.

[b]Liu & Yeh's figure for Hebei, 3.6 million, excludes Rehe and the municipalities of Beijing and Tianjin. I have added 1.6 million for Beijing and 1.2 million for Tianjin (from Perkins 1969: 212, 293), and 5 million for Rehe (6.2 million in 1948; Guan 1956: 2).

[c]7.8 million added for Rehe, Beijing, and Tianjin.

[d]Includes Rehe, Beijing, and Tianjin.

ics—Yan 1963). Unfortunately, the figures for Hebei in 1858–98 are not available, since the qingce of those years included only the Chengde prefectural totals under Zhili. To flesh out the earlier period, I have used provincial memorials to the throne on population and granary holdings (also housed in the Ming-Qing Archives) for data on the late 1770's and the early 1780's. (I am grateful to James Lee for sharing these figures and his knowledge of the archival population data with me.)

The twentieth-century figures are drawn from several sources: an enumeration for 1912; the estimates of Ta-chung Liu and Kung-chia Yeh for the 1930's; the statistical study of Guan Weilan for 1948 (whose data, though less accurate than the figures collected by the

TABLE B.2

Reported Population of Hebei and Shandong Prefectures
and Districts, 1820, 1883, and 1948

(1,000's of people)

| Prefecture/district | 1820 | 1883 | 1948 |
|---|---|---|---|
| Hebei | | | |
| Chengde | 784 | — | 6,196 |
| Yongping | 671 | 1,780 | 2,345 |
| Zunhuazhou | 702 | 816 | 1,324 |
| Shuntian | 2,935 | 3,474 | 4,403 |
| Xuanhua | 839 | — | — |
| Yizhou | 221 | 244 | 483 |
| Tianjin | 1,601 | 1,976 | 2,186 |
| Hejian | 1,616 | 2,174 | 2,947 |
| Baoding | 1,705 | 2,199 | 3,103 |
| Shenzhou | [266] | 695 | 805 |
| Dingzhou | 371 | 359 | 618 |
| Zhengding | 1,255 | 1,370 | 2,259 |
| Jizhou | 1,289 | 1,236 | 1,273 |
| Zhaozhou | 767 | 632 | 865 |
| Guangping | 1,225 | 1,102 | 1,734 |
| Shunde | 952 | 1,053 | 1,258 |
| Daming | 1,965 | 1,949 | 1,116 |
| | | | |
| Northwest Shandong | | | |
| Wuding | 2,191 | — | 2,228 |
| Jinan | 4,015 | — | 5,297 |
| Dongchang | 1,613 | — | 1,995 |
| Linqingzhou | 968 | — | 731 |

SOURCES: Guan 1956: 68–80; Liang 1980: 273; Rozman 1982: Appendix 4.
NOTE: Brackets indicate figure of questionable utility.

TABLE B.3

Reported Population of the Counties of Shuntian Prefecture, Hebei, ca. 1600 and 1883

(1,000's of people)

| County | 1600 | 1883 | County | 1600 | 1883 |
|---|---|---|---|---|---|
| Daxing | 71.0 | 180.2[a] | Pinggu | — | 40.0 |
| Wanping | 62.1 | 206.5[a] | Changping | 15.5 | 120.7 |
| Liangxiang | 14.8 | 35.2 | Miyun | 17.1 | 116.7 |
| Gu'an | 35.1 | 100.6[a] | Shunyi | 13.0 | 84.1 |
| Dong'an | 13.2 | 105.1 | Huairou | 7.3 | 50.3 |
| Yongqing | 13.2 | 82.3 | Zhuozhou | 39.4 | 87.1[a] |
| Xianghe | 9.2 | 35.4 | Fangshan | 10.6 | 79.4 |
| Tongzhou | 13.0 | 270.9 | Bazhou | 65.4 | 140.1 |
| Sanhe | 14.2 | 192.0[a] | Wen'an | 25.7 | 200.2 |
| Wuqing | 20.2 | 372.9 | Dacheng | 32.0 | 114.2[a] |
| Guoxian | 4.3 | —[b] | Baoding | 7.1 | 14.3 |
| Baodi | 36.7 | 326.6 | Ninghe | —[d] | 212.7[a] |
| Jizhou | 22.1[c] | 208.3 | TOTAL | 562.2 | 3,376.8 |

SOURCE: Liang 1980: 457.
NOTE: The 1600 figures are from the Wanli period, 1573–1620.
[a] 1882 figures.
[b] Merged into Tongzhou in the early Qing.
[c] Included Yutian, Fengrun, Zunhua, and Pinggu counties in the Ming. After 1743 Zunhua was raised to a district (zhilizhou), overseeing Yutian and Fengrun counties.
[d] Part of Baodi until 1731.

People's Republic a few years later, have the advantages of giving subprovincial breakdowns); and, finally, the 1953 census figures.

Gilbert Rozman, in his study on the Qing population (1982), has not succeeded in overcoming the basic limitations of the past research. It is difficult to go beyond the approach and method that Ho Ping-ti and Dwight Perkins adopted: to accept the 1953 figures as a reasonably credible baseline and to look on the 1393 and mid-Qing figures as distant pointers toward educated guesses about China's population in that period. The plausibility of such guesses must depend on qualitative evidence as much as these rather questionable numbers. In the absence of better data, this study uses the following working figures for the population of Hebei and Shandong: roughly 7,000,000 in 1393, rising to 50,000,000 by 1800 and 75,000,000–80,000,000 by the 1930's.

Table B.2 presents the population figures on Hebei and Shandong prefectures for 1820, 1883, and 1948. Problematical as these figures are, they furnish some basis for speculating that the ecologically less favored areas of northeastern Hebei (Yongping prefecture) and central Hebei (eastern Tianjin and Hejian) were among the last areas in

Zhili to be developed. In both areas we see a substantial population increase in the half century after 1820, a period in which population growth elsewhere leveled off.

Finally, Table B.3 presents the data on a single Hebei prefecture, Shuntian, broken down by counties, for the Wanli (1573–1620) period and for 1883. Once again, the numbers are highly problematical, for they come from periods when population registration and reporting were done haphazardly at best. But seen in conjunction with the qualitative evidence on cotton cultivation and the provincial quantitative data, they furnish some additional basis for speculating that the period 1550–1800 might have been one of relatively rapid population growth, only briefly interrupted by the Ming–Qing dynastic transition.

# Cultivated Acreage
# in Hebei and Shandong,
# 1393-1957

Data on cultivated acreage in the Ming are sketchy and unreliable. The 1393 figures shown in Table C.1 seem inflated and implausible when compared to later figures, even though a land survey was undertaken in 1368—the first of three known surveys in the Ming. The 1502 figures might reflect the results of the second survey, in 1398. The results of the third survey cannot be gauged, since the 1578 figures shown in the table apparently did not incorporate the results of the survey begun that year. Dwight Perkins (1969: 222–26) argues for using the 1502 figures as rough indicators of the cultivated acreage around 1400.

The Qing data have a double problem. The figures for 1661–1753 do not include "official land" (guantian), which probably constituted about 29 percent of the total cultivated land in Hebei at the start of the dynasty. The bannerland is included in the later figures, but those figures may undercount the acreage in both provinces because of the practice of converting a certain multiple of low-grade land into one cadastral mu for tax purposes. Perkins estimates on the basis of John Lossing Buck's 1930's data on different grades of land a possible 20 percent to 30 percent undercount as a result of this practice. If we add 29 percent to the Hebei figures for bannerland and another 20 percent or so for the undercounting, we would come to Perkins' conclusion that by the eighteenth century the two provinces had brought into cultivation approximately all the land they would cultivate down to the 1930's. Given the rising population, we come to the central fact of mounting pressures on the land from the eighteenth century on.

TABLE C.I
Reported Cultivated Acreage in Hebei and Shandong, 1393–1957

(1,000's of mu)[a]

| Year | Hebei | Shandong | Source |
|------|-------|----------|--------|
| Ming Dynasty | | | |
| 1393 | 58,250 | 72,404 | Liang 1980: 346–47 |
| 1502 | 26,971 | 54,293 | |
| 1578 | 49,257 | 61,750 | |
| | | | |
| Qing Dynasty | | | |
| 1661 | 45,977 | 74,134 | Liang 1980: 380 |
| 1685 | 54,343 | 92,527 | |
| 1724 | 70,171 | 99,259 | |
| 1753 | 66,162 | 99,347 | |
| 1812 | 74,143 | 98,635 | |
| 1851 | 72,726 | 98,473 | |
| 1873 | 73,046 | 98,473 | |
| 1887 | 86,652 | 125,941 | |
| | | | |
| Republic of China | | | |
| 1933 | 118,000 | 120,000 | Perkins 1969: 236 |
| | | | |
| People's Republic | | | |
| 1957 | 132,000 | 139,000 | Perkins 1969: 236 |

NOTE: This table must be read in conjunction with the accompanying text, which discusses the implausibility of much of the Ming data and the undercounting in the Qing data.

[a]The Ming mu was 0.1434 acre, the Qing mu 0.1518 acre, and the shi mu (used since the Republic) 0.1647 acre.

# Character List

Adachi Keiji 足立啓二
*ailong* 挨壟
Asuwei *cun*, 阿蘇衞村
  Changping *xian* 昌平縣
*ba* 壩
*badie bawan* 八碟八碗
*badie chimian* 八碟吃麵
*badie siwan* 八碟四碗
Bai Boyi 白撥一
Bai Heyi 白鶴一
Bai Hongyi 白洪一
Baizhuang, 柏莊
  Leting *xian* 樂亭縣
*baogong* 包工
*baojia* 保甲
*baozheng* 保正
*baozhong* 包種
Bi Fenglian 畢豐漣
Bi Yuanrong 畢遠蓉
Binggezhuang, 邴各莊
  Funing *xian* 撫寧縣
*bobo she* 餑餑社
*changgong* 長工
*changgong huopu* 長工活譜
*cheling* 車領
Chen Shuping 陳樹平
*chunjie qiuhuan* 春借秋還
Cong Hanxiang 叢翰香
*cuntan jingkuan* 村攤警款
*cuntan xuekuan* 村攤學款

Cuqiao gongshe 簇橋公社
*daban* 大辦
Dabeiguan (*cun*), 大北關（村）
  Pinggu *xian* 平谷縣
*da che* 大車
Dadao hui 大刀會
*da datou* 大打頭
*dainōhō* 大農法
*danshan* 單扇
*datao* 搭套
*dazonghuitou* 大總會頭
*diandi* 典地
*dianfeng* 墊封
*difang* 地方
Ding Ling 丁玲
Ding Yizeng 丁宜曾
Dong Dezhai 董德齋
Dong Jizhong 董繼中
Dong Tianwang 董天望
Dong Weizeng 董維曾
Dongfanliu *cun*, 東矾硫村
  Zhangqiu *xian* 章邱縣
Donghongyapo *cun*, 東鴻鴨泊村
  Fengrun *xian* 豐潤縣
Dongjiao *cun*, 東焦村
  Shijiazhuang *shi* 石家莊市
*dongshi* 董事
Du Fengshan 杜鳳山
Du Ruhai 杜如海
Du Xiang 杜祥

*duanqian* 端牽
Dujiangyan 都江堰
*dusi* 都司
Duyake *cun*, 杜雅科村
  Zaoqiang *xian* 棗強縣
*eba* 惡霸
*erba* 二八
*erbafenzi* 二八分子
*fajia* 發駕
*fajia zhifu* 發家致富
Fan Baoshan 樊寶山
Fang Guancheng 方觀承
Feng Menglong 馮夢龍
*fengu* 分穀
*fenlong* 分壟
*fensheng minshu* 分省民數
  *gushu qingce* 穀數清册
*fenzhong* 分種
Fu Shizhen 傅世珍
*fuchan* 副產
*fujia* 附加
Ge Shouli 葛守禮
*guanggun* 光棍
*guantian* 官田
*gugongren* 僱工人
Guo Kuan 郭寬
Guo Xujiu 郭緒九
Guo Zhishan 郭志善
Handan *xian* 邯鄲縣
Hao Xiaowu 郝小五
Hao Yonghai 郝永海
*haoxian* 耗羨
Heitingzhuang, 黑汀莊
  Linyu *xian* 臨榆縣
Hejianfu 河間府
Hou Baochen 侯寶臣
Hou Baolian 侯寶廉
Hou Changyong 侯長永
Hou Qingchang 侯慶昌
Hou Yuanguang 侯元廣
Houjiaying, 侯家營
  Changli *xian* 昌黎縣

Houxiazhai, 後夏寨
  Enxian 恩縣
Houyansi *cun*, 後延寺村
  Xianghe *xian* 香河縣
Huang Kerun 黃可潤
Huangsha hui 黃紗會
*huangzhuang* 皇莊
*huishou* 會首
*huoji* 伙計
*huozhong* 夥種
Huzhuang, 胡莊
  Pinggu *xian* 平谷縣
Huzhuang, 胡莊
  Ninghe *xian* 寧河縣
Jialing jiang 嘉陵江
Jiao Yü 焦玉
Jiaojiazhuang, 焦家莊
  Fengrun *xian* 豐潤縣
*jiazhang* 甲長
*jieshaoren* 介紹人
Jigezhuang, 紀各莊
  Jixian 薊縣
Jing Su 景甦
*jingzhengchu* 經徵處
*jizhu* 寄住
*jubao* 具保
Junxian 濬縣
Juren li 居仁里
Kong Ziming 孔子明
*laozhuang* 老莊
Lengshuigou *cun*, 冷水溝村
  Licheng *xian* 歷城縣
Li Dingguo 李定國
Li Gao 李高
Li Guangtai 李廣泰
Li Guangzhi 李廣志
Li Jinghan 李景漢
Li Maozhe 李茂哲
Li Ruyuan 李儒源
Li Wanliang 李萬艮
Li Xiufang 李秀芳
Li Yanlin 李嚴林

Li Yuan 李元
Li Zhenzong 李振宗
Li Zhuyuan 李注源
Liang Yazi 梁芽子
*lianggui* 糧櫃
  (*liangfang*) (糧房)
*liangtou cu*, 兩頭粗
  *zhongjian xi* 中間細
*lieshen* 劣紳
*lihu* 犁戶
*lijia* 里甲
*lingsheng* 廩生
*linlü* 鄰閭
Liu Qidazi 劉七達子
Liu Wanchen 劉萬臣
Liu Wenxin 劉文新
Liu Zhu 劉珠
Liu Zixiang 劉子馨
Longwo *cun*, 龍窩村
  Yutian *xian* 玉田縣
Lu Longqi 陸隴其
Lu Nan 盧楠
Lu'anfu 潞安府
Lujiazhai, 盧家寨
  Zunhua *xian* 遵化縣
Luo Lun 羅崙
Luo Xiujin 羅繡錦
Ma Fengwu 馬鳳舞
Ma Shichao 馬士超
Ma Wantong 馬萬通
Macun, 馬村
  Huailu *xian* 獲鹿縣
Michang *cun*, 米廠村
  Fengrun *xian* 豐潤縣
Min jiang 泯江
Mudan jiang 牡丹江
*mujuan* 畝捐
Nanquanfuzhuang, 南權府莊
  Jinan *shi* 濟南市
*nazu* 納租
*niangong* 年工
Nijing *zhen* 泥井鎮

Niu Xiwu 牛希武
Nuanshuitun *cun*, 暖水屯村
  Zhuolu *xian* 涿鹿縣
*paijia* 牌甲
*paitou* 牌頭
Pang Zhengxi 龐正喜
Qian Jin 錢瑾
Qianlianggezhuang, 前粱各莊
  Changli *xian* 昌黎縣
Qin Runtian 秦潤田
*qishui* 契稅
Qizhai, 祁寨
  Gaotang *xian* 高唐縣
Qu Er 屈二
Qu Yuangui 屈元貴
*quandi* 圈地
*renzhuang* 認狀
Rizhao *xian* 日照縣
Sanggan he 桑乾河
Sanyuan 三原
*sanziyibao* 三自一包
Shajing *cun*, 沙井村
  Shunyi *xian* 順義縣
Shangjie li 尚節里
*shaozhong* 捎種
*shengxu shui* 牲畜稅
*sheshu* 社書
Shi Maoer 時毛兒
Shi Yulong 時玉龍
*shonōhō* 小農法
*shoushi* 首事
*shuang gongqian* 雙工錢
*shuji* 書記
*shuoheren* 說合人
*shushou* 書手
*shuyuan* 書院
Sibeichai *cun*, 寺北柴村
  Luancheng *xian* 欒城縣
*siliang* 死糧
Sunjiamiao *cun*, 孫家廟村
  Huimin *xian* 惠民縣
Taihetang 太和堂

Taishan Laomu 泰山老母
*tanding rudi* 攤丁入地
Tangxian 唐縣
*tankuan* 攤款
Tian Genzi 田根子
Tian Kui 田奎
*tianfu* 田賦
*tianfu fujia* 田賦附加
*tianfu fujuan* 田賦附捐
Tianjinfu 天津府
Tianmen hui 天門會
Tiaoshanying, 眺山營
　　Mancheng *xian* 滿城縣
*touxian* 投獻
*tuhao* 土豪
Wang Baojun 王葆鈞
Wang Guangxin 王光新
Wang Guoxiang 王國相
Wang Kunbi 王崑璧
Wang Qinglong 王慶龍
*wangshehui* 亡社會
Wang Shizhen 王士禎
Wang Shunqing 王順卿
Wang Weishan 王維善
Wang Xizhen 王錫珍
Wang Zanzhou 王贊周
Wang Zhen 王禎
Wangquansi *cun*, 望泉寺村
　　Shunyi *xian* 順義縣
*wangzhuang* 王莊
Wu Fengxin 吳鳳鑫
Wu'an *xian* 武安縣
Wudian *cun*, 吳店村
　　Liangxiang *xian* 艮鄉縣
*xiangbao* 鄉保
*xiangshe* 鄉社
*xiangyue* 鄉約
Xiaojie *cun*, 小街村
　　Tongxian 通縣
Xiaowangzhuang, 小王莊
　　Yutian *xian* 玉田縣

Xiaoying *cun*, 小營村
　　Miyun *xian* 密雲縣
Xiaozhong he 小中河
Xincheng *xian* 新城縣
Xingbao li 興保里
Xinyan *cun*, 新堰村
　　Chengdu *shi* 成都市
*xinzheng* 新政
*xiucai* 秀才
Xu Guangqi 徐光啓
Yang Baosen 楊保森
Yang Kun 楊坤
Yang Lianting 楊連廷
Yang Mingwang 楊明旺
Yang Run 楊潤
Yang Xiuyuan 楊秀元
Yang Yuan 楊源
Yang Ze 楊澤
Yao Shanyou 姚善友
*yashui* 牙稅
Yin Heli 尹和里
*yonggong duri* 傭工渡日
Yongpingfu 永平府
You Zhaogui 游照貴
Yu Tunzi 于囤子
*yuegong* 月工
Yuncheng *xian* 鄆城縣
Zezhoufu 澤州府
Zhang Cailou 張彩樓
Zhang Chonglou 張重樓
Zhang Deyuan 張德元
Zhang Gouer 張狗兒
Zhang Linbing 張林炳
Zhang Qilun 張啓倫
Zhang Rui 張瑞
Zhang Sheng 張生
Zhang Shoujun 張守俊
Zhang Wenju 張文舉
Zhang Wentong 張文通
Zhang Yangwu 張揚武
Zhang Yueqing 張樂卿

Zhang Yuming 張玉明
*zhanggui* 掌櫃
Zhanhua *xian* 沾化縣
Zhao Er 趙二
Zhao Fenglin 趙鳳林
Zhao Wenyou 趙文友
Zhao Zigang 趙子綱
*zhengshui* 正稅
*zhidi jieqian* 指地借錢
Zhimafeng *cun*, 芝蔴埄村
　　Yutian *xian* 玉田縣
*zhonggeng* 中耕

*zhongjianren* 中間人
Zhongliangshan *cun*, 中兩山村
　　Changli *xian* 昌黎縣
Zhou Yuetang 周越堂
　　(Fengchi, Yuchi) （鳳池、玉池）
*zhuangding* 壯丁
*zhuangtou* 莊頭
Zichuan *xian* 淄川縣
Zu Xiaojiang 俎曉江
Zugezhuang, 祖各莊
　　Anci *xian* 安次縣

# REFERENCES CITED

# References Cited

The following abbreviations are used in the citations: KC, *Chūgoku nōson kankō chōsa*; MT, Minami Manshū tetsudō kabushiki kaisha; ZRD, Zhongguo renmin daxue Zhongguo lishi jiaoyanshi.

Adachi Keiji. 1981. "Shindai kahoku no nōgyō keiei to shakai kōzō" (Farm management and social structure in North China in the Qing), *Shirin*, 64.4: 528–55.

Alavi, Hamza. 1973. "Peasant Classes and Primordial Loyalties," *Journal of Peasant Studies*, 1.1: 23–61.

Alitto, Guy S. 1979. "Rural Elites in Transition: China's Cultural Crisis and the Problem of Legitimacy," in Susan Mann Jones, ed., *Select Papers from the Center for Far Eastern Studies*, no. 3, 1978–79, pp. 218–75. Chicago: Center for Far Eastern Studies, University of Chicago.

Amano Motonosuke. 1936. *Santō nōgyō keizai ron* (The agricultural economy of Shandong). Dalian: MT.

Baran, Paul A. 1957. *The Political Economy of Growth*. New York: Monthly Review.

Beijing zhengfa xueyuan. 1957. *Zhonghua renmin gongheguo tudifa cankao ziliao huibian* (A compendium of reference materials on the land reform laws of the People's Republic of China). Beijing: Falü.

Billingsley, Phil. 1981. "Bandits, Bosses, and Bare Sticks: Beneath the Surface of Local Control in Early Republican China," *Modern China*, 7.3: 235–88.

Boserup, Ester. 1965. *The Conditions of Agricultural Growth. The Economics of Agrarian Change Under Population Pressure*. Chicago: Aldine.

Brenner, Robert. 1982. "The Agrarian Roots of European Capitalism," *Past and Present*, 97, Nov.: 16–113.

Brook, Timothy. 1982. "The Spread of Rice Cultivation and Rice Technology into the Hebei Region in the Ming and Qing," in *Explorations in the History of Science and Technology in China*, pp. 659–90. (Festschrift volume in honor of the 80th birthday of Dr. Joseph Needham.) Shanghai: Shanghai guji.

Buck, John Lossing. 1937a. *Land Utilization in China*. Shanghai: University of Nanking.

———. 1937b. *Land Utilization in China: Statistics*. Shanghai: University of Nanking.

————. 1930. *Chinese Farm Economy*. Chicago: University of Chicago Press.

Chang Chung-li (Zhang Zhongli). 1962. *The Income of the Chinese Gentry*. Seattle: University of Washington Press.

————. 1955. *The Chinese Gentry: Studies on Their Role in Nineteenth-Century Chinese Society*. Seattle: University of Washington Press.

Chao, Kang. 1981. "New Data on Landownership Patterns in Ming–Ch'ing China, Research Note," *Journal of Asian Studies*, 40.4: 719–34.

————. 1977. *The Development of Cotton Textile Production in China*. Cambridge, Mass.: East Asian Research Center, Harvard University.

Chayanov, A. V. 1966a. "On the Theory of Noncapitalist Economic Systems," in Daniel Thorner, Basile Kerblay, and R. E. F. Smith, eds., *A. V. Chayanov on the Theory of Peasant Economy*, pp. 1–28. Homewood, Ill.: Richard D. Irwin, Inc.

————. 1966b. *Peasant Farm Organization*, in *ibid.*, pp. 29–277.

Chen Hengli. 1963. *Bunongshu yanjiu* (A study of [Zhang Lixiang's] "Sequel to the *Treatise on agriculture*"). Beijing: Nongye chubanshe.

Chen Ping. 1981. "Shehui chuantong he jingji jiegou de guanxi" (The relationship between societal tradition and economic structure), *Xuexi yu tansuo*, no. 1: 4–19.

————. 1979. "Dan yi xiaonong jingji jiegou shi woguo changqi dongluan pinqiong de binggen" (The crops-only small peasant economic structure is the root of our nation's protracted disorder and poverty), *Guangming ribao*, Nov. 16, 1979: 3.

Chen Shiqi. 1959. "Jiawu qian Zhongguo nongcun shougong mianfangzhi gongye de bianhua he zibenzhuyi shengchan de chengzhang" (Changes in China's rural handicraft cotton spinning and weaving industry before 1895 and the development of capitalist production), *Lishi yanjiu*, no. 2: 17–38.

Chen Shuping. 1980. "Yumi he fanshu zai Zhongguo chuanbo qingkuang yanjiu" (A study of the spread of maize and the sweet potato in China), *Zhongguo shehui kexue*, no. 3: 187–204.

Chen Wenhua. 1981. "Zhongguo gudai nongye kejishi jianghua" (Lectures on the history of China's agricultural technology in pre-modern times), 2 parts, *Nongye kaogu*, no. 1: 114–24; no. 2: 143–53.

Chen Zhengmo. 1935. *Ge sheng nonggong guyong xiguan ji xugong zhuangkuang* (Customary practices and the conditions of supply and demand in labor hiring in the different provinces). Nanjing: Zhongshan wenhua jiaoyuguan.

Chen Zhenhan. 1955. "Mingmo Qingchu (1620–1720) Zhongguo de nongye laodong shengchanlü, dizu he tudi jizhong" (Farm labor productivity, rent, and land concentration in the late Ming–early Qing), in ZRD, 1: 272–94.

*Chengde fu zhi* (Gazetteer of Chengde prefecture), 1831.

Ch'ü T'ung-tsu (Qu Tongzu). 1962. *Local Government in China Under the Ch'ing*. Cambridge, Mass.: Harvard University Press.

Chūgoku nōson kankō chōsa kankōkai (Niida Noboru, ed.). 1952–58. *Chūgoku nōson kankō chōsa* (Investigations of customary practices in rural China). 6 vols. Tokyo: Iwanami.

Chūgoku nōson keizai kenkyūjo (Beijing daxue nongxueyuan). 1939. *Santō shō Keimin ken nōson chōsa hōkoku* (Report on the village investigation in Huimin county, Shandong province). Beijing.

Cochran, Sherman. 1980. *Big Business in China: Sino-Foreign Rivalry in the Cigarette Industry, 1890–1930.* Cambridge, Mass.: Harvard University Press.

Cong Hanxiang. 1981. "Shishu Mingdai zhimian he mianfang zhiye de fazhan" (A preliminary discussion of the development of cotton cultivation and cotton spinning and weaving in the Ming), *Zhongguo shi yanjiu,* no. 1: 61–78.

Crook, David and Isabel. 1959. *Revolution in a Chinese Village: Ten Mile Inn.* London: Routledge & Kegan Paul.

Dai Yi, ed. 1980. *Jianming Qing shi* (A simplified history of the Qing). Beijing: Renmin.

Dalton, George. 1969. "Theoretical Issues in Economic Anthropology," *Current Anthropology,* 10.1: 63–102.

Dernberger, Robert F. 1975. "The Role of the Foreigner in China's Economic Development, 1840–1949," in Dwight Perkins, ed., *China's Modern Economy in Historical Perspective,* pp. 19–47. Stanford, Calif.: Stanford University Press.

Ding Ling. 1949. *Taiyang zhao zai Sangganhe shang* (The sun shines on the Sanggan River). Beijing: Xinhua.

Dirlik, Arif. 1982. "Chinese Historians and the Marxist Concept of Capitalism: A Critical Examination," *Modern China,* 8.1: 105–32.

———. 1978. *Revolution and History.* Berkeley: University of California Press.

Eastman, Lloyd. 1981. "Peasants, Taxes, and Nationalist Rule, 1937–45." Manuscript.

Eberhard, Wolfram. 1965. *Conquerors and Rulers: Social Forces in Medieval China.* 2d rev. ed. Leiden: E. J. Brill.

Elvin, Mark. 1973. *The Pattern of the Chinese Past.* Stanford, Calif.: Stanford University Press.

Engels, Friedrich. 1926. *The Peasant War in Germany.* New York: International Publishers.

Esherick, Joseph. 1982. "Missionaries, Christians, and the Boxers: Imperialism in Religious Guise." Manuscript.

———. 1981. "Numbers Games: A Note on Land Distribution in Prerevolutionary China," *Modern China,* 7.4: 387–412.

———. 1980. "On the Social Origins of the Boxer Movement," paper presented to the International Conference on the Boxer Movement, Jinan, Shandong, November 1980. Chinese translation in *Wenshizhe,* 1981, no. 1: 22–31.

———. 1976. *Reform and Revolution in China: The 1911 Revolution in Hunan and Hubei.* Berkeley: University of California Press.

Fairbank, John K., and Kwang-ching Liu, eds. 1980. *The Cambridge History of China,* vol. 11: *Late Ch'ing, 1800–1911,* part 2. Cambridge: Cambridge University Press.

Fan Baichuan. 1983. "Ershi shiji chuqi Zhongguo zibenzhuyi fazhan de gaikuang yu tedian" (The development and special characteristics of modern Chinese capitalism in the early years of the twentieth century), *Lishi yanjiu,* no. 4: 11–24.

Fei Xiaotong. 1948. *Xiangtu chongjian* (Reconstruction of the native countryside). Shanghai.

Feng Huade. 1937. "Hebei sheng Ding xian de yashui" (Brokerage taxes in Ding county, Hebei), *Zhengzhi jingji xue bao*, 5.2: 285–322.

———. 1936. "Hebei Ding xian zhi tianfu" (Land taxes in Ding county, Hebei), *Zhengzhi jingji xue bao*, 4.3: 443–520.

———. 1935. "Xian difang xingzheng zhi caizheng jichu" (The financial basis of county local administration), *Zhengzhi jingji xue bao*, 3.4: 687–750.

Feng Menglong. 1958. *Xingshi hengyan* (Stories to awaken the world). 2 vols. Hong Kong: Zhonghua. Originally published in 1627.

Feuerwerker, Albert. 1980. "Economic Trends in the Late Ch'ing Empire," in John K. Fairbank and Kwang-ching Liu, eds., *The Cambridge History of China*, vol. 11: *Late Ch'ing, 1800–1911*, part 2, pp. 1–69. Cambridge: Cambridge University Press.

———. 1970. "Handicraft and Manufactured Cotton Textiles in China, 1871–1910," *Journal of Economic History*, 30.2: 338–78.

———. 1958. *China's Early Industrialization: Sheng Hsuan-huai (1844–1916) and Mandarin Enterprise*. Cambridge, Mass.: Harvard University Press.

Frank, Andre Gunder. 1978. "Development of Underdevelopment or Underdevelopment of Development in China," *Modern China*, 4.3: 341–50.

———. 1967. *Capitalism and Underdevelopment in Latin America*. New York: Monthly Review.

Freedman, Maurice. 1966. *Chinese Lineage and Society: Fukien and Kwangtung*. London: University of London, The Athlone Press.

Friedman, Milton, and L. G. Savage. 1948. "The Utility Analysis of Choices Involving Risk," *Journal of Political Economy*, 56: 279–304.

Fu Yiling. 1979. "Ming Qing shidai jieji guanxi de xin tansuo" (New inquiries into class relations in the Ming–Qing period), *Zhongguo shi yanjiu*, no. 4: 65–74.

Fu Zhufu. 1981. "The Economic History of China: Some Special Problems," *Modern China*, 7.1: 3–30.

———. 1980. *Zhongguo jingjishi luncong* (Essays on the social-economic history of China). 2 vols. Beijing: Sanlian.

Furushima Binyū. 1955. "*Chūgoku nōson kankō chōsa dai ikkan o yonde*" (On reading the first volume of *Investigations of Customary Practices in Rural China*), in KC, 4: 3–7.

Gamble, Sidney. 1963. *North China Villages: Social, Political and Economic Activities Before 1933*. Berkeley: University of California Press.

———. 1954. *Ting Hsien: A North China Rural Community*. Stanford, Calif.: Stanford University Press.

Geertz, Clifford. 1963. *Agricultural Involution: The Process of Ecological Change in Indonesia*. Berkeley: University of California Press.

Georgescu-Roegen, N. 1960. "Economic Theory and Agrarian Economies," *Oxford Economic Papers*, 12.1: 1–40.

Griffin, Keith. 1978. "The Roots of Underdevelopment: Reflections on the Chinese Experience," *Modern China*, 4.3: 351–57.

Grove, Linda. 1975. "Rural Society in Revolution: The Gaoyang District, 1910–1947," Ph.D. dissertation, University of California, Berkeley.

Grove, Linda, and Joseph Esherick. 1980. "From Feudalism to Capitalism: Japanese Scholarship on the Transformation of Chinese Rural Society," *Modern China*, 6.4: 397–438.

Guan Weilan, ed. 1956. *Zhonghua minguo xingzheng quhua ji tudi renkou tongji biao* (Administrative divisions and statistical tables on the land and population of the Republic of China). Taibei: Beikai.

Gurley, John. 1976. *China's Economy and the Maoist Strategy.* New York: Monthly Review.

Hao Ran. 1972. *Yan yang tian* (Bright sunny skies). 3 vols. Hong Kong: Sanlian.

Hartwell, Robert. 1982. "Demographic, Political, and Social Transformations of China, 750–1550," *Harvard Journal of Asiatic Studies,* 42.2: 365–442.

Hatada Takashi. 1981. "Saikan ni atatte" (On republication), in *Chūgoku nōson kankō chōsa,* 1: 1–4. Tokyo: Iwanami. Re-issue of KC.

———. 1973. *Chūgoku no sonraku to kyōdōtai riron* (The villages of China and the theory of community). Tokyo: Iwanami.

Hebei sheng mianchan gaijin hui. 1937. *Hebei sheng mianchan diaocha baogao, 1936* (Report on the investigation of cotton production in Hebei, 1936). N.p.

———. 1936. *Hebei sheng mianchan diaocha baogao, 1935* (Report on the investigation of cotton production in Hebei, 1935). N.p.

Hinton, William. 1966. *Fanshen: A Documentary of Revolution in a Chinese Village.* New York: Random House.

Ho Ping-ti (He Bingdi). 1969. *Huangtu yu Zhongguo nongye de qiyuan* (Loess and the origins of Chinese agriculture). Hong Kong: Chinese University of Hong Kong.

———. 1962. *The Ladder of Success in Imperial China.* New York: Columbia University Press.

———. 1959. *Studies in the Population of China.* Cambridge, Mass.: Harvard University Press.

Hofheinz, Roy, Jr. 1977. *The Broken Wave: The Chinese Communist Peasant Movement, 1922–1928.* Cambridge, Mass.: Harvard University Press.

Hou Chi-ming. 1965. *Foreign Investment and Economic Development in China, 1840–1937.* Cambridge, Mass.: Harvard University Press.

———. 1963. "Economic Dualism: The Case of China, 1840–1937," *Journal of Economic History,* 23.3: 277–97.

Hsiao Kung-ch'uan. 1960. *Rural China: Imperial Control in the Nineteenth Century.* Seattle: University of Washington Press.

Hsieh, Chiao-min. 1973. *Atlas of China.* New York: McGraw-Hill.

Hsü Cho-yun. 1980. *Han Agriculture: The Formation of Early Chinese Agrarian Economy, 206 B.C.–220 A.D.* Seattle: University of Washington. Press.

Hu Hsien-chin. 1948. *The Common Descent Group in China and Its Functions.* New York: Viking Fund.

Hu Rulei. 1979. *Zhongguo fengjian shehui xingtai yanjiu* (A study of China's feudal social formation). Beijing: Sanlian.

Huang, Philip C. C. 1982. "County Archives and the Study of Local Social History: Report on a Year's Research in China," *Modern China,* 8.1: 133–43.

———. 1979. "Current Research on Ming-Qing and Modern History in China," *Modern China,* 5.4: 503–23.

———. 1975a. "Analyzing the Twentieth-Century Chinese Countryside: Revolutionaries versus Western Scholarship," *Modern China*, 1.2: 132–60.

———. 1975b. "Mao Zedong and the Middle Peasants," *Modern China*, 1.3: 271–96.

———, ed. 1978. "Symposium on China's Economic History," *Modern China*, 4.3.

Huang, Philip C. C., and Lynda Schaeffer Bell and Kathy Lemons Walker. 1978. *Chinese Communists and Rural Society, 1927–1934*. Berkeley: University of California Press.

Hymer, Stephen, and Stephen Resinick. 1969. "A Model of an Agrarian Economy with Non-agricultural Activities," *American Economic Review*, part 1, 59.4: 493–506.

Imahori Seiji. 1963. *Tōyō shakai keizai shi josetsu* (An introduction to Chinese socioeconomic history). Kyoto: Ryūgen.

Institute of Pacific Relations. 1938. *Agrarian China: Selected Source Materials from Chinese Authors*. Chicago: University of Chicago Press.

Ishibashi Hideo. 1956. "Shinchō chūki no kiho kichi seisaku" (Policies on bannerland in the capital province in the middle Qing period), 2 parts, *Tōyō gakuhō*, 39.2: 23–72; 39.3: 67–98.

Ishida Bunjirō. 1944. *Shina nōson kankō chōsa hōkokusho—tochi kōsa kōka no kenkyū* (Investigations of customary practices in China: a study of land taxes). Tokyo: Tōakenkyūjo.

Jian Bozan. 1957. "Lun shiba shiji shangbanqi Zhongguo shehui jingji de xingzhi" (On the nature of China's society and economy in the first half of the 18th century), in ZRD, 1: 338–400.

Jing Junjian (Ouyang Fanxiu). 1961a. "Ming Qing liang dai 'gugongren' de falü diwei wenti" (The legal status of "worker-serfs" in the Ming and Qing dynasties), *Xinjianshe*, no. 4: 31–39.

———. 1961b. "Ming Qing liang dai nongye gugong falü shang renshen lishu guanxi de jiefang" (The hired agricultural laborers' legal liberation from personal dependency during the Ming and Qing dynasties), *Jingji yanjiu*, no. 6: 49–74.

Jing Su and Luo Lun. 1959. *Qingdai Shandong jingying dizhu de shehui xingzhi* (The social nature of Shandong managerial landlords in Qing times). Shandong: Renmin.

Johnson, Chalmers A. 1962. *Peasant Nationalism and Communist Power: The Emergence of Revolutionary China, 1937–1945*. Stanford, Calif.: Stanford University Press.

Jones, Susan Mann. 1979. "The Organization of Trade at the County Level: Brokerage and Tax Farming in the Republican Period," in Susan Mann Jones, ed., *Select Papers from the Center for Far Eastern Studies*, no. 3, 1978–79, pp. 70–99. Chicago: Center for Far Eastern Studies, University of Chicago.

Ju Zhendong. 1977. *Hebei qidi zhi yanjiu* (A study of bannerland in Hebei), in Xiao Zheng, ed., *Minguo 20 niandai Zhongguo dalu tudi wenti ziliao* (Materials on the land question in the mainland during the 1920's), no. 75. Taibei: Chengwen.

KC, see *Chūgoku nōson kankō chōsa*.

Kahoku kōtsū kabushiki kaisha. 1940. *Tetsuro aigoson jittai chōsa hōkokusho* (Report on the investigation of actual conditions of a railroad-protection village). N.p.

Kahoku sōgō chōsa kenkyūjo. 1944a. *Sekimon shi kinkō nōson jittai chōsa hōkokusho* (Report on the investigation of actual conditions in a village in the suburb of Shimen [Shijiazhuang] city). Beijing.

―――. 1944b. *Kahoku keizai tōkei shūsei* (Compendium of economic statistics on North China). 3 vols. N.p.: Kahoku sōgō chōsa kenkyūjo.

Kao, Charles H. C., Kurt R. Anschel, and Carl K. Eicher. 1964. "Disguised Unemployment in Agriculture: A Survey," in Carl Eicher and Lawrence Witt, eds., *Agriculture in Economic Development*, pp. 129–44. New York: McGraw-Hill.

Kashiwa Yūken. 1944. *Hokushi no nōson keizai shakai* (The rural society and economy of North China). Kyoto: Kōbundo.

Kataoka Shibako. 1962. "Kahoku no tochi shoyū to ichijo benpō" (The single whip tax and landownership in North China), in *Shimizu hakushi tsuitō kinen mindaishi ronsō*, pp. 139–63. Tokyo: Daian.

―――. 1959. "Minmatsu Shinsho no kahoku ni okeru nōka keiei" (Farm management in North China during the late Ming and early Qing), *Shakai keizai shigaku*, 25.2/3: 77–100.

Kataoka, Tetsuya. 1974. *Resistance and Revolution in China: The Communists and the Second United Front*. Berkeley: University of California Press.

Kawachi Jūzō. 1964. "1930 nendai Chūgoku no nominsō bunkai no haaku no tame ni" (Getting a handle on the differentiation of the Chinese peasantry in the 1930's), *Rekishigaku kenkyū*, 290: 27–41.

―――. 1963. "1930 nendai Chūgoku no nōgyō seisanryoku kōzō to saikin no dōkō" (The structure of Chinese agricultural productivity in the 1930's and recent trends), *Keizaigaku zasshi*, 49.6: 1–29.

Kita Shina kaihatsu kabushiki kaisha chōsakyoku. 1943a. *Rōdōryoku shigen chōsa hōkoku* (Report on the investigation of labor resources). Beijing.

―――. 1943b. *Kosai mensaku chitai no ichi nōson ni okeru rōdōryoku chōsa hōkoku* (Report on the investigation of labor power in a village in the west Shandong cotton-growing area). Beijing.

Kraus, Richard Arnold. 1968. "Cotton and Cotton Goods in China, 1918–1936: The Impact of Modernization on the Traditional Sector," Ph.D. dissertation, Harvard University.

Kuhn, Philip A. 1979. "Local Taxation and Finance in Republican China," in Susan Mann Jones, ed., *Select Papers from the Center for Far Eastern Studies*, no. 3, 1978–79, pp. 100–136. Chicago: Center for Far Eastern Studies, University of Chicago.

―――. 1975. "Local Self-Government Under the Republic," in Frederic Wakeman Jr. and Carolyn Grant, eds., *Conflict and Control in Late Imperial China*, pp. 257–98. Berkeley: University of California Press.

―――. 1970. *Rebellion and Its Enemies in Late Imperial China: Militarization and Social Structure, 1796–1864*. Cambridge, Mass.: Harvard University Press.

Lau, Yee-fui, Ho Wan-yee, and Yeung Sai-cheung. 1977. *Glossary of Chinese Political Phrases*. Hong Kong: Union Research Institute.

Lefebvre, Georges. 1959. *Les Paysans du Nord pendant la revolution française*. Bari: Laterza. Originally published in 1934.

Lenin, V. I. 1956. *The Development of Capitalism in Russia*. Moscow: Foreign Languages Publishing House.

Le Roy Ladurie, Emmanuel. 1979. *Carnival in Romans*, tr. Mary Feeney. New York: George Braziller.

———. 1978. *Montaillou: The Promised Land of Error*, tr. Barbara Bray. New York: George Braziller.

———. 1974. *The Peasants of Languedoc*, tr. John Day. Urbana: University of Illinois Press.

Levine, David. 1977. *Family Formation in an Age of Nascent Capitalism*. New York: Academic Press.

Li Hongyi. 1977. *Hebei tianfu zhi yanjiu* (A study of land taxation in Hebei), in Xiao Zheng, ed., *Minguo 20 niandai Zhongguo dalu tudi wenti ziliao*. Taibei: Chengwen.

Li Jinghan. 1933. *Ding xian shehui diaocha gaikuang* (A summary of the investigation of the society of Ding county). Beijing: Daxue.

Li Shu. 1957. "Guanyu Zhongguo zibenzhuyi mengya wenti de kaocha" (Reflections on the problem of the sprouts of capitalism in China), in ZRD, 2: 742–80.

Li Wenzhi. 1981. "Zhongguo dizhu jingji zhi yu nongye zibenzhuyi mengya" (Chinese landlordism and the sprouts of capitalism in agriculture), *Zhongguo shehui kexue*, no. 1: 143–60.

———. 1963a. "Qingdai qianqi de tudi zhanyou guanxi" (Land relations in early Qing), *Lishi yanjiu*, no. 5: 75–109.

———. 1963b. "Ming Qing shidai de fengjian tudi suoyouzhi" (The feudal landowning system of the Ming–Qing period), 2 parts, *Jingji yanjiu*, no. 8: 67–77; no. 9: 55–61.

———, ed. 1957. *Zhongguo jindai nongyeshi ziliao*, vol. 1: *1840–1911* (Source materials on the agricultural history of modern China). Beijing: Sanlian.

Liang Fangzhong. 1980. *Zhongguo lidai hukou tiandi tianfu tongji* (Statistics on population, cultivated area, and land taxes in China's successive dynasties). Shanghai: Renmin.

Lippit, Victor. 1983. "The Concept of the Surplus in Economic Development," *Working Paper Series*, Department of Economics, University of California, Riverside, no. 65.

———. 1978. "The Development of Underdevelopment in China," *Modern China*, 4.3: 251–328.

———. 1974. *Land Reform and Economic Development in China*. White Plains, N.Y.: International Arts and Sciences Press.

Lipton, Michael. 1968. "The Theory of the Optimizing Peasant," *Journal of Development Studies*, 4.3: 327–51.

Liu Dunyuan and Zhang Zhongge. 1981. "Woguo yangzhu shihua" (Informal comments on hog raising in our country), *Nongye kaogu*, no. 1: 103–5.

Liu, K. C. 1981. "World View and Peasant Rebellion: Reflections on Post-Mao Historiography," *Journal of Asian Studies*, 40.2: 295–328.

———. 1978. "The Ch'ing Restoration," in John K. Fairbank, ed., *The Cambridge History of China*, vol. 10: *Late Ch'ing, 1800–1911*, part 1, pp. 409–90. Cambridge: Cambridge University Press.

Liu Qing. 1972. *The Builders*. Beijing: Foreign Languages Press.

Liu Shaoqi. 1938. "Jianchi Huabei kangzhan zhong de wuzhuang budui" (The armed forces that have persisted in the war of resistance in North China), *Jiefang*, 43/44: 49–53.

Liu, Ta-chung, and Kung-chia Yeh. 1965. *The Economy of the Chinese Mainland: National Income and Economic Development: 1933–1959*. Princeton, N.J.: Princeton University Press.

Liu Yongcheng. 1982. Qingdai qianqi nongye zibenzhuyi mengya chutan (A preliminary study of the sprouts of capitalism in agriculture of the early Qing period). Fuzhou: Fujian renmin.

———. 1980. "Qingdai qianqi de nongye zudian guanxi" (Agricultural rent relations in the early Qing), in Zhongguo shehui kexue yuan lishi yanjiu-suo Qingshi yanjiushi, ed., *Qingshi luncong*, 2: 56–88. Beijing: Zhonghua.

———. 1979a. "Qingdai qianqi diannong kangzu douzheng de xin fazhan" (New developments in tenants' rent resistance struggles in the early Qing), in *ibid.*, 1: 54–78.

———. 1979b. "Lun Zhongguo zibenzhuyi mengya de lishi qianti" (On the historical preconditions for the sprouts of capitalism in China), *Zhongguo shi yanjiu*, no. 2: 32–46.

———. 1962. "Lun Qingdai guyong laodong" (On hired labor in the Qing period), *Lishi yanjiu*, no. 4: 104–48.

*Luancheng xian zhi* (Luancheng county gazetteer), 1872. (Reprint, Taibei, 1976; 2 vols.)

MT, *see* Minami Manshū tetsudō kabushiki kaisha.

MacKinnon, Stephen R. 1980. *Power and Politics in Late Imperial China: Yuan Shi-kai in Beijing and Tianjin, 1901–1908*. Berkeley: University of California Press.

Mai Shudu. 1930. "Hebei sheng xiaomai zhi fanyun" (The marketing and transport of wheat in Hebei province), *Shehui kexue zazhi*, 1.1: 73–107.

Malone, C. B., and J. B. Taylor. 1924. *The Study of Chinese Rural Economy*. Peking: China International Famine Relief Commission.

Mansfield, Edwin. 1980. *Economics: Principles, Problems, Decisions*, 3d ed. New York: W. W. Norton.

Mao Zedong. 1940. "Xin minzhuzhuyi lun" (On new democracy), in *Mao Zedong ji*, 7: 147–206. Tokyo: Hokubōsha, 1972.

———. 1939. "Zhongguo geming yu Zhongguo gongchandang" (The Chinese revolution and the Chinese Communist Party), in *ibid.*, 3: 97–136.

———. 1927. "Hunan nongmin yundong kaocha baogao" (Report on an investigation of the peasant movement in Hunan), in *ibid.*, 1: 207–49.

Marks, Robert Brian. 1978. "Peasant Society and Peasant Uprisings in South China: Social Change in Haifeng County, 1630–1930," Ph.D. dissertation, University of Wisconsin, Madison.

Marx, Karl. 1968. "Preface to *A Contribution to the Critique of Political Economy*," in Karl Marx and Friedrich Engels, *Selected Works*. New York: International Publishers.

———. 1967. *Capital*. 3 vols. New York: International Publishers.

———. 1963. *The Eighteenth Brumaire of Louis Bonaparte*. New York: International Publishers.

Marx, Karl, and Friedrich Engels. 1959. *Basic Writings on Politics and Philosophy*, ed. Lewis S. Feuer. Garden City, N.Y.: Doubleday.

Matsuda Yoshirō. 1981. "Minmatsu Shinsho Kōtō Shukō deruta no shaden kaihatsu to kyōshin shihai no keisei katei" (Reclamation of the *shatian* in the Pearl River delta of Guangdong and the forming of gentry control in the late Ming-early Qing period), *Shakai keizai shigaku*, 46.6: 55–81.

Medick, Hans. 1976. "The Proto-Industrial Family Economy: The Structural Function of Household and Family During the Transition from Peasant Society to Industrial Capitalism," *Social History*, 1.3: 291–315.

Mendels, Franklin F. 1972. "Proto-Industrialization: The First Phase of the Industrialization Process," *Journal of Economic History*, 32.1: 241–61.

Migdal, Joel S. 1974. *Peasants, Politics and Revolution: Pressures Toward Political and Social Change in the Third World.* Princeton, N.J.: Princeton University Press.

Minami Manshū tetsudō kabushiki kaisha, Chōsabu. 1940. *Hokushi menka sōran* (A composite view of cotton in North China). Tokyo: Nihon hyōronsha.

———, Hokushi jimukyoku chōsabu. 1939. *Chintao kinkō ni okeru nōson jittai chōsa hōkoku* (Report on the investigation of a village in the suburb of Qingdao). Beijing.

———, ———. 1938–41. *Nōka keizai chōsa hōkoku: Hōjun ken* (Report on the investigation of peasant household economy: Fengrun county), vol. 1: *1937*; vol. 2: *1938*; vol. 3: *1939*. Dalian.

———, Hokushi keizai chōsajo. 1940a. *Hokushi nōson gaikyō chōsa hōkoku* (Report on the investigation of general conditions of North China villages), vol. 1: *Keimin ken* (Huimin county). N.p.

———, ———. 1940b. *Ibid.*, vol. 2: *Taian ken* (Taian county).

———, ———. 1940c. *Ibid.*, vol. 3: *I ken* (Wei county). N.p.

———, ———. 1940d. *Nōka keizai chōsa hōkoku: Kakuroku ken, 1939* (Report on the investigation of peasant household economy: Huailu county, 1939). Beijing.

———, Keizai chōsakai. 1935. *Santō shō ichi nōson ni okeru shakai keizai jijō* (Socioeconomic conditions in one village in Shandong province). Dalian.

———, Kitō chiku nōson jittai chōsahan. 1936a. *Kitō chiku nai nijūgo ka son nōson jittai chōsa hōkokusho* (Report on the investigation of actual conditions in 25 villages of the northeastern Hebei area). 2 vols. Tianjin.

———, ———. 1936b. *Kitō chiku nai sentaku nōson jittai chōsa gaiyō hōkokusho* (Summary of the investigation of actual conditions of selected villages in the northeastern Hebei area). Tianjin.

———, Kitō nōson jittai chōsahan. 1937a. *Dainiji kitō nōson jittai chōsa hōkokusho: tōkeihen. Dai ichiban: Heikoku ken* (Report on the second investigation of actual conditions of northeastern Hebei villages: statistical volume. First group: Pinggu county). Dalian.

———, ———. 1937b. *Ibid. Dai sanban: Hōjun ken* (Third group: Fengrun county).

———, ———. 1937c. *Ibid. Dai yonban: Shōrei ken* (Fourth group: Changli county).

———, Tenshin jimusho chōsaka. 1937. *Kahoku shō nōson jittai chōsa shiryō* (Materials for investigations of actual conditions in villages in Hebei province). Tianjin.

———, ———. 1936a. *Junka ken Rokasai nōson jittai chōsa hōkoku* (Report on the investigation of actual conditions in Lujiazhai village, Zunhua county). Tianjin.

———, ———. 1936b. *Kita Shina ni okeru mensakuchi nōson jijō* (Conditions of a village in the cotton-growing area of North China). Dalian.

———, ed. 1979. *Kyū shokuminchi kankei kikan kankōbutsu sōmokuroku*

(Comprehensive catalogue of company publications pertaining to the old colonies). Tokyo: Ajia keizai kenkyūjo.

Moise, Edwin. 1977. "Downward Social Mobility in Pre-revolutionary China," *Modern China*, 3.1: 3–32.

Moore, Barrington, Jr. 1966. *Social Origins of Dictatorship and Democracy*. Boston: Beacon Press.

Mori Masao. 1975. "18–20 seiki no Kōseishō nōson ni okeru shasō gisō ni tsuite no ichi kentō" (A study of charitable granaries in villages of Jiangxi province from the 18th to the 20th century), *Tōyōshi kenkyū*, 33.4: 60–98.

Moulder, Frances. 1978. "Comparing Japan and China: Some Theoretical and Methodological Issues," in Alvin Coox and Hilary Conroy, eds., *China and Japan: The Search for Balance Since World War I*. Santa Barbara, Calif.: ABC-Clio.

———. 1977. *Japan, China and the Modern World Economy*. Cambridge: Cambridge University Press.

Muramatsu Yūji. 1962. "Kichi no 'shuso satsutō' oyobi 'sagin satsutō' ni tsuite" (On bannerland rent books: the "Quzu cedang" and the "Chaiyin cedang"), 2 parts, *Tōyō gakuhō*, 45.2: 39–70; 45.3: 39–61.

———. 1949. "Ranjō ken to Jihokushi son" (Luancheng county and Sibeichai village), *Hitotsubashi ronsō*, 22.1: 180–207.

Murphey, Rhoads. 1977. *The Outsiders*. Ann Arbor: University of Michigan Press.

Myers, Ramon. 1980. "North China Villages During the Republican Period: Socioeconomic Relationships," *Modern China*, 6.3: 243–66.

———. 1970. *The Chinese Peasant Economy: Agricultural Development in Hopei and Shantung, 1890–1949*. Cambridge, Mass.: Harvard University Press.

Nanjing daxuc lishixi Ming Qing shi yanjiushi, ed. 1980. *Ming–Qing zibenzhuyi mengya yanjiu lunwen ji* (A collection of essays on the sprouts of capitalism in Ming–Qing). Shanghai: Renmin.

Nankai daxue lishi xi. 1959. *Qing shilu jingji ziliao jiyao* (Abstract of social economic materials in the *Qing shilu*). Beijing: Zhonghua.

Nee, Victor. 1979. "Toward a Social Anthropology of the Chinese Revolution," *Bulletin of Concerned Asian Scholars*, 11.3: 40–50.

Niida Noboru. 1963. *Chūgoku hōsei shi* (A history of China's legal institutions). Rev. ed. Tokyo: Iwanami.

———. 1952. *Chūgoku no nōson kazoku* (Family and lineage in rural China). Tokyo: Tōkyō daigaku shuppankai.

———. 1947. "Kahoku ni okeru kazoku bunretsu no jittai" (Actual conditions in the dissolution of families in North China), *Tōyō bunka*, 4: 1–35.

Ning Ke. 1980. "You guan Han dai nongye shengchan de jige shuzi" (Some figures on agricultural production in Han times), *Beijing shiyuan xuebao*, 3: 76–90.

Nishijima Sadao. 1966. *Chūgoku keizaishi kenkyū* (Studies in China's social-economic history). Tokyo: Tōkyō daigaku shuppankai.

Noma Kiyoshi. 1964. "'Chūgoku nōson kankō chōsa' no kikaku to jisseki—Chūgoku mondai kenkyū ni okeru shukanteki 'zen i' to sono genkai" (The intentions and actual results of the *Investigation of Customary Practices in Rural China*: subjective 'goodwill' and its limitations in the study of the China problem), *Rekishi hyōron*, 170: 1–15.

Paige, Jeffery M. 1975. *Agrarian Revolution: Social Movements and Export Agriculture in the Underdeveloped World.* New York: Free Press.

Parish, William L., and Martin King Whyte. 1978. *Village and Family in Contemporary China.* Chicago: University of Chicago Press.

Peng Yuxin. 1945. *Xian difang caizheng* (County local finance). Shanghai: Shangwu.

Perkins, Dwight. 1969. *Agricultural Development in China, 1368–1968.* Chicago: Aldine.

———. 1967. "Government as an Obstacle to Industrialization: The Case of Nineteenth-Century China," *Journal of Economic History,* 27.7: 478–92.

Perry, Elizabeth J. 1981. "Popular Unrest in China: The State and Local Society." Manuscript.

———. 1980. *Rebels and Revolutionaries in North China, 1845–1945.* Stanford, Calif.: Stanford University Press.

Polanyi, Karl, Conrad M. Arensberg, and Harry W. Pearson, eds. 1957. *Trade and Market in the Early Empires: Economies in History and Theory.* Glencoe, Ill.: Free Press.

Popkin, Samuel. 1979. *The Rational Peasant: The Political Economy of Rural Society in Vietnam.* Berkeley: University of California Press.

Potter, Jack M., May N. Diaz, and George M. Foster, eds. 1967. *Peasant Society: A Reader.* Boston: Little, Brown.

Potter, Sulamith. 1983. "The Position of Peasants in Modern China's Social Order," *Modern China,* 9.4: 465–99.

Prazniak, Roxann. 1980. "Tax Protest at Laiyang, Shandong, 1910," *Modern China,* 6.1: 41–71.

Qian Hong. 1957. "Yapian zhanzheng yiqian Zhongguo rogan shougongye bumen zhong de zibenzhuyi mengya" (The sprouts of capitalism in certain handicraft industries in China before the Opium War), in ZRD, 1: 238–71.

Qu Zhisheng. 1931. *Hebei mianhua zhi chuchan ji fanyun* (The production, marketing, and transport of cotton in Hebei). Beijing: Shehui diaocha suo.

Rawski, Evelyn. 1972. *Agricultural Change and the Peasant Economy of South China.* Cambridge, Mass.: Harvard University Press.

Ren Meie, Yang Renzhang, and Bao Haosheng. 1979. *Zhongguo ziran dili gangyao* (An outline of China's physical geography). Beijing: Shangwu.

Riskin, Carl. 1975. "Surplus and Stagnation in Modern China," in Dwight Perkins, ed., *China's Modern Economy in Historical Perspective,* pp. 49–84. Stanford, Calif.: Stanford University Press.

Rozman, Gilbert. 1982. *Population and Marketing Settlements in Ch'ing China.* Cambridge: Cambridge University Press.

Schran, Peter. 1969. *The Development of Chinese Agriculture, 1950–1959.* Urbana: University of Illinois Press.

Schultz, Theodore W. 1964. *Transforming Traditional Agriculture.* New Haven, Conn.: Yale University Press.

Schwartz, Benjamin I. *Chinese Communism and the Rise of Mao.* Cambridge, Mass.: Harvard University Press.

Scott, James C. 1976. *The Moral Economy of the Peasant: Rebellion and Subsistence in Southeast Asia.* New Haven, Conn.: Yale University Press.

Shang Yue. 1957. "Qingdai qianqi Zhongguo shehui de tingzhi, bianhua he fazhan" (Stagnation, change, and development in Chinese society of the early Qing period), in ZRD, 1: 160–238.

Shanin, Teodor. 1972. *The Awkward Class: Political Sociology of Peasantry in a Developing Society: Russia 1910–1925.* London: Oxford University Press.

Shenyang nongxue yuan. 1980. *Yinghan nongye keji cidian* (English-Chinese dictionary of agricultural technology). Beijing: Nongye.

Shimizu Morimitsu. 1951. *Chūgoku gōson shakai ron* (On the village society of China). Tokyo: Iwanami.

*Shuntian fu zhi* (Gazetteer of Shuntian prefecture), Guangxu period (1875–1908).

*Shunyi xianzhi* (Shunyi county gazetteer), 1933. (Reprint, Taibei: Chengwen, 1968; 2 vols.)

Skinner, G. William. 1980. "Marketing Systems and Regional Economies: Their Structure and Development," paper presented to the Symposium on Social and Economic History in China from the Song Dynasty to 1900, Beijing, Oct. 26–Nov. 1, 1980.

———. 1979. "Social Ecology and the Forces of Repression in North China: A Regional Systems Framework for Analysis," paper presented to the North China Workshop, Cambridge, Mass., Aug. 1979.

———. 1977a. "Regional Urbanization in Nineteenth-Century China," in G. William Skinner, ed., *The City in Late Imperial China*, pp. 211–52. Stanford, Calif.: Stanford University Press.

———. 1977b. "Cities and the Hierarchy of Local Systems," in *ibid.*, pp. 275–351.

———. 1971. "Chinese Peasants and the Closed Community: An Open and Shut Case," *Comparative Studies in Society and History*, 13.3: 270–81.

———. 1964–65. "Marketing and Social Structure in Rural China," 3 parts, *Journal of Asian Studies*, 24.1: 3–44; 24.2: 195–228; 24.3: 363–99.

Skocpol, Theda. 1979. *State and Social Revolutions: A Comparative Analysis of France, Russia, and China.* Cambridge: Cambridge University Press.

Smith, Arthur H. 1899. *Village Life in China.* New York: Fleming I I. Revell.

Smith, Thomas C. 1977. *Nakahara: Family Farming and Population in a Japanese Village, 1717–1830.* Stanford, Calif.: Stanford University Press.

———. 1959. *The Agrarian Origins of Modern Japan.* Stanford, Calif.: Stanford University Press.

So, Alvin. 1982. "Gentry and the Capitalist World System: A Study of the Political Economy of the South China Silk District," Ph.D. dissertation, University of California, Los Angeles.

Sorokin, Pitirim, and Carl C. Zimmerman. 1929. *Principles of Rural-Urban Sociology.* New York: Henry Holt.

Stalin, Joseph. 1940. *Dialectical and Historical Materialism.* New York: International Publishers.

Sun Jingzhi. 1957. *Huabei jingji dili* (An economic geography of North China). Beijing: Kexue.

Sun Yutang and Zhang Jiqian. 1979. "Qingdai de kentian yu dingkou de jilu" (Qing dynasty records on cultivated land and population), in Zhongguo shehui kexue yuan lishi yanjiusuo Qingshi yanjiushi, ed., *Qingshi luncong*, 1: 110–20. Beijing: Zhonghua.

Tawney, R. H. 1932. *Land and Labor in China.* London: Allen & Unwin.

Tilly, Charles. 1979. "Proletarianization: Theory and Research," working paper no. 202, Center for Research on Social Organization, University of Michigan.

———. 1975a. "Revolutions and Collective Violence," in Fred I. Greenstein and Nelson W. Polsby, eds., *Handbook of Political Science*, vol. 3: *Macropolitical Theory*, pp. 483–555. Reading, Mass.: Addison-Wesley.

———. 1975b. "Food Supply and Public Order in Modern Europe," in Charles Tilly, ed., *The Formation of National States in Western Europe*, pp. 380–455. Princeton, N.J.: Princeton University Press.

———. 1975c. "Western State-Making and Theories of Political Transformation," in *ibid.*, pp. 601–38.

———. 1964. *The Vendée*. Cambridge, Mass.: Harvard University Press.

———, ed. 1978. *Historical Studies of Changing Fertility*. Princeton, N.J.: Princeton University Press.

Tōadōbunkai. 1917–20. *Shina shōbetsu zenshi* (Comprehensive gazetteer of China's different provinces), vol. 4: *Shandong*; vol. 18: *Zhili*. Tokyo: Tōadōbunkai.

*Tudigaige shouce* (Handbook for land reform). 1951. Beijing: Xinhua.

Tudiweiyuanhui. 1937. *Quanguo tudi diaocha baogao gangyao* (Abstract of the report on the nationwide investigation of land). Nanjing.

Uchiyama Masao. 1980. "'Chūgoku nōson kankō chōsa' to Chūgoku shi kenkyū" (The *Investigations of Customary Practices in Rural China* and the study of Chinese history), *Rekishigaku kenkyū*, 484: 50–60.

Wakeman, Frederic Jr. 1966. *Strangers at the Gate: Social Disorder in South China, 1839–1861*. Berkeley: University of California Press.

Wallerstein, Immanuel. 1979. *The Capitalist World-Economy*. Cambridge, Eng.: Cambridge University Press.

———. 1974. *The Modern World-System: Capitalist Agriculture and the Origins of the European World-Economy in the Sixteenth Century*. New York: Academic Press.

Wang Yeh-chien. 1973a. *Land Taxation in Imperial China, 1750–1911*. Cambridge, Mass.: Harvard University Press.

———. 1973b. *An Estimate of the Land Tax Collection in China, 1753 and 1908*. Cambridge, Mass.: East Asian Research Center, Harvard University.

Wang Youmin. 1934. *Hebei sheng mianchan gaikuang, 1934* (The general situation of cotton production in Hebei province, 1934). Zhengding: Shiyebu Zhengding mianye shiyan chang.

Wang Yuhu. 1980. "Zhongguo nongye fazhan zhong de shui he lishi shang de nongtian shuili wenti" (Water in the development of Chinese agriculture and the historical problem of water control on farmland), (Beijing nongye daxue) *Kexue yanjiu ziliao*, 8005: 1–12.

———. 1979. *Zhongguo nongxue shu lu* (Notes on China's agricultural treatises). Beijing: Nongye.

Wang Yuquan. 1980. "Zhongguo lishi shang de nongmin de shenfen" (The status of peasants in Chinese history), paper presented to the Symposium on Social and Economic History in China from the Song Dynasty to 1900, Beijing, Oct. 26–Nov. 1, 1980.

Watson, James L. 1982. "Chinese Kinship Reconsidered: Anthropological Perspectives on Historical Research," *China Quarterly*, 92: 589–622.

Wiens, Mi-chu. 1980. "Lord and Peasant: The Sixteenth to the Eighteenth Century," *Modern China*, 6.1: 3–40.

Wilkinson, Endymion, ed. and tr. 1978. *Landlord and Labor in Late Imperial China: Case Studies from Shandong*. Cambridge, Mass.: East Asian Research Center, Harvard University.

Wittfogel, Karl August. 1957. *Oriental Despotism: A Comparative Study of Total Power*. New Haven, Conn.: Yale University Press.

Wolf, Arthur P., and Chieh-shan Huang. 1980. *Marriage and Adoption in China, 1845–1945*. Stanford, Calif.: Stanford University Press.

Wolf, Eric R. 1969. *Peasant Wars of the 20th Century*. New York: Harper & Row.

———. 1966. *Peasants*. Englewood Cliffs, N.J.: Prentice-Hall.

Woodside, Alexander. 1978. "The Ch'ien-lung Reign." Manuscript for *The Cambridge History of China*, vol. 9.

Wu Shiqian. 1979. "Guanyu Baxian dangan" (On the archives of Ba county), *Zhongguo shi yanjiu dongtai*, 4: 4–7.

Wu Zhi. 1936. "Shandong sheng mianhua zhi shengchan yu yunxiao" (Cotton production, transport, and marketing in Shandong province), *Zhengzhi jingji xue bao*, 1: 1–90.

Xingzhengyuan nongcun fuxing weiyuanhui. 1934a. *Henan sheng nongcun diaocha* (Investigation of rural Henan province). Shanghai: Shangwu.

———. 1934b. *Shaanxi sheng nongcun diaocha* (Investigation of rural Shaanxi province). Shanghai: Shangwu.

Xu Dixin, ed. 1980. *Zhengzhi jingji xue cidian* (Encyclopedia of political economy), vol. 1. Beijing: Renmin.

Xu Guangqi. 1956. *Nongzheng quanshu* (A comprehensive work on agriculture). 2 vols. Beijing: Zhonghua. Originally published in 1639.

Xu Xinwu. 1981. *Yapian zhanzheng qian Zhongguo mianfangzhi shougongye de shangpin shengchan yu zibenzhuyi mengya wenti* (Commodity production in the cotton handicraft spinning and weaving industry in China before the Opium War and the issue of the sprouts of capitalism). N.p.: Jiangsu renmin.

Yagi Yoshinosuke. 1943. *Keizai ni kansuru Shina kankō chōsa hōkokusho, tokuni Hokushi ni okeru kosaku seido* (Report on the social-economic aspects of the investigation of Chinese customary practices, especially the tenancy system in North China). Tokyo: Tōakenkyūjo.

Yan Zhongping. 1963. *Zhongguo mianfangzhi shi gao* (A draft history of cotton spinning and weaving in China). Beijing: Kexue.

Yang, C. K. 1959. *Chinese Communist Society: The Family and the Village*. Cambridge, Mass.: M.I.T. Press.

Yang, Martin. 1945. *A Chinese Village: Taitou, Shantung Province*. New York: Columbia University Press.

Yang Xuechen. 1963. "Qingdai qidi de xingzhi ji qi bianhua" (The nature of bannerland in Qing times and its change), *Lishi yanjiu*, no. 3: 175–95.

Yao Shan-yu. 1942. "The Chronological and Seasonal Distribution of Floods and Droughts in Chinese History, 206 B.C.–A.D. 1911," *Harvard Journal of Asiatic Studies*, 6.3/4: 273–312.

Ye Duzhuang. 1948. *Huabei mianhua ji qi zengchan wenti* (Cotton in North China and the problem of increasing its output). Nanjing: Ziyuan weiyuanhui, jingji yanjiusuo.

Ye Xian'en. 1983. *Ming-Qing Huizhou nongcun shehui yu dianpu zhi* (Rural

society and the tenant-serf system in Huizhou during the Ming-Qing).
Anhui: Anhui renmin.

Yoshida Kōichi. 1977. "20 seiki zenhan Chūgoku no ichi chihō shijō ni
okeru menka ryūtsū ni tsuite" (On the circulation of cotton in one local
market in China during the first half of the 20th century), Shirin, 60.2:
1 35.

———. 1975. "20 seiki Chūgoku no ichi mensaku nōson ni okeru nōminsō
bunkai ni tsuite" (On the differentiation of the peasantry in one cotton-
growing village in 20th-century China), Tōyōshi kenkyū, 33.4: 1–34.

Young, Ernest P. 1977. The Presidency of Yuan Shih-k'ai. Ann Arbor: University of Michigan Press.

Young, John. 1966. The Research Activities of the South Manchurian Railway Company, 1907–1945: A History and a Bibliography. New York:
East Asian Institute, Columbia University.

Yue Chen, ed. 1980. Zhongguo jindai nongye jingji shi (A history of China's
agricultural economy in the modern period). Beijing: Zhongguo renmin
daxue.

ZRD, see Zhongguo renmin daxue . . .

Zhang Peigang. 1936–37. "Qingyuan de nongjia jingji" (The economy of
peasant families in Qingyuan), 3 parts, Shehui kexue zazhi, 7.1: 1–65;
7.2: 187–266; 8.1: 53–120.

———. 1935. "Jibei Chadong sanshisan xian nongcun gaikuang diaocha" (A
study of general rural conditions in 33 counties in northern Hebei and
eastern Chahaer), Shehui kexue zazhi, 6.2: 267–311.

Zhang Ruide. 1979. "Ping-Han tielu yu Huabei de jingji fazhan" (The
Beiping–Hankou railroad and North China's economic development),
M.A. thesis, Taiwan Normal University.

Zhang Shiwen. 1944. Nongcun shehui diaocha fangfa (The method of doing
rural investigations). Chongqing: Shangwu.

Zhang Weihua et al., eds. 1980. Qufu Kongfu dangan shiliao xuanbian (Selections from the Kong lineage archives in Qufu), vol. 1, part 1. Shandong:
Qilu shushe.

Zhang Youyi, ed. 1957. Zhongguo jindai nongyeshi ziliao, vol. 2: 1912–1927;
vol. 3: 1927–1937 (Source materials on the agricultural history of modern
China). Beijing: Sanlian.

Zhao Quancheng. 1955. Qingdai dili yange biao (A study of the changing
geography of the Qing period). Beijing: Zhonghua.

Zhongguo kexue yuan dili yanjiu suo jingji dili yanjiu shi. 1980. Zhongguo
nongye dili zonglun (Overview discussion of the agricultural geography of
China). Beijing: Kexue.

Zhongguo mianfang tongji shiliao (Statistical source materials on the history of China's cotton textiles), 1950. Shanghai: Shanghai shi mianfangzhi gongye tongye gonghui choubeihui.

Zhongguo renmin daxue Zhongguo lishi jiaoyanshi, ed. 1957. Zhongguo
zibenzhuyi mengya wenti taolunji (Essays on the question of the sprouts
of capitalism in China). 2 vols. Beijing: Sanlian.

Zhongyang renmin zhengfu nongyebu. 1950. Huabei dianxing cun diaocha
(Investigations of representative villages in North China). N.p.

# INDEX

# Index

Hejian prefecture, 112, 118, 187, 324–25
Henan province, 55, 87, 89, 112, 115, 119, 131–32, 277, 280, 290
Herskovits, Melville, 5
"High level equilibrium trap," 18–19, 20, 169, 181–84
Hinton, William, 39, 82–83, 306n
Hirano Yoshitarō, 28f
Ho Ping-ti, 10, 60n, 321, 324
Hog raising, 73, 150–54 passim, 181
Homicide cases (Qing), 33, 47–48, 88–101 passim
Hong Kong, 29
Hongdong county, 114
Hou Baolian, 272
Hou Changyong, 272
Hou lineage, 235
Hou Qingchang, 271–72
Hou Yuanguang, 243, 273
Houjiaying village, 35, 46, 77, 319; rent relations in, 78, 203–8 passim, 212, 215, 272; wage labor in, 197, 215; disasters in, 212f; lineages in, 234–37 passim, 273; political structure in, 241, 242–43, 273–74; marriage practices in, 256; atomization of, 271–74, 291
House building, 220, 222
House clusters, 65, 220
Houxiazhai village, 35, 46, 76, 114, 264, 315; food prices in, 109; lineage in, 117, 234ff, 260–61, 265; landownership in, 117, 238, 259–60, 265; rent relations in, 203ff, 235, 259, 260–61, 284; disasters in, 212f, 262; degreeholder in, 233; political structure in, 237–38, 241, 260, 262–63; solidarity in, 238, 259–63, 290; year-laborers in, 255; taxes in, 284
Houyansi village, 315
Hsiao, K. C., 26, 232ff
Hsü Cho-yun, 60
Hu Hsien-chin, 234
Hu Rulei, 12n
Huaian county, 101
Huailu county, 36, 51, 103f, 224
Huang Sha hui (group), 290
Huaxian (county), 233
Hubei province, 122
Huimin county, 206
Huixian (county), 290
Hunan province, 122, 257, 278
Huzhuang village: Ninghe, 206, 319; Pinggu, 313f
Hymer, Stephen, 195

Ideological indoctrination, 224
Imahori Seiji, 29
Imperialism, 21–23, 293; and Chinese capitalism, 11, 13, 18f, 301f; and high-level equilibrium trap, 18–19; and commercialization, 23, 121, 194. See also World economy
Incipient capitalism analysis, 11–16 passim, 138–39, 294
Income, 158, 265, 296, 314; managerial farm, 72–73, 118, 158, 173–77; of middle peasants, 107, 158, 254; from handicraft production, 118, 132, 192; of poor peasants, 158, 186–89 passim, 197, 216, 296, 298f, 309–10; rental, 174–78 passim; of officials, 178, 242–43, 247. See also Wages
Indemnity payments, state, 302
India, 122–34 passim, 166–67, 191
Inflation, 209, 279
Influenza epidemic, Indian, 166–67
Inheritance, see Partible inheritance
Innovations, 4, 9, 18–19, 20, 169, 179–82
Institute of Economics: Beijing, 13n, 38, 322–23; Nankai, 129; Shanghai, 302
Institute of Geography, 62
Insularity, village, 23, 30, 65f, 219–24, 244–49 passim, 304f
Intensification, agricultural, 115, 179–80, 182; of labor use, 8, 10–11, 15, 62, 161–68 passim, 182; of land use, 10f, 15, 61f, 110, 139, 180
Interest rates, 189–90, 301
Intermediaries, in rent relations, 207–8
Interplanting, 61–62, 180–83 passim
Involution, agricultural, 8–16 passim, 155–56, 185, 216, 296–98, 302, 309; and village politics, 32; managerial farms and, 139, 155, 296ff, 307; collectivization and, 307. See also Intensification; Marginal productivity of labor; Poor-peasant economy and society; Surplus labor
Irrigation, 55–64 passim, 149, 180–81, 220, 234; for wet-rice, 58, 63n, 263; with chemical fertilizer, 181, 183

Japan, Meiji, 19n, 281
Japanese field studies, see Mantetsu surveys
Japanese invasion and occupation, 21, 39, 212, 270, 278; and cotton economy, 23, 128–34 passim, 302; self-defense organizations and, 30, 244f; and Baxian archive, 51n; Manchuria

Library of Congress Cataloging in Publication Data

Huang, Philip C., 1940–
    The peasant economy and social change in North China.

    Bibliography: p.
    Includes index.
    1. Peasantry—China—History.  2. Agriculture—Economic
aspects—China—History.  3. China—Rural conditions.
I. Title.
HD923.H83  1985        338.1'0951        83-40106
ISBN 0-8047-1220-4